A TIME TO SPEAK

John J. Walsh OSA

A Time To Speak

HOMILIES FOR THE THREE-YEAR CYCLE

the columba press

First published in 2000 by
the columba press
55A Spruce Avenue, Stillorgan Industrial Park,
Blackrock, Co Dublin

Cover by Bill Bolger
Origination by The Columba Press
Printed in Ireland by Colour Books Ltd, Dublin

ISBN 1 85607 303 3

Contents

Foreword

'Neither a borrower nor a lender be', was the injunction of Polonius to Hamlet in the play of that name. The person who sets out to put into print homilies for Sunday Masses throughout the three year liturgical cycle is very likely to infringe on both of these pieces of advice, at least in the realm of ideas, and I must plead guilty as well. Few of the ideas in this book can be claimed as being original. Most of them I have gleaned from reading, listening, and especially from the text of, and commentaries on Sacred Scripture. My hope is that the contents of this book may be a source of help to others who have the demanding task of putting together a homily week after week throughout the whole year. This would make me a happy 'lender' indeed.

The criticism may be levelled that, in the text, there are too many references to St Augustine. But Augustine is not, as it were, the property of the religious orders associated with his name. He is in fact the man for all Christians, the most quoted theologian in the documents of Vatican II. His career was one of wide experience, having been, in his own words, one of those 'whose starved spirits lick shadows'. This graphic expression was an admission that he had been trying to satisfy, with pursuits which had no real substance, his inner yearning for a spiritual dimension in life, something which is a common occurrence among the younger generation of our own time, especially in the United States. The great drawback in this era is that there are so many agencies, such as films, television, radio, newspapers, all clamouring for the attention of those who look on, listen to, or read them. The producers responsible for these exercise a virtual monopoly in their particular area, with responsibility to precious few. To gain attention, the homilist has got to compete with these, using his own particular techniques. For example, ask a question to set the congregation thinking, or mention briefly something without the remotest connection with religion, and make them wonder as to the purpose it serves.

But, however important the homily, we must remember that the Mass is infinitely greater, and bearing this in mind a certain aura of sacredness accrues, as well, to the homily, being part of a magnificent whole. 'To me there is nothing so consoling, so piercing, so thrilling, so overcoming, as the Mass', John Henry Cardinal Newman wrote in the story of his conversion and ordination to the priesthood in the Catholic Church. 'It is not a mere form of words; it is a great action, the greatest action that can be on earth. It is not the invocation merely, but – if I dare use the word – the evocation of the Eternal. He becomes present on the altar in flesh and blood, before whom angels bow and devils tremble.' *(Loss and Gain: The Story of a Convert)*

Year A

'In the presence of God and of Christ Jesus,
who will judge the living and the dead,
and in view of his appearing and his kingdom,
I solemnly urge you: proclaim the message,
and whether it be welcome or unwelcome,
persist with it.'
(2 Tim 4:1f)

FIRST SUNDAY OF ADVENT
Is 2:1-5; Rom 13:11-14; Mt 24:37-44

Today, the first Sunday of Advent, marks the beginning of a period of preparation for the celebration of the birth of Christ, our Saviour, at Christmas. All the readings in the Mass advise us most urgently to make ourselves ready, to be on the alert, to turn aside from our sinful ways, and give more time to God in our lives. 'Come, let us walk in the light of the Lord', Isaiah says in the first reading. Let us not live lives of darkness and of sin, St Paul admonishes his listeners; but let us put on the armour of God's grace, and appear in the light, meaning that our consciences should have nothing to hide at any time, but rather be open to the promptings of the Holy Spirit directing them. 'Be vigilant, stay awake', the gospel warns, at any moment you may be called upon to make an eternal choice, and that as unexpectedly as the people who were swallowed up by the Flood, in the time of Noah.

Outwardly, people may appear the same, like the men working in the fields or the women grinding at the millstone, but inwardly they have responded differently to the graces God has given them. Thus they are in varying states of preparedness for what is to come, with the result that while some will be taken into God's kingdom, others will be left or rejected. This is true of every single individual, for as we pass through life we are all being faced with a choice between two ways, either that of slavery to evil tendencies in our lives, which we call sin, or, on the other hand, that of grace, which is allowing Jesus Christ be our guide and exemplar in all that we do.

It is only when we sincerely try to model our lives on that of Christ that our spirits will experience real freedom. Jesus himself said to the Jews (Jn 8:32), 'If you persevere in my word, you will indeed be my disciples. You will learn the truth, and the truth will make you free.' Persevering in the word of Jesus demands that we listen to it, as it comes to us from out the scriptures and from within our consciences; also that we think about it and study its requirements, and that we put into action what we have learned. The true disciple of Christ asks the question, 'What am I setting before myself as the main purpose of my life?' My career, the acquisition of material possessions, the pursuit of pleasure, or the service of God and my neighbour? The truth of Jesus will teach us what things are really important and what are not. Furthermore, discipleship of Christ brings its own rewards. It brings freedom from fear, fear about oneself, fear about one's ability to cope with life, fear about contradiction and opposition from others, fear about death and the uncertainty of life thereafter. 'In love there can be no fear', St John wrote (1 Jn 4:18), 'but perfect love casts out fear; because to fear is to expect punishment, and anyone who is afraid is still imperfect in love.'

If we end up having no love or reverence towards God, no respect or consideration or pity towards others, then we will have reached the stage of choosing to be lost, as Jesus, in his prayer at the Last Supper, said of Judas. 'Father, I kept those you had given me true to your name. I have watched over them, and not one is lost except the one who chose to be lost.' This is what should really frighten us, that the choice of our own destiny for all eternity rests entirely with ourselves.

If the Son of Man comes unexpectedly and finds us wanting, then we, who were part of the divine plans and designs from the moment of creation, we who were born to love, to be united with our Creator for ever in heaven, we will depart this world, and find ourselves unloving, frustrated by our rejection of love, utterly incapable of any response to the love of the God who will still love us. To prevent such a tragedy, it is necessary for us from time to time to take a critical look at ourselves, at the kind of lives we are leading, the response we are making to God's grace. We should take note of our patterns of behaviour, but far more importantly our sets of values, what we regard as important in life.

Advent is a time when we ought to do precisely this. 'Come, let us go up to the mountain of the Lord,' the first reading tells us, 'to the Temple of the God of Jacob, that he may teach us his ways, so that we may walk in his paths.' The second reading is of special significance in that it finally brought about the conversion of St Augustine after he had opened the New Testament at random at that very passage, and please God it will help us to look into our own lives and, if needs be, change them too.

SECOND SUNDAY OF ADVENT
Is 11:1-10; Rom 15:4-9; Mt 3:1-12

If pilgrims in the Holy Land go east on the road from Jerusalem down to Jericho, that road where the man, in Jesus' parable about the Good Samaritan, fell among robbers, they end up, just above the entrance to the Dead Sea, in one of the deepest areas on this earth which lies open to the skies, more than 1,200 feet under the level of the sea. It was in this region, while our Lord was on earth, that a community of people dwelt on the cliff-tops overlooking the Dead Sea, people who regarded the rest of the Jews as being so wicked that they withdrew into this barren region to keep themselves from being contaminated. These were the Essenes, oddly enough never once mentioned in the New Testament, an extraordinary group of men, women and children, who prayed daily together and meditated on the ancient Hebrew Bible, of which they made numerous copies, some of which survive as the Dead Sea Scrolls.

They purified themselves regularly in ritual washings, and practised celibacy, relying on a steady influx of recruits for their continued existence. In a perpetual struggle to survive in the sweltering heat of this wilderness, and sustained by the belief that the end-time was at hand, they lived apart from the world. They did not try to change it.

In today's gospel we have the story of the man whom many scripture scholars would link with the Essene community – John the Baptist. He also had been living in this wilderness up till now, eating the only food available there, namely locusts and wild honey, and also attaching great importance to ritual washing, so much so that we always refer to him now as the Baptist. But John, in contrast to the Essenes, was not satisfied just to remain apart from the world. He set out to convert the world, and not because the end of the world was near, but rather the beginning. 'The kingdom of God is close at hand,' he said, and the challenge he put to the crowds which flocked to hear him, down in the Jordan valley, can be summarised in one sentence: 'Change your lives' – 'Repent.'

This also was to be the call of Jesus when he began his public mission, 'The time has come and the kingdom of God is at hand. Repent and believe the Good News.' And this call is addressed to us as well. The changing of our lives is a life-long process, but it must begin here and now, and the call to do so comes to all without exception. We ask why did John make such a bitter attack on the Pharisees and Sadducees who came to be baptised, by addressing them as a 'brood of vipers'. It was simply because the Pharisees, deeming themselves perfect, saw no need for change, while for the Sadducees, who did not believe in a life hereafter, change was pointless, because their hopes did not extend beyond the present life. They preferred to go through this life oblivious to any possibility of life after death.

The fact that these people nevertheless came to listen to John is testimony that they felt something lacking in their approach to life, and that in spite of themselves they were drawn to this charismatic and truly ascetic figure calling them to repentance. 'He shall drink no wine or strong drink,' the angel said of John to his father Zechariah. For some of us there is perhaps a lesson here too.

In this period leading up to Christmas, it is well to recall that in the Bible drunkenness is strongly condemned, precisely because it makes people forgetful of what they are, of their eternal destiny, of their duty to be true to themselves. 'Woe to those,' Isaiah wrote (5:11), 'who from early morning chase after strong drink, and stay up late at night getting drunk.' In this area human nature does not change. St Paul, convinced from the moment of his conversion that every true Christian gives witness to the mystery of the cross, puts it very forcibly for us, 'You cannot belong to Christ, unless you crucify all self-indulgent passions and desires' (Gal 5:24). John the Baptist, a stern and uncompromising figure, threatened his listeners with hell-fire, if they did not mend their ways.

Jesus too was firm. 'Go and sin no more' was his frequent warning, but the firmness of Jesus was coupled with a marvellous understanding and compassion for those caught up in the snares of sin. And this it is which makes us confident that, in spite of all the moral turmoil within us, our lack of commitment to the following of the gospel message of Christ, and the evils of our time, the love of God will finally prevail.

FEAST OF THE IMMACULATE CONCEPTION
Gen 3:9-15, 20; Eph 1:3-6, 11-20; Lk 1:26-38

At the end of the wonderful series of apparitions at the grotto of
Massabielle in Lourdes in 1858, when the only witness to these,
Saint Bernadette Soubirous, asked once again for the name of
her heavenly visitor, she was told, 'I am the Immaculate
Conception'. Four years prior to this, on the 8th of December
1854, the dogma of the Immaculate Conception had been proclaimed by Pope Pius IX in these words: 'At the first instant of
her Conception, by the grace and privilege of Almighty God,
and in consideration of the merits of Jesus Christ, the Saviour of
the human race, the Virgin Mary was preserved and exempted
from all stain of original sin.' But the little girl had never heard
these words before, nor did she have any idea as to what they
meant. The only thing she was certain of was that almost every
day for a fortnight her soul had been held spellbound, not by
reflecting on a dogma, but rather by the visible presence of some
mysterious person, who by her every word and gesture conveyed
a sense of that purity and goodness and graciousness that can
only be associated with a heavenly being.

The child was convinced that she was confronted by one who
was never touched by the slightest taint of wickedness or evil,
one who was holy in a profound and radical way. Thus in a
purely intuitive manner – by contemplation – she had come to
grasp the basic truth of the doctrine of the Immaculate Conception, that the Blessed Virgin was as holy as ever a creature
can possibly be, that never once was she in any way guilty of the
slightest imperfection, never once gave way to the suggestions
of evil, or injustice, or impatience, or criticism of others, or complaint against God about what she had to suffer, despite one day
being remembered and venerated as 'Our Lady of Sorrows'.

What the Church, in this feast, adds to this is that God
adorned Mary, from the first instant of her existence, with every
kind of grace, the fullness of grace, in view of the merits of Jesus
Christ her Son, that is, on account of the redemption to be effected
by her Son alone. Mary never knew that state which we call original sin, and which consists precisely in the lack of divine grace,
in everyone born into this world, something that came about as
the result of the fall of our first parents. In a particularly unique
way, we can apply to Mary the words of St Paul about all the

redeemed (Eph 2:10), that she is God's work of art. It is God himself who made her what she is, and gave her a new form of life because of Christ Jesus, and God who long ago planned that she should spend this life in bringing redemption to others. For, being exempt from any inclination to sin – what we call concupiscence – and being raised above the level of all human beings, she would become their representative and their advocate with God.

The fervour generated by all this grace lifted Mary's spirit towards God with an urgent impulse of all her being, an impulse of faith and love. Because those most favoured by God are also those who thirst after him most, who yearn to be united with him, and to do his will in all things. And God, who is love, made Mary the most lovable of any object of love, her personality more attractive than that of any other human being. Hence, in this perfect being, who never in the least way yielded to sin, or was attracted to it, God would become man.

The Immaculate Conception of Mary has a message too for all of us here and now. It tells us clearly that God has set plans for each of us from the moment we came into being; that he surrounds the life of each of us with redemptive love, that within the limits of God's plans for us we can give ourselves or refuse ourselves to God. God does not force himself upon us; each one of us is asked, as was Mary, to say 'fiat', 'let it be done to me according to your Word'.

If we imitate the response of Mary, we too will become Christ-bearers. In a spiritual way he will be born in us, and through us make himself present to those around us. We will carry the light of faith and the flame of love through the darkness of this world, until we come to the place where we belong, in God's eternal radiance, where there is never any change or shadow of alteration. May the Blessed Virgin, whose first beginning was holy and pure, pray for us, that we too may become what God wants us to be. Amen.

THIRD SUNDAY OF ADVENT
Is 35:1-6,10; Jm 5:7-10; Mt 11:2-11

The book which comes last in the Canon of Sacred Scripture is the Book of Revelation, or the Apocalypse. It was written at a period of persecution and tremendous hardship for the members of the infant Church. Anyone who reflects on the last sentences of that book cannot but be touched by the longing there expressed that God might come and release his people from the suffering they were enduring.

The Church is referred to as the Bride, (the Bride of Christ), and the author says 'The Spirit and the Bride say, "Come". Let everyone who hears say, "Come". ...The one who guarantees these revelations repeats his promise: Indeed, I am coming soon. Amen, come Lord Jesus.' In this period leading up to Christmas, we too should be giving voice to that same intense longing. 'Courage, do not be afraid. Look your God is coming', the liturgy reminds us. Our God is coming to save us. We might this morning ask ourselves what salvation means to us. From what does Christ save us? The answer, in the main, is twofold. He saves us firstly from sin, and secondly from death. But most of us can admit that we tend to be offhand and casual about sin, and rather dubious about salvation from death, the inevitable end of every living thing.

However, about sin, if we look about us, we can see the very definite results of sin in the community, in society. It can lead to divisions and strife, to violence against innocent victims, to extortion and robbery. Where there is bitterness and lack of compassion, where there is selfishness and the relentless pursuit of one's own interests and desires without regard for the rights of others, there is sin.

In complete contrast the example of Christ, and even more so the merits gained by Christ, who was completely at one with the will of the Father and the promptings of God's Holy Spirit, Christ who gave of himself for others, who was the one for others, even to the extent of laying down his very life for them, all these can bring about a change in those who sincerely invite Christ into their lives, a change which can counteract the evil tendencies which are the results of sin. And if we ask how Christ has conquered death, the answer is that by his resurrection he has removed the fear of death from those who have faith in him, for he has given a solemn promise that, if we but believe, we also shall rise from the dead as he did. Instead of feeling doomed to extinction, we can say in the words of scripture 'Oh death where is thy sting, death where is thy victory?' (1 Cor 15:55).

Furthermore, on his final night on earth, Jesus left us, as his last testimony, this Holy Eucharist which we are now celebrating, as a sign and guarantee that this will come to pass. 'They who eat my body and drink my blood shall have life in them, and I will raise them up on the last day.' If our faith in the promises of Jesus wavers, we are reassured by his answer to the query of John the Baptist in today's gospel, 'Are you the one who is to come or have we got to wait for someone else?'

Obviously John also was going through a crisis of faith, for before his imprisonment he had said of Jesus, 'I am the witness that he is the Chosen One of God' (Jn 1:34). Jesus' reply to the disciples of John, who had put the question, was to go back and tell John, not what Jesus was saying, but rather what he was doing. John, with his knowledge of the O.T., would then understand that in the healing of the sick, the lame, the blind, was clearly revealed the sign which the prophet Isaiah declared would denote the coming of the promised Messiah. God was at work in the actions of Jesus.

But the significance of the blind seeing, the deaf hearing, goes deeper than any physical cure. In Christ those who are blind to the truth about themselves and God have their eyes opened, in Christ those who falter in their pursuit of what is honourable and just and pure have their steps strengthened, in Christ those who were deaf to the voice of God and conscience begin to listen, in Christ those who were dead and powerless in the grip of sin are restored to newness and richness of life, in Christ the poorest are endowed with the riches of God. This is the season when we are called to live in the thought of Jesus as he once came, and as he will come again for each one of us. It is the time to desire his second coming from our affectionate and grateful remembrance of his coming on that first Christmas (Cardinal Newman).

FOURTH SUNDAY OF ADVENT
Is 7:10-14; Rom 1:1-7; Mt 1:18-24

In the second reading today, which is the introduction to the Letter to the Romans, St Paul describes himself as 'a servant of Christ Jesus who has been called to be an apostle, and specially chosen to preach the Good News that God promised long ago through his prophets'. We might consider the question, where in the scriptures can we find this promise of God? To do this we should bear in mind that there are two ways in which we can get to the meaning of a passage in scripture. There is, first of all, the literal sense, or what message the author wanted to convey when writing it. And then, there is the message which the Holy Spirit wants to convey to us as we read the passage.

The first reading today from the prophet Isaiah, which is known as the Emmanuel prophecy, is one of the most famous passages in all the Old Testament that illustrate the two senses in which scripture may be understood. Taken literally, it shows Isaiah urging King Ahaz to have faith in God, that the royal line of David will survive, because the newly wedded queen will give birth to a son, a promise fulfilled in the future King Hezekiah. But if taken in the hidden sense, as St Paul obviously does, as well as St Matthew in the gospel reading, this passage from earliest times had a message also from the Holy Spirit. It can be seen as a solemn promise from God that a Redeemer will be born of a virgin, and that his name will be Emmanuel, meaning 'God with us'.

The challenge of all three readings is that of a call to faith. In each a chosen individual is being asked to make an act of faith. King Ahaz was called upon to have trust in God, and not try God's patience. St Paul became aware, again by faith, that his mission was to preach the word to the gentiles, and this, by the way, only after many years' reflection on the message imparted to him after being struck down while on the road to Damascus. Finally, St Joseph, as we see in today's gospel reading, was the first living person after Mary, who was asked to make an act of faith in Christ. He was called upon to believe that the child Mary was carrying was of divine origin – a most difficult thing for him to do, since it seemed to run counter to his marital rights. Indeed the mystery of a virgin birth must have been a far greater stumbling block for him than for us who have become so familiar with it. We have come to accept that God works in mysterious ways that confound human wisdom, ways demanding reflection and faith. Perhaps Joseph was helped by reflecting on God's promise to Abraham, one most unlikely to be fulfilled, that he would be the father of a great people, even though he was an old man, and his wife Sarah had been sterile from her youth. Yet fulfilled it was.

Perhaps we too should ask ourselves, what particular act of faith is God asking of me at this time. Part of the answer is to be found in the New Testament where it states that what makes a person acceptable to God is not obedience to the Law, but faith in Christ Jesus (Gal 2:16). This faith is not merely intellectual assent; it is an entrusting of ourselves to Christ, uniting ourselves with Christ. For we believe that, at the first Christmas, not only did the Blessed Trinity come down to us in visible form in God the Son made man, but that in and through the Son made man it has been made possible for us to be drawn into the glorious intimacy of the most holy Trinity.

For us Christmas should be a time of joy, not so much because Christ became one with us, as that he made it possible for us to become one with him. Yet the whole significance of St Luke's account of the birth of Christ is that the people of Israel did not receive the 'expected one' when he arrived. We get hints of this from the utterances of the two great prophets of the Old Testament, Jeremiah and Isaiah, who lived several hundreds of years prior to the birth of Christ. He was treated like an alien by his own people, like a traveller, as Jeremiah puts it, who has stopped but for a night. Again, according to Isaiah, the ox knows its owner, and the ass its master's manger, but Israel rejected its messiah; there was no room for him at the inn. Do we close our hearts to Christ? Let us listen to St Paul's last words to his converts at Corinth, 'Examine yourselves to make sure you are in the faith; test yourselves. Do you acknowledge that Jesus Christ is really in you? If not you have failed the test' (2 Cor 13:5). We can put Christ back into Christmas by putting him first into ourselves.

CHRISTMAS DAY

Vigil: Is 62:1-5; Acts 13:16-17, 22-25; Mt 1:1-25
Midnight: Is 9:1-6; Tit 2:11-14; Lk 2:1-14
Dawn: Is 62:11-12; Tit 3:4-7; Lk 2:15-20
Daytime: Is 52:7-10; Heb 1:1-6; Jn 1:1-18

In the countryside close to Bethlehem, on the first Christmas night, St Luke tells us, there were shepherds watching over their flocks, when an angel of the Lord appeared to them, and the glory of the Lord shone round them. At first fearful and bewildered, the shepherds were reassured by the angel. 'Do not be afraid', he said to them, 'here is a sign for you. You will find a baby wrapped in swaddling clothes and lying in a manger'.

'Here is a sign for you.' In the Old Testament there were many such signs which were regarded as visible evidence of the presence and purpose of God. For example, in the greatest of these, when Moses received the Tables of the Law from God on Mount Sinai, we find the traditional signs of that time denoting the presence of God, peals of thunder, lightning, flashes of fire, the ground shaking. The reaction of the people was one of fear and awe, and they said to Moses, 'Do not let God speak to us, or we shall die.' Yet, while Moses was speaking to God on their behalf on the mountain, their faith grew weak, to the extent that they fell into idolatry and worshipped a golden calf.

Four hundred years later, on the same mountain, we have another sign, a further self-revelation by God, this time to the great prophet Elijah, who stood in a cave while the Lord passed by. Then, we are told, there came a mighty wind, followed by an earthquake and by fire, but God was not in any of these; he was no longer associated with the forces of nature. But after the fire there came the 'whisper of a gentle breeze', or taking the Hebrew literally, 'a still small voice', and when Elijah heard this he covered his face, because he felt himself in the presence of God, and no one, it was believed, could gaze upon the face of the Almighty God and live. Elijah regarded God as a Spirit who was beyond human comprehension. Yet again, while all this was taking place, the people of Israel were in a state of revolt against God, and lapsed into idolatry.

Let us in the light of these two signs try and understand the sign granted to the shepherds of Bethlehem, that of the baby in the manger. For it is here, we can say with certainty, that we have the greatest self-communication of all time by God to the human race. There is nothing of the fire or lightning of Mount Sinai, but the glory of the Lord. There is no dreadful rumbling of earthquake or thunder, but a heavenly host praising God and proclaiming peace to the world. And although there is the still small voice, which somehow recalls that which was heard by the prophet Elijah, it is rather the first earthly sound made by a new-born child. But in complete contrast to the other two signs, this new sign of the baby in the manger, is not one to instill terror into the hearts of those privileged to gaze upon him.

Later on in his public life, Christ in a reference to the Cross was to say, 'I, when I am lifted up from the earth, will draw all people to myself' (Jn 12:32). And in the humility of his birth, in the gathering of some lowly shepherds drawn to his manger, he was from his first moments on earth already preaching the lesson of self-abandonment that he would preach in so complete a way during his last moments on Calvary. What one among us is not touched by the helplessness of a new born babe. The infant lying in the manger, on the threshold of life, is a sign to melt the heart, to draw all people, as would the crucified one on the Cross with the last agonising breath of his life.

But the tragedy is that this sign, like the other two, would be met largely with unconcern, misunderstanding and disbelief. Christ would be rejected by the leaders of Israel, the Pharisees, Scribes, Priests, and the majority of its people, because he did not correspond to their expectations of what the Messiah should be. We should not travel down that road, nor turn our backs on the actions of the Holy Spirit by trying to hold on to our own concepts of God.

Rather let us open our minds, let us be drawn, let our hearts be melted by the consideration of God assuming a tiny, frail human form, and being laid in a manger. May our faith in Christ then be reborn this Christmas day, because only faith can guarantee the blessings that we hope for, or prove the existence of those things which at present remain hidden from our view' (Heb 11:1).

THE HOLY FAMILY OF JESUS, MARY & JOSEPH
Sir 3:3-7, 14-17; Col 3:12-21; Mt 2:13-15, 19-23

The poet, William Wordsworth, writing about the French Revolution as it appeared to enthusiasts said, 'Bliss was it that dawn to be alive, but to be young was very heaven.' The same perhaps could be said about Christians in the Apostolic Age, which had a glory and splendour about it that inspired people to acts of heroism in spreading the gospel and living up to its demands. But as early as 100 AD things were beginning to change. The thrill of the first years, to a certain extent, had passed. Christianity had become a thing of habit, the wonder had faded, and there were some who wanted to adapt the teaching of Christ to the secular philosophy and outlook of the day. What's new, you might say. The infant Church was in real danger of breaking up into opposing factions under the influence of emerging heresies.

St John, the only surviving Apostle, saw only one remedy for this, and in his First Letter to the Christian communities he expressed it in this rather surprising sentence, 'If God has loved us so much, then we also ought to love one another' (4:11). Note he did not say 'we also ought to love God', but rather 'we ought to love one another'. In other words the immediate response to God's love as it envelops each one of us should be to have respect and consideration and love for one another. This is the way we manifest our love for God.

On this, the Feast of the Holy Family, we could find no more apt advice for all Christian families, especially those which are in danger of splitting up under the stresses and strains of this modern age. Following the advice of St John, we can say that from the moment husband and wife are joined together in marriage, the only way for them to be faithful to God is by being faithful to each other; the concrete way they express their love for God is by the pure and steadfast love that they have for each other. If this love between a husband and wife persists, then their children will grow up in God's love. We can even say that when the children respond to their parents' love for them, then they too are responding to God himself. That which sustains the married relationship of such a couple will be, not so much the house they live in, or the material things they possess, or the securities they have built up for the future, but rather this true love, which they show to each other, and the children God grants them.

The perfect model for any family has got to be the union of Mary and Joseph, who had no possessions, no securities, not even a house to call their own, during the period covered by today's gospel story. We find the protective instinct of Joseph trying to shield Jesus and Mary from the hostility of King Herod. And just as the day would come when Joseph would no longer be there to supply this protection, so no modern father or mother can hope to control indefinitely the situations in which their children find themselves. After all Jesus was only twelve when, lost in the Temple, he began to see the will of his Father for himself in a way completely incomprehensible to both Mary and Joseph.

Mary in the Incarnation being disturbed, Joseph in his dreams being urged to go against traditional custom, Jesus in the Temple acting as he did, all these show that tensions did exist within the Holy Family, tensions which were in no way the consequence of sin, but rather an indication of evolution and growth. It is within the family that spiritual and moral values, attitudes towards each other, towards life, towards God himself, are being passed on, and this not so much by a process of indoctrination, as by a free and natural initiation.

We can only guess as to the extent to which the attitudes of Jesus were formed by Joseph, the man of inner vision, the man of respect for the law, of seeing love as greater than the law, and by Mary, not the meek, male-dominated woman portrayed by commentators in the past, but the one, who could make such far-reaching decisions as she did at the Annunciation, the mother who did not try to hold on to her Son, who displayed such remarkable inner strength and calm in the face of all kinds of adversity, in standing by her Son to the end, even to his death on a Cross.

May families always look to Jesus, Mary and Joseph for guidance, for inspiration, for courage, in the glorious but demanding task to which God has called them. Not only will the Holy Family be a model, it will be a source of grace to them as well.

MARY, MOTHER OF GOD
Num 6:22-27; Gal 4:4-7; Lk 2:16-21

In the gospels we read that the most common reaction of those
who witnessed the actions, or heard the words of Jesus was one
of astonishment and amazement. For example, at the
Transfiguration of Christ on Mount Tabor, when his face shone
like the sun, and his clothes became dazzlingly white, and
Moses and Elijah appeared speaking to him, Peter spoke for all
three Apostles present, when he said, 'Lord, it is wonderful for
us to be here.' But when they heard a voice speaking from the
cloud that covered them, all three fell on their faces, overcome
with fear. Ordinarily, we have to say with the Letter to the
Hebrews (11:1), 'It is only faith which can guarantee the blessings that we hope for, or prove the existence of those realities
which at present remain unseen.' And by way of example, it
adds, 'It was for faith that our ancestors were commended.'

To nobody is all this more readily applicable than to the one
who was the first to believe in Christ, our Mother in faith, as well
as Christ's earthly Mother, the Blessed Virgin Mary. There are
many of us who, in our approach to Mary, place her on a lasting
pedestal, and look on her after the manner of the three Apostles
gazing on the transfigured Christ. All too often we imagine her
as the Madonna of the Christmas card, serene, immobile, seated
forever in the immaculately clean stable of golden straw and
glistening snow outside, with adoring angels hovering over-
head. Such a figure is simply not real. For the plain fact is that
Mary, on earth, knew neither triumph nor heavenly spectacle.
No one has ever lived, suffered, died in such simplicity, in such
deep unawareness of her own supernatural dignity.

What evidence do we have for this, you may ask? And the
answer is there in the few short sayings attributed to her in the
gospels. For, in her own eyes, Mary was the handmaid, the servant
of the Lord, depending entirely on God's will, and sustained by
God's goodness. The fathers of the Vatican II Council acknowledged this when they stated that Mary stands out among the
poor and the humble of the Lord, who confidently await and
receive salvation from God (*LG* 55). Indeed, in the first four centuries of the Church, Christian writers placed greater emphasis
on the simple faith of Mary at the Annunciation, than on her
divine motherhood. The Virgin believed, and in her faith

conceived, or as St Augustine strikingly wrote, 'She first conceived Jesus in her heart, before conceiving him in her womb.'
Mary, whom we venerate as the Mother of Good Counsel, wants
above all to be our guide and counsellor in this area of faith. She
wants to beget faith in us, to be our Mother in faith. That is why,
in the gospel of St John, she is present at the beginning and the
end of Christ's public life.

She is there at the wedding feast of Cana, fully believing
before Jesus had worked a single miracle. It was only after the
changing of water into wine that Jesus' disciples began to
believe in him. In fact it was Mary herself who brought about
this very sign by her request to Jesus to intervene. 'Do whatever
he may tell you', she told the attendants, words which only one
who believed totally in the power of Jesus could utter. Cana was
the first of the signs recorded by St John, in order to bring us, as
it did his first disciples, to believe in Jesus. But as to the Mother
of Jesus, she is represented as already believing before it.

Significantly, John's gospel also is the only one to record the
presence of Mary at Calvary. 'Near the cross of Jesus stood his
Mother' (19:25) is the terse statement we read there. When all the
signs and wonders of the public mission of Christ seemed, in the
estimation of many, to have been a delusion, and all but one of
his carefully chosen Apostles had deserted him, his Mother was
still there witnessing him draw his last breath, and still believing. For Mary's faith in her Son had never been founded on the
evidence of astounding miracles or visions, but rather on a complete, absolute, childlike trust in the mysterious ways of God our
Father. Nor did her role as Mother on earth cease when her Son
departed this world. For in his dying moments, Jesus had ensured
its continuation when he said to John, 'Behold your Mother'.
Here Jesus reveals that his own natural Mother will henceforth
be the Mother of the disciple also, the disciple who was a figure
of all of Jesus' true disciples, you and I included. At that moment
Mary assumed a new role in God's plan of salvation for the
human race, that of spiritual Mother to us all.

SECOND SUNDAY AFTER CHRISTMAS
Sir 24:1-2, 8-12; Eph 1:3-6, 15-18; Jn 1:1-18

St Luke, in chapter nine of his gospel, has a very curious reference to Christ. 'Now it happened', he says, 'that as he was praying alone, his disciples were with him'. How could he be alone,
you might ask, if the disciples were with him? It could perhaps
mean that he was praying out of hearing, but not out of sight, of
the disciples, or more likely that for once he was away from the
throngs of people who pursued him everywhere seeking
favours from him. And one very good reason for this latter was
the locality in which he then was, the vicinity of a northern town
called Banyas, a Greek name meaning the town of Pan. It was a
place shunned by all strict Jews, because for centuries it had
been a centre of pagan worship of the fertility god Pan, and also
the spot where Herod's son Philip had built the city of Caesarea
Philippi around a great white marble temple dedicated by his
father to the godhead of Caesar Augustus. This was regarded by
the Jews as being idolatry. The fact that Jesus came here at all
shows the extraordinary freedom of his spirit. He could disregard taboos, mingle with and sometimes cure Samaritans,
sinners, tax-collectors, gentiles, from whom members of the
religious establishment of the day among the Jews kept their
distance.

It was on this occasion near Caesarea Philippi that Jesus
posed to his disciples the surprising question, 'Who do you say I
am?' It is a question which every year, during the celebration of
Advent and Christmas, Christ addresses to us also. Finding an
answer was something which occupied the minds of the first
Christians for quite some time, something also which led to
several heresies in the first centuries AD about the nature and
person of Christ.

The Church uses the scriptures, and in particular the gospels,
to awaken in us a response in faith to this mystery. In what is the
first gospel to be written, St Mark tells us nothing about Christ's
life before his public ministry, but he begins with an account of
the work of John the Baptist as being the fulfilment of a prophecy
by Isaiah. What Mark is saying is, that the story of Jesus really
began far back in Israel's history, and that his public life, his
death, and his resurrection show us that he is God.

Matthew and Luke in their accounts of the birth of Jesus,

which we read every year at Christmas, go a step further. They are saying that it was evident from the moment, not only of his public life, but of his birth, that Jesus was a divine person. Matthew traces the genealogy of Christ back to Abraham, the father of Jewish faith and also of ours. By this he is indicating to us, that the promises made long ago to Abraham, that he would be the father of a great people, were now about to be fulfilled in the life and work of Jesus. Luke traces the genealogy of Jesus back even further, to the first man Adam. The story of Jesus, he is saying, really began with the creation of man, and what God was doing through the life and death of Jesus, was to create, not only a new Israel, but a new humanity, for himself. It is well to remember that St Paul saw Christ as the second Adam, the new Adam, in whom all humanity would be renewed.

Today the beginning of the gospel by St John goes back to the moment when time began. Its very first words, 'In the beginning', show us what John has in mind. For these are the same words with which the Bible begins its account of the creation, 'In the beginning, was the Word, and the Word was God.' And in that first chapter, no less than ten times we read, 'God said', that is God spoke the Word. 'God said, "Let there be light" – God said, "Let there be a firmament" – God said, "Let the waters come together"' – and so on. The creative Word of God was at work, and the story of Jesus, St John is telling us, is the story of this Word, after becoming flesh.

John emphasises also that what took place as the work of God in the life of Jesus, was not a kind of afterthought on the part of God, a means of plugging a gap, of setting right a defect which had appeared in creation because of the original sin of which Adam and Eve were guilty. No, Christ is, and always was, at the very centre of God's plans for creation, and every created thing derives its meaning from him. Our task, then, for the new year should be to put Christ at the very centre of our lives, so that, as we read at the offertory, by the mystery of the water and wine in the Mass 'we may come to share in the divinity of Christ, who humbled himself to share in our humanity'.

THE EPIPHANY OF THE LORD
Is 60:1-6; Eph 3:2-3, 5-6; Mt 2:1-12

'Arise, shine out Jerusalem, for your light has come; the glory of the Lord is rising on you, though night still covers the earth and darkness the people. ... The nations come to your light ... everyone in Sheba will come bringing gold and incense'. These sayings of the prophet Isaiah must have been very much in the mind of St Matthew when he described the coming of the Magi to worship the new-born Saviour of the world in Bethlehem. So too must have been the words, which were recorded by Matthew but uttered by Jesus during his public life, when he praised the Roman centurion, a gentile, a foreigner, for his great faith, 'I tell you solemnly, nowhere in Israel have I found faith like this. And I tell you that many will come from the east and the west to take their places at the feast in the kingdom of heaven, but the subjects of the kingdom (meaning the Jews) will be turned out in the dark' (8:10+).

Roughly twenty-five years after his death on Calvary, this acceptance of Christ by the gentiles was described in his gospel by Matthew, in his beautiful story of the Wise Men from the east being drawn to Bethlehem by a star that shone especially bright in the darkness of the night sky, resulting in the epiphany or revelation to them of God in the person of the infant Jesus. The Apostles when trying to understand the events of Christ's life had been taught by Christ himself to look for their meaning in certain passages of the OT, and so it is more than likely that Matthew linked the star of Bethlehem, shining serenely in the sky while night covered the earth and darkness the peoples, with a prophecy in the Book of Numbers, which promised, 'A star shall come forth out of Jacob, and a sceptre shall rise out of Israel' (24:17).

Originally, this was seen as a reference to the founding of the royal house of David from which the Messiah would come. But Matthew went on to link the star with Bethlehem, which was the city of David, and moreover the town foretold by another prophet (Micah) as being the place chosen by God where the promised Messiah would be born. Since the royal line of David had long since vanished, the Messiah would not be a political leader but rather a spiritual one, and his coming, to a large extent, would be ignored by his own people.

It was mainly the gentiles, represented by the Wise Men, who were to be drawn to this Star of Bethlehem, and came to believe in God's greatest self-revelation, through the person of Jesus Christ. We are told nothing of what the Magi said, but the gospel, in a concrete way, describes the sublime act of their perfect faith in him, whom they sought, 'Falling to their knees they paid him homage'. Then they offered him gifts, gold as befitting a royal person, frankincense reserved for the worship of God, and myrrh, a substance used in dressing wounds and embalming bodies, signifying that this child was truly man, capable of suffering, and destined one day to die.

You may perhaps say that we have no gold, or frankincense, or myrrh. That is true, but we have something more valuable, precious treasures that we can present to Christ, our Saviour and our King. We bring gold to Christ when we try and make him king of our hearts. We offer frankincense when by our worship and prayer we proclaim his divinity. And we can, in some small way, alleviate the pain of the wounds he suffered for us by applying the myrrh of our own sufferings, our sorrow, our humiliations and tears.

The departure of the Magi from their own country is symbolic of every response of faith. When we make an act of faith, we abandon something, the kind of outlook which urges us to rely only on the tangible material world, and we allow ourselves to be drawn, as were the Magi, by someone who, although invisible, is more real than the world of sense around us. But we must always remember that we could never begin to seek God, draw nearer to God, unless God had already found us. The desire for God, the secret thirst for salvation that arises within us, is not begotten of any human emotion, but rather kindled by God himself.

When we are baptised in this faith we become the enlightened; we carry within us the light of faith; we are marked with the sign of God; we become Magi to others in our turn. As Pope St Leo the Great once said, 'Whoever preserves in himself, or herself, the brightness of a holy life, becomes for many a star which lights the way to the Lord.'

THE BAPTISM OF THE LORD
Is 42:1-4, 6-7; Acts 10:34-38; Mt 3:13-17

During the week we celebrated the Feast of the Epiphany of the Lord, which recalls the manifestation or showing forth of God in the person of Jesus Christ, before the gentile world, represented in the persons of the wise men who came from the east. But rather strangely, in the Orthodox Churches of the east, for example in Greece, Russia, Armenia, it is today that the Epiphany is celebrated, and it is not the Magi story but the Baptism of Christ which is central to the readings even as you heard it read just now. The reason for this is that the Eastern Churches, which always focused on the mystical aspect of the Christian faith, regarded the entire life of Christ as a whole series of epiphanies, or revelations of the divinity, of which Christ's Baptism in the Jordan, by John, was the first and most important.

We begin to see the reason for this when we recall how Jesus, after his resurrection, appeared to his Apostles in the Upper Room, and told them, 'You will receive power when the Holy Spirit comes upon you; and then you will be my witnesses to the ends of the earth' (Acts 1:8). Thus the primary function of the Apostles was to bear witness. And if we ask what witness, we find the answer in what St Peter demanded, when the Apostles met to choose a successor to Judas Iscariot, 'You must choose someone, who has been with us the whole time that the Lord Jesus has been travelling round with us, someone who has been with us, right from the time of the baptism of John, until the day when Jesus was taken up from us, and he can act with us as a witness …' (Acts 1:21). Thus the starting point for the testimony of the Apostles, who were the special witnesses chosen by the Holy Spirit, was that event which we recall in the liturgy today, namely the Baptism of Jesus by John.

We may wonder why Jesus, who was absolutely sinless, submitted to this baptism by John, a baptism which was purely symbolic, a sign of the repentance which John preached, but not a sacrament. Jesus himself saw it as a compliance with the wishes of the Father. He humbled himself, and proclaimed himself as being one with sinful humanity, without however condoning its sins, or being in any way guilty of sin himself. When Jesus comes out of the water, we have the first revelation in scripture of the Blessed Trinity of persons in the one true God, the Son being baptised, the Holy Spirit descending on him in the form of a dove, the Father saying, 'This is my beloved Son; with him I am well pleased.'

St John, in his first Letter stated, 'If anyone acknowledges that Jesus is the Son of God, God lives in him, and he in God' (1 Jn 4:15). This should be a source of great consolation to us, because by our baptism we have acknowledged the divine sonship of Jesus, and so we have become temples of God's Holy Spirit; we are set apart for the worship of God, and like the Apostles we too are commissioned to give witness to the continuing presence on earth of Christ, putting into effect his work of salvation.

Today it is difficult for us, who have, as a general rule, become members of the Church at infancy, to understand the joy which the oath of allegiance to God, taken at their baptism, brought to the adult converts to Christianity in those early days of the Church. For them this sacrament was the conscious and blessed beginning of what they called the 'Way', the road to God mapped out by Christ. Jesus, we say, was king, priest and prophet, and his first public act as prophet was his baptism.

Prophets had a habit of linking some striking symbolic actions with what they wanted people to learn. For example, Jeremiah carried a yoke on his shoulders to let Israel know it was in bondage. Isaiah never married to let Israel know how spiritually poor and barren she was. Jesus himself cursed the fig-tree which being withered next day symbolised Jerusalem's rejection of the salvation offered her. Jesus' baptism also was a prophetic action, in that by it he was telling people that they were in need of conversion, and should turn to God once more, as John the Baptist was telling them.

Jesus' baptism moreover was for Israel a sign of its repentance and salvation. And so likewise should our baptism be for all of us. If John came across to the people as a grim ascetic, threatening them with inexorable judgment, Jesus comes across as a giver of hope. John was the prophet of woe; Jesus the prophet of salvation.

SECOND SUNDAY OF THE YEAR
Is 49:3, 5-6; 1 Cor 1:1-3; Jn 1:29-34

In the readings today we have two sayings which can be applied
in a special way to Christ, the first from as far back as seven
hundred years in the Old Testament era, 'I will make you the
light of the nations, so that my salvation may reach to the ends of
the earth', the second from Christ's contemporary, John the
Baptist, 'Yes, I have seen and I am the witness that he is the
Chosen One of God.' We can say that these point equally to each
one of us, who are followers of Christ, for we are called to be a
light to the nations, and also to give witness that Jesus, the
Chosen One of God, is still continuing his mission of salvation.
With the absolute certainty that comes from our religious belief
in the truth of the gospels, we can say that the risen glorified
Christ is present here and now. He is present in the Church in a
special way, in the celebrations of the liturgy, in the sacrifice of
the Mass, in particular in the Eucharistic species in the
Tabernacle, in his word, since he himself speaks when the
Scriptures are read in church, present when the Church prays
and sings. 'Where two or three are gathered together in my
name, there am I in the midst of them' (Mt 18:20).

That saying, incidentally, makes quite clear also the importance and the real necessity of being part of the worshipping and
believing community, as against those who would claim that
they are quite capable of working out their own salvation, while
remaining apart from that community. However Christ comes
to all of us as One unknown, as once he came to those by the
lake-side in Galilee who as yet did not know him. 'Follow me',
he said to them, 'and I will make you fishers of men'. And to
those who answer this call, whether they be wise or simple, he
will reveal himself in the hardships, the conflicts, the sufferings
which they will encounter in doing so, and in return, as an
indescribable mystery, they will learn from their personal experience who he is.

Jesus' ministry began in Galilee, and it was not something
static, but rather a dynamic crusade. He never said, 'I have come
to teach', but 'I have come to cast fire upon the earth, and how I
wish it were already kindled' (Lk 12:49). This fire is that which
sets apart and purifies those meant for the kingdom. He was not
some high-minded teacher calmly indoctrinating people with

words of wisdom, but rather the strong Son of God, spearhead-
ing an attack against the devil and all his works, and calling on
people to make up their minds on which side of the battle they
would be. 'It was to destroy all the devil had done that the Son of
God appeared', St John wrote (1 Jn 3:8). And during those three
short years of his public preaching there was a tremendous
sense of urgency about everything he did and said. 'There is a
baptism I must receive, and how great is my distress till it is
over', was how he described his task (Lk 12:50). How are we to
respond, we should ask ourselves, to his call.

The first assembly of the Council of Churches met in
Amsterdam in 1948, and issued a report, agreed upon by all,
which begins from basics, and states what every Christian believes. It proclaims our Lord Jesus Christ to be our God and
Saviour, the Son of God made man, who gave the Holy Spirit to
dwell in his Body the Church. Always keep in mind that Church
is never to be equated with the small group that exercise a minis-
terial role within it, much less so with the hierarchy that directs
that group. What was handed on of the teaching of Christ by the
Apostles, the report states, comprises everything that serves to
make the people of God grow in faith and live their lives in holiness. In this way the Church in her doctrine, in her life and in her
worship, preserves and hands on to every generation all that she
herself is, and all that she believes.

But Christ is not only the one we remember and experience
from our links with the past. He is the one who brightens our
future, who stands on the shores of time and beckons to us. Thus
we can say that every time we celebrate the Holy Eucharist together, not only are we made mindful of the past, but we are, as
St Paul said, proclaiming his death until he comes (1 Cor 11:26).
For by his death he continues to honour and worship God the
Father, to make atonement for our sins, to intercede for us and
for others, and to ask the Father's blessing on all who have gone
before us. And when the time comes for us to follow them, God
grant that each of us may be able to say with John the Baptist, 'I
have seen, and I am the witness that Christ is the Chosen One of
God'.

THIRD SUNDAY OF THE YEAR
Is 8:23-9:3; 1 Cor 1:10-13,13; Mt 4:12-23

'Direct each thought, each effort of our life, so that the limits of
our faults and weaknesses may not obscure the vision of your
glory, or keep us from the peace you have promised.' That beautiful opening prayer sums up in short the longing of every human
heart for acceptance by God and for enduring peace. The
tragedy is that so many people try to satisfy this longing while
turning their backs on God, with the result that their search for
inner calm and serenity becomes fruitless. 'Peace I leave with
you, my peace I give to you; not as the world gives do I give to
you', Christ said in his final discourse to his Apostles at the Last
Supper as recorded by St John (14:27). Peace, or in Hebrew
'Shalom', was the common word of greeting and farewell
among Jewish people. It still is. But in St John's time the word
did not just mean an absence of war, trouble or bitterness. It was
an expression of that harmony and union with God and our
neighbour that comes from following the wishes of God's Holy
Spirit.

There is a great difference between the peace of the world
and the peace which comes from God through the action of
Christ. The peace which the world offers is the peace of escape
from turmoil and hassle. The peace of Christ is that which enables us to rise above sorrow and suffering, the common lot of
all mankind. Indeed, St Paul states the Christ himself 'is our
peace' (Eph 2:14), meaning that reflection on Christ wounded
and nailed to the Cross is enough to melt the hearts of the most
bitter opponents, and sustain people in times of adversity.
Human pain, suffering and misery, however, are conditions
which God never wished for mankind.

Why is it then, you may ask, that God's wishes are not being
put into effect? The answer, in part, lies in the free-will that God
has granted us. He respects that free-will; he does not impose
solutions, or exert force and pressure on people. As with the
Blessed Virgin Mary at the Annunciation, God comes to each
one of us with an invitation, a request, and then leaves us free to
respond. If we reject God's requests, it can only lead to unhappiness and inner anguish. If, on the other hand, we acquiesce to
the wishes of God, then we will become possessed of an inner
calm and serenity that nothing will ever disturb. The prayer of

Jesus, 'Let not your hearts be troubled, neither let them be afraid', will be a reality in us.

However, the wonder is that God chose the most unlikely places to give witness before the world to his providential care and concern for those in trouble. In the person of Jesus Christ he was born into a remote and isolated region of the vast Roman empire, one of a race described by the first century pagan historian Tacitus as 'a most contemptible mob ... a repulsive people'. That was how the cultured Roman regarded the Jews. Nor does the enigma of God's selection stop there; for he chose the most despised province of the Jewish state, Galilee, in which his Son would grow up. Galilee of the nations, or in other words 'heathen Galilee' (NAB) was how it was described, a land where people walked in darkness. And finally, God chose Nazareth, a village then so obscure that its name was never even once mentioned in the OT.

Quite often in ancient times it was even customary for its inhabitants, when going to Jerusalem for the festivals, to claim they were natives not of Nazareth but of Cana. Bartholomew, the future Apostle, before he had met Jesus, summed up attitudes well when he said to Philip, 'Can anything good come out of Nazareth?' (Jn 1:46). When the Son of God became man he emptied himself of some of the special attributes of his divine nature, so as to become like us in all things except sin. Such is the mystery of the Incarnation. And side by side with it is the mystery of God's choice of this most backward place in which the divine Incarnation would unfold. Surely it is true that in the most unexpected circumstances Jesus began to show himself as healer of the sick in body, and light of those whose spirits lived in darkness.

His choice of place in which to deliver a message to people continues to surprise us, – a refuse dump along the cliffs outside the town of Lourdes, the church gable-end in what was poverty-stricken Knock, an isolated hollow in the mountainous moorland around Fatima. God is forever confronting us with the unexpected, and as for us, we can only say with the Blessed Virgin, 'My soul glorifies the Lord', or with the writer of the Psalms, 'What God is great like our God?'

FOURTH SUNDAY OF THE YEAR
Zeph 2:3, 3:12-13; 1 Cor 1:26-31; Mt 5:1-12

Today's gospel reading which recalls Christ's preaching of the Beatitudes is one which causes a lot of soul-searching for Christians, something which is evidenced by a certain feeling of unease every time we hear them. Yet Christ never intended that they should be anything other than an encouragement to us. They make no demands, they are not a law, they do not lay a new yoke on Christ's disciples. They are a description in eight striking sentences of the marvellous freedom which the truly devout soul enjoys. Jesus is speaking from experience, because he himself lived the Beatitudes in his own life, and it is only by living them also in our lives that we can discover how true they are.

Although they are not set commands, they are nevertheless revolutionary; and how revolutionary can be seen when they are compared with the beatitudes advocated by the Wisdom books of the Old Testament. These latter describe as happy the man who has a good wife, obedient children, faithful friends, the one who succeeds and prospers in all he puts his hand to. But surprisingly, according to Jesus, the happy and blessed are not the propertied, not the contented or the successful, but rather the poor, the hungry, the mourners, the despised and persecuted. We may begin to understand this if we can answer the vexed question, 'Whom did Jesus have in mind when he spoke about the "poor in spirit"?' Was it those lacking in material goods, or those with plenty of resources without being over-attached to them, or perhaps the people who were convinced that material things mean nothing and that God means everything? The fact is that the vast majority of the population of the Graeco-Roman world in those times enjoyed very little material prosperity.

In line with the Old Testament, it would seem that St Matthew's 'poor in spirit' was a reference, not so much to those lacking worldly possessions, but rather to those who found themselves in humble circumstances and continued to make do without complaint, those whose spirits remained free despite their lowly social standing and their servile behaviour, which were in such stark contrast to the arrogance and assertiveness of those who controlled the sources of wealth, and also were its principal beneficiaries. Hundreds of years prior to Christ we read in one of the Psalms, 'This poor man called, and the Lord heard him, and saved him from all his distress' (Ps 34:6). Such a person willingly became detached from material things because he knew that they would not bring him complete happiness or security, and so he turned to, and relied on God, for he was confident that God alone would give him help and hope and strength. However this does not mean that material poverty is a good thing. It simply is not. Jesus, for example, would never regard that state as blessed where people live in slums without having enough to eat, and where health degenerates because conditions are all against it.

Yet paradoxically, it is also true that Jesus himself never initiated any social reform, or campaign to assist the poor and the exploited. 'Do not store up treasures for yourselves on earth, where moth and rust consume and thieves break in and steal, but rather lay up treasures for yourselves in heaven' he said in the Sermon on the Mount (Mt 6:19+). So firmly did he refuse to be cast in any such role that he was even referred to as the friend of publicans or tax-collectors, themselves the greatest exploiters of people at that time. The truth is that despite his miraculous feeding of the multitudes Jesus' concern never stopped short at the material goods, or lack of them, in peoples' lives.

It was on people themselves, the human person as he, or she, stood in relation to God, that he focused his mission. 'Seek ye first the kingdom of God and his saving justice, and all these other things will be given you as well' (Mt 6:33). And there is absolutely no doubt that his sympathy, his concern, went out to the humble, the toilers and heavily-laden, the outcasts like sinners and publicans who lived a despised existence on the verge of Jewish society. The people who have only God to turn to, the powerless, those who mourn, those who are persecuted, abused and calumniated on account of Christ, all these will be comforted. They will have mercy shown them. Theirs will be the kingdom of heaven; in them the love of God will reveal itself as the meaning of life; they will be called children of God, they shall see God.

FIFTH SUNDAY OF THE YEAR
Is 58:7-10; 1 Cor 2:1-5; Mt 5:13-16

In India when two people meet, instead of shaking hands, as we do in the West, they have the beautiful custom of joining hands, as if in prayer, and bowing towards each other, a gesture which appears so very meaningful and symbolic to westerners. Truly it has been said, that the only way to counter the sign of the clenched fist, which Isaiah mentions today, is with the sign of the joined hands, which denotes generosity and respect, and one might even say readiness to pray for others. If you allow your life to be moulded by such attitudes, then as the first reading also states, your light will rise in the darkness, and your shadows become like the noon-day. The gospel is even more emphatic, 'Your light must shine in the sight of men, so that, seeing your good works, they may give the praise to your Father in heaven.'

Does it strike you, however, that there seems to be a contradiction between this saying of Christ to his disciples, and the fact that Christ spent all his own life – with the exception of three years – in the obscurity of the backward little village of Nazareth, and that seemingly with little effect, for the inhabitants refused obstinately to see anything in him other than 'the carpenter, the son of Mary'; so much so, as St Mark tells us, that even Christ himself was amazed at their incredulity. 'He could work no miracle there because of their lack of faith', Mark says bluntly (6:5f). Is Jesus then consistent in cautioning me not to hide my light under a tub, while all that time at Nazareth he seemed to act like the man in his own parable, the man who received but one talent and was condemned for not putting it to good use. The message and the mystery of Nazareth are not easy to unravel. What Christ was called upon to practise at Nazareth was the heroism of the ordinary, the daily, often dull, routine, which requires its own kind of courage. Nazareth then was the scene of a hidden life, the ordinary everyday life of a family, made up of work and prayer, marked only by hidden virtues, and only God and Christ's closest relatives and neighbours were witnesses to any of it. Here in fact we have mirrored the lives of the majority of us. What sets Jesus apart from the rest of us is that he possessed the one basic talent, beside which all others are worthless. This was his ability to remain in God, to anchor his whole life firmly in the Father, to let the Father be the guiding force in his life. In his own words, 'The Son can do only what he sees the Father doing, and whatever the Father does the Son does too' (Jn 5:19). But this close relationship with God is not something we can earn, or plan for ourselves. It is God's miracle, God's doing. It is like the man in the parable, who scatters seed on the land. Night and day, while he sleeps or when he is awake, the seed is germinating, sprouting, growing. But how, he does not know. Concealment, we might even say, is the way God's glory is revealed in the world. Thus for the people of Nazareth, Jesus would remain just 'the carpenter'; while it was only through the mystery of the resurrection that the light of Christ's true identity was revealed to his very chosen disciples. So it was too with many of the great saints, who never tried to create an impression of holiness, but strove inwardly to remain always close to God, 'in loving attentive expectancy', as St John of the Cross said. These words could admirably describe the short life of another great Carmelite saint. St Teresa of the Child Jesus died about a hundred years ago at the age of 24, after nine years in her Convent at Lisieux.

Very few people took notice. According to her natural sister, Pauline, several of the other nuns even said that Teresa had been doing nothing, had come to Carmel seemingly to amuse herself. Yet in the following twenty years this community sent out over 750,000 copies of her *Abridged Life*, and 250,000 copies of *The Story of a Soul*, the account of her life written under obedience by Teresa herself. Within 28 years she had been canonised a saint in Rome before 50,000 people in St Peter's Basilica and an estimated half million in the Square outside. Two years later little Teresa Martin who had never once left her convent was proclaimed Patroness of the Foreign Missions. How did this come about? Reflecting on St Paul's assertion that there are three virtues which endure, faith, hope and love, and the greatest of these is love, Teresa saw her mission in life. 'In the heart of my mother, the Church', she said, 'I shall be love'. And in the concealment of her convent God's glory was to be revealed in a very special way before the whole world.

SIXTH SUNDAY OF THE YEAR
Sir 15:16-21; 1 Cor 2:6-10; Mt 5:17-37

Thus says the Lord God, 'A new heart I will give you, and a new spirit I will put within you; and I will remove from your body the heart of stone, and give you a heart of flesh' (Ezek 36:26). Here God, using figurative language, is addressing us from out the Old Testament about spiritual realities. I wonder how many of you recall the name Philip Blaiberg. Over thirty years ago (2/1/68), he was the first person ever to receive a new physical heart in a transplant operation carried out by Dr Christian Barnard. He was to live a further 19 months, but during all that time his entire body instinctively, vehemently, and ceaselessly fought to reject the implanted heart, even though without it he had no hope of survival.

This struggle is a picture very often of the way our divided yet real self strives to resist the life of Christ in us, the new heart he wants to create in us, that inner spiritual life-source which we too need so absolutely. To allow the vitality and power of Christ become part of us involves pain, and darkness, and mortification, and purification, not because Christ wants to inflict suffering on us, but because the impure and evil elements of our sinful nature do not want to be transformed. 'Lord make me pure', Augustine before his conversion used to pray, 'but not yet'. It was a hard struggle before grace prevailed. The great difference, however, between the reaction of the body to an organ transplant, and this reluctance to put Christ at the very centre of our lives, is that you only have to make up your mind finally to follow where God wants to lead you, and it is within your power to travel that path.

The first reading states quite clearly that each person has free will. God does not force his commandments on us, neither is he responsible for the evil which exists in the world. As the reading says in such a thought-provoking and rather frightening way, 'Man has life and death before him; whichever a man likes better, will be given him.' In other words everyone decides the way his/her soul shall go. St Paul, in the second reading, says that the weakness and the foolishness of the Cross were the things that God chose for his Son. And even though these things are a greater stumbling block than ever for our present-day culture, the Cross, nevertheless, is the only way to arrive at all that God has prepared for those who love him.

God's claim to obedience, so well exemplified for us in the person of Jesus Christ, is an absolute, total demand, claiming the whole person, not only in outward action but in one's inner attitudes, in one's heart. Thus not only is it wrong to cause bodily injury to another; we must not even harbour evil intent, or anger, or contempt against others. This sharpening of the demands of the law, to the point of the seemingly impossible, must have caused dismay among Christ's listeners at the Sermon on the Mount. And when Christ went on to say that not only must they not commit adultery, but that it was possible, by lustful looks alone, to commit adultery in the heart, then the surprise and astonishment among his Jewish audience must have been overwhelming.

But what Christ was saying was that the entertainment of lustful thoughts betokens an interior attitude of extreme selfishness, an attitude which tends to regard another person as an object, a means, of satisfying one's own inordinate and sinful cravings for self-gratification, and that this stands in absolute contrast to the loving desire and respect for each other which those in holy wedlock should have. People outside marriage, and sometimes even married couples, often cite love as a reason for setting aside all moral restraints in their relationship. But, on the contrary, it is a fact that true love does impose restraints, the restraints of consideration for, and respect for, and regard for the dignity and the happiness of the person loved.

Is Christ then demanding the impossible in asking us to extend the constraints of the moral law to our thoughts and imagination also? Is St Paul indeed, when he says, 'In your minds you must be the same as Christ Jesus' (Phil 2:5)? The answer would be yes, it is impossible, but for the saving grace which Christ is always ready to offer us, to help us attain these ideals. 'In Christ all things are possible.' For he is the one who is our advocate with the Father, the one who pleads with sighs too deep for words, that our sins may be wiped away, and that the holiness and purity of God may shine forth in all we are and do.

SEVENTH SUNDAY OF THE YEAR
Lev 19:1-2, 17-18; 1 Cor 3:16-23; Mt 5:38-48

In the teaching of the catechism, about a generation ago, there was a much used image of God symbolised by an ever-watchful eye, with a warning finger in front of it, and written underneath, the words, 'God sees you'. It may well have been an attempt to express visually the feelings of Job in the Old Testament, where he became obsessed and frightened by the thought that God was scrutinising his every action. 'Will you never take your eyes off me, long enough for me to swallow my spittle?', he cried (Job 7:19). Or it could have been an illustration of a saying in the Book of Ecclesiasticus, 'Their ways are always under his eye, they cannot be hidden from his sight' (17:15).

But such a concept of God, instead of drawing souls to him, can also have disastrous results, as for example in the person of the French writer and philosopher, Jean-Paul Sartre, who died in 1980. He stated in his autobiography that, in the middle of an innocent boyhood prank, he suddenly realised that, in his own words, 'God sees me'. And this so frightened him that, by deliberate choice, he cursed God, and became a bitter atheist for the rest of his life. In his writings, for part of which he refused the offer of a Nobel Prize, he painted a picture of man as a responsible but lonely human being adrift in a meaningless world, with a terrifying freedom to choose, that brought with it anguish or enduring anxiety. But God, from whom we come and to whom we go, instead of fixing a cold and calculating eye on us, bestows life and joy and, if we but have faith in him, a sense of being cared for – cared for, not because of what we do, or indeed the choices we make, but for our own sakes. God, we might say, even turns a blind eye on our faults, as shown by the Parable of the Prodigal Son; he is indiscriminating in his compassion; he is a Father who is prodigal in his forgiveness.

Never should we see God as a threat to our lives. Rather does he want us to live, to grow, to come to maturity and fulfilment. To err is human, to forgive divine, and this readiness to forgive is the unique attribute of our God. 'Father forgive them', Christ prayed for his executioners, 'because they know not what they do'. As the gospel points out, God treats all alike. He causes the sun to rise on the bad people as well as the good, his rain – a blessing in parched Israel – to fall on honest and dishonest alike.

And in our attitudes too, Christ tells us, there must be no spite, no hatred, no vindictiveness towards others. 'Be ye perfect as your heavenly Father is perfect', he tells us. 'Be holy, for I, the Lord your God, am holy', the first reading says. Strange as it may seem, the principle of 'an eye for an eye' was not a barbaric practice, but rather a call to the people of the Old Testament to exercise restraint towards those from whom they differed. It became known as the Law of Recompense or Retaliation (*Lex talionis*). But if we read the story of the creation in the book of Genesis, we see how quickly the disorders in society, caused by sin, spread after the Fall of our first parents, recounted in chapter three. Chapter four describes for us the first murder; and the spirit of hatred and feuding between families and clans that spread amongst mankind is exemplified by the reference to Lamech saying in the same chapter: 'I killed a man for wounding me, a boy for striking me. Sevenfold vengeance is taken for Cain, but seventy-seven-fold for Lamech.'

The pursuit of such vendettas – which by the way we have witnessed in our own times also in the wiping out of whole villages, even cities, by way of retaliation – brings about the virtual collapse of society. We have seen it in our own country, in the sectarian violence promoted in the name of religion, in the collapse of the very fabric of community life within certain areas of our cities, with the resulting unhappiness and longing to get away from it all on the part of many. It is striking how quickly even the very first Christian communities became divided and partisan, some taking Paul's side, others that of Apollos, and so on, as described in the second reading from the Letter to the Corinthians. But tensions, it can be said also, seem to give more purpose to a community. They oblige people to spend more time in prayer, in dialogue, in working at the restoration of unity. 'As the Lord has forgiven you', St Paul warns, 'so you also must forgive. Put on love which binds everything together in perfect harmony. And let the peace of Christ rule in your hearts' (Col 3:12-18).

EIGHTH SUNDAY OF THE YEAR
Is 49:14-15; 1 Cor 4:1-5; Mt 6:24-34

Although it is impossible for us to penetrate to the inner make-up of the mind of Jesus, we can nevertheless gain insights into it from meditating on passages of the New Testament, such as today's gospel reading. 'I am telling you not to worry about your life and what you are to eat, nor about your body and how you are to clothe it. Surely life means more than food and the body more than clothing ... Set your heart first on the kingdom of God and his righteousness, and all these other things will be given you as well. So don't worry about tomorrow; tomorrow will take care of itself. Sufficient for each day are the things that go wrong on that day.' From all these sayings, and from the recorded events of his public mission, the thing which strikes us especially is the absence of constraint in the life of Christ. He seemed to pass as free as the wind through all our man-made structures of duty and obligation. He steadily disobeyed the demands of what we regard as self-interest and self-preservation. His whole manner of life, and even more so his manner of dying, was a challenge to necessity, to the order of toil, hunger, passions, the struggle against nature, the struggle to hang on to life. Christ confounded his critics by conforming to no set pattern.

For a few brief years he emerged from his hidden existence in Nazareth, and became a wandering preacher, without a purse, very often without a place to lay his head. He expected people to lend him a boat, or a beast to ride on, with as little hesitation as he himself was prepared to give to them his coat or his cloak, should the need so arise. His sternest reprimand for his Apostles was reserved for Peter who counselled caution in the face of danger to his life. For him, even death was not a necessity. 'I lay down my life for my sheep ... No one takes it from me; I lay it down of my own free will' (Jn 10:15, 18). His entire preaching and career was a denial of the easy notion, held by the rich and healthy, that people get their deserts in this life.

It did not worry him that he was criticised for consorting openly with publicans and sinners, the despised ones of Jewish society. By so doing, he is telling us that people do not have to be good for God to accept them. God bestows his gifts freely. He is under no constraint to distribute them in the manner of wages by way of reward for good behaviour. Even while the human race was still in sin, God loved it, by sending his own divine Son to redeem it. The secret of Christ's influence on people with whom he came in contact was, perhaps, the unmistakable difference between him and all others, the fact that although he was in this world, he appeared to be motivated and governed by values nowhere found in it. He was beyond comparison with others, nor did he try and offer concrete proof of his credentials, like the prophets of the Old Testament.

Nevertheless, people of all kinds were drawn to him, men, women, children, tax-collectors, even people of ill-repute in society, and he showed concern for all, something Jewish rabbis never did. Although he humbly said, 'Happy is the one who does not take offence at me' (Mt 11:6), he was always in control of every situation. He could see through the remarks of his opponents, refute their objections, answer their questions, or force them into answering them themselves, with the result that even the Scribes, as St Luke remarks (20:40), dared not ask him any further questions. As to ordinary people, so great were the numbers drawn to him, to listen to him, to be cured of their illnesses, or just to witness the miracles worked by him, that he had to take his disciples aside to rest awhile.

St Matthew, in today's gospel, says that whether we are rich or poor, whether we are good or bad, whatever the activity we are engaged in, our lives are intended to bear witness to the supreme generosity, love, and freedom of the providence of God which watches over all of us. Our spirits, then, must always be free to reach out to God, and not become bogged down by concern for purely material needs, the daily demands of life. Because if we become engrossed in the provision of the necessities of life, we can, so easily, lose sight of the value of life itself. This does not mean that we should never take all the necessary steps for the prudent handling of life. But worry must not cloud out our vision of life's meaning. Each day should be lived as it comes, each task fulfilled as it appears, and then the sum of all our days will enable us to partake finally of the glorious freedom of the children of God.

NINTH SUNDAY OF THE YEAR
Deut 11:18, 26-28; Rom 3:21-25, 28; Mt 7:21-27

It is very easy nowadays to live a shallow existence in our modern world. What used be once referred to as the thinking man or
woman is fast becoming part of an endangered species. It is an
era of continual distraction – radio, television, computer games,
cyberspace or virtual reality, the internet enabling people on
opposite sides of the world to exchange typed messages at the
touch of a key. There are some individuals who spend up to 40
hours a week linking up with other people involved in this
latter. Our Irish missionary priests in Ecuador find it extremely
difficult to persuade their parishioners – mostly very poor people
– to give up watching television all through Sunday morning.

It has been said that in the US 'being busy' has been glorified
to such an extent that one of the most embarrassing situations
for the true American is to be caught thinking – doing nothing,
just thinking. It goes without saying that against such a frenetic
background the practice of perseverance in any prayer apart
from the Mass is becoming more difficult to pursue. There is
moreover within the Church itself a minority of people who are
ready to look with disdain on what they regard as mere religious trimmings, and who would go so far as to deride as 'craw
thumpers' and persons to be pitied all who would take seriously
St Paul's exhortation to keep on praying at all times.

At first sight today's gospel, and indeed our Lord's own
words, seem to lend weight to their arguments, that we should
concentrate on doing our duty and not waste our time on novenas,
and rosaries, and such like. After all, Christ had spelt it out clearly
to his disciples, 'Not everyone who says to me "Lord, Lord",
will enter the kingdom of heaven, but the person who does the
will of my Father in heaven.' Is the possibility and the very
necessity of prayer, we may well ask, being here called into
question?

We might begin to reply by admitting that a truly profound
prayer life can only be achieved by devoting effort, and time,
and perseverance to it. In modern times there are many businesses which demand round the clock attention, thus destroying
the old habits of private and family prayer. For others the morning has become the most intense part of the day, and the evening
the most profane and distracting section. But to interpret the

words of Jesus in the gospel as praise for anyone who by-passes prayer is precisely to distort them.

In fact, according to the gospel, the criterion by which Jesus judges us is whether he 'knows us', whether there exists between him and us a truly personal bond and relationship. There could possibly be certain individuals with the ability to drive out devils, to work miracles, to foretell the future, all done in the name of Christ, but were they without this knowledge of Christ, without a close spiritual affinity linking them with Christ, they could well face complete rejection by him. He does not mince words when he says, 'I shall tell them to their faces: Away from me, I have never known you.'

If there is one thought we might all profitably take away with us this morning, it is this: that prayer is the way we come to know Christ; that it is an essential part of the Christian life; that in effect, as somebody has said, one can no more believe without prayer, that one can swim without water. The basic expression of faith is not, 'I believe in the Bible, or in the doctrines of Christ and his Church, or in observing the commandments.' Faith is rather a turning to the mysterious and hidden being whom we call God, with the words, 'I believe in you, I trust in you, I commit myself entirely to you'. And every prayer is in a way a repetition in endless variations of this personal response, 'I believe in you'.

Faith is to be practised as a real part of our everyday life, and hence we should not pray merely as the mood strikes us. Nor, however, should we regard prayer as an obligation, a duty which presses upon us, or purely a repetition of set formulas, like the 'Lord, Lord' of the gospel. Prayer must instead be a loving expression of our living faith. There was a stage in the history of the Church when every-day work was seen as service to the world, and hence as a distraction from God. But following the advice of St Paul that our lives should be lives of continuous prayer, we should regard our entire working activity as an in-direct form of prayer, prayer without words. No matter what you do, do it for the glory of God.

FIRST SUNDAY OF LENT
Gen 2:7-9, 3:1-7; Rom 5:12-19; Mt 4:1-11

Contradiction, it has been said, is the hall-mark of what is false. We see this exemplified in the gospels, where they tell us that accusations were laid against Jesus at his trial, by false witnesses, and how the falsehood of these witnesses was revealed by their contradiction of one another. Jesus foretold, moreover, that just as he himself had encountered opposition, so would the Apostles and indeed the Church in which they were about to play such an important role. And in the century which has recently come to a close, the Church of Christ, in its teaching, has once more met with sustained criticisms, the inaccuracy of which very often is evident from the contradictions inherent in them.

For example at the beginning of the past century, the accus-ation was that religion was the opium of the people; it dulled the sensibilities of its followers, their reactions, their ability to make decisions for themselves. Nowadays, the Church, because it has stressed the existence of sin in the world, is accused of giving rise to a guilt complex in people. People are over-reacting to this concept of sinfulness which is preached to them. Yet we have only to look about us to see the presence of evil in society, to con-clude that the actions of some within it, not only threaten the very fabric of that society, but are an abhorrence to God.

As we see from the story of our first parents, evil enters the world because people refuse to obey God when he speaks to them through their conscience, that inner God-given awareness of what is good and evil, which clearly points out the road they must follow, and what they must steer clear of. Here, however, I would like to stress that, in putting into practice what God is asking of us, there are two extremes to be avoided. On the one hand, there are people who refuse to admit to any imperfection in their lives, and also some others who, through their continual disregard for their God-given awareness of what is just, and pure, and holy, have lost the very sense of evil. On the other hand, there is in every local community a minority of basically very good people whose consciences become clouded over with a persistent and confused feeling of guilt. They become obsessed with the thought of sin in everything they do, and this scrupu-losity is bound up with a false image of God, whom they regard as a threat hanging over them, one whose slightest whim must not be ignored, at the risk of eternal damnation. And, let us be honest, there is an element of this latter in the approach of very many of us to Lent also.

We are inclined to regard the season of Lent as a time when we have to make a special effort to placate a demanding and vengeful God in order to remain in his good grace. But if you want to get the Church's correct thinking on how we should regard God and Lent, then read through, and meditate on, the first preface for Lent in your missals, a preface which is such a beautiful and inspiring statement of what our approach to both God and Lent should be. 'Father, ... each year you give us this joyful season', it says – not the gloomy season, notice, that so many regard it as – 'this joyful season when we prepare to celebrate the Easter mystery with mind and heart renewed. You give us a spirit of loving reverence for you, our Father, and of willing service to our neighbour'.

Here we have the perfect blue-print for Lent. This is the season, it is telling us, when we should make a special attempt to say yes to the love of God. We do this by our personal attitude towards God, by our openness to the promptings of his Holy Spirit within us, by becoming willing instruments of God's loving and providential care as it reaches out to those around us who stand in need of it. Lent of course is also a time of repentance for each of us, and if we face up to the fact that there are elements of hatred and bitterness, selfishness and undue craving for sensual pleasure, pride and greed, dishonesty and disregard for the rights of others, in our lives, then as St John in his First Letter tells us, 'God who is faithful and just will forgive our sins, and purify us from everything that is wrong.'

What God is asking of us, then, during the season of Lent is to offer up as penance the sacrifices necessary to avoid sin. By sacrifice we mean essentially a more faithful carrying out of our daily duties, and leading a life of purity, of Christian virtue, of charity towards our neighbour, of prayer. And all this should be undertaken, not through fear, but by way of a response in love to the God who loves us.

SECOND SUNDAY OF LENT
Gen 12:1-4 2; Tim 1:8-10; Mt 17:1-9

During the Consecration of the chalice, the celebrant at every
Mass, recalling the words of Jesus at the Last Supper, says, 'This
is the cup of my blood, the blood of the new and everlasting
covenant.' That word covenant, which is central to the theme of
all the readings today, has lost most of its significance for people
in the modern world. But for the majority of people in ancient
times it was the only means of ensuring their very survival.
There were two kinds of covenants, or what we might term
treaties, agreements which were entered into by two countries,
or tribes, or communities, or even individuals. There were
covenants between equals, but more often there were covenants
where one of the parties was far more powerful than the other,
in which case the weaker party pledged allegiance to the
stronger in return for promises of protection, whenever needed.

This latter was to take on a unique significance in the history
of Israel, in that its people were the first to enter into a covenant
with God himself. And thereafter the history of Israel was largely
the history of the promises of this chosen people to serve God,
and the promises God had made, beginning with Abraham, as
shown in the first reading, 'I will bless you and make you a great
nation, ... and all the tribes of the earth shall bless themselves by
you.' It was God who took the initiative in this. He invited the
people into a covenant relationship, a relationship which was
not that of slaves, but of first-born children graciously redeemed
by God, a relationship which was meant to be the basis of the
community.

The covenant was always ratified by sharing a meal and offering a sacrifice. And so it is that the new and eternal covenant
between ourselves and God is ratified by the Eucharist, which is
both a meal and a sacrifice. God has nothing to gain from any
covenant, but enters it freely, in order to show his bountiful
mercy. The central event in the whole of the Old Testament was
the covenant at Mount Sinai, and the establishment of the Law
by Moses, who was regarded as the friend of God. But the Jews
lapsed from observance of the Law and the covenant, in times of
prosperity, when they had established themselves in the
Promised Land. It was then that God raised up prophets to recall
the people once more to renewed observance of the Law. One of

the greatest of these was Elijah, and we read in the Book of Kings how he became wearied and despairing because the people turned their backs on the true God and fell into idolatry. It reached the stage where Elijah went out into the wilderness and wished he were dead. But after being fed miraculously his courage was restored, and he travelled south for forty days and forty nights, until he came to Mount Sinai. Moses had wandered for forty years in the desert after receiving the Law on Mount Sinai, and we see that Elijah's journey was a symbol of this, but in reverse. He was going back to the sources of the Jewish faith. And at Sinai God appeared to Elijah also, God's covenant was renewed in him and his fervour was restored. From the time of Elijah on, the aim of the Old Testament prophets was to return to the standards of the Mosaic tradition.

Now we can perhaps begin to see why it is that in today's gospel we have Moses and Elijah appearing side by side with Christ at the Transfiguration on Mount Tabor. Moses represents the Law and the covenant at Sinai, and Elijah represents the prophets who, at a much later period, helped to keep the Mosaic tradition alive. In Christ we have the new and everlasting covenant which has evolved between God and man. And just as Elijah travelled through the desert for forty days to be renewed in the Sinai covenant, so we are spending these forty days of Lent in preparation for the renewal of the Christian covenant in us. God also is telling us during this season to listen to Christ, to open our hearts to him. For the Christian covenant is especially a covenant within, a covenant of the heart.

God is asking us to show our love for him, not by mere external observance, by going through the motions in our practice of Christian virtue. We will be saved, not just because we are members of Christ's Church, not because we comply with all the external requirements which that membership entails. What comes first and foremost is an inner personal commitment to Christ, and let us pray that we may all acquire this once more during this season, at the end of which we recall and celebrate the glorious events of the first Easter.

THIRD SUNDAY OF LENT
Ex 17:3-7; Rom 5:1-2, 5-8; Jn 4:5-42

For us who live in such a rainy climate, it is very difficult to
grasp the vital necessity and deep significance of water for the
people of biblical countries. Even today neighbouring countries
in the middle-east threaten to go to war over the sharing out of
water from rivers that flow through their territories. It has been
said that a person in ancient times who dug a well received as
much honour and gratitude from a Jewish community as would
the donor of a hospital, for example, in ours. When it did rain in
Israel, there was a feeling of gratitude to the Almighty, and awe
at the strength and power of the water, as it gushed through the
wadis and dried-up river beds. Water was seen as the life-giving
principle not only for man and beast but for the parched land
and crops.

It was God who blessed the people by sending them this rain,
and when the heavens remained shut up, they believed that it
was because the people's faith in God was found wanting. This
lack of faith we see in the first reading, where the Israelites in the
desert were tormented by thirst, and how they began to grumble
and complain against Moses. Moreover they even accused God,
as we so often do when confronted with difficulties. 'Is the Lord
with us or not?', they said – does God care about us? They were
thinking on a purely natural and material level. Yet, God did not
forget them, as we see, when water in abundance flowed out
from the rock after Moses struck it. It is interesting that, in the
Psalms, God is often referred to as 'my rock, my fortress, my
deliverer', and that St Paul echoes a tradition of the Rabbis,
which claimed that the rock followed the Israelites while they
journeyed through the desert. But Paul is not thinking in purely
material terms either – 'They all drank from the spiritual rock
that followed them', he states, 'and that rock was Christ' (1 Cor
10:4). And in today's second reading Paul also speaks about the
love of God being poured into our hearts by the Holy Spirit,
which has been given us.

In the gospel we see the faith of the half-pagan Samaritans
being contrasted with the faith of the Jews which, quite often,
was a superficial thing – a faith which was miracle-hungry,
seeking after signs and wonders, a faith which was blinded by
nationalism, and saw God as a kind of national asset for Jews

alone, one who was bound to bring about Jewish aspirations, if they but offered up the required sacrifices in the Temple at Jerusalem and observed certain laws of external conduct. The Jews, for example, were not supposed to drink the same water, nor even drink from the same vessel as a Samaritan. This explains why the Samaritan woman was surprised when Jesus asked her for a drink.

Then there followed a gradual self-revelation by Jesus to her. She had responded by recognising him as no ordinary Jew, but one who was greater than Jacob, who dug the well, one who was a prophet, the promised Messiah, the Saviour of the world. He went on to tell her that the hour was coming when people would worship God, not in Samaria, not in Jerusalem, but in Spirit and in truth. This was a clear reference to the new covenant spoken of by Jeremiah the prophet, a covenant in which God reveals himself internally to each person, so that one does not have to be instructed by others about the things of God, but rather listen to the Holy Spirit of God speaking within oneself.

For the Christian this internal revelation of Christ becomes the inner source of trust in, and prayer to, the Father. Remember always that there must never be a contradiction between our lives and our worship. We must continually remind ourselves during this period of Lent, that if we continue to sin in our daily lives, then our worship of God can become as empty and meaningless as that of the Jews in early times, who combined it very often with worship also of pagan gods. But if we open ourselves in faith to the Spirit of Christ, then the gift of God will become a spring inside us welling up to eternal life, as Jesus promised.

This message, I think, is brought home to us in those two places of tremendous faith, Lourdes and Fatima, for in each of them there was found a miraculous spring of water, a sign of the deep faith and devotion which would come to so many modern counterparts of those Samaritans at their well. Together with Knock they are places where some persons find bodily healing, but many, many more, discover afresh the wonder of God's love for them and inwardly are never thirsty again.

FOURTH SUNDAY OF LENT
Jer 1:4-9; Acts 13:46-49; Lk 10:1-12, 17-20

One of the problems which vexed the Jewish religious authorities in ancient times was the connection between suffering and sin. This was understandably so before belief in the resurrection came to be accepted generally by them. For if the devout and upright person was to be rewarded by God, and there was no life after death, then the reward for a life well spent would obviously have to come in the life-time on earth of that person. But how was it that frequently the wicked seemed to prosper in this world, while the good people very often were seen to be burdened with suffering and misfortune? Even Jesus' own disciples seemed to go on the assumption that where there was suffering there must be sin.

And so they put the question to Jesus, as we read in today's gospel, 'Who sinned, this man or his parents, for him to have been born blind?' But Jesus refused to apportion blame to either. He simply remarked that, in the divine scheme of things, the whole episode was intended to show that, in the man born blind, God was at work through Jesus. In other words, the miracle performed in the cure of the blind man was a sign that Jesus, to quote his own words, is 'the Son of Man', the one who shares in the divine power, a power that can transform people and give them new life, and even enable them to become children of God.

We are inclined to think that conversion to God is a once-off occurrence in time. But not so. Conversion, or turning to God, is an on-going event. God is for ever on this earth saying to us, 'Now is the time', and hence there is no standing still. The Pharisees were the ones who wanted everything to remain static and fixed. They were typical of the people in every generation who condemn anyone whose idea of religion is not theirs, and they were adamant that theirs was the only way of serving God.

For sheer drama what takes place in today's gospel story has been described as one of the most brilliant scenes in the whole of the New Testament. In a few sentences, the inner character of each of those involved is revealed by St John. The former beggar stands before his betters, as the Pharisees saw themselves, and is relentlessly badgered by them in an attempt to force him into denying that he was cured by Jesus. But being brought up in a hard school he displayed an extraordinary strength of will by not allowing himself to be browbeaten by his questioners. His refusal to comply with their purpose is a lesson to all of us, who have had the grace and knowledge of God bestowed on us in the sacrament of baptism, in order that we may give witness to Christ before the world.

In response to this prolonged questioning, he stuck to the fact of his own cure, and refused to be drawn into speculation about explaining it. He even dared to suggest that because of their continuing interest the Pharisees were perhaps considering becoming Jesus' disciples too. This led, on their part, to the last resort of those who find themselves losing in arguments – abuse followed by insult. They called him a sinner through and through since he was born.

As to the parents of the blind man, their fear is quite palpable. They were in dread of being debarred from the synagogue, and so, rather than commit themselves in any way, they referred to their son himself all further questions about the cure. But the real defendant in the whole case was Jesus, and he was being judged in his absence. 'We know that this man is a sinner', the Pharisees said referring to Jesus. The man born blind, in response, confronted them with an argument they could not answer. If Jesus had performed a miracle, then he could not be a sinner, because God does not grant the wishes of a man who is evil. It is the prayer of the good man which God always responds to.

And so a new light came to the man born blind, an inner one. He believed in Christ and worshipped him. If the Pharisees had only realised the extent of their own blindness there would be hope that they might keep searching for the light. But because they were sure that their beliefs were beyond question, their wilful, and hence sinful, blindness to the light remained. At St Paul's conversion when his sight was restored his first words were, 'Lord what am I to do?' His advice to the Romans on this is directed at us too. 'Let us give up all things we prefer to do under cover of the dark; let us arm ourselves and appear in the light. Let us live decently as people do in the daytime' (Rom 13:12f).

ST PATRICK'S DAY
Jer 1:4-9; Acts 13:46-49; Lk 10:1-12, 17-20

> Christ be with me, Christ within me, Christ behind me,
> Christ before me,
> Christ beside me, Christ to win me, Christ to comfort and
> restore me.

This is a brief quotation from the ancient hymn called 'The Breastplate of St Patrick', which authorities agree was written by St Patrick himself. A breastplate in time of war gave bodily protection, but for Patrick the term meant a spiritual guard, a protection of faith against the devil, against wicked human beings and vice.

From his writings we can see that Christ was central to Patrick's spiritual life, that he was filled with the ideals of Christ, the thirst of Christ for the eternal salvation of souls. The longer of his two writings, his 'Confession', gives us some insight into the kind of person he was. Above all he was an ascetic, who started a tradition that lives on to this day in St Patrick's Purgatory, Lough Derg. He was brought to Ireland as a slave at the age of 16, and in the harsh existence he endured as a shepherd amongst hostile strangers he acquired a deep humility which comes to the surface everywhere in his writings, a humility which stood him well as he battled to reach an understanding of the future which God had mapped out for him. He speaks of himself as a sinner, the least learned of men. But this was perhaps the pious exaggeration of a man in mature old age looking back on his youth.

What is certain is that he was to acquire a wide knowledge of, and intimate familiarity with Sacred Scripture, and modern analysis of his two works has revealed references to the writings of at least twenty of the great theologians of the early Church. But out of this sense of his own unworthiness there developed a tremendous trust in God, something that later stood by him as he tried to cope with a hostile pagan environment. Like the shepherd children of Fatima, the boy Patrick turned to God in prayer, as often as 100 times during the day, he tells us, and as often again at night.

From this rich experience of almost uninterrupted conversation with God his whole character and outlook changed. There developed in him a remarkable nobility of spirit, which made him ignore the hardships he had endured, as well as a keenness of spiritual vision which enabled him to gain insight into souls. Deep in the hearts of the very people who had enslaved him he became aware of a sense of hopelessness and misery in their search for meaning to life. This had the result of enkindling in him the flame of the crusader for God.

Patrick, who had been kept in bondage for years by the Irish, did not seek revenge, or even just redress for the loss of his liberty. No; his sole aim became that of bringing light where darkness prevailed, of sowing hope where people looked beyond life on earth with nothing but despair. Having made good his escape, Patrick was consumed by a burning missionary zeal for the conversion of his former captors, themselves held captive by the pagan beliefs which governed their lives.

This he felt was given sanction by a vision one night, in which he seemed to hear the people who lived by the Wood of Voclut, near the Western Sea, crying out to him with one voice, 'We appeal to you, holy youth, to come and walk once more among us.' This wood incidentally, in the 7th century was claimed to be along the western shore of Killala Bay. And so it came about that Patrick responded to this call, and returned to win souls for God, to confront unbelievers, to travel continuously, to resist the establishment of the day, to spread throughout the land the good news of salvation.

Today we need many of these traits which so characterised Patrick, his humility, his honesty and lack of pretence, his energy in a noble cause, his fearlessness in the face of opposition, his loyalty to the gospel he preached, and above all his life of intense prayer and union with God from his earliest years onwards. 'My enemies think that being Irish is a cause of shame', he wrote.

We ourselves should be ashamed of being Irish in this time of change, only if we fail to uphold those ideals which Patrick's life exemplifies for us. Our generation will only be remembered, if it can reach out, and assimilate, and put into practice the rich heritage left by St Patrick, and in turn hand it on intact, even hopefully enriched, to the generations which will come after us.

FIFTH SUNDAY OF LENT
Ex 37:12-14; Rom 8:8-11; Jn 11:1-45

The story of the journey of each of us to God is a story of fresh beginnings. Saint Bernard, the Cistercian Abbot of Clairvaux, used to say each morning, 'This day I will begin to serve my God anew.' In ancient Greek mythology there was a fable about the Phoenix, a bird which was reputed to live an immensely long time. And when it sensed at the end of every five hundred years that death, as a possibility, was drawing near, it built a kind of funeral pyre around itself, and set fire to it. Then from the ashes of this fire the Phoenix rose again, rejuvenated and resplendent, to begin a new cycle in its existence.

All this of course was a myth, but year after year in our lives, Lent, in a very real sense, is, or should be, a time of revitalisation, of renewal, a time when we once again dedicate our lives, in a fuller way, to Almighty God. And, very appropriately, all three readings for this Sunday are concerned with resurrection to newness of life.

In the OT reading, Ezekiel, the great prophet of the exile in Babylon, speaks about the hope of Israel's return from exile to their own native soil, an event which he compares with a rising again from the grave. God will put his Spirit within his people, and they will awake to a new awareness of his sustaining presence among them. St Paul, in the second reading, refers to the way in which Christ has burst the bonds of death and decay by his resurrection, and how in rising from the dead, he has taken on a new and totally transformed existence.

The Spirit which raised Christ from the dead is, moreover, received by all Christians, at the moment of baptism, and this indwelling Spirit is a sign in our mortal bodies – a sign which betokens a new life within us, which can never be destroyed, even with the death of our bodies. The state of each one of us, in this life, is governed by two forces, which in a way, we might say, are in conflict with one another – the life of the Spirit, and the death of the body. These two are emphasised in the high-point of the gospel story about the raising of Lazarus, where Christ says, 'I am the resurrection. If anyone believes in me, even though he dies, he will live, and whoever lives and believes in me will never die.' If a person has faith in Christ and places all his trust in him, then he will be possessed by the Spirit of the risen Jesus, raised up into a new plane of existence, and for him death loses all its destructive power. 'Yes it is my Father's will', Jesus had promised by the Sea of Galilee, 'that whoever sees the Son and believes in him shall have eternal life, and that I shall raise him up on the last day' (Jn 6:40).

Seeing the Son, for us, is to regard him with the inner eye of faith, and acknowledge that he is truly the Son sent by the Father. Indeed, whoever sees the Son, sees the Father who sent him, as Jesus himself pointed out (cf. Jn 12:45). But, just as the customary circular grave stone of that time shut off Lazarus in the tomb from the outside world of light and life, so we, by the manner of life we lead, can erect a barrier between ourselves and Christ – Christ who wants to be our light and our life. This obstacle to the grace of God can be an accumulation of compromises, neglect, self-deception, settling for a second-rate form of Christianity.

Lent is a time for removing these obstacles, for renewing the life of Christ's holy Spirit within us. The goal of life in this world should be to please God, and both Christians and Jews aspire to this ideal. We can arrive at this goal only by allowing the Spirit of Jesus to dwell in us, to direct us, to permeate our whole being, to the extent that we live for God. Without the Spirit which is the true source of Christian life, the body, through the influence of sin becomes inert. 'People who are taken up solely with material things can never be pleasing to God' (Rom 8:8).

Let us take courage and inspiration from the consoling words of St Paul to his Corinthian community, 'Though this outward nature of ours may be falling into decay, the inner nature is renewed day by day. Yes, the troubles of this life, which are soon over, though they weigh little, train us for the carrying of a weight of eternal glory, which is out of all proportion to them' (2 Cor 4:16f).

May this Lenten season leave each one of us with a clearer, and more real, vision of that eternal glory which God has promised will be ours, if only we have a deep and lasting faith in his word, and are obedient to the message he addresses to us through his divine Son, Jesus Christ our Lord.

PASSION SUNDAY
Is 50:4-7; Phil 2:6-11; Mt 26:14-27:66

'He was oppressed and was afflicted, yet he opened not his mouth. Like a lamb that is led to the slaughter, and as a sheep before its shearers is dumb, so he opened not his mouth' (Is 53:7). These words of Isaiah really evoke a response deep down within true followers of Christ, in as much as we are aware how aptly they apply to God's only beloved Son, and the way he died for all of us. If you dwell prayerfully on them they will surely enkindle within you a love that can change your whole life. For, in the words of St Peter, 'without having seen him you will come to believe in him, and so you will be filled already with a joy so glorious that it cannot be described' (1 Pet 1:8). On the other hand, unless you have a sincere love of Christ, you are not true followers of his. You cannot say you love him unless you have a feeling of gratitude to him, and this gratitude will not exist unless you appreciate what he suffered for you. Indeed we might go so far as to say that it is impossible that anyone can have attained to the love of Christ without feeling distressed at the thought of his bitter sufferings, and regret having contributed to them by his/her own personal sins. Having heard the Passion narrative there is no real necessity to retrace in great detail the events there described. But it is well to bear in mind that Christ was no stranger to hardship, privation and suffering, long before that final day of his life.

Being in the form of God, St Paul says, from the moment he came on earth, he emptied himself, taking the form of a slave, becoming as human beings are (Phil 2:6f). He, the most high God, became a poor man, and suffered the hardships of the poor, at times having not even a place whereon to lay his head. He endured hunger and thirst, and after journeying on foot all day long, surrounded by crowds of people seeking favours, he oftentimes remained whole nights at prayer on the mountains. Despite his love and compassion for all who came to him, he was subjected to hatred, contempt and persecution, in particular by the Pharisees and priests, who openly planned his death. Many attempts had been made on his life. St John recalls how his enemies tried to stone him (8:59), and Luke describes how his own townspeople at Nazareth attempted to throw him over a cliff (4:30). But because his hour had not yet come, he walked through the midst of the mob and went away. Yet, how deeply grieved he must have been at this rejection and antagonism. 'How sharper than a serpent's tooth it is to have a thankless child', King Lear, in Shakespeare's play, said. And how deeply grieved Christ, who was God incarnate, must have been at being spurned by the very people he had chosen, before all others, to live amongst.

Both in soul and body, Jesus was to be handed over to the malice of the evil one, to the powers of darkness, whose hour this was. With his loud cry to the Father, 'Not my will but thine be done', he had finally steeled himself for what lay ahead. So terrible was the inner struggle he had to surmount that the perspiration pouring from his face became great drops of blood falling to the ground. A further bitter pill was the knowledge that one of his very own would betray him, that most of the other Apostles would forsake him, and that Peter, his designated successor, would swear repeatedly that he never even knew him. With his arrest his sufferings would become more physical, as described in the passion narrative. But most terrible of all was his feeling of being abandoned by God, his inner spirit shrouded in a darkness that reflected the murky darkness that enveloped Calvary as the end drew nigh. It was this latter that made him cry aloud, 'My God, my God, why have you forsaken me?' To him the words of scripture could surely be applied, 'Attend all you who pass by, and see whether there be any sorrow like unto my sorrow' (Lam 1:12). That the person so suffering was the eternal Word made flesh, yet still true God from true God, is a profound mystery.

Thus the face cruelly disfigured was the face of God himself. The forehead streaming with blood, the hands and feet nailed to the Cross, the body lacerated with scourges, the side pierced with a lance, these were the forehead, the hands and feet, the sacred body, the side of the eternal God himself, made visible in Jesus. Why such suffering? We can only say with Isaiah, 'It was for our transgressions he was smitten, for our sins he was brought low. On him lay the punishment that brings us healing, through his wounds we are made whole' (53:5+). God, our Father, grant that your Son's suffering for us may not be in vain.

EASTER SUNDAY
Acts 19:34, 37-43; Col 3:1-4 or 1 Cor 5:6-8; Jn 20:1-9

During the past week we have been recalling the last hours on earth of Jesus Christ, our beloved Redeemer. We have followed in thought his prayer and agony in the Garden of Gethsemane, his condemnation by Pontius Pilate, his crucifixion, the placing of his body in the tomb by the few who had remained faithful to the end. And the feeling uppermost in our minds should have been one of compassion, the ability and willingness to suffer with a person who suffers, something which is the mark of a love that is truly sincere.

But the ability to rejoice with one who rejoices is even a greater sign of love. For, in certain ways, it is easier to have compassion for those weighed down by affliction and sorrows, that to enter honestly and wholeheartedly into the joy of another, to be glad because he/she is glad. So, our prayer during this Easter Mass should be to ask for the grace to be intensely glad, to rejoice in the great glory and joy of Christ Jesus, our Lord, on this blessed day. And not only must we ask for this grace, we must keep on asking, for the joy we are seeking is not something we can arouse in ourselves through our own efforts. It is something which must come from the bounty of God – a pure gift, which will enable us to be intensely glad, and to rejoice at the resurrection of our Lord, at the happiness that he is now experiencing.

Today's liturgy is full of this joy, the joy of a new life. For Christ is alive, and we should never allow anything to fill our hearts with so much grief, that we forget that Christ has conquered death. Whether the day is calm or stormy, whether I am in good health or bad, whatever comes my way, nothing can alter the fact that Christ has left the tomb, that he is present, even now, in all those who have faith in his word. If I can really grasp the significance of the resurrection of Christ, then I shall always be happy. 'All I want', said St Paul, 'is to know Christ, and the power of his resurrection' (Phil 3:10). Christianity, then, is compounded of far-reaching hope, and of a deep joy, that is not simply a concession to weak human nature, but a privilege and a duty. For a sad Christian is really not an authentic Christian, but a sorry one indeed.

We can get rid of all sadness only if we allow the Spirit of the risen Jesus to possess our souls. If you take up a Bible and read the next nine verses after today's gospel passage from St John, you will find an illustration of this in perhaps the most touching of the post-resurrection appearances – that to Mary Magdalene, for whom as for all the other followers of Christ, the previous days had been such a shattering experience. So broken-hearted is she that she mistakes the risen Christ for the gardener, until he says the one word 'Mary'. At that moment we can almost sense the astonishment and the relief of Mary from the pent-up grief and emotion which had made her oblivious to her surroundings. She can manage to say only one word, 'Rabboni', which means 'Master', and she gives expression to her joy by clasping the feet of her risen Lord.

Is it possible for us also to experience the risen Christ in any kind of sensible way. We should remember that Christ when alive had said, 'Destroy this temple (meaning his body), and in three days I will raise it up.' In so saying he was promising a sign, but one which was to be a secret sign, for, though many saw the risen Christ, no one witnessed the actual resurrection. It was to be received by many, but on faith alone. 'Blessed are those who have not seen, and yet believe', Jesus said to the doubting Thomas. But he had also said much earlier, 'Those who have my commandments and keep them, are those who love me, and those who love me will be loved by my Father, and I will love them and reveal myself to them' (Jn 14:21).

How does Christ reveal himself? Definitely not in any sensible or physical way, but purely on the level of faith. 'Those who love me will keep my word, and my Father will love them, and we will come to them, and make our home with them' (14:23). This indwelling of God, in a way, is grasped by its effects on our lives, effects which imply a presence within us of which they are a shadow, a voice within us of which they are the echo. Christ may be holding communion with us, without our knowing it. By opening our hearts to what he is saying we may briefly have to follow him in travail and hardship, but we will most assuredly also follow him in glory.

SECOND SUNDAY OF EASTER
Acts 2:42-47; 1 Pt 1:3-9; Jn 20:19-31

Year by year, we observe the season of Lent, often we might add with a kind of grim determination. In the Holy Week cere-monies we have vividly portrayed for us the sufferings and death of Jesus Christ our Saviour. But as the first Preface for Masses during the season of Lent pointed out, all this was by way of preparation for celebrating the mystery of the events of the very first Easter, with mind and heart renewed. And during this season following on our celebration, what God is asking of us is to reflect on the glorious resurrection of Christ, and what it means for us. The fact that in doing so we are confronted with mystery should not put us off. Even in the domain of secular science, it is now admitted in the words of a great writer on the history of science (Jacob Bronowski: *The Ascent of Man*, p. 353), that 'no event, not even atomic events, can be described with certainty'. Our knowledge is so far from being absolute, and our information so limited, that we have to treat all data with humility.

It is precisely with such humility that we must approach the scriptural accounts of Christ's resurrection, and not with the kind of obstinacy shown by the Apostle Thomas, who refused to believe until he had touched the wounds on Christ's body. Thomas failed in two ways: he wanted to verify the faith by physical means, and as well he was not prepared to accept what the rest of the Christian community had by now come to believe. However, we should never imagine that, because of the visions of the risen Christ which all the Apostles were privileged to experience, the road to faith was an easier one for them than it is for us. Indeed St Luke states quite clearly that when Christ, in the Upper Room, had shown them his hands and his feet, 'they still thought it was too good to be true'. It was not only Thomas who doubted. They all had to grapple with the question of what really had occurred. And their message for us, and that of Mary Magdalen also in her search for the body of Christ, could well be summed up in the inspired words of the prophet Jeremiah (29:13), 'When you seek me you shall find me, if you search for me with all your heart'. This risen Lord was no phantom or hal-lucination, but rather so real that one could touch or cling to him. The Jesus who had died was in very truth the Christ who had risen again.

At the Last Supper, Christ had said to the Apostles, 'You are sad now, but I shall see you again, and your hearts will be full of joy; and that joy no one shall take from you'. And in today's gospel reading we can see how Christ kept his promise, 'The disciples were filled with joy when they saw the Lord.' For us also, Jesus must be, not a figure in a book, not a memory from the past, but rather a living presence, one who is with us here and now. To those who, like Thomas, would argue that this is making too great a demand on our credulity, Christ replies, 'Happy are those who have not seen, and yet believe.' Because, as St Augustine pointed out, 'Faith is to believe, on the word of God, what we do not see.' It is like taking a step in the dark while trusting absolutely in what God is promising to us as the consequence.

The resurrection of Christ was a unique happening that lies beyond all human reasoning or understanding. 'Only faith can guarantee the blessings that we hope for, or prove the existence of realities that are unseen ... It is by faith that we understand how the world was created by God, so that what is seen was made out of what cannot be seen' (Heb 11:1, 3). The first chapter of the Bible tells us that the universe began in a single flashing act of creation, when God willed all things into being, out of nothing. The resurrection of Christ, of which we are celebrating the octave, is a mystery also. The risen glorified body of the Lord is a new creation. The disciples were filled with joy when they saw the Lord. Faith, joy – a faith which leads to and is the cause of joy – that is the message for us today. But there is more. For in our following of Christ, even though we have not as yet passed through the portals of death, we also can become part of this new creation initiated by Christ. We might even begin to speak of a third creation, for by our faith in the saving effect of Christ's death and resurrection, as St Paul tells us, we become something extra. We are made children of God himself. We are no longer slaves, but friends, and so on this day we should ask that we may receive and our joy, like that of the Apostles, may be full (Jn 16:24).

THIRD SUNDAY OF EASTER
Acts 2:14, 22-33; 1 Pt 1:17-21; Lk 24:13-35

The most precious thing we have as Christians is our faith, our
firm belief that God exists, that he has revealed himself in the
person of Jesus Christ, his divine Son, that by our following of
Christ we attain the privilege of being accepted as children of
God, and that having lived in communion with God, in him
alone we will ultimately find true happiness. When we are completely united with God, then there will be no more sorrows or
trials; we will become sharers in his divine life, and our own
lives will be complete. The articles of this our faith are more
certain than all the discoveries of human wisdom, because they
are founded on the very word of God, who cannot lie. Of course
divine revelation, and the articles of faith which are based on it,
can seem obscure and at times difficult to grasp, but as Cardinal
Newman once said, 'Ten thousand difficulties do not make one
doubt' (*Apologia* p. 239). And as to difficulties, even the chosen
disciples of Jesus himself had a number of these, in particular in
coming to terms with his resurrection from the dead. He had said
to them at the Last Supper, 'I will see you again, and your hearts
will rejoice, and that joy no one will take from you' (Jn 16:22).

But the two disciples on the road to Emmaus were anything
but joyful. Very obviously they were not leaders in the community, but they represented all the followers of Christ generally.
The two were troubled, and as yet did not understand why
Jesus' body was missing from the tomb. Neither, at first, did
they recognise Jesus, but once recognition came they did not
hesitate to believe. This was in complete contrast to the
Apostles, who recognised the risen Jesus straightaway, but
hesitated to trust their senses. The two at Emmaus, we are told,
recognised him in the breaking of bread, and the words used
leading up to this, 'took, blessed, broke, handed', are precisely
the terms used by Luke in describing the institution of the
Eucharist at the Last Supper.

This has a very special message for us, as to where principally
we should seek to find Jesus. For we can take as addressed to us
also the promise of Jesus to his disciples, 'I will not leave you
orphans; I will come to you. Yet a little while and the world will
not see me, but you will see me; because I will be alive, and you
also will live' (Jn 14:18). Christ is telling his followers, ourselves

included, that they will have a new life, a life which will be the result of Christ's Holy Spirit dwelling within them. At the very moment the disciples at Emmaus recognised Christ, we are told that he had already vanished from their sight. This statement is probably intended to bring home to us that Jesus' miraculous appearance is hardly necessary when one has his presence in the Holy Eucharist. Of course we cannot see Christ, or be aware of his presence in any physical manner. We cannot look at him, hear him, or converse with him. But still in a spiritual, immaterial, inward way, we can really possess him, be aware of him. And, wonderful to say, such possession and awareness can be more real and more present than that which the Apostles enjoyed in the days of his flesh, precisely because it is spiritual, because it is invisible.

Luke says that while Jesus spoke with the two on the road, their hearts burned within them. But at the time this was happening they were not aware of it. Afterwards when Jesus had said the blessing over the bread, it was then their eyes were opened, their faith in him renewed. This is a clear declaration that it is only by faith that the presence of the risen Jesus is recognised, and not by visual means, because Jesus, we are told, had already vanished from their sight when they recognised him. He had passed from being seen without being known, to that of being known without being seen.

This simple and charming story has one great lesson for us all. It tells how the two disciples begged Christ to stay with them, and how they enjoyed his companionship. The very word 'companion' derives from two Latin words, 'cum' meaning 'together with', and 'panis' which means 'bread', implying that companionship is the result especially of eating together, breaking bread together, something which is at the heart of the Eucharist. Like the disciples who begged Christ to stay with them, we too must really want him to be present in our hearts and in our lives in order to share in his companionship. This we should do every we time we celebrate the Eucharist together.

FOURTH SUNDAY OF EASTER
Acts 2:14, 36-41; 1 Pt 2:20-25; Jn 10:1-10

There is at present a greater sense of urgency than at any time during the century recently ended, about the need for men and women who will carry on the Church's tradition in Holy Orders, in the Foreign Missions, and in the different religious congregations and secular institutes that have been so much to the forefront in bringing the gospel message to people throughout the world. Each year on this day, which has been designated Vocations Sunday, we are all asked to reflect on this situation, and on what we can do in any way towards improving it.

A vocation to the priesthood or Religious life is a mysterious and sublime reality which can only come from God himself. And yet the prayers of all of us have an important part to play in God's plans for the salvation of the world. No one should ever say such a role is not for me, for God oftentimes chooses the most unlikely candidates to fill it. In the first years of the Church, when its members were being actively persecuted, when many had to flee for their lives or go into hiding, who could ever possibly imagine that one of their most fanatical persecutors would become the greatest missionary of all in spreading the gospel message among the gentiles?

Yet, as the liturgy has been recalling for us during the last week, this precisely is what happened in the case of Paul, or Saul as he was originally named. Here was a man who fully agreed with the stoning of St Stephen for his Christian faith, an act which was in contravention of Roman law at the time, the one who held the garments of those engaged in carrying out the killing, the one who afterwards proceeded to round up and bring to trial more members of the Christian communities, from as far away as Damascus, one hundred and forty miles from Jerusalem. And yet this was the man destined to become God's chosen instrument in bringing the name of Christ before gentiles and Jews alike, both in Asia Minor and southern Europe. So extraordinary and sudden was the change in Saul that for a time many Christians mistrusted him. Apart from the vision granted him on the road to Damascus, the ground for this conversion must have been prepared by the heroic witness of St Stephen and the prayer offered to God by the saint for his executioners. However hard Paul tried, he could not blot out from his mind the manner in which Stephen died. The blood of the martyrs was already becoming the seed of converts to the infant Church. Of course, it is true that we are not called upon to be martyrs in order to promote the spread of the faith, although the kind of life each one of us leads can be a powerful influence in drawing others to Christ. But there is one thing we can do, and that is pray. Christ himself said to his followers, 'Pray therefore the Lord of the harvest to send out labourers into his harvest' (Mt 9:38). Without specific, habitual, insistent prayer, there can be no success in gaining vocations. We must ask not only for an increase in vocations, but also for the perseverance of those who have been called, for their sanctification, and for the success of their missionary endeavours.

Our holy father the Pope frequently exhorts Christian families, whom he calls the first seminaries and source of religious vocations, to try and foster within the family circle a climate of Christian prayer, which will enable their children to be open to the voice of God calling them, and to respond generously in a joyful and persevering way to what God is asking of them. If parents pray with their children, and are seen praying by their children, then they are most certainly sowing the seeds of those vocations which will be needed to minister fulltime to the spiritual needs of the future. But it is not only families, it is the whole community which should be involved in this task. For a community which is poor in vocations makes the whole Church poorer, but a community rich in vocations makes the entire Church richer.

We should remember, also, that the concern of the Virgin Mary for the infant Church after the Ascension of her divine Son is something which continues to this day. We commend to her care the needs of our missionaries, the needs of religious engaged in teaching, nursing, looking after the disabled and orphaned, the need for more dedicated souls to live lives of faith and love within the cloister, praying for the salvation of the whole world. May there always be men and women, within the Church, who are willing to carry on such works of service for others.

FIFTH SUNDAY OF EASTER
Acts 6:1-7; 1 Pt 2:4-9; Jn 14:1-12

At the heart of every great civilisation in the history of mankind there has been some form of religion, which when it declined was followed gradually afterwards by the break-up of that civilisation. Are Western countries, we might ask, on the slide to decadence therefore, because they concentrate their energies almost solely on the acquisition of wealth and political power, to the near total exclusion of religious values? Of course we should seek higher standards of living, and work so as to pay for the good things we enjoy, but unless we are ambitious also for the higher gifts of the spirit we can end up as a nation without a soul, devoid of moral values.

As against this, the history of God's chosen people Israel, as we see in the Bible, is proof that a low material culture can become the vehicle of a truly great religious tradition. 'Man', one of the Fathers of the early Church (Eusebius) wrote, 'man, the beloved creation of the divine Word, is meant to form a bridge between God and the material universe'. The first Christian heresies, on the one hand, sought to convert Christianity into a religion of pure spirit, claiming that the material world is essentially evil. The prophets of modern progress, on the other hand, would say, 'We must concentrate all our energies on developing our material assets; as for religion, it is immaterial', in other words it serves no useful purpose in promoting the welfare of the human race.

But there are only three great enduring factors which can sustain the true aspirations of the human soul, faith, hope and love, and only these can span the gap between ourselves and the God who created us for himself. The Church, which Christ the eternal Son of God founded, is continually reminding us of the faith which we have received, and of our duty to increase and hand it on to the next generation. As to love, some would even claim that it has been over stressed in recent times, to the point of becoming almost a kind of sentimentalism largely divorced from any moral code. However Scripture assures us that the greatest of the cardinal virtues is love.

But we should ask ourselves what about the virtue of hope and its significance in our lives. Hope which for the Jews was, and still is, so very important, has for Christians become almost the forgotten virtue. 'Trust in God still and trust (or hope) in me', Christ told his disciples in his farewell discourse at the Last Supper. 'Hope is to us like an anchor, safe and sure', the Letter to the Hebrews tells us (6:19), and in the ancient world the anchor was the one great symbol of stability for the seafarer, who, relying on sail-power, was forever at the mercy of the uncertain winds. An ancient proverb maintained that 'a ship should never depend on one anchor, or a life on one hope' (Epictetus).

And so it is that the hope mentioned by the writer of Hebrews is anchored in two unalterable truths, first the promise given by God, who cannot lie, to shower blessings on Abraham and all his descendants (and such are we also), and secondly the oath by which God confirmed this promise, thus making it into a most solemn and sacred pledge. If throughout our lives we continue to hope and trust in God's mercy then we can pass with confidence through the veil that separates us now from God, that veil through which the risen Christ has passed as our forerunner.

Christ's promise to his Apostles at the Last Supper is made to us also, 'I am going now to prepare a place for you, and after I have gone and prepared a place for you, I shall return to take you with me so that where I am you also may be.' The longing for happiness hereafter is obviously a response to the virtue of hope implanted in us by God. No matter what happens we should continue to trust that with the grace of God we may persevere to the end, and so obtain the joy of heaven, which God will bestow on us as a reward for the good works accomplished under the guidance of the Holy Spirit, who pleads for us with sighs too deep for words.

The great Carmelite saint, St Teresa of Avila, whose writings on prayer merited for her the title of Doctor of the Church, composed this little prayer to keep her hope alive: 'Hope, Oh my soul, hope. You know neither the day nor the hour. Watch therefore, for everything passes quickly … the more you strive, the more you prove the love you have for God, and the more you will rejoice one day with your beloved One, in a happiness and rapture that can never end.'

SIXTH SUNDAY OF EASTER
Acts 8:5-8, 14-17; 1 Pt 3:15-18; Jn 14:15-21

In his prayer at the Last Supper, Christ pleaded with his divine Father that his disciples and followers might be characterised by their union with him, and form a united family with Christ himself as their head, so that people looking at their example would plainly see that God was at work in and through them. That his prayer was answered is clearly evident from the comment of pagan neighbours on the behaviour of members of the early Church, 'See how the Christians love one another.'

Regrettably, the same cannot be said today about many Irish people who would claim to be Christian. For the last forty years or so we have witnessed a gradual decline in moral and social standards in this country. Sadder still, many of our people see the only cure for this as being a more stringent law-enforcement campaign. Social standards, they claim, can only be upheld by making stricter laws and imposing more severe penalties on those who break them. But the lesson of history is that a multiplicity of legal restraints and harsher penalties should only be tried as a last resort, for they can never be the ultimate cure against evil.

Christ's way to change society was never to counter wrongdoing with force, but rather to change people from within, to put a new spirit within them. The request of the Apostles, James and John, that they be permitted to call down fire from heaven on a Samaritan town, because the inhabitants refused them permission to enter it, was met with a rebuke from Jesus, as was Peter in Gethsemane when he wanted to use the sword against those about to lay violent hands on Jesus. A change in society requires some form of moral crusade, for a society is valuable only in terms of the calibre of its people, their sense of justice and honesty, their self-restraint, their appreciation of beauty and excellence of thought and discourse.

Freedom itself is valuable only if individuals exercising it are filled with a sense of virtue and purpose. In Ireland at present we have a dedicated group who place great store on preserving the ecological balance of nature. But in America some years ago, an essay in *Time* magazine declared that belief in God would seem to be an ecological necessity in order to preserve the balance of human beings in US society. However in seeking a solution for the trials of our times, we, as Christian believers, must never forget that we have God on our side. 'I shall ask the Father, and he will give you another Advocate to be with you always', Christ says to us in today's gospel. This Advocate is the Holy Spirit, who comes to our assistance, who, as St Paul puts it, 'pleads for us, with sighs too deep for words' (Rom 8:26). Jesus, in his conversation with the Samaritan woman at the well, spoke about being born again of water and the Holy Spirit. Christians who are so reborn learn how to live a life of union with Jesus, by acting in accordance with the promptings of his Holy Spirit dwelling within them.

We have numerous examples of this in the history of the Church, in saintly souls, such as Venerable Matt Talbot, to mention just one who, although a man of little learning, laboriously waded through many great and difficult theological treatises, and gained marvellous insights into the things of the spirit. St John mentions how Christ, in his discourse in the Temple, spoke about the Spirit which those who believed in him were to receive, 'for there was no Spirit as yet, because Jesus had not yet been glorified' (7:37+). In today's gospel Christ makes a solemn promise to his Apostles, 'I will not leave you orphans; I will come back to you.' And St Paul keeps on reminding his first converts from paganism in Corinth, 'We are those who have the mind of Christ' (1 Cor 2:16), as well as those in Rome, 'The Spirit of God has made his home in you. In fact, unless you possessed the Spirit of Christ you would not belong to him' (Rom 8:9).

The departure of Jesus from this world does not mean that he is now remote from those who put their trust in him; he has not left us orphans. In fact it is by our faith in him, our union with him – 'you in me and I in you', as he says in the gospel – that we are drawn into the hidden life of the Blessed Trinity, which we describe as heaven. The first Christians looked forward with longing to the Second Coming of Christ; but it is quite true to say that this coming is taking place every single day. And our prayer should be the same as that of the early Christians: 'Maranatha – come Lord Jesus.' Amen.

ASCENSION OF THE LORD
Acts 1:1-11; Eph 1:17-23; Mt 28:16-20

The Ascension of our Lord and Saviour was an event which must have been recalled with joy and thanksgiving by the Apostles and disciples of Jesus Christ. Reflection on the Ascension of the Lord should make us aware that we live in a world of mystery, with one bright beacon lighting the way ahead, and that oftentimes through a sea of troubles and difficulties. Without this light, which is the glory which surrounds this final event in the earthly history of Jesus, we would not know where we are, what will become of us, what we are to believe, and what the ultimate meaning is of life on earth. But if we have the generosity of heart to risk everything, and accept God's word, then we will be able to go forward in the knowledge that our Redeemer lives, and is even now at the right hand of the Father, making intercession for each and every soul on earth.

'Who shall separate us from the love of Christ?' the New Testament asks (Rom 8:35-39). Indeed nothing can, for in 'all things we are conquerors through him who loved us'. We can remain certain that 'neither death nor life, … nor things present nor things to come … nor height nor depth, nor anything else in all creation, will be able to separate us from the love of God in Christ Jesus our Lord'. 'He then led them' – the specially chosen witnesses of his post-resurrection appearances – 'out as far as Bethany, and lifting up his hands he blessed them. And it came to pass that while he blessed them, he parted from them and was taken up into heaven' (Lk 24:50f). At that moment every thought and feeling they ever had about him must have come crowding back into their minds. He was leaving them at a crucial moment. He personally had endured contradiction, rejection and the cross. Their Calvary was still to come.

Their first feelings must have echoed the words of the Canticle of Canticles in the Old Testament, 'My Beloved had withdrawn himself and had gone. My soul grew faint at his flight. I sought him but I could not find him; I called to him, but he gave no reply' (5:6). The cry of their hearts might well have been the plea, 'We beseech you, Oh Lord, do not leave us comfortless.' This was the first reaction on their part, a purely human one, which surely tended to override every other feeling, as Christ ascended into heaven before their eyes.

But, in a truly wonderful way, their sorrow and anxiety gave way to more lofty and noble emotions. For we are told, 'they returned to Jerusalem with great joy, and were continually in the Temple praising God'. They had seen Christ being raised up on high, and their spirits were lifted up with him to a new spiritual plane, making them determined and confident in facing up to the prospect of trials such as Christ himself had endured. Christ had suffered and entered into joy, and so would they, after his example, although to a lesser degree. 'Was it not necessary', Jesus had asked the disciples on the road to Emmaus, 'that the Christ should suffer these things, and so enter into his glory?' And so it was that from the moment of Pentecost onwards, the Apostles would no longer hesitate in the face of opposition and persecution. We are told in the Acts of the Apostles (5:41) that they were even 'glad to have the honour of suffering humiliation for the sake of the name', meaning of course Jesus, who by his resurrection had received the name 'Lord'. Christ suffered and entered into joy; so did the Apostles in their measure, and so do we.

But the Apostles were not allowed to bask in the glow of this new-found consolation. They were commanded to preach to all the nations, to baptise them and lead them to obey the teachings of Christ. At some point or other in the life of each of us there is pain and sorrow and trouble. But we must be tried in order to triumph, humbled in order to be exalted. 'If you can have some share in the sufferings of Christ, be glad, because you will enjoy a much greater gladness when his glory is revealed', St Peter, by way of encouragement, tells us (1 Pet 4:13). Then when the time comes to leave this world, you will also be able to say with St Paul, 'I have fought the good fight; I have finished the race: I have kept the faith' (2 Tim 4:7), and 'all there is left for me now is the crown of justice reserved for me, which the Lord, the just judge will give to me on that day; and not only to me but to all who have longed for his coming'. Lastly Jesus says, 'Let not your heart be troubled. I go to prepare a place for you … and I will come again, and will take you to myself, so that where I am, you also may be' (Jn 14:1+).

PENTECOST SUNDAY
Acts 2:1-11; 1 Cor 12:3-7, 12-13; Jn 20:19-23

'In the beginning God created the heavens and the earth ... and God's Spirit hovered over the water.' Thus begins the account of creation in the Bible, which saw the Spirit of God as bringing about the birth of all living creatures. The Spirit was the source of life. In the first chapter of St John's gospel, John the Baptist says to his followers, 'The one on whom you see the Spirit come down and rest is the one who is going to baptise with the Holy Spirit.' In other words there is going to be a new creation; mankind is going to be born again in the Spirit. This had been foretold in the Old Testament. The prophet Isaiah (11:1+) had said repeatedly that the Spirit would rest on the 'shoot that springs from the stock of Jesse', Jesse being the father of king David, from whom Christ was descended.

Jesus was conceived by the Holy Spirit, was visited in a special way by the Holy Spirit at his baptism, was led by the Holy Spirit out into the desert for 40 days to be confronted by Satan. We can say that everything Christ did during his public life was done under the guidance of the Holy Spirit and by his power. Those who would sin against, or revile, the Holy Spirit, according to Christ, would be guilty of a sin which would never be pardoned. Moreover, Christ made a solemn promise that after his Ascension there would be an outpouring of the Holy Spirit on his followers which would surpass everything that had gone before. Those who were thus privileged were granted signs and gifts which clearly could only come from God, the most striking one being the gift of tongues, by which foreigners who did not speak Aramaic were able to understand every word said in that language, by Christ's disciples.

But the work of the Holy Spirit was not confined to these extraordinary happenings. He was active, and continues to be so, in the everyday life of each individual Christian, as well as in the Church as a whole. We are all temples of the Holy Spirit, who grants to each one the gifts of salvation which that person longs for. 'If the Spirit of him who raised Jesus from the dead is living in you, then he who raised Jesus from the dead will give life to your own mortal bodies, through his Spirit living in you' (Rom 8:11). God had sent his Son into the world in order that through him it might be possible for us to be adopted as children of God. And the proof that we are children of God is 'that God has sent the Spirit of his Son into our hearts: the Spirit that cries "Abba, Father"'. This Spirit is a Spirit of joy, of love and of service. Today's feast marks the birthday of all of us as Christians.

But we should not regard ourselves as being a step above all others. 'God has chosen the weak and insignificant people of this world to confound the strong' Sacred Scripture warns (1 Cor 1:27). We are to give witness before the world to the wonders brought about in very ordinary people by the healing and saving powers of the Holy Spirit. Such was the effect on the Apostles, who from being timid and fearful men – hiding in the Upper Room – became courageous and fervent proclaimers of the gospel. Their reaction was like that of the reluctant prophet, Jeremiah, who in the face of opposition said: 'I will not think about the Lord; I will not speak in his name any more. But then, there seemed to be a fire burning in my heart, imprisoned in my bones. The effort to restrain it wearied me; I could not bear it' (20:9).

We see the same response to the Spirit's urging, in the Apostles Peter and John, when they rejected the demand of the Sanhedrin authorities that they refrain from preaching in the name of Jesus. 'We cannot promise to stop proclaiming what we have seen and heard', they said (Acts 4:20). Regardless of opposition, of persecution, of the refusal of the majority of their own people to listen to them, they would remain steadfast in their newly-found faith, and in their fidelity to the mission entrusted to them by Jesus Christ. The first Pentecost saw the beginning of something which would change the whole world.

We too are called to play a role in this mission of the Holy Spirit, but we must begin by allowing the Holy Spirit to change us in a special way this day. 'In your goodness, Lord, give us the Holy Spirit, who alone can teach us to think and do what is right, so that we, who without you cannot exist, may live in obedience to your loving will.' Let us then keep our hearts open to what the Holy Spirit is telling us, and offer ourselves daily as willing instruments for God's plan for the salvation of the world.

THE MOST HOLY TRINITY
Deut 4:32-34, 39-40; Rom 8:14-17; Mt 28:16-20

There was a time in the course of Western civilisation when practically all peoples in Europe were more or less agreed about the existence of God. The only divisions that crept in arose from the beliefs they held about God, and the fact that there was hatred and bitterness between the different groups was really an indication also of the intense passion with which they held to those beliefs. But this is not the case nowadays. Not only are there many who openly profess their lack of faith, but the very quality of life we pursue tends to promote a kind of atheism in all of us. Especially in our large cities, people are at a distance from the things of nature, surrounded by a world which is a largely human creation.

The result is that all of us, even the rural-based of our population, are bound to suffer in some degree God's apparent remoteness from this kind of situation, God's silence, God remaining hidden to the end of our earthly days. For the many living things of nature, and incredible elements of the universe, in a most powerful way, can speak to us of God. And several of the great saints, like for instance St John of the Cross, withdrew regularly into the countryside to encounter God. For most of us, it is in times of sorrow, of pain or great anguish, that we find ourselves turning almost instinctively to a God who cares about us, a God who has a bond of kinship with us, since he has identified with the suffering of mankind in the person of Jesus Christ, who has gone ahead of us, bearing his Cross also.

Today we celebrate the Feast of the most Holy Trinity, the mystery of God's inner life. The mystery will remain for all of us as long as we live in this world, even though the veil which covers it is lifted ever so little. Revelation assures us that, not only is our God a personal God, he is three Persons, Father, Son and Holy Spirit, while remaining one God. And although we cannot even begin to give a logical explanation for this, our faith enables us in some small measure to experience the presence of God. How this can happen is stated by St Augustine in a most beautiful passage from his 'Confessions' (p. 211). 'What do I love when I love my God?' he asks. Then he continues; 'Not material beauty or beauty of a temporal order; not the brilliance of earthly light, so welcome to our eyes; not the sweet melody of harmony and song; not the fragrance of flowers, perfumes and spices; not manna or honey; not limbs such as the body delights to embrace. It is not these that I love when I love my God. And yet, when I love him, it is true that I love a light of a certain kind, a voice, a perfume, a food, an embrace; but they are of the kind that I love in my inner self'.

In other words, since God is pure spirit, these, as pointers to God, must be taken in a spiritual sense. But then he poses the truly fundamental question, 'What is my God?' The earth, the sea, and all living things in them replied; 'We are not your God. Seek what is beyond us.' 'Tell me something of my God', he then demands. And loud and clear they answered, 'God is he who made us.'

Many scientists today, who study the origin of the universe, maintain that, keeping in mind the complexity of the world we live in, it now requires a greater act of faith to be an atheist than to believe in the existence of a divine creator. God is creator, and he continues to create, to shape our lives, if only we surrender our will to his. And if we place our lives in God's hands, then, in his own good time, he will make us sharers in the blissful existence of the Father, Son and Holy Spirit. Indeed, as St John in the New Testament tells us, in a very mysterious phrase, 'We shall become like God, because we shall see him as he really is.'

Seeing God, in other words, will change us utterly, and for ever afterwards. Seeing God, or salvation, is a pure gift that always comes from the Father. It was made visible and realised in his divine Son made man, and it is only through the action of the Holy Spirit that it is made effective in each of us. In the New Testament we are told that 'in one Spirit we have access through Christ to the Father' (Eph 2:18). But the descent of God to us must be answered by an ascent of the human soul to God. We will be successful in this, if and only if, we break free from the sinful pursuits which hold us captive. Then like mirrors, as St Paul says, we will reflect the brightness of the Lord, until finally we are turned into that image which we reflect (2 Cor 3:17f). All glory to the Father, the Son, and the Holy Spirit, for ever and ever. Amen.

THE BODY AND BLOOD OF CHRIST
Deut 8:2-3, 14-16; 1 Cor 10:16-17; Jn 6:51-58

For devout Jews, the world over, the place of greatest attraction in Jerusalem is not of course any Christian shrine but rather the Western Wall, or as non-Jews prefer to call it, the Wailing Wall. The reason is that it is the only surviving portion of the great Temple which once stood there for over a thousand years, and which was central to Jewish worship of God. Since the final burning of the Temple by the Romans in 70 AD, it has been the custom of devout Jews to express publicly here their grief over the destruction of this sacred place, which they looked on as the sign of God's presence in their midst. While the Temple stood it was a tradition that everyone, young or old, should go up there at least once a year. This was not done grudgingly, but with great joy, as we see from the Psalms: 'I rejoiced when I heard them say, "Let us go to God's house", and now our feet are standing within your gates, Oh Jerusalem.' Even during the exile in Babylon, when the Temple lay in ruins for close on 70 years, their thoughts kept going back to it. 'By the streams of Babylon we sat and wept, when we remembered Zion', Zion being the hill on which Solomon erected the first Temple. 'It was there they asked us, our captors, for songs ... "Sing to us", they said, "one of Sion's songs". Oh how could we sing the song of the Lord on alien soil?' (Ps 137)

We are told in the Old Testament that when it was first consecrated the 'glory of the Lord' enveloped it – a sign that God had taken possession of his sanctuary. The most sacred part of the Temple was the Holy of Holies, the place in which was kept the Ark of the Covenant, which Moses had made. But to us, it comes almost as an anti-climax to read in the Book of Kings (1 Kg 8:9): 'There was nothing in the Ark except the two stone tablets Moses had placed in it at Mount Sinai'. Hence we might say that the destruction of the Temple was permitted in order to make way for a more real and uninterrupted visible presence of God in this world. There was a promise of this in the discourse of Jesus with the Samaritan woman at the well. 'The hour is coming', he said, 'when you will worship the Father, neither on this mountain nor in Jerusalem ... The hour will come ... when true worshippers will worship the Father in Spirit and truth' (Jn 4:21).

Central to this worship is, not a building, but a person, the sacred Body and Blood of Jesus Christ, the focus of all our attention in today's feast. It was at the Last Supper, on the very night he was betrayed, that Jesus made good his promise, both for his immediate followers and for all of us in this generation as well. By instituting the Eucharist he gave the Church a memorial of his death and resurrection, a sacrament of love, a sign of unity, a bond of charity, so that the minds of all taking part in it would be filled with grace and thereafter rest secure in the pledge of future glory which it grants to people of faith. St Peter in his discourse to the household of Cornelius, the Roman centurion, said, 'They killed Jesus by hanging him on a tree. Three days afterwards God raised him up, and allowed him to be seen, not by all, but only by such witnesses as God had chosen beforehand, by us who ate and drank with him after his resurrection from the dead' (Acts 10:40f). In other words, a witness to Jesus' resurrection was one who shared in the Eucharistic meal with Jesus, after God had raised him from the dead. And so it is that every time we celebrate Mass together we too are giving witness before the world to the resurrection of Jesus. But there is another reason why we join in this celebration, and Jesus himself states it very definitely. 'Unless you eat the flesh of the Son of Man, and drink his blood, you will not have life in you' (Jn 6:53).

Without the Mass you will become like dead branches that wither away because they have ceased to draw sustenance from the parent stock. On the other hand, for the person who receives Christ at the table of the Eucharist there is a solemn promise of eternal life, of resurrection on the last day. The first reading today spoke of the manna by which God preserved the lives of the chosen people in the vast and inhospitable desert wastes, where they had been wandering for forty years. But no matter how extensive and efficient the securities with which we surround our earthly existence, a life without Christ is a starved life, a meaningless journey with nothing at the end. Whereas for the person with faith and trust in the loving providence of God, this bread come down from heaven becomes the guarantee of life everlasting.

TENTH SUNDAY OF THE YEAR
Hos 6:3-6; Rom 4:18-25; Mt 9:9-13

Throughout the gospels we are told, time and again, how Christ
had pity on the multitudes. It is not immediately so apparent to
us what it was in the multitudes that drew forth this pity on the
part of Christ. It was not because they were for the most part
poor – he himself also belonged to that category. It was not
because they were ignorant about what their conduct should be,
what kind of lives they should lead. They had the prescriptions
of the Mosaic Law, which covered every possible eventuality or
situation likely to arise in their lives. However, it is in Christ's
dealings with the sick that we get a clearer insight into the
motives that gave rise to his pity. For again and again we see
that Christ's primary concern on such occasions was with the
condition of the soul of the sick person.

When, for example, in Capernaum a paralytic was brought to
him on a stretcher Jesus' first words were, 'Courage, my child,
your sins are forgiven'. The thoughts of the Scribes on hearing
this were, 'This is simply blasphemy; it is so easy to say your
sins are forgiven.' But back came the challenge of Jesus, 'Which
is easier to say, "Your sins are forgiven", or to say, "Get up and
walk"?' And then to make quite clear he had authority to forgive
sins, he said to the paralytic, 'Rise, take up your bed and go
home', and the man did so (Mt 9:2+).

Indeed, it is stated emphatically in today's gospel that the
reason Jesus became one of us is to call sinners, to help sinners,
to enable them conquer their sinful tendencies. Moreover, this
mission of Christ is an ongoing one. For all of us, without exception, are sinners, and to deny that such is our state, is to deny
that we have any need for the redemption which Christ has
gained for us by his death and resurrection. To make such a
claim would be to align ourselves with the Pharisees. 'If we say
that we have no sin, we deceive ourselves', St John says, 'and the
truth is not in us' (1 Jn 1:8).

It is remarkable that the people who have protested their sinfulness loudest of all, have been the holiest among the human
race, namely the saints. Whenever St Philip Neri, one of the outstanding saints of the 16th century, saw a criminal being led to
his execution – a common sight in Rome at the time – he would
say, 'There, but for the grace of God, go I.' We, who for no merit

of our own have been given the gift of faith, should see the Church as the means by which Christ continues to this day, his seeking out of sinners, his ministration to them, his healing of their broken relationship with their heavenly Father.

This same Church has been blamed for exaggerating the role of sin, for giving rise to guilt complexes in perfectly innocent people. But such an attitude is, as St Paul says, to make nonsense out of logic. For we have but to look around us to see the stern reality of sin in the world. Wherever any nation or individual exercises a tyranny over another, wherever there is exploitation of the poor, the weak, those who cannot fight back, wherever there is cheating, selfishness and disregard for others, there we see humans causing suffering, even death, instead of promoting life, harmony and peace, peace which is the Old Testament word for redemption. Where there is peace, whether in the individual soul, the community or a whole nation, there is redemption.

We should bear in mind that, unfortunately, we are not yet fully redeemed; that we are born into a community of sinners, wherein, even setting aside our own spiritual shortcomings, we are continually being confronted with, and affected by the sin of others. We should never be ashamed to admit our own sins, no matter how great, before the priest who represents Christ in the sacrament of penance, for the priest himself also stands in need of repentance. But if we strive with all our might to change, to distance ourselves from the cause of our evil habits, to seek from God the graces that will keep us faithful, then from the God, who will not be outdone in generosity, we will receive the assurance that, sinners though we are, he loves us, that his grace is more powerful than all our sinful activity, that he accepts us as we are, even with all our faults. For as St John points out, 'God is greater than our hearts, and he knows everything'. We, however, can never in this life fully understand the enormity, the malice, the inevitability of sin. All we can do is turn to God daily and plead, 'Lead us not into temptation, but deliver us from evil.'

ELEVENTH SUNDAY OF THE YEAR
Ex 19:2-6; Rom 5:6-11; Mt 9:36-10:8

Today's gospel recalls the selection of the twelve Apostles by Jesus. It was the first step towards the foundation of what we refer to as 'Our Holy Mother the Church'. And indeed the Church exercises the role of a mother in regard to each of us. For it was in the Church that each of us received a new life in the waters of baptism. Through the Church we were initiated into the teachings of Jesus Christ, are guided by the light of the Holy Spirit, as well as being sustained on our way through life by the grace of the sacraments. And from the Church we receive the example of holiness, in particular that of the Blessed Virgin Mary, who was preserved from the least stain of sin, as well as a multitude of people who attained sanctity to a truly heroic degree.

Both Christ and his Apostles were to experience opposition and persecution, even to the giving of their lives for the message they preached, and we, their followers today, can expect no better, although we are less likely to have the complete sacrifice demanded of us. Were the Church to disappear it is certain that before long all knowledge of Jesus, and what he stood for, would be lost to the world, as well as any credible meaning for life on this planet. However, we have a God-given guarantee that the gates of hell will never prevail against the Church.

We might, this morning, reflect on our own individual role in the Church, a role which St Peter, obviously from reflection on the last words of today's first reading, sets out in rather lofty terms. 'You are a chosen race, a royal priesthood, a consecrated nation, a people set apart to sing the praises of God, who called you out of the darkness into his wonderful light. Once you were not a people at all, and now you are the people of God; once you did not know God's mercy, but now you have been given that mercy' (1 Pt 2:9f). After ascending into heaven, Christ, to quote his own words, did not 'leave us orphans'. He would remain almost tangibly with us, not in any physical way as while on earth, but rather the now glorified Christ, who is in heaven, continues to reach out to us, to speak to us, to minister to us, in and through the other members of the Church, and especially through those called by him to play a special role within that Church. This continuing activity in the world of the glorified Lord is the Church. It is the glorified body of Christ, living now at this moment, which continues to fulfil the function his earthly body had during his life on earth. We speak of the Church as the sacrament of Christ, that is, the visible sign of his presence here and now.

We cannot, and should not, ignore the visible element in the Church's make-up. No matter how well-intentioned we may be, there is a danger of being led astray, if we attempt to find God by ourselves, in a direct encounter of spirit with spirit, ignoring the believing community, of which we should be an integral part. The dangers of such an approach have been shown up in the work of individual priests among alcoholics and drop-outs in American cities, and even more so by the worker-priests in France some years ago. In very many cases instead of winning souls for Christ, it was the priests themselves who became estranged from the Church, and that principally because they were trying to get through to individuals who were completely turned in on themselves, pandering to their own needs and incapable of forming personal relationships.

Nowadays all engaged in missionary activity try and come together at regular intervals, so that by contact with fellow believers, they are inwardly renewed, and have the opportunity to gain inner strength from the visible faith of the community of which they had been part. We should never cease to wonder at the marvels, the wells of salvation, within Christ's Church, and why we have been called to be part of it. Why should we be called? God's special call went out to Moses, although Moses was a murderer, to David although he was to be an adulterer, to Saul, later to be called Paul, who was a fanatical persecutor of the first followers of Christ. We should rejoice in our election by God, but not take vainglorious pride in it. None of us was chosen because of any merit on our part. Rather we should see ourselves as being servants, however unprofitable, of the gospel of Christ, and witnesses before the world of Christ's power to change people's lives, and bring peace into their hearts, as he promised, 'My own peace I give you, a peace the world cannot give, this is my gift to you' (Jn 14:27).

TWELFTH SUNDAY OF THE YEAR
Jer 20:10-13; Rom 5:12-15; Mt 10:26-33

Early in the 20th century, there was a famous scholar and society man in Dublin, highly regarded for the wisdom of his opinions on any subject (J. P. Mahaffey), who was once asked if he was a Christian. His answer was, 'Yes, but not offensively so'. By this he meant that his aim was not to allow his Christianity to distinguish him in any way from others, that it should not upset them, should not intrude on the society he kept, nor put obstacles in the pursuit of the life of pleasure that he loved. This could very easily be a description of the Christianity of many of us here and now also. While we are quite prepared to admit that we are Christians, we are, by and large, careful not to take religion too seriously. We rarely in any practical way so model our lives according to our religious beliefs, that they will be a silent reprimand to others who adhere to purely worldly standards. The fact, however, is that the really genuine Christian can never escape the injunction of Christ to be different from the world.

The task which the following of Christ places before us is not to conform to the standards of this world, but rather to transform those standards. Sin entered this world through one man, and through sin death, and thus death has spread throughout the whole human race, because everyone has sinned. The world's great sin is really unbelief, and the task of the Church is to challenge this unbelief, while relying on the guidance of the Holy Spirit who is our Advocate with God, now that Christ has ascended into heaven. The last words spoken by Christ to his Apostles, according to St Matthew, were, 'Go, therefore, make disciples of all the nations; baptise them in the name of the Father, and of the Son, and of the Holy Spirit, and teach them to observe all the commands I gave you. And know that I am with you always; yes, to the end of time.'

Although we are in this world, we must keep our gaze fixed on the world to come, and live for God by pursuing the spiritual standards given us by Christ. 'As for me', St Paul said, 'the only thing I can boast about is the cross of our Lord Jesus Christ, through whom the world is crucified to me and I to the world' (Gal 6:14). But the task of Christians is not, as it were, to wage any kind of vendetta against the world. Indeed, the world is also the object of God's love, and he wishes to save it. 'For God sent his Son into the world, not to condemn the world, but so that through him the world might be saved' (Jn 3:17). We should never, then, be taken aback by encountering the opposition of people whose lives are governed by purely worldly motives.

When the Apostles were apprehensive about the future, Christ encouraged them, 'Don't be afraid.' Don't be anxious about the trouble the future may bring, about your material needs, not even about threats to your lives. The most important revelation about God to emerge from the gospels is that he is a caring God, a compassionate forgiving God, a God who is on our side. Our attitude to God must be that of the psalmist when he says, 'In God I trust – I shall not fear' (Ps 56:11). Instead of dominating my actions by fear, God gives me the courage to be myself, to be guided in everything I do by Christian beliefs which have become part of me, transformed me, as they did the disciples of the Lord. The only thing I should fear is the loss of God, the loss of trust in God. This lack of trust begins when I look for security through my own efforts, in the works and wealth of my own making. Jesus criticised the feverish efforts, the anxious haste and worry of those worldly people, who refuse to grant God any part in their lives. 'In God I trust – I shall not fear.'

Jesus himself on the night he celebrated his final Passover meal with his Apostles, was about to enter a stage where he would suffer more than anyone had ever suffered, or ever will suffer in time to come. Yet, he remained tender, affectionate and caring towards them, and, although he knew they would all be scandalised when confronted with the awful tragedy of his passion and death, he was in no way reproachful towards them, not even towards the one who, while at table with him, was all the time plotting his betrayal. When in Gethsemane the reaction of his human nature to the terror of what lay ahead was such that his sweat fell to the ground like great drops of blood, nevertheless, his prayer to his heavenly Father was still, 'Not my will but yours be done.' No matter how awful the future may seem, this should be our prayer too.

THIRTEENTH SUNDAY OF THE YEAR
2 Kgs 4:8-11, 14-16; Rom 6:3-4, 8-11; Mt 10:37-42

In the scripture readings, last Sunday, we were told by Christ not to give way to fear, that to be a follower of his requires courage. Today's readings – in particular the first one and the gospel – go further. They impress upon us that being a good Christian requires generosity as well, and moreover the ability and the willingness to rise above self-seeking, a readiness to allow oneself to be used by God for his divine purposes. The prophet Elisha, in the first reading, is described as 'a holy man of God', and we should keep in mind that in Old Testament times a person was described as 'holy', not because of the achievements of his piety, or the state of mystical union he had acquired with God, but because he was the bearer of God's word, God's message to his people, a message which was of benefit to them in coping with the anxieties and problems which confronted them in their everyday existence.

We have a lesson to learn from the hospitality of the good woman who kept 'open door' for the prophet, and arranged things so that he could enjoy privacy and peace apart from the others in the household. The upper room, with its meagre furnishing, was a place where he could not only attain bodily rest, but also, more importantly, renew his inner spiritual strength by communing with God in the solitude it provided. This simple and beautiful little story is a reminder to us that we also should be willing to go apart, to distance ourselves periodically from what can be described as the super-excitement and overstimulation of modern living, and commune with our Maker as well.

If we do so, we will discover that all the time God is standing at the door of our hearts, knocking for admittance into that private domain within us, as the Book of Revelation describes it. Stating it in very human terms, we might even say that God at times is 'dying' of coldness. He knocks on the door to every heart, and how few there are who willingly open to him. For very often this inner room is already occupied, and by none other than ourselves. We see how in the case of the woman who kept a welcome for the man of God, the generosity she showed was to be rewarded by the birth of a son. And for the people of the Old Testament, who were not as yet believers in the resurrection of the body after this life, this was the way they saw themselves surviving, through the offspring with which God had blessed them while on earth.

People of outstanding virtue, of great faith and openness to God, undoubtedly set something in motion which does not stop with themselves. We will never fully understand in this life, how profound is the influence which one truly saintly soul has on the human race. We Christians, whether good or bad, have been signed with the mark of God, as was Elisha the prophet. Each one of us can say with St Paul in today's second reading: I have, through the waters of baptism in Christ Jesus, been made into something special for God. God has committed to me some work, some definite service, which he has not given to any other being.

If my heart is open to the prompting of the Holy Spirit, I shall do this work, perhaps even without consciously intending it. In my own special way I may, for example, end up being an angel of peace, a preacher of truth, a source of consolation and encouragement to others, but always provided I put God before my own interests, before family ties and relations, even before my own life, as Christ urged his Apostles in the gospel reading. But this is not a programme to be worked out apart from our ordinary everyday calling. The gospel speaks about a simple thing like a cup of cold water, given in Christ's name, not going unrewarded.

But incidentally, lest we belittle the following of Christ, it is well to keep in mind also that water was, and to this very day is, a most precious commodity in the Holy Land and neighbouring countries. Sanctity is attained, it has been said, by doing the little things in life well, and sanctity is in no way a little thing. In the light of the readings, and by way of practical example, it is fitting for us, here in this church, to be mindful of the debt we owe to so many unselfish people, who, week in week out, make it possible for us to worship God in a more meaningful and sacred way, in clean and decorative surroundings, when together we celebrate the Blessed Eucharist. To quote the words of Christ himself, such people also will most certainly not go without their reward.

FOURTEENTH SUNDAY OF THE YEAR
Zech 9:9-10; Rom 8:9, 11-13; Mt 11:25-30

If you live unspiritual lives, you are doomed to die; but if by the
Spirit you put an end to the misdeeds of the body, you will live.
In saying that St Paul was being faithful to the traditions of the
Old Testament, and so were the first Christians in adhering to
the doctrine of what was referred to as the 'Two Ways', the
choice between two kinds of life which face everyone during
their brief sojourn on earth. On the one hand there is the life
dominated by sinful human nature, a life focused and centred on
oneself. Such a life follows only one law, namely its own desires.
It takes what it likes, where it likes. It is motivated and controlled
by passion, or lust, or pride, or ambition. To allow the things of
this world so to dominate one's life is self-extinction, spiritual
suicide. And those who follow such a course become totally unfit
to stand in the presence of God, because they become resentful
towards the law and control of God, and end up regarding him
as an enemy.

On the other hand there are those for whom God is the focal
point of their lives on earth. Their lives are given direction by
God's Holy Spirit, a direction which finds them daily drawing
nearer to heaven. For such, death is only a temporary interruption
on the way. These, it could be said represent extreme states of
the Two Ways, whereas, in reality, most of us pursue a course
that goes back and forth between the two.

One of the great heresies of our time, surely, is that happiness
and peace of mind, and provision for the future can be bought
with money. This, rather surprisingly, is especially true about
the poorer people in society. The rich are all too well aware from
bitter experience that not every day of their lives is filled with
bliss. Despite having the luxuries that money can buy, they can
suffer from the strains and tensions that go with money, which
quite often can lead to the breakdown of personal relationships
within the family circle, resulting in broken marriages, and separation from the children.

One of the great reasons why family members fall out,
especially in rural Ireland, it has been said, is disputes over land
and wills. Because of consumerism in our society the very capacity
to love has become rarer, a certain sociologist has claimed (Eric
Fromm). Since God speaks to us from the scriptures, it is very

profitable to follow the evolving moral attitudes towards riches which we find in them. In the Book of Genesis, worldly possessions were regarded as a sign of God's special blessing. We have, for example, an obviously exaggerated description of the wealth of Abraham, his flocks and herds, his silver and gold. Here the inspired writer is simply stating, in the language of his own time, that God loved Abraham in a very special way indeed, that Abraham, by the very fact of being rich, was a just man, since poverty was a curse, a punishment for sin.

But in the Book of Job, this view is questioned. 'The Lord gives, the Lord also, for his own purposes, can take away. Blessed be the name of the Lord.' Later on during an age of great prosperity in the Northern Kingdom of Israel, the minor prophets, like Amos and Hosea, even denounced the rich, because of their luxury, their injustices, and their exploitation of the poor. At this point the concept of poverty had reached a crossroads. There was the road which led nowhere, the way of the bitter, despondent, cynical, and – let's face it – even the greedy poor, that Christ said would always be with us. And then there was the road travelled by those who came to be known as the 'poor of the Lord', those with nobody else to turn to, who in every aspect of their existence, depended entirely on the Lord, those who could declare with utter sincerity, 'Our help is in the name of the Lord, who made heaven and earth.'

Christ identifies with these latter in today's first reading. 'See your king comes to you, humble and riding on a donkey.' And it is to these very people that he addresses himself in the gospel, 'Come to me all you who are overburdened, and I will give you rest. Learn from me, for I (too) am gentle and humble of heart, and you will find rest for your souls.' At the Last Supper he had said to the Apostles, 'Peace I leave with you, my peace I give you. Not as the world gives, do I give to you.' And the gift of Christ was not that of this world, but rather the gift of God's Holy Spirit, a gift more precious, more enduring than silver or gold, or anything that this passing world can offer.

FIFTEENTH SUNDAY OF THE YEAR
Is 55:10-11; Rom 8:18-23; Mt 13:1-23

When the Second Vatican Council was in session the army of newspaper men present found much of the discussions rather dull or over their heads, and to inject more life into their reports they portrayed the entire thing as a struggle between two opposing groups of those participating in the discussions. On the one hand, there were those they labelled conservatives, the cardinals and bishops who wanted to retain the status quo, and, on the other, those who became the darlings of the media, the progressives, who were all for fresh thinking, for new approaches. But the interesting thing was that the progressive policy was, in many respects, a return to the sources of Christianity, an attempt to go back to the mind, and the attitudes and the thinking of the early days in the Church. Many of those ideas which were regarded as new, when put forward by the so-called progressives, were really old ideas, which were brought to birth in the age of the Apostles.

Let us this morning try and go back to the age of the Apostles, and capture the fears, the anxieties, the problems that confronted the early Church. The first reading really sets the picture for us. It highlights a correspondingly dark age, further back in the history of the Old Testament, hundreds of years before the Apostolic age. It is taken from that part of the Book of Isaiah, which is called the Book of Consolation. At that time everything seemed to be in a disastrous mess for the Jews, the chosen people of God. The Temple was destroyed, all the leading citizens, the ruling and moneyed classes, were in exile in Babylon, and, to make matters worse, there were many rather weak-willed people among the exiles who had fallen away from the faith of their ancestors, and were putting their trust in the pagan gods of their conquerors.

But God, through the preaching of the prophet Isaiah, kept reminding the faithful not to despair, to keep trusting him when he said that his word would not fail. 'The word that goes from my mouth does not return to me empty, without carrying out my will and succeeding in what it was sent to do.' This, almost precisely, was the situation in the Apostolic Church also, as we see from the gospel. The Christians encountered opposition and persecution on all sides – from the Jews who regarded them as bringing the Law into disrepute, as being blasphemers because they claimed that Christ was a divine person – from the gentiles, who mocked at the folly of the Cross, and at Christian belief in the resurrection of Jesus. Moreover, many of the new converts to Christianity, the 'false brethren' as St Paul described them, had fallen away in the face of opposition and persecution.

The gospel parable speaks of the man who hears the word and welcomes it at once with joy, but when put to the test, does not persevere. When some trial or persecution comes on account of the word – that is the gospel teaching – he loses courage and falls away at once. Christians, at present, do not have to contend with active persecution for their faith, at least in this country. Yet our faith, as Christ predicted, will of necessity be challenged from time to time, and indeed at present we have to stand up for our beliefs in the face of a more subtle opposition than that encountered by the early Church, in particular the veiled sarcasm, criticisms and mockery of those who have it in their power to inform public opinion.

Faced with such, we should ask ourselves whether in us the word of God is succeeding in what it was sent to do, whether we try to understand with our hearts, so as to be converted, to be strengthened and healed by our loving God. We should always bear in mind what St Paul said to the faithful who were suffering for their beliefs in pagan Rome, 'I think that what we suffer in this life can never be compared to the glory, as yet unrevealed, which is waiting for us' (Rom 8:18).

Nor, indeed, should we ever forget that the principal message in the gospel parable of the sower is that, despite all the frustrations we may encounter as we go through life, the grain which is scattered by the heavenly sower will yield a return out of all proportion to what was sown, even at times a hundred times greater. No matter, then, what ups and downs we encounter as we go through life, we should never despair, because we are assured by sacred scripture that God's kingdom will finally triumph. 'God so loved the world that he sent his only-begotten Son, so that no one might perish, but might have eternal life' (Jn 3:16).

SIXTEENTH SUNDAY OF THE YEAR
Wis 12:13, 16-19; Rom 8:26-27; Mt 13:24-43

In the eighth psalm of the Old Testament, the writer poses the question to God, 'What are human beings that you care for them, or mortals that you keep them in mind?' In so doing, we might say that he was trying to come to a greater understanding of both the motives of God and the nature of humanity. For by the very fact that we have come about through the creative action of God, that God has made us in his own image as scripture tells us, it follows that as God for us remains forever the great unknowable, so there must be an element of mystery also about each one of us.

One of the things in us which remains inexplicable is the urge which arises at times, in all of us, to cast off, as it were, the stamp of the divine we bear, to wipe out that imprint of God on our inner being, to turn a deaf ear to the voice of God which throughout our lives continues to address us through our conscience. There were two requests which, all through his life, St Augustine kept repeating in his prayers, 'That I may know God, and that I may know myself.' Knowledge of God is purely a gift of the Holy Spirit given out of generosity.

In trying to acquire self-knowledge, however, there are two extremes to be avoided. There are souls – admittedly few in number – who have almost a pathological fear of admitting to any imperfection in their lives. They go to confession and say, 'I have committed no sin', and when the priest suggests that there may perhaps be something in their past lives for which they can be sorry, they remain adamant in their refusal to admit to any such. One might well ask the question, how then can there be contrition, which is a necessary part of the sacrament, or indeed what purpose does the sacrament of reconciliation serve for such people? For if somebody were to go through life without ever sinning, then that person would have no need for redemption or for a redeeming Christ.

By way of direct contrast there are those who might be described as tortured souls, by whom the most trivial actions are deemed to be evil and sinful. They are haunted by the spectre of damnation, and God, who is love, becomes for them a kind of despot scrutinising all their actions, ready to exact retribution for their least fault. They forget that one of the divine attributes, as today's reading from the Book of Wisdom points out, is forbearance, that while the common tendency of humans is to lapse, to deviate from the path of true virtue, the mark of the truly strong, the divine, is to forgive. 'Disposing of such strength', the first reading today states, 'you are mild in judgment, you govern us with great lenience … you have given your children the hope that, after sin, you will grant repentance'. While in all truth and humility, we must confess that none of us is perfect, to regard ourselves as beyond redemption is to belittle the redemptive power of the life and death of Jesus Christ, our Saviour. Each of us has been given his or her own special talents and virtues, but each one falls short, in varying degree, of the ideal which God proposes to us individually in our inmost being. We all have good in us, but we also have evil. As it was said once, 'There is so much good in the worst of us, and so much bad in the best of us, that it hardly becomes any of us to speak badly about the rest of us.' The gospel reading adds further emphasis to this when it likens the kingdom of heaven, or the Church, to a mixture of wheat and darnel, or weeds. At an early stage the darnel is very much like wheat, and so the landowner does not try to separate the two, but waits until harvest time. Likewise, God does not immediately separate the bad from the good, but gives them every chance, here and now, to change and amend their ways. It is when we are united with Christ, when the Holy Spirit pleads for us before God, that we become pleasing to God.

We should find great consolation, then, when we recall the mercy, the graciousness of God, who, as St Paul points out, loved us while we were still sinners, and loved us to the point of dying for us. 'No one can have greater love than this', Christ himself said, 'to lay down his life for his friends' (Jn 15:13). The repentant thief, having been forgiven on his cross on Calvary, did not have time thereafter to perform any good deeds, or to put the commandments into practice. He threw himself on the mercy of God, and his sins became as if they had never existed. It is by doing this that we too can draw near to our God.

SEVENTEENTH SUNDAY OF THE YEAR
1 Kgs 3:5, 7-12; Rom 8:28-30; Mt 13:44-52

The words of popular songs, most people would agree, are by and large repetitive and without very much meaning, but some lyric writers at times have an uncanny knack of getting to the heart of human situations, what people are looking for in life. There was one song some years ago, which intentionally or not, parodied the approach of many of us to God in the prayer of petition, and one of its lines went, 'Lord, please send me a Mercedes Benz'. At first this appears a bit silly and rather amusing, but then when we start seriously to examine those things we keep asking of God, we begin perhaps to have second thoughts. How often is our prayer an attempt to manipulate God, to make God change his mind, to pressurise God into bringing about the kind of things that we want in our lives. If so, we would do well to ponder over the significance of this saying from a famous spiritual writer (Meister Eckhart) of the Middle Ages, 'To use God is to kill him.'

If our prayer is only inspired by concern for material things, then when these are not granted, prayer, in our estimation, becomes pointless. And as soon as we cease to pray, our faith begins to vanish. For every prayer is an act of faith in God, and without it God is removed from our lives; for us God becomes, as it were dead. This is the lesson we should learn today from the Old Testament reading, which suggests that God was pleased because Solomon did not ask for a long life, nor for riches, nor for the downfall of his enemies, but instead sought something spiritual – that inner wisdom which would enable him to discern good from evil, and consequently make the right choices in life.

Every day of his life the devout Jew – and Jesus in a preeminent way was one such – repeated these words from sacred scripture, a tradition which is maintained up to this very day, 'Hear Oh Israel: the Lord our God is one Lord; and you shall love the Lord your God with all your heart, and with all your soul, and with all your might. And these words which I command you this day shall be written on your heart, and you shall teach them diligently to your children, and shall talk of them when you sit in your house, and when you walk by the way, and when you lie down, and when you rise' (Deut 6:4-7).

This in effect is what Christ too is saying to us in the gospel, through the parable of the man who sells all he owns, in order to acquire the treasure he desires, and likewise through the story of the merchant prepared to part with all he possesses for the sake of the one pearl of great value. For the hidden treasure and the pearl that is worth everything, both symbolise something far more precious, the grace and love of God, which come to us in Jesus Christ. It is these latter which will guide our prayer towards the things that really matter, in particular towards the acceptance of God's holy will for us. As St Paul reminds us in the second reading, for those who love God, everything will turn to their good.

Genuine prayer is the act of coming before God with a generous heart and with open hands. There are so many things in my life that I cling to, and hold tight with clenched fists – my work, my position, the friends I have, the esteem of others for me, my ideas, my views on things, the image of myself I like to project to others. If, however, I come before God with an open mind, and open my fists, these things may still remain. And if I am prepared to wait long enough with fists open, with mind uncluttered by longing and selfish desires, the Lord will inevitably come. He will look at the things I have been clutching in my hands, may even be surprised that there are so many. Then perhaps he will begin to ask, 'Would you mind if in turn I take out this little item?' And I perhaps answer, 'Of course, that's why I have come here with open hands.' Then again the Lord may take a second look, and ask, 'Would you mind if I put something else in your hands?' And once more I answer, 'Of course, you may.'

This truly is always the heart of prayer. It is putting into practice the lesson learned by Job, who had travelled a long and painful road before becoming resigned to God's will, no matter what he demanded, a lesson summed up in his own words, 'The Lord gives, and the Lord also takes away.' My response should likewise be, 'Blessed be the name of the Lord; may the will of my Lord, in all circumstances, be done in me, even as it is done in heaven. Amen.'

EIGHTEENTH SUNDAY OF THE YEAR
Is 55:1-3; Rom 8:35, 37-39; Mt 14:13-21

In the Israel of two thousand years ago, there was great significance attached to the sharing of a meal. It was almost regarded
as being a sacred action which demanded that the host put aside
any resentment or ill-will towards his guests, and treat them in a
most courteous and honourable manner. This sharing of a meal
played an important role in Christ's public life also, but for him
there was something uniquely special in it, something of a
sacramental character which conveys a message to us. It is
hardly surprising then that the miraculous feeding of the multitude is recounted more frequently than any other single episode
in the four gospels; in fact, it appears six times in all.

We might wonder why did the evangelists lay such stress on
this event – indeed why did they regard it as being so important a
part of the faith of the early Church? If we look more carefully at
the wording used by the evangelists to describe the miraculous
feeding by Christ of large groups of people, we begin to see the
answer to our query. The people were ordered to sit down, and
this was in effect more by way of gaining their attention, of getting them to concentrate on what was about to happen. There
was more or less an accepted formula to describe what then
followed. Jesus took the bread, raised his eyes to heaven, and
said the blessing – this is not to say that he blessed the bread, but
rather that he blessed God, that is, gave thanks and praise to
God, for having given the bread. Having done this Jesus then
gave the bread to his disciples, who in turn distributed it to the
people.

The use of these terms should make it quite clear to us that
the miraculous events in question are closely linked with the
Eucharist. Indeed, in the whole gospel of St John, there is no
mention whatsoever of the institution of the Blessed Eucharist at
the Last Supper, but instead the miraculous feeding of the multitude becomes a sign, that helps us focus on the nature of the
Eucharistic mystery, on the necessity of it, on the consoling and
healing value of it. For us, who hear so much about want in our
own times, about the endless struggle of some people to obtain
food that will satisfy their hunger, it is well to recall and meditate
on the rather extraordinary and somewhat mystifying saying of
St Augustine, that 'Christ is food, seeking hunger.' It could,

possibly, be linked with the beatitude which states, 'Blessed are those who hunger and thirst after justice, they shall have their fill.'

The presence of so many people mentioned in the gospel story – five thousand, not counting women and children – bears clear testimony to the inner hunger of mankind for the bread of Christ. But people are not always quite certain what this bread is, what exactly they are seeking. They long for Christ, whether intentionally or not, but their understanding of him is very often blurred and unreal. They have perhaps been brought up in a way that sees God as an avenging God, one who will mercilessly punish their least transgression. Instead of the liberation preached in the gospel, this approach begets a feeling of uneasiness, even of rebellion; and understandably so, since one does not halt the course of human longing, of search for meaning to existence, by confronting it with a wall of fear. Today, and perhaps during the coming week, we might reflect on our own seeking, what we hunger for, and how Christ can satisfy this hunger. 'Why spend money', the first reading asks, 'on what is not bread … on what fails to satisfy?'

'Come to me', says the Lord, 'listen, and your soul will live'. For those who respond to this invitation there is clear evidence that Christ fulfils this promise, especially in our churches, where the troubled in mind, the broken in spirit come and kneel before the tabernacle, and go away touched and strengthened by Christ's healing presence there. He fulfils it in the confessional, where penitent souls seek forgiveness, and go away reassured in the belief that God's love is greater than their sins. He fulfils it at the foot of the altar, where, during the Mass devout souls receive the only food that will satisfy their inner yearnings. No matter, then, how heavy your crosses, St Paul says, no matter how frequent your falls, come, eat, and be refreshed, for nothing can come between you and the love of God, made visible in Christ Jesus, our Lord, even as it is in the holy Eucharist which we are now celebrating.

NINETEENTH SUNDAY OF THE YEAR
1 Kgs 19:9, 11-13; Rom 9:1-5; Mt 14:22-33

Shortly after the ancient Roman Republic had become an empire, with supreme power vested in the person of the emperor, the pagan religion began to lose its attraction for people, especially when they were forced to worship the reigning emperor as a god, and more and more Romans were attracted to what were called 'mystery religions'. These mystery cults, introduced mainly from the east, with their special initiation rites shrouded in secrecy, became very popular. The charge has been levelled against the Catholic Church, in modern times, that a lot of the mystery which originally was part of the liturgy – even the mystery surrounding the person of Christ – has been pushed into the background; and as a result that the Church itself has lost some of the fascination and the attraction it formerly had. But the first reading today, about the pilgrimage of the prophet Elijah to the holy mountain of Sinai, or Horeb, never fails to fascinate the thoughtful reader.

The great prophet, who had been so fearless in confronting and defeating, on Mount Carmel, the army of false prophets who were followers of King Ahab, and even more so of his queen, Jezebel, suddenly lost heart in the face of continuing opposition from the queen, to such an extent that he wished he was dead. For him it was a real crisis of faith. How could God really be Lord when Jezebel's power continued undiminished, and she still posed a threat to his life? God, however, was to restore his faith by means of that strange pilgrimage to the holy mountain, Horeb or Sinai, where he was to encounter the divine presence in a special way, a way that shows clearly the development in the Old Testament understanding of God. When he gave the commandments to Moses on this mountain, God's presence was made manifest in a storm, earthquake and lightning. But for Elijah these were only the heralds of the Lord's coming. For he was not in the wind, or the earthquake, or the lightning, but rather in 'a voice of a gentle stillness', an awesome vocal silence.

The whole revelation was a lesson to the fiery prophet, who had overturned pagan altars and slaughtered 450 false prophets, that the days of violence were past, and that God in his own hidden way would bring about the welfare of Israel. It was not the fearful and tremendous forces of nature, but rather this whisper of a gentle breeze that denoted the presence of God, and made Elijah cover his face with his cloak, for, as the Jews believed, no human being could look on the divine countenance and live. From now on the power of God is not to be seen in natural phenomena, for God is superior to all such. In fact he controls them; he uses them for his own purposes, for God is in no way material; he is pure Spirit.

We see this further exemplified in today's gospel, in the person of Jesus, who shows himself the complete master over the elements which whipped up the lake into such mountainous waves, that the disciples despaired of ever reaching the land. Wherever, then, there is storm and unrest, God brings calm, where there is inner turmoil and depression, God generates peace and spiritual renewal. Leading up to the first reading, Elijah's prayer was, 'Lord, I have had enough. Take away my life.' But after his encounter on Horeb, all this was changed. 'I am filled with jealous zeal for the Lord of hosts', we find him saying.

Likewise, at the outset of the gospel story, the disciples were in desperate straits in their boat, and that at a time, the fourth watch, between three and six in the morning, when human resistance is at a low ebb. We can understand how their first reaction to the appearance of Christ walking on the water was one of terror. But those few words from Christ, 'Courage ... do not be afraid', bring about a change so dramatic that Peter ventures to get out of the boat, and walk on that very element which up to then had inspired such alarm in them all. In his momentary hesitation Peter is reassured by the sustaining hand of Jesus.

The message for us is quite clear. When fears and problems assail us, when God seems so remote and forgetful of our plight, then we should cry out, 'Lord, save us, we perish.' This little prayer should also be an act of faith in God, and conversely, every act of faith is another form of prayer, because in making it our thoughts are turning to God. And God will not only hear our call, he will respond favourably to it, provided we do not waver in our trust in him.

THE ASSUMPTION OF THE BVM
Apoc 11:19, 12:1-6, 10; 1 Cor 15:20-27; Lk 1:39-56

The events leading up to Christ's final moments on earth are very well catalogued in all four gospels. But in contrast the end of Mary's life is more or less shrouded in mystery. In former times there was one school of thought which maintained that since Christ's life on earth ended in death, so should Mary's. And there was another which spoke of Mary's departure from this world not so much as a death but as a 'dormition', in other words a falling asleep. These latter would claim that Mary, in spirit, had already experienced death with her divine Son on Calvary, when the sword of sorrow pierced her soul, that sword predicted by Simeon, at the presentation of the child Jesus in the Temple. Indeed there is a very beautiful church on Mount Zion in Jerusalem, which was built for the Benedictine monks in the nineteenth century, and which is called the 'Church of the Dormition of the Virgin Mary'.

There are opposing traditions, as well, as to where Mary spent her last days on earth. One says Jerusalem, while the other, which is particularly favoured by Greek Orthodox Christians, maintains that it was close to Ephesus where the grave of the Apostle John is venerated, and where a house said to be the last home of Mary is a centre of pilgrimage to this day. In all of this there is one question we might reflect on: why do pilgrims frequent the Holy Sepulchre in Jerusalem, or the final resting place of St Peter in Rome, while there has never been any spot from earliest Christian times which came to be universally regarded as the burial place of the Mother of our Lord and Saviour, Jesus Christ? Is it conceivable that those early Christians, who were so loving, reverent and careful about the bodies and graves of the saints and martyrs, would neglect her who was the Queen of martyrs and saints, who was the very Mother of God himself?

The answer is supplied by the dogma declared in 1950 by Pope Pius XII, which states: 'The Immaculate Virgin preserved free from all stain of original sin, when the course of her earthly life was finished, was taken up body and soul into the glory of heaven, and exalted by the Lord as Queen over all things, so that she might be more fully conformed to her Son, the Lord of lords and conqueror of sin and death.' While the statement does not tell us how her stay on earth ended – it just says, 'when the course of her earthly life was finished' – its wording, nevertheless, confirms that her holy, inviolate body was never interred in any earthly grave, but was assumed into the presence of God without undergoing corruption.

This Assumption is a truly unique participation in her Son's Resurrection, and a guarantee of the resurrection of all other Christians too. Furthermore, Mary by her obedience, faith, hope and burning charity always cooperated with her divine Son in restoring supernatural life to souls. For this reason she is indeed a mother to each and every one of us, in the order of grace. This motherhood of Mary began even at the moment of the Annunciation, when she gave her consent in faith to God's plans for the role she was called upon to play in our redemption, a role she would fulfil without faltering, even to being a spectator at the death on the cross of her only-begotten Son.

What is more, it will continue without interruption until the eternal salvation of all the elect is achieved, which means that after her Assumption this saving role did not cease, but continues to be active in gaining redeeming graces for all of us. 'Dust you are, and into dust you shall return', God had said to our first parents, Adam and Eve, because they had sinned. But Mary had never been touched by the least stain of sin, and therefore never would her body crumble into dust. For she who had been linked so closely with Christ, when he conquered sin by his passion and death, should surely share in the reward gained by him in his resurrection. This, then, is why the Church – which is all of us – by this feast pays honour to Mary, who has been taken up, body and soul, into heaven to be with her Son forever.

This feast is a call to us to renew our hope also of being with Christ one day; it is meant to comfort each one of us on our pilgrim way to the eternal home he has prepared for us, if only we are faithful to the graces he grants through our Mother Mary who pleads for us. Let us keep praying that we may be found worthy to be, as Mary now is, with her Son Jesus for ever in heaven.

TWENTIETH SUNDAY OF THE YEAR
Is 56:1, 6-7; Rom 11:13-15; Mt 15:21-28

The people of Israel, when chosen by God as his own special people, regarded themselves as being uniquely favoured, and rightly so. But by way of conclusion from this they began to regard all other people as being just so much material for stoking up the fires of hell. Yet we have God proclaiming through the prophet Isaiah, 'Foreigners who have attached themselves to the Lord, to serve him, and to love his name – these I will bring to my holy mountain. I will make them joyful in my house of prayer' (Is 56:6). I wonder how those Jews, who so abhorred all gentiles, could ever reconcile this saying with their own attitudes.

However, lest we feel like condemning their bigotry, it is well to remember that up to the middle of the nineteenth century it was the firm conviction of many Catholics that only members of the Catholic Church could be saved, and those outside the Church could only be saved by belonging to the soul of the Church, whatever that really meant. As with the Jews, this was a flawed argument that in effect tried to set bounds to the scope of God's grace, to see him as a kind of sectarian God, serving the interests of a limited and select group. But Sacred Scripture – both Old and New Testaments – warns us against such a narrow and biased outlook. God's house will be called a house of prayer for all the peoples, and God will make them all joyful in this house.

This was what God was proclaiming through the prophet Isaiah, as given in the first reading. St Paul, who regarded himself as being privileged to be chosen as an apostle for the pagans, reiterates that God will show his mercy to all mankind without exception. Moreover, the gospel story foreshadows the breaking down of racial divides when it tells us how Jesus cured the daughter of a Canaanite woman. The Canaanites, we should remember, were the traditional ancestral enemies of the Jews. They were regarded as a sinful race that embodied all that is wicked and godless, a race, according to Jewish thinking, to be wiped off the face of the earth. It was the only occasion recorded in the gospel when Jesus was ever outside Jewish territory, and what transpired there foreshadows the spread of the gospel to the entire world.

It marked the dawn of a new era, when membership of God's

holy and chosen people would no longer be restricted to followers of the Mosaic Law only. Confirmation of this is found in the
last words of Jesus to his disciples before his Ascension, 'All
authority in heaven and on earth has been given to me. Go,
therefore, make disciples of all the nations; baptise them in the
name of the Father and of the Son and the Holy Spirit, and teach
them to observe all the commands I gave you.' Indeed the heart
of the Christian message lies in this: that irrespective of class, race,
nationality or colour, whether we are sophisticated and learned,
or uneducated and ignorant, whether we are rich or poor, we are
all called to be members of the newly constituted family, which
has God as Father, and Jesus Christ as brother.

As St Paul pointed out to the people of Colossae, we are the
people of God; he loved us and chose us for his own, and not
because of any merit of ours, or the colour of our skin, or because
we are morally or intellectually superior to others. God's choice
of us to live out the gospel of Christ to the full is really a mystery.
And just as certain people within the state, such as members of
the armed forces or police, wear a distinctive uniform, so must
we Christians be distinguishable among the rest of mankind by
a kind of uniform also, not in any material way, but spiritually.
'You must clothe yourselves', says St Paul, 'with compassion,
kindness, gentleness and patience'.

Christ's message, which is that of love towards others, must
live in all its richness in all our hearts. Everything we do or say,
then, should be done in the name of the Lord Jesus, as we give
thanks through him to God the Father. It is only then that we
become really Christian, that barriers are broken down, that we
can go forward, sustained by, and sustaining, the community
which has been brought into being by the preaching of the message of Christ. Finally, you might ponder over, and bring away
with you, this saying of St Augustine, when speaking from
Hippo, as bishop to the people of his diocese, about the union
that should exist between them, 'What I am for you terrifies me;
what I am with you consoles me. For you I am a bishop, but with
you I am a Christian.'

TWENTY-FIRST SUNDAY OF THE YEAR
Is 22:19-23; Rom 11:33-36; Mt 16:13-20

In the gospel reading you have just heard, the intention of Jesus was to discover what understanding of himself and his mission his specially chosen disciples had learned, as well as their concept of the role they were to play when he was gone. So he put to them the very direct question, 'Who do you say that I am?' Even now this is a question which he continues to address also to each one of us. What does God really mean to me; what does Christ, the incarnation of God, mean? And, like the disciples in Caesarea Philippi, we will be able to respond if and only if for a brief period we put aside the daily concerns that occupy our minds.

It is interesting to read how one man in the present era conducted this soul-searching in complete isolation, which however was forced upon him. It is the account by a French journalist, Jean-Paul Kauffman, of how he survived three years captivity in Beirut, during the war in Lebanon. Despite all the horrors of his ordeal there, he seemed almost glad that he had undergone this solitary confinement, because of what he called the spiritual cleansing it brought about within him. Had he not experienced it, he believed, he would perhaps have died in utter ignorance of the meaning of life in this world.

'The closeness of death hanging over me', he wrote, 'helped me put my thoughts in order, ... it enabled me to cleanse my soul. God became very significant for me. Never have I prayed with such intensity ... In the darkness and silence I felt close to God ... This one and only uncreated, holy God, so far beyond the real understanding of humans, is the most impressive reality in the world, and yet so completely beyond the compass of the human mind'. And drawn by the challenge of that question to Peter, 'Who do you say that I am?', in order to find an answer, he read and reread the Bible, one of only two books to which he had access, the other being Tolstoy's *War and Peace*.

The question for us is what source do we consult in our quest for Christ. We must bear in mind that, important though it is, the New Testament is based on something else, namely the recollections of the message and teachings of Jesus which were preserved in the first Christian communities. In other words the Church was already in existence before the writing of the New

Testament. Hence it is that to encounter Christ we must first turn to the community of the Church today, where the Jesus tradition is enshrined, not so much in writing as in the lives of those who make up the Church, for literacy was never a Christian prerequisite.

The Church is the result of the mission of Christ and the Holy Spirit, and the visible sign of the continuation of that mission. Christians in the first century used to say, 'The world was created for the sake of the Church.' Indeed God created human beings so that they might be partakers of his divine life. This communion with God can only be attained by the bonding together of people in Christ, and this union is the Church. It was St Augustine who first stated that the Church is Christ. It was inaugurated by his preaching of the gospel, and by his choice of twelve men with Peter as head. And it was finally to come into being from the pierced heart of Christ as he slept the sleep of death on the cross. It is only with the eyes of faith that we can recognise the visible Church, of which we are members, as being a spiritual reality that enables us to be sharers in the divine life. This happens because, in a new and spiritual way, Christ remains at the centre of this worshipping community, as well as in each individual member, through the sacrament of the Eucharist. Moreover the reality of redemption through Christ is brought about also by encounter, conversation and communion with other human beings who are followers of Christ.

The Church is not the creature of times and places, the result of secular politics or the whims of individuals. The Roman empire persecuted it for three centuries, and then a flood of heresies tried to change it. Barbarian hordes invaded its territory; the so-called Reformation attacked it from within. That it survived is a sure sign of its divine origin. We should love the Church as our mother in the order of grace, and also see it brought to perfection in the Blessed Virgin Mary, who as St Augustine said is 'clearly the mother of the members of Christ ... since she co-operated out of love so that there might be born in the Church the faithful, who are members of Christ their head.'

TWENTY-SECOND SUNDAY OF THE YEAR
Jer 20:7-9; Rom 12:1-2; Mt 16:21-27

There are three things in particular which the readings in the Mass today teach us. The first is that God calls each one of us in a unique way to bear witness before the world to certain eternal values, by what we believe, what we say, what we do. That call may not be as insistent as the one which came to the prophet Jeremiah, on whom it brought insult, derision, and suffering throughout his whole life. But if our minds are open to the promptings of God's Spirit the call will be unmistakable. The second lesson is how we respond to God's demands. Are we prepared to live by these, to change our ways in accordance with the insights granted us, and not just model our lives on the behaviour of the people around us? The third lesson is, how far are we prepared to go in defence of our principles, in pursuing the demands of our conscience, especially when these run counter to the standards of the world around us. Are we ready to act according to the example of Christ, Christ who tells us that unless we renounce ourselves, take up our cross daily and follow him we cannot be numbered among his faithful disciples. John Paul I, who was Pope for only 33 days, while being Cardinal Archbishop of Venice, was asked to write something each month for the city's Catholic paper. This took the form of a letter addressed to some important person in past history.

His final letter was to Jesus and part of it goes like this. 'When you said, "Blessed are the poor, blessed are the persecuted," I wasn't present with you. Had I been, I'd have whispered in your ear, "For heaven's sake, Lord, change the subject, if you want to keep any followers at all. Don't you know that everyone wants riches and comfort? … You're promising poverty and persecution. Who do you think is going to follow you?" But you went ahead unafraid, and I can hear you saying you were the grain of wheat that must die before it bore fruit; and that you must be raised up on a cross, and from there draw the whole world up to you. today this has happened; they raised you up on a cross. You took advantage of that to hold out your arms and draw people to you. And countless people have come to the foot of the cross, to fling themselves into your arms.' This was a lesson the disciples of Jesus were slow to learn. They wanted him to be a conquering Messiah, a warrior leader who would drive out the Romans from their country.

But Jesus' way was that of the cross to which he would be condemned by the religious leaders of the day. Peter reacted almost violently while reproaching Jesus, 'God forbid that this should happen to you.' The response of Jesus, however, was most severe, likening Peter to Satan in tempting him to turn aside from the path that would lead to suffering and death, and consequently to his resurrection. What in effect Peter also had been advising was, 'Lower your standards. Give people what will please them and they will become followers of yours.' And this was precisely what Satan had urged upon Jesus during his forty days' fast in the wilderness at the start of his public mission. It requires courage and a special grace to pursue a call in the face of rejection and mockery. The prophet Jeremiah did not want to do it, but the sense of mission to which he was called by God prevailed in him. For St Paul God's love was the only thing that really mattered and even the prospect of death did not deter him from preaching this to others. Jesus, whose life was so much shorter than that of Jeremiah or Paul, never once gave way to his opponents while proclaiming the kingdom of God by word and example.

It is so easy for us Christians to identify with society and its standards. Lying, stealing, killing, for example, are condemned by society. But the more subtle ways of committing these are often not even regarded as moral issues. Lying is evil, but the commercial world can so easily get away with bogus advertising and deceptive packaging; stealing is evil, but what of useless food products, inflated prices, or perpetual idling in paid employment; killing is wrong, but what of industrial pollution, the continued marketing of harmful drugs such as in the thalidomide case, or of poisoned olive oil as in Spain where approximately one million people were affected. Taking up one's cross and following Christ can mean being faithful to the teaching of Christ when turning one's back on it could bring ill-gotten wealth, or short-lived pleasure, or promotion to higher office in society. Being a true disciple of Christ can often mean speaking what people do not want to hear, or doing what people do not want to do.

TWENTY-THIRD SUNDAY OF THE YEAR
Ez 33:7-9; Rom 13:8-10; Mt 18:15-20

During the early days of heart-transplant operations, the mile-
stone for a patient was to survive a year afterwards. One particular patient who had attained this goal, described how before
the operation all he wanted was to die, but after he had survived
it, the world seemed a different place to him. 'When you have
faced death', he said, 'and been given another chance of life, you
notice everything'. As a French philosopher Sartre said, 'The
peak of love's joy, if it exists at all, is to feel that life is worth living'. His year's reprieve from death had brought this man a
fresh vision of the wonder of living. Christ's declaration in the
gospel that there is more to life than just eating, or drinking, or
the provision of clothing and shelter, now seemed very true. But
if it happens that we can become blind to the wonders of nature,
how much more likely are we to ignore the marvels of divine
revelation, which is the foundation of our religious beliefs. For it
may so easily happen that our religious vision and understanding of life on earth can become blurred and recede into the
background of our minds.

A convert in mature years, like the great English writer and
commentator, G. K. Chesterton, could marvel at the wild extremes
of truth to be found in the Church's teaching; for example, the
Virgin giving birth – a seeming contradiction in terms, the
divine death – an even greater contradiction, the sacredness of
marriage being praised on the same level as dedication to God
by a life of celibacy in a religious order, and so on. The sense of
almost childlike wonder before the truths of revelation, or
before God's creation, is something which, perhaps to a certain
extent, the modern person has lost. So wonderful are the discoveries and advances in new technology that they are almost taken
for granted. Twentieth century people have become carried
away by the hustle and bustle of complete change which has
swept so rapidly through their world. Historically speaking
they have, one might say, become dislocated, cast adrift from
their moorings in the past. There is such little continuity linking
them with that past, which seems light-years away. And there is
a vagueness about the future – in fact there is the fearful possibility that there may not be a future, if one considers the nuclear
holocaust that could be unleashed on the world by national

leaders hungry for power. In the face of all this, however, our response must not be one of despair and helplessness. Far from being a thing of fear, our belief in the providential care of God should be a liberating force. There may be some who, like the orthodox Jew in the time of Christ, maintain that people are not being religious unless they are enduring some kind of discomfort. Those who go down that road end up as victims to pessimism. But then, I cannot lock myself up in the secret room of my own heart and let others sink further into disillusion. Our Christian faith tells us, quite literally, that we are all members of one family, that our aim and prayer must be to become 'one Body, one Spirit, in Christ'.

In today's readings, God is telling me that I must be filled with concern for my brothers and sisters, in particular should they lose the vision of their immortal destiny, and the urge to strive for it. In the first reading God is calling me to be a prophet. This has nothing to do with foretelling the future. In the OT, a prophet was a person of God, one filled with the Spirit of God, one who had given himself up to be a servant of God, a witness before the whole world to the things of God. 'Son of man', we were told in the first reading, 'I have appointed you as sentry to the House of Israel.' A prophet was a sentry, a watchman, a familiar figure in the defence system of the land. A sentry always stood apart, on a tower or rampart. He noticed everything; he tried to see the significance of any movement around him, to spot any signs of danger for his community.

Likewise the committed Christian must be concerned about others, about the dangers that threaten them. Christ never said that it was none of his business if people were being exploited, or being led astray, or leading sinful lives. But neither did he reveal an individual's sins to his face. And so we are to be prophets by giving open witness to Christian virtues in our own lives, by wooing the wrong-doers back to the true path, by praying for them, and by manifesting always an active love for them, as did Christ Jesus. A certain saint never tired of telling those who came to see him that many, many souls are lost, because they have nobody to pray for them. Let us always do that faithfully.

TWENTY-FOURTH SUNDAY OF THE YEAR
Sir 27:33-28:9; Rom 14: 7-9; Mt 18:21-35

In that gospel reading Peter asked Jesus how often he should forgive his brother, and in the parable following was told that not only should he do so time and time again, but he should also forgive his brother from his heart. But there is still more. In the Sermon on the Mount, Jesus had widened the act of forgiving to include even one's enemies. 'Love your enemies, do good to those who hate you, bless those who curse you, pray for those who persecute and calumniate you' (Lk 6:27f). Sadly, the majority of us who try to live up to Christian standards feel that the love of God and of our fellow human beings is not exactly a priority in our lives.

But we should bear in mind that love does not consist solely in making great sacrifices. Indeed, great sacrifices without love are worth nothing, and neither are wonderful deeds, great achievements or heroic endurance. All of these latter were present in the life of St Paul. He was a man of profound spiritual knowledge, with a vast understanding of the mysteries of revelation. He could have answered thousands of questions on theological problems which have vexed the greatest minds down the centuries. So wonderful were the gifts God had given him that no one who met him could go away without being wiser about the path a soul should take to come close to God.

Such was this great apostle who devoted his unique talents to the spreading of Christ's message to the gentiles. Yet, of himself he could say, 'Though I speak with the tongues of men and of angels, and have not love, I am become as sounding brass, or a tinkling cymbal. Though I have the gift of prophecy, and understand all mysteries and all knowledge, and even have all faith so as to remove mountains, yet if I have not love, I am nothing' (1 Cor 13:1+). Thus being blessed with faith and eloquence and knowledge is not proof that one has also the gift of love. Even martyrdom, in itself, is no passport into paradise, as Paul said, 'Though I give my body to be burned, and am without love, it will do me no good whatever.' Jesus urged his followers, 'If you love me, keep my commandments.'

However, it is quite possible to be obedient, but remain without love, to obey God through fear of being punished by him. This generally happens when people pursue the things of this world, but are restrained from doing so to the full, by the kind of religion they profess. Those who go further than themselves, they look upon as being ungodly, whereas those who do not go as far as themselves, they regard as being superstitious, and scoff at them by labelling them conservatives.

The fact is, however, that if we turn away from evil out of fear of being punished, we are in the position of slaves. Jesus makes our whole duty consist in loving God, and at the same time also loving our neighbour. 'We know we have passed from death to life, because we love one another', St John wrote in his first letter (3:14), and 'Everyone who loves is born of God, and knows God, because God is love' (4:7). Moreover, 'Anyone who lives in love, lives in God, and God lives in him' (4:16). We can say that love is the seed of holiness, and begets all kinds of excellent qualities and virtues that single out a truly saintly person from ordinary souls. 'Love, and do what you will', St Augustine used to say, meaning that all who are motivated by love, in everything they do, are incapable of doing wrong to anyone. Indeed, holiness is really love of the divine law.

When as infants we were baptised, we received the Holy Spirit, and the Spirit thus given is the Law of God written on our hearts. In the Letter to the Hebrews we have confirmation of this where it says, 'I will put my laws into their minds, and write them on their hearts' (8:10). To know and believe that one is immensely loved by God gives ultimate meaning to life on earth and provides the foundation for true, real, and meaningful happiness.

Faith, however, should never beget a condescending attitude towards others, especially people of different religious persuasion to ourselves – regarding them as poor misguided individuals – nor should our faith lead to a feeling of complacency and smugness in ourselves. For faith is more a gift than an achievement on our part. It leads to the knowledge that we are loved by God as we are, and this frees us from worrying about our own perfection, our own happiness. It gives us the freedom of the children of God who place their trust completely in his love for them.

TWENTY-FIFTH SUNDAY OF THE YEAR
Is 55:6-9; Phil 1:20-24, 27; Mt 20:1-16

'My thoughts are not your thoughts,' the first reading warns us, 'my ways not your ways – it is the Lord who speaks.' God, in other words, is completely different from what human beings imagine. From the time of the ancient Greeks up to the beginning of the twentieth century, much effort, and at times zealous fervour, went into formulating proofs for the existence of God. But such proofs seem to have lost their appeal for our generation, which seems more concerned with what we mean, when we speak of God.

Although most of us believe that God created us, there are others who go so far as to declare that God is no more than something of our own creation. At one stage those who did not subscribe to the existence of a divine being claimed that belief in such a one merely made human beings shy away from work, while expecting God to do it for them. But many psychiatrists in recent times have become concerned that a lack of spirituality in turn can lead to its own mental upsets. Because when pressures become too great, and demands are impossible to meet, it is not the presence of a divine friend but rather the absence of one that can drive people to despair. The hope, in this world, of attaining a complete understanding of the nature of God is something, not only that can end up in many a blind alley, but, ultimately, is truly impossible to reach. For the finite human mind is incapable of encompassing the infinite.

The English writer, C. S. Lewis, famous for his insights into Christianity, after his wife had died from cancer, compared our idea of God with a house of cards. If one has a skilful and steady hand it is possible to build a quite elaborate structure, a kind of oriental temple, with playing cards. But because our limited image of the divine can easily become an idol, God occasionally shakes the table on which the cards are built up, and the whole thing collapses. Indeed we might well go so far as to say that this shattering is one of the marks of God's presence. For Lewis, the death of his wife was a crushing experience, which caused his image of God to crumble. It was only after the lapse of time that he came to look on his experience as a grace from God, because his understanding of the divine had increased further. One can very easily make the common mistake of trying to reduce God to one's own level. St Thomas Aquinas, on his deathbed, begged that all his writings on the nature of God be destroyed, so convinced was he of their limitations. His request was never carried out, but this warning by him to his followers remains. If you believe you can comprehend God it is quite certain he is not God that comes to your mind. God indeed is infinitely greater than any concept of him the human mind can form, even though it be endowed with the genius of a Thomas Aquinas.

We will have made considerable progress in our knowledge of God, St Augustine declared, when before we know who he is, we have first learned who he is not. God's ways certainly are not our ways, as we see in today's gospel parable. At first glance it seems to go contrary to our sense of justice. It is preceded by, and ends with the same sentence, 'The last will be first and the first last.' And so it happens when the landowner comes to pay his workers. His bailiff, or steward, is told to start with those who worked only an hour, and give them one denarius each. Thus those who had worked a full day saw the latecomers receiving as much as had been agreed for them in the early morning. Had they themselves been paid first, they would have gone off without being aware of what the rest got.

Any modern trade unionist would be appalled if his employer dealt with his staff in that manner. And we have a certain sympathy for those who had borne the heat and burden of the day, and received just as much as those who worked for just one hour in the cool of the evening. How could the landowner, who of course stands for God in the parable, treat his dependents in such a shabby way. Thus it comes as a rude awakening to us to learn that the whole thrust of the parable is that nobody can bargain with God, or claim the right to a reward from God. What Jesus is here stating in a rather striking way is that God is not in the business of bargaining, that a life of eternal happiness hereafter is a sheer gift that comes from God's generosity. In no way can it be earned. By way of response the important thing for me is my love for God and for my neighbour. But perhaps more important still is God's love for me as I am, as well as for the members of the community of which I am part.

TWENTY-SIXTH SUNDAY OF THE YEAR
Ez 18:25-28; Phil 2:1-11; Mt 21:28-32

When a good man commits sin, he will be punished, we were
told in the first reading, and when a wicked man repents he will
be saved. This looks very much like stating the obvious, but
obvious it was not for the Jews, who for a long time believed that
the whole community became guilty when one person from
within it committed sin, and that, moreover, the sins of parents
were punished in their children. For example, when the
Apostles saw the man who was born blind, they asked Jesus
who was responsible for this, the man himself or his parents.
And at the trial of Jesus, when Pilate, after washing his hands,
said, 'I am innocent of this man's blood. It is your concern', the
assembled onlookers all cried out, 'His blood be upon us and on
our children.' But as far back as the time of the prophet Ezekiel,
over 600 years before Christ, God had been revealing to the Jews
that all individuals are personally responsible for their own
misdeeds.

This theme is developed further by Jesus in the gospel parable
of the two sons, the meaning of which is quite clear. The Jewish
leaders who had pledged obedience to God had reneged on
their promises, whereas the tax-collectors and public sinners,
who, at first, had refused to keep God's commandments had
now been converted by the preaching of John the Baptist.
Generally speaking, people belong to one or other of two categ-
ories, (i) those whose profession is better than their practice,
putting on a show of piety and fidelity, but failing to live out
these; and (ii) those who, despite a rough exterior, are at heart
generous and upright.

Promises are never a substitute for performance, nor can fine
words take the place of good deeds. 'If you love me, keep my
commandments', Christ said (Jn 14:15). But our promise to do
so, very often, falls short of fulfilment, far more than we ourselves
imagine. While we may be quite sincere in desiring to fulfil
them, unknown to ourselves we slip into doing the exact opposite. The son who promised to obey his father was quite polite. 'I
go, sir', he said, but obviously there was no sincerity in his
response. It was not in keeping with his habitual frame of mind,
which as a rule showed him shying away from any work. Thus
the moment the words were out of his mouth they were forgotten.

In like manner, many of us can fail to keep our promises, and not from deliberate disloyalty, but because we have gradually acquired the habit of not doing so. It perhaps already has become part of our nature. By continually ignoring the dictates of our conscience, our will can reach the stage where it is incapable of responding, even though we deceive ourselves into thinking it can. Thus a person can say, 'If the worst comes to the worst, if perhaps I have a serious health problem, or at least reached a stage where death is immanent, I can always make a confession and repent.' But thus to quieten one's conscience, by what might be described as doomsday planning, is to make the foolish presumption that when the time comes, one will be able to repent, despite repeatedly having refused to do so.

The very fact that one refuses to express sorrow for one's sinful ways now, should be a clear message that there is a greater difference, than one imagines, between promising and the ability to carry out our promises. Once we have become willing slaves to sinful tendencies, Scripture warns us, 'our iniquities like the wind will sweep us away' (Is 64:6). At every stage of our lives, deeds, not vain hopes or wishes, must be our watchword. Neither lip-service of God, nor being a Christian merely in name, will suffice to merit the eternal vision of the glory of God.

We are told in the Book of Genesis (15:6) that 'Abraham put his faith in God, and on account of this faith he was considered to be free from sin'. The question is what is faith, and how can people be certain that they have faith. Some would say that faith lies in the awareness of one's own sinfulness and the infinite holiness of God, being conscious of one's own weakness and inability to attain salvation, longing for redemption by Christ, and living for him and loving him with all one's heart. But all these emotions do not constitute faith, however necessary and admirable they may be, because they are emotions, or simply good thoughts, unless they are acted upon. And if they are not accompanied by good works they are quite dead. 'As the body without the spirit is dead', Sacred Scripture warns, 'so faith without good works is also dead', good works entered into with cheerful and joyful commitment.

TWENTY-SEVENTH SUNDAY OF THE YEAR
Is 5:1-7; Phil 4:6-9; Mt 21:33-43

One of the most striking statements of St Jerome, Doctor of the Church and translator of the Bible, is that to be ignorant of the scriptures is to be ignorant of the power of God and his wisdom. 'Ignorance of the scriptures is ignorance of Christ', he said. today is Emigrant Sunday, and if we turn to these same sacred scriptures, we come up against the theme of exile again and again, right from the very time that Adam and Eve were cut adrift from the state of happiness and original justice that was theirs in Eden. As we contemplate the scripture stories that dwell on this theme, there is one thing that becomes very clear to us. No matter the hardship and suffering, the alienation and exile that people often endure, the Lord ordains that out of it all, good will come to them and to others, on condition that they put their trust in the providence and love God has for them.

Thus the patriarch Abraham, in answer to a divine call, departed from his own country, his own people, and religion, and settling in an alien country which was to become one day the promised land, he became, as St Paul never tires of reminding us, the father in faith of all of us ever since. Likewise, Jacob, the grandson of Abraham, was sent away into a strange land by his father Isaac. He parted with all he had grown up with, and was never to set eye on his mother again or hear her voice. He was to endure harsh conditions while serving a man who, although an uncle of his, was a hard task-master. When finally he returned to the land of his forefathers he was once more forced into exile in Egypt because of famine that afflicted his people.

But in God's own time all these sufferings and upsets were to be rewarded, for in Egypt his family was delivered from famine and became very powerful. Moses, one of his descendants, was compelled to leave Egypt, and wander in the desert for most of his life with an unwilling band of followers. God, however, was with Moses, having chosen him to bring this motley group together as a nation, and lead them to the borders of the land that was destined to be their permanent home. To mention another exile from the Old Testament, we have the touching story of Ruth, born outside the Jewish faith, who nevertheless was prepared to leave her own country in order to look after her aging mother-in-law, Naomi, herself a Jewish widow seeking to return to Israel. Despite opposition from Naomi, Ruth pleaded, 'Do not press me to leave you, or to turn back from following you. Wherever you go, I will go. Wherever you live, I will live. Your people shall be my people, and your God my God' (Ruth 1:16). Having prevailed by these immortal words, Ruth was to be rewarded by in a very special way, in that she became the great grandmother of King David, the ancestor of Christ himself. 'By the streams of Babylon we sat down and wept, when we remembered Zion.' This was how the Psalmist described the reaction of those in the greatest exile of all, numerically speaking, the rounding up and deportation to Babylon of the most influential people in every sector of Jewish society, following on the destruction of the Temple in Jerusalem.

But not only did the Jewish faith survive this calamity, it even emerged enriched and spiritually more profound, especially in the area of prayer. It is very likely that the custom of the gathering together, or synagogue, for the purpose of prayer, worship and scripture reading, began during the exile in Babylon. What is certain is that those exiles, who later returned to their native land, came back spiritually renewed and with a new understanding of their God-given heritage. In all of these events people of faith saw God's hand at work, leading and guiding them towards a goal that often remained hidden from them, but which ultimately formed part of God's plan, not only for the Jews, but for the salvation of the whole human race. Perhaps also, these exile stories prefigure the reality which underlies the whole New Testament, namely, the voluntary exile from heaven of God's own Son, Jesus Christ, who became as it were a slave in order to restore mankind to friendship with God.

When we recall the millions who went into exile from this country, and pray for them, we can take pride also in the good they have effected in other people. If with the eyes of faith I see God at work in the world, and look towards heaven as my final home, then like St Paul I will be able to say, 'It is, now, not I who live, but Christ who lives in me.' And when that happens, neither am I any longer an exile, but part of God's family.

TWENTY-EIGHTH SUNDAY OF THE YEAR
Is 25:6-10; Phil 4:12-14; Mt 22:1-14

With the exception of St Patrick, it is perhaps true that no foreign saint exerted a greater spiritual influence on this country of ours – without ever actually setting foot on it – than did St Bernard of Clairvaux in France, the monk who in the 12th century really established the Cistercian Order as a force for good throughout the length and breadth of Europe. While travelling to Rome to receive appointment as bishop of Armagh, St Malachy, himself a monk, called on Bernard, and even expressed a wish to join his Order, but was refused permission by the Pope.

On his return journey, Malachy left some Irish monks in Clairvaux to learn the Cistercian way of life, and when these came back to Ireland the first Cistercian monastery was set up in Mellifont, Co Louth. The fact that this foundation bore quick results, and the Order spread rapidly throughout the country, was due in large to the zeal and devotion of Bernard which he passed on to all who came in contact with him. Every morning, in his monastery at Clairvaux, Bernard would ask himself this question, 'Bernard, Bernard, why have you come here?' And by keeping his mind focused on the meaning of life, he was to change not only himself, but the values of Europeans as well. It is imperative that, from time to time, we all should ask ourselves this same question also, and especially when we are gathered together as a worshipping community to celebrate the Eucharist. 'Why am I here?' To find an answer we might turn to the parable of the wedding feast in the gospel reading. The king here referred to is God, the wedding feast is a celebration of the advent of the Messiah, or Redeemer, who is the son of the king, in other words, Jesus the Son of God. Those sent out with invitations were first the prophets and later on the disciples of Christ.

But those originally invited, namely the Jews, chose to ignore God's messengers, and even used violence against them. The burning of their town, by way of retribution, refers to the destruction of Jerusalem. Finally those called in from the streets were the sinners and gentiles despised by the Jews. The behaviour of the Jews recalls for us the saying of St Augustine, 'God created us without our cooperation, but without our cooperation he cannot save us.' We should never regard this parable as applying only to another age, because the call to share in the heavenly banquet of the Messiah is an on-going call. Moreover, Christ is appealing to us here and now not to consider how much we will be punished if we turn a deaf ear to his invitation, but rather to reflect on what we will lose if, like the Jews, we spurn his call. We must always keep in mind that the invitation extended to us is one that comes out of God's generosity. Those in the highways and byways could never, by any stretch of the imagination, have expected an invitation to the wedding feast, still less deserve it.

The treatment meted out to the man in the parable who had no wedding garment, at first sight, seems to us rather harsh. But the gospel is insisting that when we come to the Eucharistic banquet we should be in the state of friendship with God. The parable has nothing to do with the clothes we wear to church, but it has everything to do with the interior spirit and reverence that should motivate us when we come into God's house. How often does it happen that we come with no preparation whatsoever, that spiritually speaking we are only half alive, mere shadows, satisfying our consciences by sitting out the time for what we perhaps regard as an institutional obligation imposed by the Church, which we fulfil in a routine fashion as if it were simply a social custom.

If every single person in this congregation had a sincere desire to respond to the call of Christ, then our coming together would be true worship of God indeed. And we would not be in the least upset or concerned if asked the question, 'Why have you come here?' We should make it a habit to renew daily, and especially during the Sunday Mass, our dedication to the following of Christ. Then when burdens and crosses weigh heavily upon us we can take courage by contemplating the eternal banquet, the reward God has prepared for all who love him. 'Come you that are blessed by my Father', Christ promises, 'take possession of the kingdom which was prepared for you from the foundation of the world'. At this heavenly banquet God will wipe away all tears from our eyes. Death shall be no more, nor mourning nor crying shall be anymore, for the former things will have passed away (Rev 21:4).

TWENTY-NINTH SUNDAY OF THE YEAR
Deut 30:1-4; Eph 1:3-10; Jn 11:45-52

Before being called by Christ to be one of his twelve Apostles, St Matthew was a tax collector operating in a customs house, somewhere in the north of Galilee. Since this profession required that he be able to read, write and especially keep records, these skills he would put to good use in writing his gospel account of Jesus' mission. His literary style, as an evangelist, may be more artificial than that of St Luke, but there is no doubt that the gospel excerpt you have just heard is truly dramatic. The question put to Jesus, as to whether it was permissible for Jews to pay tribute to Caesar, gives a clear insight into the minds and strategy of the Pharisees. They were endeavouring to walk Jesus into a political trap that would set him at odds with the Roman authorities, who were the rulers of Israel at that time, or, failing that, would discredit him before his own people. To avoid giving rise to suspicion of their intent, they decided not to get involved personally themselves. They sent some of their disciples along to Christ instead. It is quite likely that the leaders of the Pharisees stayed in the background because they wanted the followers of Herod, the Roman appointed tetrarch of Galilee, to take part also in the plot against Jesus, even though these Herodians, who openly advocated cooperation with the Romans, were normally their most bitter enemies.

The feigned tributes to Jesus by this delegation, mention of his honesty, his fearlessness, his disregard for the status of those he encountered, all this flattery coming from people who normally were hostile to Christ merely highlights the hypocrisy of their praise. Then the trap was sprung: 'Tell us what is your own opinion? Is it lawful to pay taxes to Caesar or not?' Were Christ to answer, 'Pay the tax', then he would stand accused of collaboration with the Roman oppressors, and would incur the scorn of ordinary Jews each of whom had to pay a poll tax, from the age of twelve for women and fourteen for men. Were he to advocate non-payment, he could be arrested for sedition by the Roman authorities. Jesus' response, however, 'Give to Caesar the things that are Caesar's, and to God the things that are God's', left them confounded, and they slunk away. But Jesus' reply left the matter in suspense, because it did not touch upon the right of the Romans to rule Israel, nor did it enumerate precisely the things of Caesar or those of God.

These opposing claims of God and state were left to be decided by the informed conscience of each individual, and still are to this day. What must be kept in mind is the warning of Jesus, in the Sermon on the Mount, that 'no one can serve two masters … one cannot be the slave of both God and wealth' (Mt 6:24). Wealth in early OT times was seen as created by God, and bestowed on patriarchs, kings and leaders who had roles of special responsibility. Later on, wealth ceased to be regarded as a gift from God. 'Woe to those who join house to house and field to field, until everywhere belongs to them', Isaiah warned (Is 5:8), and Jesus himself said, 'Alas for you who are rich; you are having your life of ease now' (Lk 6:24). The world and all its resources were created by God for the benefit of all human beings without exception, and this must usually obtain alongside the right to private property, whether inherited or acquired by personal enterprise. It is the task of government to seek a balance between these objectives that will lead to the common good of all those governed. And taxation is still one of the most common means of achieving this.

But, just as with the Jews in the time of our Lord, people nowadays do not take kindly to having a share of their earnings taken from them in the form of tax. But, whereas the taxes then in Israel, for the most part, went to swell the coffers of the authorities in Rome, where slavery was a substantial economic factor as well for all its citizens, taxes collected nowadays, in this country for example, go towards caring for the sick, the elderly, the permanently disabled, the huge cost of maintaining the infrastructure of the state. We should never forget that we have a dual set of responsibilities, towards God and towards our neighbour in society. In the latter, state authorities have a major role to play, and have a right to our cooperation in their endeavour to bring about the material welfare of all citizens. We fulfil our obligations towards achieving that by obeying the just laws of the state, by paying our lawful taxes, and by helping to bring about the common good at all times.

MISSION SUNDAY
Deut 30:1-4; Eph 1:3-10; Jn 11:45-52

In the first chapter of St Mark's gospel we read how Jesus, after choosing his first four disciples, began his public mission by preaching at the synagogue in Capernaum, the town where Peter lived. When at sundown the sabbath had ended, he continued late into the night curing people of all kinds of diseases. Yet before dawn next morning, he slipped away to a lonely place and prayed there by himself. His disciples set out to look for him, and, having found him, told him with a certain enthusiasm, 'Everybody is looking for you.' They wanted him to cash in on his newly acquired popularity in the town, but his response was, 'Let us go elsewhere to the neighbouring towns so that I may proclaim the message there also, for that is what I came out to do.' And he went through the whole of Galilee, proclaiming the message in their synagogues and casting out devils.

'That is what I came out to do', is rather a peculiar saying. It could mean, 'I came out from Capernaum', or it could refer to Jesus' coming forth from God the Father. It is quite possible that the entire passage could be stated like this, 'I have come forth from God, to bring the gospel to all people.' Mark then goes on to describe how a leper came to Jesus and pleaded, 'If you want to, you can make me clean.' And Jesus being moved with pity for him said, 'Of course I want to. Be cured', and he was. Despite being warned not to speak of what happened, the man went away and started telling everybody about his cure.

As everything in sacred scripture has a divine purpose we might ask, 'Why did Mark include this miracle in his gospel? Has it got a message for us from the Holy Spirit who inspired Mark?' Some would say yes, that just as the man was cleansed from his leprosy, and then told everyone about it, so it is that every Christian who has been cleansed from the stain of original sin in baptism, has a duty to go forth and give witness before the world to Christ's teaching. For as the gift of miracles is given to saints, not for their own benefit, but for the benefit of others, in the same way the precious gift of faith was not given to us solely to achieve our own personal salvation, nor to be kept hidden away like the man who buried his talent in the ground for purely selfish motives. We are called to play some active role in the Church's task of winning souls for Christ.

The gospel message has not been heard, or scarcely so, by close on two billion human beings at present, mainly in Africa, Asia, Latin America, the Pacific islands, and their number is increasing daily. In all other countries, including our own, there are three kinds of unbelief that one can encounter, and it is here we can do something for Christ. (i) There is the atheist who, having rejected God, sets about attacking the very idea of God with a fervour that is almost religious in a perverted sense, an attitude which in extreme cases can verge on the psychotic. (ii) There are those who accept the existence of God and the fact of revelation, but still find themselves unable to believe. (iii) Finally, there are those who are nominally Christian, who even receive the sacraments now and again, but have almost entirely lost their faith, because they never engage in true Christian activity. They cling to the outward forms of religion, but without a living faith in God they have, in practice, become sceptics, a condition which leaves them worse off than the atheist, who at least becomes excited at the mention of God. To regard atheists and sceptics as being beyond redemption would be to doubt the power of the grace of God, but conversion among them is very rare. It is among the millions in the second group, that those called to be ambassadors for Christ are more likely to evoke a response.

In an obscure way this group are in a search for peace in God, but keep drawing back from a final commitment in faith to God. The barriers they have built between themselves and God cannot be broken down by reasoning with them or by force of argument. For human intelligence is incapable of penetrating fully the depths of the supernatural mysteries of our faith. The solution lies not with the mind, but with the will. It is with the will that we believe, that is, no one can believe unless he/she wills to do so. As St Augustine learned in his own conversion, the main reason why the will draws back from accepting the faith is that it fears to pay the price of faith, to sacrifice those things which the will craves. Faith is a gift which demands in turn the gift of oneself to God. We should pray for that faith, and fervently beseech God that the light of faith may never die in our country.

THIRTIETH SUNDAY OF THE YEAR
Ex 22:20-26; 1 Thess 1:5-10; Mt 22:34-40

Since Vatican II Council, many earnest Catholics complain that over-emphasis is being placed on the love of God and of our neighbour, and not enough on obedience to God, and observance of his commandments. But over-emphasis on commandments can itself give rise to a whole set of fears. Why, for example, do we fear death? Partly, we might say, because it marks our entry into the unknown, but even more so because of our sense of guilt. If people felt that they could easily meet God, then to die would only be a great adventure, as Blaise Pascal, the great French scientist and religious philosopher said. He died in 1662 at the age of thirty-nine, after having received in an ecstasy of joy the Holy Viaticum, praying as he half rose from his bed, 'May God never abandon me!' Sadly, his death perhaps may have been hastened by the fact that in the latter half of his life he was won over to Jansenism which regarded all human nature as being corrupt, and this led him to overdo mortifications and self-punishment because of this exaggerated sense of human depravity and sinfulness.

But where does the sense of sin in a soul come from? It comes from our feeling of being governed by law. So long as one sees in God only the law of justice, he/she must ever be in the position of a criminal before the judge, with no hope of acquittal. But this is precisely what Jesus came to abolish. He came to tell us that God is not law, but love, that the centre of God's being is not legalism but grace, that when we die we go out, not to a judge, but to a Father, who awaits his children coming home. Because of that Jesus gave us the victory over death, its fear banished in the wonder of God's love. 'We know, brothers and sisters, beloved by God, that he has chosen you', St Paul wrote to the Church at Thessalonika (1 Thess 1:4).

In the Old Testament the term, 'beloved by God', was reserved for great figures like Moses, Solomon, and so on. But here it is applied to the Thessalonians, who were gentiles, and it ushered in a new era in attitudes towards God. St Augustine posed the question, 'Does love bring about the keeping of the commandments, or does the keeping of the commandments bring about love?' And his answer was, 'Who can doubt that love comes first? For the one who does not love has no reason for keeping the commandments.'

On the other hand an over concentration on law, on external observance, betrays the suspicion that Christ is an ineffectual Saviour. He may let me down, unless I have a record of good behaviour to back up my claim to an eternal reward. This outlook of course is an extreme one, as is that which regards God as the kind and friendly God, for ever at our beck and call, ready with a solution for our every need. Nor can we say that the role of God lies between these two extremes, for we cannot pin down God. Neither can we analyse our faith completely, and put God under the microscope, and use him to become masters of our own destiny. When it comes to an encounter with God in our lives, what matters is the experience of God which he grants us deep down in our souls.

In his hymn, 'Lead kindly light', Cardinal Newman wrote, 'I loved to choose and see my path, but now lead thou me on.' It is the heart which feels God and not reason. That is what faith is – God reached-out-to by the heart, not by reason (Pascal). Perhaps during the coming week, we could ask ourselves, 'Is it possible for me to encounter God in my life? What does God mean to me?' I have heard some people say, in a kind of disgust with their lives, 'How can God be really interested in me? How can he possibly love me?'

But the fact is that he does; and if we constantly remind ourselves that this is so, that he actually died for each and every one on this earth, then this very thought can change our whole lives. For we have but to look around us and see the power of even human love, how some characters seem to grow and blossom forth under its influence; and how others – especially in the case of children – become stunted and imbalanced, where love is wanting in their lives. And the message of today's readings is that the love of God should not stop short with each of us, but that it should radiate out from us so as to encompass those with whom we live, those in the community of which we are part. We should never forget that incisive saying of St John, the evangelist, 'Since God has so loved us, then we ought to love one another.'

FEAST OF ALL SAINTS
Apoc 7:2-4, 9-14; 1 Jn 3:1-3; Mt 5:1-12

In the account of the conversion of Saul, later to be known as Paul, which we find in the Acts of the Apostles (Chap. 9), we read how he set out for Damascus in order to arrest and take back to Jerusalem, any men or women that he could find, who were known to be 'followers of the Way'. This name, 'followers of the Way', is the one by which those who adhered to the teachings of Christ were first known. When people followed the Way, then they were serving God according to the patterns of conduct which became the distinguishing mark of the Christian community. They were putting into practice in their daily lives the teachings of Jesus, who had said, 'I am the Way, the Truth and the Life' (Jn 14:6). Jesus had an extraordinary attraction for people, to the extent that they were prepared to change their whole lifestyle, once he had challenged them with the invitation, 'follow me'.

Today we recall all the dedicated men and women of faith, down through the centuries, who have tried to follow this call of Christ, to the best of their ability. We do so by one of the most loved feasts in the Church calendar, the Feast of All Saints. Originally, this feast was meant to commemorate the numerous martyrs in the early centuries of Christianity, whose names were never recorded. But later it came to include all those who while on earth had striven to lead blameless and holy lives, without having to die for their beliefs. We might even say that to a certain extent we ourselves are included, especially if we recall that the New Testament refers to all baptised Christians, even while they were still living, as saints, a holy people. We read in the Acts of the Apostles (9:32) how 'Peter visited one place after another and eventually came to the saints living down in Lydda.' And the Letter to the Hebrews ends with these words, 'Greetings to all your leaders and to all the saints. The saints of Italy send you greetings.' This is a joyous feast, one in which we celebrate the victory of Jesus Christ, the Lamb of God, over the powers of evil.

Even though it is now a celebration in faith, we take courage from the example of so many fervent Christians, who have gone before us, and also so many good-living people, thank God, who are all around us here and now. Heartened by their example, we look forward to the day when we will all celebrate the feast in heaven, in the great assembly of all the faithful departed, which St John described in the first reading. This vision of John is an encouragement to us to persevere in our Christian way of life. For the majority of us it is not martyrdom we have to undergo, such as that which faced so many brave people, in the early centuries of Christianity, as well as in the post-Reformation period here in our own country. It is not open atheism or heresy that we now have to contend with, but rather a persistent, growing, and subtle temptation to discard the Christian values and practices that we have inherited.

The countless saints we recall today, apart from the difficulties peculiar to their time, had to contend more or less with the same failings, inclinations, and opposition that face us here and now. Their greatest lesson to us is that they never forgot God, nor ceased trying to live holy lives. Even though what we shall be in the future has not yet been revealed, we should keep reminding ourselves of the wonderfully encouraging message of St Paul (1 Cor 2:9), 'No eye has seen, nor ear heard, neither has it entered into the heart of anyone, what God has prepared for those who love him', words which surely spurred on many of those early unnamed saints we commemorate in this feast, in their following of the Way, which is Christ. We could meditate with profit as well on how Christ, while on earth, himself lived out the Beatitudes mentioned in the gospel.

Moreover, we could see the lives of the saints, and those of the good people we have known but have now gone to their reward, as so many reflections of the perfection of Christ, the poor in spirit – the sick, the aged, the underprivileged, the meek – those who have carried their crosses without complaint, the hungry – who strove for what was right, the pure in heart – who always put God first, the peacemakers – who tried to reconcile and not divide, the persecuted – who because they were faithful to high ideals were rejected by lesser people. Let us today thank God for all his saints and let us pray that we too may one day be numbered with them in heaven. Amen.

THIRTY-FIRST SUNDAY OF THE YEAR
Mal 1:14 - 2:2, 8-10; 1 Thess 2:7-9, 13; Mt 23:1-12

One of the mottoes of commercialism is to avail of any opportunity that presents itself to one. The world's first passenger
service by railway was started in England in 1825, and within 20
years or so special 8-day return tickets were being issued in
Lyons in France to people wishing to go by rail to the little village of Ars, roughly 15 miles away. What was the attraction of
Ars, you might ask? Well, there was a parish priest there, John
Mary Vianney, whose whole life was devoted to the care of
souls, who during the last 10 years of his life spent between 16 to
18 hours daily hearing confessions. Into this little village of 200
or so inhabitants, more than 300 pilgrims came daily, rich, poor,
clerics, lay people, all seeking peace of mind, advice, God's forgiveness, bodily cures, or just the opportunity to touch this tiny,
charismatic, little man, who to this day is remembered as the
'Curé d'Ars'. In the last seven years of his life, the annual total of
such pilgrims increased from 80 to 100 to close on 120,000 people.

Yet the first 28 years of his life, in certain respects, seemed a
complete disaster. Despite having near average intelligence, he
lacked a basic education. Feeling called to the priesthood when
he was 19 years, he entered a school where the average age of
the pupils was 12, with the aim, in particular, of gaining a
knowledge of Latin. But it was a subject he never mastered.
Worse still, he was conscripted into the army, and because of
poor health, without intending to do so, he ended up a deserter
finding refuge in a remote village, and living under a false name
(Jerome Vincent). Later, availing of an amnesty granted by
Napoleon to deserters, he succeeded in getting into a seminary,
and despite being dismissed after failing once again his final
exam, he was at last ordained at the age of 29 when a priest, who
was his friend and mentor, made a special plea for him on the
basis of his holiness and sincerity.

But from there on, with crowds making such demands on
him, he had to undergo terrible trials. In particular for 34 years
he suffered nightly attacks from the devil, who tried by every
means to disrupt his few hours of sleep, by creating all kinds of
noise heard also by independent witnesses, by pushing his bed
and appearing to tear the bed clothes, and by shouting, 'I'll get
you yet, Vianney'. These attacks were always exaggerated before

a big public sinner was due to come to his confessional. The fact that John Vianney was a truly extraordinary saint, and now is declared patron and exemplar for all pastoral clergy, brings to mind the words of the New Testament, 'God has chosen the foolish in the world to shame the wise, the weak in the world to confound the strong. Those whom the world regards as common and despicable are the ones God has chosen; those who are nothing at all to show up those who are everything' (1 Cor 1:27+).

All three readings today are, by implication, concerned with two things: the duties and obligations of those in the priesthood, and as well their shortcomings and failures. Without in any way making an excuse for the latter, it can be said that, morally speaking, priests by and large are no better and no worse than those to whom they minister, those to whom they preach. If only the just should be permitted to preach in church, then who would dare open their mouths. And so it is that a priest has to take the risk of speaking freely each Sunday, for as Pope Pius XII said, 'This free speech belongs to the Church, and without it an injury would be done to both pastor and people.' The priest is an instrument in the hands of God, and God sometimes uses the weakness and imperfection of the instrument to confound the proud and the mighty.

Moreover, God wants us to lift our gaze beyond the limitations, the shortcomings of the instrument, to the perfection, the loving care, of the Almighty One who uses this instrument. What is required of the faithful is a discernment of faith which hears God himself speaking through the agency of his chosen ministers, as well as a willingness to pray that the word of God may take root in their lives, and yield an abundant return, just like the grains of seed in the parable of the Sower. What we must keep in mind is that we are all a 'priestly people, God's only people', and that the task of building up God's kingdom on earth devolves on every one of us. For this we are privileged to have been chosen, and we must never cease working and praying that with our cooperation God's plans for the salvation of the whole world may come to fruition.

THIRTY-SECOND SUNDAY OF THE YEAR
Wis 6:12-16; 1 Thess 4:13-18; Mt 25:1-13

Our present day western civilisation derives, in great part, from Greek, Roman and Jewish cultures. But in attitudes, in ancient times, towards life after death, there could be no greater gap between, on the one hand, the Graeco-Roman tradition, and on the other, the Jewish tradition. In particular, when confronted with the inevitability of death, the response of the person without faith was, and today is, one of despair. On a pagan tombstone from the classical period can be read the grim inscription, 'I was not, I became; I am not, I care not.' This reflects the thinking of the living rather than the state of the dead person. In the words of a pagan Greek poet (Theocritus): 'There is hope for those who are alive, but those who have died are without hope.' One of the greatest lyric poets, the Roman writer, Horace, who died the year Christ was born, had this advice for the reader: 'Enjoy the present day, trusting in tomorrow as little as you can' (*Carpe diem, quam minimum credula postero*). No wonder then that the motto of the time was, 'Eat, drink, and be merry, for tomorrow we die.'

In the Jewish tradition, belief in resurrection after death did not gain acceptance until the first century before Christ. But there was belief in a shadowy existence of the departed in a place called Sheol, where they could neither know God nor praise him. If we take the Book of Ecclesiastes, for example, written about 300 BC, we find its author agreeing, yes, there can be a certain happiness in eating, drinking and being content with one's work while on earth, but because of the futility of earthly pursuits and possessions, there is in human beings a God-given yearning for something deeper, especially for the meaning of all experience and all time. And God is the only one who is wise, the only one who knows.

In a beautiful last chapter, full of vivid imagery, the author of Ecclesiastes describes how, without being touched in the least by the passing of man to his eternal abode, the things of nature carry on with their own pursuits. Even those who mourn the passing from this life of one of their own are already walking to and fro in the street before, as the writer says, 'the silver cord is snapped, or the golden lamp (of life) is broken, or before the dust returns to the earth from whence it came, and the spirit to

God who gave it'. There is some element in each person which this world is not worthy to retain; it is of God, and after its sojourn here it returns to God.

The greatest change in attitude to life hereafter came about with belief in the resurrection of Christ. 'For us', St Paul wrote to the Philippians (3:20), 'our homeland is in heaven, and from heaven comes the Saviour we are waiting for, the Lord Jesus Christ, and he will transfigure these lowly bodies of ours into copies of his own glorious body'. We should not therefore, he tells us in the liturgy today, remain without understanding concerning those close to us who have passed away.

We should not grieve as others do, who have no hope of resurrection, or of eternal life. Note, he does not tell us to avoid being sorrowful, for sorrow over the death of a loved one is a natural reaction, but rather not to be like others, who have no hope. The necessity of losing somebody in death causes us anguish, but hope consoles us. Our human frailty is tried by the one, but our faith is strengthened by the other. The liturgy this month asks us to respond in two practical ways. Firstly, it tells us to be prepared, not to let things go too late. No tolling funeral bell can cause greater anguish than the words 'too late'. Those who live all their lives close to Christ will never be unprepared to enter his presence, will be with Christ even in death, and will finally share in his glorious resurrection. Secondly, it invites us to assist with our prayers those who have gone before us.

St Monica was always anxious to be buried alongside her husband, but when she was dying at Ostia, the port of Rome, she had only one last request to make of her son, Augustine, not yet a priest, 'Lay this body anywhere', she said, 'let it not be a care to you. This only I ask of you, that you would remember me at the Lord's altar wherever you may be'. We too should keep in mind that in death life is changed, not taken away. If we do this, then God will fill the emptiness caused by death in our own lives. He will renew in us the hope of our resurrection, and he will reassure us that those we lose on earth we shall see again in heaven. This is our Christian hope; this is our God-given trust.

THIRTY-THIRD SUNDAY OF THE YEAR
Prov 31:10-13, 30-31; 1 Thess 5:1-6; Mt 25:14-30

We are told clearly in the second reading today that no one has
any idea when the Day of the Lord, or the Last Day, will come. It
will steal upon us like a thief in the night. It is necessary therefore for the true followers of Christ to stay awake, to be sober, to
be prepared, to live in expectation of the Lord's coming, however
sudden it may be. It is truly fascinating to read how in ancient
Egypt, thousands of years before the Christian era, each Pharaoh
from the moment his reign commenced started to prepare for his
death. A large portion of his time was devoted to planning his
final burial place, making it secure against possible intruders,
preparing and filling it with great quantities of the most precious
and beautiful objects intended to serve his needs in the next
world.

It is truly saddening to discover how very often, within a
brief period, his former subjects, who had willingly cooperated
in the preparation of his tomb, were driven by greed to desecrate
and pillage it, no matter how secret or impregnable it was. It
calls to mind our Lord's saying: 'Lay up for yourselves treasure
in heaven, where neither moth nor rust consumes and where
thieves do not break in and steal' (Mt 6:20). On the day we die,
we must leave behind forever all earthly goods, riches, honours
and pleasures. And we each might profitably ask the question,
'What kind of person will I then be when all these possessions
are taken away from me?' The only thing we will carry with us
beyond the grave will be the virtues we have acquired in this
life.

On these final Sundays of the Church year, the liturgy keeps
reminding us that no one can foresee when the day of final
reckoning will be, but that for each one of us it will most certainly
come. And the best way to prepare for its coming is through
faithfully, and humbly, and watchfully fulfilling our obligations
to God and one another. When it does come, Scripture tells us,
God will judge each person, and of two people, who have lived
side by side all their lives, one will be taken and the other rejected.
This is a warning that intimacy with a saintly person will not
necessarily be a guarantee of salvation for those who have always
lived close to that person. The judgment of God is an individual
judgment. We cannot discharge the obligations to God we have

promised in baptism, by employing a substitute, or by associating with some good-living person. 'One will be taken and another left.'

The life of each of us is lived out in the shadow of eternity, in the certainty that day by day by our behaviour we are drawing closer for ever hereafter, to the enjoyment or loss of God's presence. But the fact that we do live in the shadow of eternity should never give rise to fearful or hysterical forebodings in us. What it does mean is that, every day, we must so live as to be ready to meet God. When confronted with these thoughts we find ourselves anxiously posing the question: 'Will I be saved?' And while, in this life, we can never have a guarantee that we will be numbered among God's elect, still there are signs that God's grace is at work in us, signs such as perseverance in prayer, selfless love, trust in the mercy of God, and concern for others.

Indeed, Christian tradition puts before us two very practical signs of final perseverance, namely devotion to the Blessed Virgin Mary and to the Sacred Heart, for God has attached very special graces to both these devotions. If I want to know for sure whether or not I still possess the living love of God which would ensure my readiness to meet him when he comes, then I have only to examine my self to see whether I truly love the Mother of God, and whether from time to time I say to myself, quietly but sincerely: 'Heart of Jesus, Son of the Eternal Father, have mercy on me.' If I can honestly say, 'Yes, I am really trying to love Christ and his Blessed Mother', then I can be sure that the love of God is still alive in me, that it has not vanished under the pressures of daily living, or been choked by indifference and routine. To isolate Mary from God's plan of salvation would be to deprive it of one of its most central parts.

As St Augustine has said, 'All the elect are, in this world, hidden in the womb of the Most Blessed Virgin, where they are cherished and nourished until such time as she brings them forth to glory after their death.' Mary, Mother of Good Counsel direct and so guide us, that when your Son comes he may find us watching and ready. Amen.

OUR LORD JESUS CHRIST, UNIVERSAL KING
Ez 34:11-12, 15-17; 1 Cor 15:20-26, 28; Mt 25:31-46

When we listen every Sunday to the gospel being read out for us, we should keep in mind the advice of Christ to the Jews, that they should examine carefully the sacred scriptures, because these same scriptures bear testimony to Christ who is the Saviour of the world. His opponents were already formulating plans to kill him, because he spoke of God as his own Father. 'You search the scriptures', he told them, 'believing that in them you can find eternal life. Now it is these scriptures that testify to me, and yet you refuse to come to me to find life' (Jn 5:39). If we were to search thoroughly through the gospels in particular, we would find, however, that in them Jesus, as a rule, did not preach about himself, nor even about God, but rather about the kingdom of God.

Since there cannot be a kingdom without a king, we might, on this the feast of Christ the King, reflect on how this title is associated with Christ in the New Testament. Peculiarly, Jesus is represented as being a regal figure, mainly at the beginning and the end of the gospel story. 'Where is he who has been born king of the Jews', the Wise Men inquired, and, having found him, conferred on him the gifts reserved for royalty. 'The Lord will give to him the throne of his father, David', the Angel had said to Mary at the Annunciation, 'and he will reign over the house of Jacob for ever, and his kingdom will have no end' (Lk 1:32f).

Then in the final days of Christ's story, when he entered Jerusalem for the last time on Palm Sunday, the evangelist Matthew says it was to fulfil the prophecy, 'Behold, your king is coming, riding on a donkey', and the people cried out, 'Blessings on the king who comes in the name of the Lord' (Lk 19:38). Later again, the charge brought against Jesus at his trial was that of declaring himself a king, setting himself up, in opposition to Caesar. And when Pilate, who through his spies knew full well that this charge was pure fabrication, put this question to Jesus, 'Are you the king of the Jews?', he got the rather enigmatic reply, 'It is you who say it' (Mk 15:2).

What Jesus implies is that the title of king being associated with him is, verbally speaking, correct, but that neither the Jews, nor Pilate, had even begun to understand what that kingship entailed. 'Mine is not a kingdom of this world', he declared. Again and again, this same title is used by different individuals throughout the Passion narrative. By Pilate: 'This is your king; shall I crucify your king?' By the soldiers: 'Hail, king of the Jews.' By the jeering crowd: 'He is the king of the Jews; let him come down from the cross, and we will believe him.' It is quite possible that the crowd's reason for saying this was the inscription on the cross, over Jesus' head, 'This is Jesus of Nazareth, the king of the Jews.' And the last request made to Christ while in this world was that of the good thief: 'Jesus, remember me when you come into your kingdom.'

For people in a modern world which puts such great emphasis on democratic rule, however much abused from time to time, there is great difficulty in understanding the original meaning of the kingdom. To equate it with earthly power, with dominion over the nations, Christ regarded as a temptation of the devil, and we see how he fled from those who, after the miraculous feeding of the multitude, wanted to make him that kind of king, whether he liked it or not. For if we look at some of the events of Christ's life we begin to see that he transcends all our thoughts of greatness and power.

At Bethlehem, we see majesty in the midst of the poverty of the manger. In the Temple, we see wisdom coupled with uneducated youth. In his public life, we find authority linked with a breaking away from the strait-jacket of the law. On Calvary, we see victory attained through the scandalous death on a cross. The only throne that Christ the King will ever occupy is the throne of people's hearts. For his kingdom is founded not on power, but on love and service; and, especially in today's gospel, this is the lesson he would have us, also, take away with us and put into practice. And if we are faithful, we will hear, on the last day, the response of our King, 'Come, you whom my Father has blessed, take for your heritage the kingdom prepared for you since the foundation of the world' (Mt 25:34). Having hopefully heard these words, we shall have reached our final destination , the kingdom that has no end, when the kingly role of Christ on earth will finally be made clear to us.

Year B

'The spirit of the Lord has been given to me, for the Lord has anointed me. He has chosen me and sent me to bring good news to the oppressed, to bind up the brokenhearted, to proclaim liberty to captives and freedom to those in prison.'
(Is 61:1)

FIRST SUNDAY OF ADVENT
Is 63:16-17, 19, 64:1, 3-8; 1 Cor 1:3-9; Mk 13:33-37

'My heart is ready, Oh God; I will sing, sing your praise.
Awake my soul; awake lyre and harp. I will awake the
dawn.'

That is the first verse of Psalm 107, and it is full of hope and
expectancy, looking forward to a new dawn, a new era. Today is
the First Sunday of Advent and it marks the beginning of a new
year in the Church liturgy celebration of the mysteries of Christ,
our Redeemer. The term 'Advent', which means coming or arrival,
is used especially in connection with the first coming of Christ at
his birth, and also in looking forward to his second coming at
the end of time. In the readings of the last few Sundays, and in
particular today's, we find a tremendous yearning for the coming of a Redeemer, a Messiah. The first reading is part of one of
the most impressive poems in the whole Bible.

Most of the influential people in Jewish society had been carried off into exile by the Babylonians in 586 BC, and, after fifty
years, at last they were being allowed return to their own country.
But the Temple in Jerusalem still remained in ruins, no sacrifice
was being offered to God, no voice lifted in prayer to the
Almighty in the place where once that Temple had stood. It was
a period of gloom and utter desolation. The prophet, Isaiah,
called by divine providence to be the mouthpiece of the returned
exiles, confesses that they all have been sinners, blown hither
and thither at the mercy of the winds of change in their fortunes.
He raises a heartbroken cry to God, to return, to tear the heavens
open, and by his renewed presence among them to free them
from the shackles of their sinful habits, and thus end their disappointment and frustration.

Advent also is a time when we should call upon God to
renew us in heart and soul, so that we may be able to celebrate
his divine Son's coming among us in a truly religious way. But
neither should we forget that, Sunday after Sunday throughout
the entire year, the heavens in a divine sense are truly opened,
and Christ comes down to us in the sacrament of the Eucharist.
He comes to visit each of us personally, to grant our inmost
needs, to keep us, as St Paul tells us, steady and without blame
until the last day, so that we may be witnesses to his presence

before the whole world. There is a clear message for us, as well, in the gospel parable of the man who set off to travel abroad, after warning his servants, whom he had left in charge, to watch out for his return. This is a very definite reference to the Ascension of Jesus into heaven, and to his expected second coming, what the first Christians called the 'parousia'.

From earliest times then, the Church is asking its members to look forward with confidence to their eternal destiny, and not to heed the crosses they encounter. So earnestly did the first Christians take to heart this injunction that, whenever they met, they greeted one another with a saying in the Aramaic language which became a watchword among them, a kind of password which identified them as being followers of Christ. St Paul used it as part of his farewell greeting to the Corinthians at the end of his first letter to them – 'marana tha', which means 'Come Lord Jesus'. We are troubled, however, when we consider that life on earth for everyone is full of trials. We are troubled in view of temptations to come, so much so that we ask the Father repeatedly in the Lord's Prayer not to lead us into temptation, but deliver us from evil. We are especially troubled at the thought of leaving this world for a destination hidden from us, and yet we pray every day that God's kingdom may come.

We want to be rewarded with the vision of God hereafter, and yet we depart from this world against our will, whereas the saints regarded this world as a place of exile, and heaven as their true home. It was a custom of St Augustine to urge his people to sing Alleluia to God, as travellers sing along the road, in order to shorten their journey, or as workers do to sweeten their toil. So rejoice, for religion is not a sad thing. But at the same time keep pressing forward, advancing in true faith, in virtue, in right conduct. St Paul advised the Thessalonians to look forward to the Lord's coming, and with such thoughts to comfort one another. 'Be happy at all times', he advised them, 'pray constantly, and for all things give thanks to God, because this is what God expects you to do in Christ Jesus' (1 Thess 5:16-18). From such considerations we too should find consolation, as we prepare this Advent season for the coming of Christ.

SECOND SUNDAY OF ADVENT
Is 40:1-5, 9-11; 2Pet 3:8-14; Mk 1:1-8

When the risen Christ had appeared to the two disciples on the
road to Emmaus, and had listened to their tales of woe, he
responded with a mild rebuke, 'You foolish men! So slow to
believe the full message of the prophets. Was it not ordained that
the Christ should suffer and so enter into his glory' (Lk 24:25f).
Then starting with Moses, and going through all the prophets,
he explained all the passages of scripture that were about himself. In the words of St Thomas Aquinas, whereas God speaks
indirectly to us through the works of spiritual writers, he speaks
directly to our minds in Sacred Scripture. And if we go back to
the Old Testament prophets we find that the collapse of the
monarchy in Israel followed by the exile in Babylon, led to an
intense awareness of the nature of the special relationship
between the Jewish people and God.

They were to be a holy people, a people consecrated to God
in a way that distinguished them from all other nations. This
new insight was put into writing by one of the greatest – some
would go so far as to say, the greatest – of the OT prophets,
whose name we do not even know. For want of a better title, he
is referred to as Second Isaiah, or Deutero Isaiah, because his
writing is to be found in the same scroll as that of the prophet
Isaiah who lived almost two centuries earlier. An entire copy of
this scroll was found among the Dead Sea Scrolls in a cave near
Qumran, and is now housed in a special building called the
Shrine of the Book, beside the Israeli Museum in Jerusalem. His
message is contained in some of the greatest poetry ever written,
a work of great power and beauty, the opening lines of which
are given in the first reading today. It begins, 'Comfort, Oh comfort my people, says your God. Speak tenderly to Jerusalem.'
Hence the whole work as far as chapter 55 has been called 'The
Book of Consolation of Israel'. The author urges the people to
have hope, and describes a messenger or look-out on the hills of
Jerusalem joyfully gazing down at the returning exiles, in
essence a new Exodus greater even than the one led by Moses
out of Egypt. The Lord himself, he says, is watching over them,
even as a shepherd watches over his flock.

The double mention of a 'joyful messenger' who is ordered to
proclaim to the people of Judaea, 'Here is your God', is taken up

by St Mark in the gospel, who associates the title with John the Baptist, whom the people of Jerusalem and surroundings went out to see, repenting of their sinful ways. But whereas the Baptist speaks of the tree, that does not bear fruit, being cut down and thrown on the fire, and the chaff being burned in a fire that will never go out, Second Isaiah, on the contrary, is full of sympathy, and refers to God as a shepherd feeding his flock, gathering the lambs into his arms and carrying them in his bosom. According to him, the new kingdom of God is at hand, but the most prominent places in it will be occupied by the poor and lowly, not the powerful ones of this world.

The most surprising and important illustration of this by the writer is to be found in what are called the four 'Songs of the Suffering Servant of the Lord', which are associated in a special way with the liturgy of Holy Week every year, as a portrayal of the passion of Christ. Why are they surprising? Because their author was living about 500 years before Christ, a time when there was as yet no belief in resurrection, and virtue was held to be rewarded by success and happiness in this life. But he depicts the ideal Servant of the Lord – although completely innocent – as been chosen by God to undergo rejection, humiliation and overwhelming suffering, followed by a shameful death.

Yet, in fact, all this is the Servant's free offering of himself on behalf of sinners, whose iniquity and guilt he has taken on himself, and for whom he asks God's forgiveness. His reward will be the eternal redemption of the human race, and the Servant will bring light to those who live in darkness and the shadow of death. For the people of faith who looked forward to this redemption, there is in the Songs of the Suffering Servant, especially in the fourth one, as it were a detailed description of what the promised Messiah would undergo, and how victory would be achieved by his suffering. Such a profound insight into the meaning of suffering has no parallel in the entire Old Testament. And the man who conceived it is telling us today to make ready in our lives a way for the Lord. This too is what the season of Advent is asking us to do.

THE IMMACULATE CONCEPTION OF THE BVM
Gen 3:9-15, 20; Eph 1:3-6, 11-12; Lk 1:26-38

We could perhaps put forward three reasons why we celebrate the Immaculate Conception of the Virgin Mary as a feast within the Church liturgy. Firstly, and very obviously, because we want to recall, and rejoice in, the tradition going back to the age of the Apostles, that Mary from the first moment of her conception was untouched by the least stain of sin. Secondly, because this privilege of Mary was part of God's preparation for the coming on earth of his divine Son, so we also should regard it as an invitation to us to prepare for our annual celebration of that first coming of Christ at Christmas. Thirdly, because in the person of Mary, free from sin and full of grace, we see the happy beginning of the Church without spot or wrinkle, which Christ will present to his Father at the end of time (GS 37). From the very beginning, from the first moment of her conception, God had chosen this unique person, and endowed her with the perfection of every virtue, so as to make her worthy of the divine motherhood, to which he would call her at the appointed time.

But it was from the merits of her own Son, he who was God-made-man, that all these graces would flow. Hence we have the strange paradox of the mother being the first heir to the holiness of her Son, and the mother being redeemed by the shedding of the precious blood of the one, who, humanly speaking, had received that blood from her very self. This is the special day in the preparation of Advent, when we should try and meditate on, even try and penetrate, the mystery of how God came among us, how God became part of what constitutes human history.

Outwardly there was nothing to make one suspect the fullness of grace that was Mary's. Although she was uniquely privileged in giving birth to the Son of God, in nourishing him, in cherishing him, in watching him grow, Mary's greatness lies in the realm of the spiritual even to a greater extent than in her divine motherhood. For her soul, from the moment she was born, was the very special temple of the Holy Spirit, to the extent that he was the sole guide of her passions, her emotions, that in her was perfect innocence of life, that she at every moment of her life was the Immaculate one. As St Augustine stated, where there is question of sin, at no time did God wish that Mary be in the least degree tainted with that. For all other human beings, however, life has been a continuous battle with the powers of evil from the dawn of history, and will continue to be so till human life on this planet is no more.

Finding ourselves in the middle of a moral battlefield, we have to struggle constantly to do what is right, and it is only at great cost to ourselves, and with the assistance of divine grace, that we can progress towards achieving our own inner goodness. It is in the light of this consideration that we begin to appreciate the spiritual richness that was Mary's, Mary in whom was accomplished the magnificent and complete victory of good over evil, of love over hatred, of grace over sin.

The reading from the Old Testament in this Mass recalls how God addressed the serpent, the evil tempter of our First Parents, in the garden of Eden. 'I will put enmity between you and the woman, between your offspring and her offspring. He will crush your head and you will strike his heel.' God was here giving notice that the serpent would finally be crushed by a Saviour born of a woman, and not only did this victory demand that the Saviour be sinless, but that his mother should also be immaculate. In our trials and difficulties, therefore, in our struggle, as we go through life, with the powers of evil, victory will be ours if we have faith in Mary's Son, and have, moreover, enlisted the aid of her whom we know and love as the 'refuge of sinners'.

Since Jesus, with his dying breath on the cross, gave Mary as mother to John the beloved disciple, it is fitting that she, who played such an important role in the drama of our redemption, be venerated as mother to each of us also. By so doing, we her children, for whom she submitted in a supreme way to God's plans for salvation, will be repaying, however inadequately, the praise and thanks we owe to her. While we express our gratitude to Jesus, as well, for allowing us to share in a mystical way in Mary's motherhood, our daily prayer should be, 'Oh Mary, conceived without sin, pray for us who have recourse to thee'. If our prayer comes from the depths of our wretchedness, Mary will hear and answer our cry.

THIRD SUNDAY OF ADVENT
Is 61:1-2, 10-11; 1Thess 5:16-24; Jn 1:6-8, 19-28

'I baptise with water', John the Baptist told his questioners, 'but there stands among you – unknown to you – the one who is coming after me; and I am not fit to undo his sandal-strap'. The one coming after him is, of course, the Messiah or promised Redeemer, whose coming, the Jews believed, would usher in a new and glorious era for their people. In the alternative opening prayer for today's Mass, we are told that 'the world rejoices in hope of the Saviour's coming, and looks forward with longing to his return at the end of time.' But we can say that, even now, Jesus Christ, our Saviour dwells among us in his Church, invisibly, yes, but nonetheless in a very real way. Of course, we do not yet see him face to face, but still it is true that, as Sacred Scripture assures us, 'we know in part', and we see 'through a glass dimly' (1 Cor 13:12), which is much more than those, who do not know Christ, are able to do.

This is because the sacrament of baptism by which we have become children of God is a source of spiritual awareness and enlightenment within us. In baptism the divine presence is granted to us who are baptised, filling us, body and soul, and setting us apart from all who are not Christian. We have been made members of the kingdom of God, at the centre of which is Christ, and the light of which is Christ's glory. And that is not all. As Christ at the Last Supper, in his priestly prayer addressed to the Father, said, 'The glory that you have given me, I have given them' (Jn 17:22). St Paul, writing to the Christian community in Corinth, develops that promise even further, when he tells them, 'All of us ... reflecting like mirrors the glory of the Lord, grow brighter and brighter, as we are transformed by the Lord, who is Spirit, into the image that we reflect' (2 Cor 3:18). And St John in his first Letter (5:18) wrote, 'We know that those who are born of God do not sin, because the One who was begotten of God (in other words Jesus) protects them.'

The true Christian then is not only born again in baptism, but is born of God. That is not to say that by baptism we are freed of concupiscence or the inclination to sin, or that those who fall into sin remain born of God. No! Until they repent, they remain solely born to judgment. And indeed, to a greater or lesser degree, none of us is completely without sin. In the gospel account of the woman taken in adultery, Jesus challenged any one without sin among the crowd surrounding her to cast the first stone at her, and no one did. But the Spirit of Jesus helps us in our weakness, and pleads for us with sighs too deep for words (Rom 8:26).

Baptism, moreover, is a means and pledge of God's mercy, God's pardon, his acceptance of us for Christ's sake. It even gives us the grace to change our nature. 'I will baptise you with water for repentance', John the Baptist told his followers, 'but the one who follows is greater than I. He will baptise you with the Holy Spirit and with fire'. In the Old Testament age, fire was regarded as a purifying element, more refined and powerful than water. It was a symbol of God intervening in human affairs, and of his Spirit coming to purify the soul.

We should never forget our own baptism, or look back at it purely as a ceremony of our infancy, and of little account thereafter. For baptism is a pledge of supernatural grace, a real blessing and gift from God to its recipients, who in turn should place their hopes of being heard by God in the promises of his favour guaranteed to them by the reception of this sacrament. Jewish initiation rites, such as circumcision, had no trace of blessing or grace in them. Christian baptism does what the Jewish rites were never able to do; it grants divine merits directly to the soul of the person baptised.

Although Christ now sits at the right hand of God in heaven, he has, in another sense, never left this world since his birth as one of us. For his Holy Spirit is still really present, especially in the hearts of believers, and he continues to reveal himself to those who seek him with faith in his promises. After he had breathed his last on the Cross, and when the soldier pierced his side with a lance, there flowed out blood and water. But by the influence of the Holy Spirit, this blood and water continues to flow, as if the Cross were still standing among us, and the baptismal water is a visible sign that the blood of Christ is applied to the souls of all who are baptised, even as we are.

FOURTH SUNDAY OF ADVENT
2 Sam 7:1-5, 8-12, 14, 16; Rom 16:25-27; Lk 1:26-38

Today we have in the Reading from the Book of Samuel one of the most important prophecies of all time, for the chosen people of the Old Testament – the prophecy of Nathan. It was stated in the form of a contrast. David is not to build a house (a temple) for God, but on the contrary God is to build a house (a dynasty) for David, and this house will never fall. 'Your house will always stand, and your throne will be established for ever', was the definite promise. From that time on, the Jewish people firmly believed that the royal line of David had a lasting place in God's plans for Israel, that the monarchy would never collapse.

But collapse it did, before the forces of Babylon, and Israel's hopes were shattered. How could God go back on his promise to David? This test of their faith in God led to deep reflection on whether other interpretations of Nathan's prophecy were possible. Thus there were some individuals who saw God's promise being fulfilled by means of the people themselves carrying on the tradition of Temple worship and sacrifice, without any ruling king. They saw themselves as being a priestly people, a kingly people, God's holy people.

Others maintained that the promise would be fulfilled by a Messiah, an anointed one, a descendent of King David, who would restore Israel to a position of prestige once more among the nations. In the light of Christ's coming, we are inclined to look back and see how prophetic were these our ancestors in faith, and yet in ways how mistaken also they were. For most of them God's plan of redemption for the whole world was never grasped. Before we begin to feel superior in any way, we should ask ourselves what the significance of Advent is for us, what are our expectations, what are we looking forward to. We might say that we are waiting for the coming of Christ, but surely Christ is here already. Yes, indeed, but for us, as well, he is here in a hidden way. We too are being asked, as were the Jews, to make an act of deeper faith, to make God present in a more compelling way in our everyday lives.

'To have faith is to be sure of the things we hope for, to be convinced of the things we cannot see' (Heb 11:1). And nowhere is such faith more in evidence than in the Annunciation as recorded in the gospel reading today.

A simple young woman, the virgin Mary, is told by the Archangel, Gabriel, that she is going to be mother of the promised Messiah, the Son of God and descendent of King David, the one foretold by the prophets of Israel, over the centuries. To add to the mystery of this announcement is the definite promise that while becoming a mother she will remain a virgin, and that compliance with God's plan is to be left to her own free choice. 'Rejoice so highly favoured', the angel said, implying that from her very conception Mary had been the recipient of God's grace and favour, and had been chosen for a long time past for the part she was being called upon to play in the redemption of the human race. She had received the perfection of holiness, and was transformed by the grace of God, purified and sanctified. Her name in Hebrew, Miryam, means 'exalted one'. 'How will this be done', she asked the angel, 'since I am a virgin?'

This does not indicate a resolution by Mary to remain a virgin – after all she was betrothed to Joseph – but rather her great longing for virginity, which was evoked in her by God, preparing her to become the mother of the Messiah in a virginal manner. In a famous 6/7th century Greek hymn (*Akathiste*) the composer gives further meanings to the greeting of Gabriel, of which these are a few. 'Rejoice, you by whom joy will shine forth! Rejoice, because you are the throne of the great king! Rejoice, womb of the divine incarnation! Rejoice, you by whom creation is renewed! Rejoice, you by whom and in whom the Creator is adored! Rejoice, unspoused Spouse! Virgin!'

St Paul said of the Corinthians, 'You are a letter from Christ, written not with ink, but with the Spirit of the living God, not on tablets of stone, but on tablets of human hearts' (2 Cor 3:3). Mary also, we can say, is a letter from the Holy Spirit, a letter that has come down to us, not in written documents, so much as in the veneration of millions of Christians, ever since those tragic moments when the Apostle St John, at the foot of the Cross on Calvary, accepted her as his Mother and ours, and took her into his own house.

THE NATIVITY OF OUR LORD
Vigil: Is 62:1-5; Acts 13:16-17, 22-25; Mt 1:1-25
Midnight: Is 9:1-6; Tit 2:11-14; Lk 2:1-14
Dawn: Is 62:11-12; Tit 3:11-14; Lk 2:15-20
Day: Is 52:7-10; Heb 1:1-6 Jn 1:1-18

For the people of the Old Testament, light and darkness were more than natural phenomena. They tended to associate them very often with virtue and wickedness in the community, and also with the day of the Lord's coming. Indeed, at Qumran on the Dead Sea shoreline, during the life-time of Jesus, light and darkness were seen as two opposing kingdoms, and the sun's victory over darkness was held to be a symbol of the triumph of faith over the blind pursuit of evil. 'In the beginning God created the heavens and the earth … and darkness was upon the face of the deep. And God said, "Let there be light, and there was light".' Thus begins the Bible account of the first creation, and when it was ended, 'God saw all that he had made, and indeed it was very good.'

But this original goodness and justice was to be shattered, because of our first parents' abuse of the freedom of will granted them by God, so that once again, as the prophet Isaiah describes it (Is 60:2), 'darkness came to cover the earth, and thick darkness the peoples'. To dispel this darkness, a new creation was needed, and the ideal of goodness and perfection became a living reality, when the light of Christ came into the world. 'The people that walked in darkness have seen a great light; for those who lived in a land of deep shadow a light has shone' (Is 9:2). For God, who had created man in his own image and likeness, had now identified with the human race, and by assuming the body of a child in the image of man, had lowered himself and become one of us.

It has become a tradition to associate snow with Christmas, and when it does come, shrouding everything with its white mantle, a stillness settles over the countryside, especially at night-time. That combination of darkness and stillness was the setting for the first Christmas. As the Book of Wisdom states, 'When all things were in quiet silence, and the night was in the middle of her course, your almighty Word leaped down from heaven, from your royal throne' (Wis 18:14f). It was as if God was saying a second time, 'Let there be light' – let the gloom and

darkness, which to such an extent exemplify the fallen and corrupt nature of the human race, be lifted, ushering in a new age of
glory to God and peace on earth among all its people. And so an
angel of the Lord appeared to some humble shepherds tending
their flocks in the enveloping darkness, and the brightness of the
Lord shone round them. 'Do not be afraid', the angel reassured
them. 'Listen, I bring you news of great joy, a joy to be shared by
the whole people. Today a Saviour has been born to you; he is
Christ the Lord.'

These words are addressed to us also. We too must listen, listen
in the stillness of our hearts, and, like the shepherds, we must
hasten, and with eagerness draw near to Christ. 'And the
shepherds came with haste, and found Mary and Joseph, and
the infant lying in the manger.' They 'found' implies effort on
their part; they had to search. But their search was not in vain.
'And seeing, they understood the word that had been spoken to
them concerning this child.'

Likewise, we must search for Christ, hasten to him with
eagerness, and in the quiet times of prayer, when we are alone
with God, understanding of our need for Christ will come to us.
St Augustine says that prior to conceiving Christ in her womb,
Mary first conceived him in her heart, in a spiritual manner, by
her faith. The Church in faith is referred to as the Spouse of
Christ, in other words, its members are called to be brothers and
sisters of Christ. It is more difficult, Augustine goes on, to
understand that the Church is the Mother of Christ. But this is
also true, and it was Christ himself who first gave it that title,
when he declared, 'Anyone who does the will of my Father in
heaven, is my brother and sister and mother' (Mt 12:50). The
Church is the Mother of Christ in that, by obedience to the will
of the Father, she brings Christ into being in the world. But we,
its members, are the Church, and thus we can give birth to
Christ, become mothers of Christ, in a purely spiritual way, by
doing God's holy will.

And Augustine is quite adamant, 'This is something that is
not out of your reach; it is not beyond you, it is not incompatible
with you. You have become children; be mothers as well'
(Sermon 72A). In the final sentences of the Bible, Christ makes
this promise, 'I shall indeed be with you soon.' May our response
be 'Amen, come Lord Jesus' (Rev 22:20).

152 A TIME TO SPEAK

THE FEAST OF THE HOLY FAMILY
Gen 15:1-6, 21:1-3; Heb 11:8, 11-12, 17-19; Lk 2:22-40

The most renowned preacher of the 19th century, a Frenchman named Jean-Baptiste Lacordaire, was once asked by an admirer how long it took him to prepare one of his sermons, and his reply was, 'All my life'. What he was really implying is that the human spirit is not transformed overnight by the grace of faith, but in most cases has to undergo a long and gradual process, before it can be an influence for good in others. Furthermore, it is becoming more and more certain that the first years of life are the most important ones in bringing this about.

Deep down within us, most of us can say that our attitudes, our inhibitions, our cultural and religious convictions, by and large, reflect the kind of family background from which we came. For family is a way of growing up together, a way of mutual discovery, exploration, remembrance, as can be observed when family members come together late in life, and recall their child-hood days. Our first experience of serving one another, playing, working together, of affection, tenderness, and indeed of misunderstanding and hurt also, happens within the family. Family is a gift, the total giving of themselves by the parents to one another, and to the offspring begotten of their union. That break-ups occur in the family circle is only to be expected in a society which regards with a certain admiration, and even envy, those who have the ability to gain the greatest possible rewards for themselves from society, while giving as little as possible in return.

Is it any wonder that of 50,000 parents, who responded to a query by a marriage counsellor in an American newspaper some years ago, a depressing 70% said that given the choice again, they would not have children; it wasn't worth it (*Time*, 5/3/79). Nowadays, not only is there a reluctance to have children, the very idea of entering a marriage contract is compounded with fear. This may be for financial considerations, or apprehension that, were the marriage to fail, wealth and property would have to be shared equally in a divorce settlement. Instead of pledging life-long commitment to each other, we find couples – especially in America – placing more trust in premarital pacts drawn up by solicitors. What can be said is that such attitudes arise primarily from a loss of faith in God, which in turn leads to a break-down of trust in others. Marriages collapse when people lose the vision of the family as a sacrament, as the visible sign of God's grace at work in the hearts of those involved, uniting them by shared life, joy, sorrow, celebration, by common striving for goodness, virtue, holiness. Indeed, the best preparation for loving the world at large, is to cultivate that intimate friendship and affection which should characterise our relations with those immediately about us.

Today we might ask ourselves, why did Christ spend all but three years of his life in such a backwater as Nazareth, a place not mentioned even once in the Old Testament. Residents, when they went south to Jerusalem, were often ashamed to admit they were Nazarenes. 'Can anything good come out of Nazareth?' was a proverbial saying of the Jews. Yet Nazareth was the scene of Christ's hidden life – the ordinary every-day life within a family specially chosen, made up of work and prayer, marked only by hidden virtues, a life to which only God, and Christ's closest relatives and neighbours, were witnesses. Here, in varying degrees, are mirrored the lives of most of us. What sets Jesus apart from the rest of us was his ability to remain in close union with God, to anchor his whole life firmly in the Father.

'You must believe me', he told his disciples, 'that I am in the Father, and the Father is in me' (Jn 14:10). In the concealment of Nazareth, the Spirit taught Jesus to see himself as set apart from other people, to understand that he was Son in a way no one else was, or ever would be again. For Jesus was a member of another family as well, the family of God, that was Father, Son, and Spirit, and yet uniquely one. Remember that, ultimately, we too are called to be sharers in that family, sharers by adoption, yes; but able to address God as our Father also, in and through Jesus Christ, our Lord. May we so use the supernatural grace granted to us in this world that, on leaving it, we will hear addressed to us too the words of God at the baptism of Jesus, 'This is my beloved child, with whom I am well pleased'.

MARY, MOTHER OF GOD
Num 6:22-27; Gal 4:4-7; Lk 2:16-21

The most common objections which are held by other Christian
Churches, not in communion with Rome, against the teaching of
the Roman Catholic Church, centre around the degree of
importance attached by Catholics to two figures, namely the
Pope and the blessed Virgin. I recall once hearing on BBC Radio
a clergyman, who was also a teacher of theology in an Anglican
seminary, describing the Catholic attitude to Mary as being
Mariolatry, something which is tantamount to a charge of idolatry. Theologians with such an outlook usually maintain that all
Christian faith should be rooted firmly in sacred scripture, and
also, some others would add, it should reflect the traditions of
the early Church. Yet these very maxims were combined together
as a necessity for faith, just a hundred years after the NT was
completed, by a man who was the first truly great creative
scripture scholar (Origen), a man who spent most of his life writing commentaries on the gospels, and sowing the seeds of the
traditions of that period. 'I do not hesitate to affirm that among
all the scriptures the gospels have pride of place', he wrote, 'and
among the gospels, pride of place belongs to that according to
John. Yet no one can grasp its meaning unless they have leaned
upon the breast of Jesus, and also, from Jesus, accepted Mary, to
be their own Mother.'

In what sense, and for what reason, you might ask, should
we regard Mary as our Mother? In the last few minutes of his
life, Jesus, seeing his mother and the disciple he loved – in other
words John – at the foot of the cross, said to his mother,
'Woman, this is your son.' Then to the disciple he said, 'This is
your mother.' By using the word 'woman' in preference to
mother, Jesus showed that he was addressing Mary solely on the
level of pure faith, and not on account of the blood-relationship
that united the two of them. Her attention, moreover, was not
directed simply to the beloved disciple, but to all the future
generations of disciples represented at Calvary by that single
disciple. Out of love, Mary cooperated with her Son, so that – as
St Augustine puts it – there might be born in the Church the
faithful who are members of Christ their Head. Mary, being
clearly designated the Mother of all the disciples of Christ, thus
becomes Mother of the whole Church. This, indeed, was the title

bestowed on her by Pope Paul VI personally towards the end of the Vatican Council.

From this it follows that every time we acknowledge Mary as our Mother we are also clearly asserting our union with Christ. If Mary is our Mother, then her one desire will be that not one of us may ever be separated from Jesus or from her, but that we may all be one Body, one Spirit, in Christ. This union is symbolised in the very last reference to Mary at the foot of the cross, which is to be found only in John's gospel, 'From that hour the disciple took her to his own.' This, of course, could mean that following on the events of Calvary John's house would become Mary's dwelling place also. But it is more likely that those words should be taken in a spiritual sense, namely that John made a place for Mary in his interior life, his life of faith. Here, in a symbolic way, Mary is being declared the model or type of the Church, and John represents all the true disciples of Christ. The more the Church resembles Mary, the more she becomes the Bride of Christ; the more she becomes the Bride, the more she resembles the Bridegroom, who is Christ; and the more the Church resembles the Bridegroom, the more she resembles God himself.

In acceding to the request of Jesus to become the son of Mary, John became a true believer in regard to the relationship between Mary and the Church. His first and most important task in acquiring the grace of God for what lay ahead was to become a son of Mary. Only then would he go out and preach the gospel and thus take on the role of apostle. The task of Mary was also made clear. She is to preserve the identity between all Christians and Christ, that they may all be one Body, one Spirit, in Christ. She is charged with continuing the prayer of Christ at the Last Supper, with watching over Christ's disciples, with helping and protecting them from the powers of the evil one. And, correspondingly, we are charged with cherishing Mary as the parting gift to all of us also by our dying Redeemer. 'From that hour, the disciple took her to his own', and likewise should we. We must then see, and venerate Mary as our Mother, as the one who will watch over us as we make our pilgrim way to be with the Father, for ever.

SECOND SUNDAY AFTER CHRISTMAS
Sir 24:1-2, 8-12; Eph 1:3-6, 15-18; Jn 1:1-18

'How beautiful on the mountains are the feet of one who brings good news.' This poetic line from the first reading of the Christmas Day Mass contains an example of what is called the 'transferred epithet' much employed in poetry, something we were taught in our school-days. It really is not the feet which are beautiful, but rather the good news. And it sums up beautifully the significance of Christmas for all God's people. For this holy season is a recalling of the good news of how God revealed himself in the person of his Son made man, the last and greatest divine revelation to the human race. 'Speak tenderly to the heart of Jerusalem', God tells his prophet Isaiah (Is 40). Here and now Jerusalem stands for the Church, and we in this post-Christmas period should begin to examine our hearts to see what response has been evoked in them by the tender image of the omnipotent God under the form of a helpless infant. We should ask ourselves what kind of Christians we are? What kind of religion do we profess?

We must be clear about one thing, that in order to be genuine, our religion must be personal; it must be sustained by personal contact with God within our hearts, our conscience. Unless our religious upbringing has fostered this personal element – however vague, however implicit – within us, then deep down we are already unbelievers, even if we keep up a somewhat routine contact with the Church, a kind of social mechanical performance without the least inner significance. The reaction of Christ to such is plain for us, in his remarks about the very people who always seemed to do the right thing – the Pharisees. 'These people honour me only with lip-service, while their hearts are far from me' (Mt 15:9).

One of the ways by which we make personal contact with God is through God's written word, the Sacred Scriptures, and especially in those extracts from them used in the liturgy of the Mass. In them God himself is truly present, speaking to his people. Through them Christ is still proclaiming his gospel. The Vatican II document on Divine Revelation emphasises this when it says, 'In the sacred books of the Bible, the Father who is in heaven meets his children with great love and speaks with them; and the force and power in the word of God is so great that it remains the support and energy of the Church, the strength of faith for her children, the food of the soul, the pure and lasting source of spiritual life.' St Paul, furthermore, writing to his disciple Timothy, says, 'Remember ... how ever since you were a child, you have known the holy Scriptures. From these you can learn the wisdom that leads to salvation, through faith in Christ Jesus.' And when he goes on to say, 'All Scripture is inspired by God, and can profitably be used for teaching, for refuting error, for guiding people's lives, and teaching them to be holy' (2 Tim 3:15f), we must remember that he is referring to the writings of the Old Testament. Most of the New Testament had not even been written at the time.

Convinced of the authenticity of their faith, the people of the Old Testament used to scorn and mock the idols which were worshipped by the pagan nations all round them. 'They have eyes and they cannot see, they have ears and they cannot hear', was how they referred to their images of stone and wood (Ps 115:5f). Although such images are long gone, we can see that for those who turn their back on the one true God, they have been replaced to this day by more subtle objects of worship. The false gods of today's world are very real but far more sophisticated.

As for ourselves, when the Scriptures are read for us, or by us, we must endeavour to hear, to see what they convey to us, not simply as so many pieces of information about people and events remote from us, but rather as the means used by God's Holy Spirit, to awaken something within us, which may well be a call to us to live a new and deeper life in Christ. We are asked to respond on a personal level to God's word which either looks forward in the Old Testament to the coming of Christ, or in retrospect in the New Testament explores the significance for us of his life. 'I shall not call you servants anymore, because a servant does not know his master's business', Christ said in his farewell discourse to his disciples (Jn 15:14f), 'I call you friends, because I have made known to you everything I have learnt from my Father.' It is up to us to reflect on the message of Jesus Christ, and hopefully be his friends also.

THE EPIPHANY OF THE LORD
Is 60:1-6; Eph 3:2-3, 5-6; Mt 2:1-12

'Where is he who has been born king of he Jews? We have seen
his star in the East and have come to worship him.' In the gospel
of the Mass a few days ago, we read about the two disciples of
John the Baptist, who saw Jesus passing by and followed him.
And then Jesus turned round and put this disconcerting and
rather abrupt question, 'What are you looking for?' They, however, could not put into words the mysterious attraction for
them which surrounded the person of Christ, what was drawing
them to him. And so they replied, rather sheepishly, 'Master,
where do you live?' 'Come and see', Christ said, and for all the
rest of that day they stayed with him. They could not tear themselves away from the enjoyment of his presence. What they were
seeking, although unable to put it into words, was God. To state
it very precisely, the greatest difference between Christianity
and other religions lies not so much in our seeking God, but
rather the other way round, in God seeking us.

The very question of the two disciples, 'Where do you live?',
was prompted by the Holy Spirit, who always takes the initiative.
The reformer, and founder of the monastery of Clairvaux, St
Bernard, used to say to his monks, 'However early you may
wake up and gather for prayer in your chapel, on a cold mid-
winter's morning, or even in the dead of night, you will always
find God awake before you, waiting for you. Rather was it he, in
the first place, who awakened you to seek his divine presence.'
But, you may well ask, how can we possibly seek God, whom
we cannot see, whom we cannot even know?

St John, in his First Letter, supplies the answer, when he
speaks of 'the one who has existed from the beginning ... we
have heard, we have seen with our own eyes ... we have
watched and touched with our hands ... the one who was with
the Father, and has been made visible to us.' Here John, with all
the emphasis he can muster, is saying to us, 'We' – namely the
other disciples and himself – 'have seen the Son of God. In
Christ, God has revealed himself to us'.

This revelation, moreover, is meant for the whole of
mankind. The touching story of the Magi, which we recall on
this feast, is a symbolic expression of all these truths. There is an
obvious link between it and the prophecy of Balaam, in the Book

of Numbers (24:17), which gave rise to the star of David tradition. Balaam, like the Magi, was from the East, from the banks of the Euphrates river, we are told. He too was a wise man, a soothsayer. Although called upon to curse Moses and his followers, he found himself, against his will, repeatedly blessing them, under the influence of God's irresistible Spirit.

He foresaw the coming of a powerful leader among the Israelites. 'I see him, but not in the present; I behold him, but not close at hand. A star shall come forth out of Jacob, and a sceptre arise out of Israel.' This star, in the immediate sense, was a reference to King David. But in the ancient East, a star signified a divine presence as well. And so, it is only in the person of Christ that we find the prophecy of Balaam being completely fulfilled. For Christ was both King and God. 'Where is he that is born King of the Jews?', the Magi asked.

Christ would be a king too, a leader of his people, and so the Magi offered him gold, the symbol of royalty. The star which had guided the Magi to Bethlehem, and stood over where the child was, was for them a sign of his divinity, and so they offered him frankincense. Finally they had been inspired to bring him myrrh, which was used to dress wounds and embalm the dead. This gift signified that Jesus was man, a man capable of suffering, who would one day die.

Unlike Balaam, the Magi came willingly with exceeding great joy. When the shepherds came to Bethlehem, they also told what had been revealed to them, and returned glorifying and praising God. When the Magi found the child of their search they fell down and adored him. In that first Epiphany the child Jesus was the object of worship, a kingly figure holding court and receiving homage, although his only throne was his immaculate Mother's arms and his kingly court a cave. But scripture, in the psalms, calls us also to worship, to adore the Lord in his holy court, and bow down before his holy temple, the temple which was the human form that shrouded his divinity.

THE BAPTISM OF THE LORD
Is 55:1-11; 1 Jn 5:1-9; Mk 1:7-11

We know from reading the gospels that wherever Jesus went during his public life he generally attracted huge crowds; and the most common reaction of people to his preaching and the way he responded to all who sought favours from him, was one of astonishment. It seems as if Matthew, Mark and Luke ransacked the Greek dictionary, in search of words to express this amazement at Jesus' words and actions. Thirty-three times in all they make use of four particular Greek words which translated mean, 'to marvel, to be amazed, to be astounded, to be astonished'. This sense of wonderment in the presence of Jesus is connected, to a certain degree, with two things: firstly, his miracles, and secondly, his teaching. Perhaps, the most revealing wonder of all is in the description, by Mark (10:32), of the last journey of Jesus to Jerusalem. 'They were on the road going up to Jerusalem, and Jesus was leading the way; and the disciples were filled with awe, while those who followed were afraid.'

Here it seems the astonishment was not so much about what Jesus said or did, but about the person of Jesus himself. When meeting him face to face, people felt that they were in the presence of somebody who was closer to God, than anyone they had ever seen or encountered before, one who appeared to have the wisdom of God on his lips, and the power of God in his hands. It is hardly any wonder that the reaction of those closest to him was such that they were prepared – even as Peter himself said – to die for him. The feeling of amazement on the part of the disciples is further illustrated in St Matthew's account of Jesus walking on the waters of the lake (14:33). Thinking they were seeing a ghost, they were terrified. But he reassured them, 'Courage! It is I! Do not be afraid.' Peter even had the temerity to say, 'Lord, if it is you, bid me come to you across the water.' But the words 'if it is you' betray a lack of trust, and this was further evidenced when Peter began to sink, and had to be rescued by Jesus.

The storm having been calmed, and both in the boat once more, the men in it, we are told, 'bowed down before Jesus, and said, 'Truly you are the Son of God.' Indeed, from the very beginning, the concept of Jesus as 'Son of God' was central to the faith of his followers. In all four gospels the public life of Christ begins with his baptism by John the Baptist, during which he is proclaimed the Son of God. The Spirit descended on him, like a dove, and a voice from heaven said, 'You are my Son, the beloved; in you I am well pleased.'

The importance attached, by the Apostles, to being present as a witness to this happening, can be seen when they came together after the Ascension to appoint a successor to Judas. The requirement was that the person selected should have been with them right from the time of the baptism of John, until Jesus was taken up from them. As we read through the gospels, we are presented with a picture of Jesus as one whose life was begun, spent and ended in the awareness that he was Son of God in a particularly unique way. That conviction sustained him throughout his whole life and mission.

His baptism marks his decision to accept that mission from God. He offers himself to God, that God may use him as he wishes. This is the beginning of the gospel account of that close personal relationship between Jesus and God, in which Jesus is uniquely 'Son', and God for him is uniquely 'my Father'. After his resurrection Jesus had said to Mary Magdalen, 'Go and find the brothers, and tell them: "I am ascending to my Father and your Father, to my God and your God"' (Jn 20:17).

By not using 'our', he distinguishes between his own relationship with God and that of others. All who believe in the divine nature of Jesus will come to eternal life. 'If anyone acknowledges that Jesus is the Son of God', St John in his first Letter says (4:15), 'God lives in him, and he in God'. John also (Jn 3:17) declares, 'God sent his Son into the world, so that through him the world might be saved. No one who believes in him will be condemned, but whoever refuses to believe is condemned already, because he has refused to believe in the name of God's only Son.' God, moreover, has sent the Spirit of his Son into our hearts, enabling us to cry, 'Abba, Father'. Such intimacy with God is open to everyone, an intimacy which will only reach its complete fulfilment when we come face to face with God in the world hereafter.

SECOND SUNDAY OF THE YEAR
1 Sam 3:3-10; 1 Cor 6:13-20; Jn 1:35-42

Is it not a fact that many of us Christians are so busy talking to
God, telling him in exact and minute detail all the things he
should be doing for us, that we rarely or never listen to what
God is saying to us. Today's first reading might well be called
'The boy who listened to God.' Whether it is pandering to our
failings, or the intention of those who selected these readings to
keep them as short as possible, unfortunately, eight verses have
been left out before the ending, precisely the very eight which
tell us what God revealed to the boy Samuel. What have we to
learn from events and sayings so far remote from our present
day world, you might ask? Well, 'all scripture is inspired by
God, and can profitably be used ... for guiding people's lives and
teaching them to be holy' (2 Tim 3:16). And the only scripture St
Paul had in mind when he wrote those words was the Old
Testament. Moreover, the period in question had much in
common with ours, in that religious practice and divine worship
had declined.

This happened because the Israelites, having reached the
promised Land and gained a military victory over the native
Canaanites, were in danger of losing out in the ideological struggle
that followed between the two groups. The Israelites were
tempted to copy the ways of the more highly cultured and
sophisticated Canaanites, even though the pagan gods of these
were sexual in nature and were worshipped in rites that were
sexual also. A strong comparison could be drawn here with the
people of our own country and their reaction to outside influences and example in the past century, some of which of course
are good and desirable, but others evil and retrograde, such as
abortion, drug-culture and crime.

Samuel, who beyond doubt was the greatest spiritual leader
of Israel since the days of Moses, was to be the last of the leaders,
or Judges, as they were called, who were elected to hold the different tribes together. Under his spiritual guidance Israel was to
become a monarchy with Saul its first king, while his successor
King David, himself the ancestor of Jesus, was the one to consol-
idate that monarchy. What did God reveal to Samuel? We
should remember that at the time, Eli then an old man, was both
Judge and high priest. The Lord God disclosed to Samuel the

wickedness of the House of Eli, how in particular his two sons
had been cursing God – the Bible very bluntly says they were
scoundrels, caring nothing for God – and how Eli, although himself a good man, had failed to correct them. And the Lord stated
most solemnly that no sacrifice or offering would ever wipe out
the guilt of the House of Eli. At the beginning of this sorry saga,
the sacred author tells us that the eyes of Eli were beginning to
grow dim, he could no longer see. But this physical blindness
was an external sign of a much more serious interior blindness
to the misdeeds of his own family, supposedly placing all their
confidence on the mere externals of religion, like the offering of
sacrifice, while within they were concerned not with the things
of God, but with their own ambitions. All this profound spiritual
assessment was made by a mere boy, because he listened to
what God was revealing to him in the depths of his soul, and
saw that the corruption of its leaders was the reason why Israel's
fortunes were declining.

There are tremendous lessons to be learned from this story
from scripture, but they will never be clear to us unless we are
open to God's message. This has become more and more difficult, with so many agencies trying to monopolise our attention.
Thirty years ago a Professor of Literature at Cambridge (C. S.
Lewis – *Christian Reflections*) described the trend like this, and it
has worsened since. 'How then, it may be asked, can we either
reach or avoid God? The avoiding, in many times and places,
has proved so difficult that a very large part of the human race
failed to achieve it. But in our own times and place it is extremely
easy.'

'Avoid silence, avoid solitude, avoid any train of thought
that leads off the beaten track. Concentrate on money, sex, status,
health and above all on your own grievances. Keep the radio
(and TV) on. Live in a crowd. Use plenty of sedatives. If you
must read books, select them very carefully. But you'd be safer
to stick to the papers. You'll find the advertisements helpful,
especially those with a sexy or a snobbish appeal.' Any combination or all of these will drown out the voice of God within. How
true it is that one person who prays and listens attentively to
God's Holy Spirit, is worth more than a thousand ordinary souls
who never listen.

THIRD SUNDAY OF THE YEAR
Jonah 3:1-5, 10; 1 Cor 7:29-31; Mk 1:14-20

On the first Easter Sunday morning, when the women were coming away from the tomb, where the body of Jesus had been laid, they met the risen Jesus coming towards them. 'Do not be afraid', he said, according to St Matthew (28:10), 'go and tell my brothers that they must leave for Galilee; they will see me there'. In St Mark's gospel, a young man in a white robe, within the tomb, asks the women to tell Peter and the other disciples, 'He is going before you to Galilee; it is there you will see him' (16:7). Even before his death, Jesus had told the Apostles after the Last Supper, 'After I am raised up, I shall go before you to Galilee' (Mk 14:28). This begins to make us wonder, why the insistence by Jesus on Galilee as a meeting place after his resurrection? 'It is there you will see me' supplies a clue, for 'to see Jesus' can also mean to 'have faith in Jesus'. In Galilee therefore there would be a rekindling, a resurgence of their belief in Jesus and his mission after the trauma of the previous days that shattered their wishful dreams of a conquering Saviour, establishing a kingdom, where they themselves would have the places of honour.

Today's gospel reading tells how the public life of Christ began when he went into Galilee, and there proclaimed the Good News from God. Galilee was the birthplace of his mission. It was here, by his miracles of healing, of casting out devils, that the powers of evil which held so many people captive were broken. Here also, all the apostles were called and commissioned to help in, and carry on, his role of Saviour of the world. Galilee was the place most suited to start such a mission.

It was the most fertile region of Palestine, and the most densely populated. The great roads from north to south, east to west, passed through it. Many battles were fought in it, and strangers settled in it, leading to a regular injection of fresh blood. But above all its contact with outside influences made the people open to new ideas. It was the most fertile ground for the seeds of a new gospel. In stark contrast to Galilee was Judaea, the most southern part of Palestine, isolated and secluded from foreign influence, its religious attitudes dictated by hardline extremists hostile to any change. The mind-set of its people, especially in Jerusalem, was an open book to Jesus, and he knew the fate that awaited him there. So fixed and inward-looking were they in their approach to religion, that Jesus shed bitter tears as he looked down on the temple area from the Mount of Olives. 'It cannot be', he said, 'that a prophet should perish away from Jerusalem. Jerusalem, Jerusalem, you that kill the prophets and stone those that are sent to you. How often would I have gathered your children, as a hen gathers her brood under her wings, and you would not' (Lk 13:33f). As much as three or four hundred years before Christ, this narrow racialism of the Jews was strongly condemned in the Book of Jonah, from which the first reading is taken today.

Far from being a droll account of Jonah's adventure with the great fish – whale is never mentioned – we have here a highly sophisticated satire on the narrow-minded Jewish thinking on God. God, it is saying, is not only the God of the Jews, but God of the gentiles also, even God of the people of Nineveh, their most hated enemies. The worst fear of Jonah, who here characterises the attitudes of the Jews, is that the Ninevites may repent, and God being a merciful God, may pardon them. And so Jonah, who wanted them punished, attempted to flee rather than call the people of Nineveh to repentance; but it was God's will which prevailed. The message for us is that no limits can be set to divine mercy, forgiveness and love, that these reach out to people of all kinds of faith in God, or none.

The call of Christ to repent is addressed to us too, here and now. It demands a complete change in our attitude towards God and our neighbour, something we have to do again and again and again as we go through life. Our response, if sincere, has got to be an on-going endeavour, not something which is over and done with, in a day. But since we are not yet perfect, our response can be somewhat erratic, a thing of ups and downs as we try to cope with the obstacles in our way. As you trust in Christ to save you, trust him too for each day's problems, St Paul said (Col 2:6f). Live in vital union with him. Let your roots grow down into him, and draw up nourishment from him. Let your lives overflow with joy and thanksgiving for all he has done for you.

FOURTH SUNDAY OF THE YEAR
Deut 18:15-20; 1 Cor 7:32-35; Mk 1:21-28

'Those who deal with the world should not become engrossed with it', the New Testament tells us, 'because the world, as we know it, is passing away' (1 Cor 7:31). However, Jesus had said that no one, not even himself, knew the day or the hour when he would come again to judge the world. He told his listeners, nevertheless, to be on the alert. 'As it was in Noah's day, so will it be when the Son of Man comes. For in those days before the Flood, people were eating, drinking, taking wines, taking husbands, right up to the day Noah went into the Ark, and they suspected nothing till the Flood came and swept them all away. It will be like this when the Son of Man comes' (Mt 24: 37+).

Today 2,000 years later, what Jesus said is still true. No one knows the day or the hour, but still hardly anyone believes that the world, as we know it, will end in our lifetime. And yet for the first time, the fragile nature of our earthly environment and existence is beginning to cause alarm to scientists and cosmologists. For nowadays, we actually have the power to end the earth's capability to preserve life by causing excessive radiation and pollution, by upsetting the balance of food-chains worldwide, destroying the atmospheric layers that act as a shield around our planet. Technology in attempting to exploit our resources is coming nearer to the point where these can become exhausted, with nothing remaining bar the evil effects of the methods employed.

However, even though heaven and earth pass away, Jesus has given a firm assurance that his message will never pass away (Mt 24:35). We might find confirmation of this from two tourist centres in present day Rome. The better known perhaps, the Colosseum, built some ten years after the death of the Apostle St Peter, was the focus of attention in its time, with its shows, its blood sports, its spectaculars. But when one goes into it today, it is just a gaunt shell, a dead place, as dead as the Empire at the centre of which it once attracted vast multitudes. And just 300 yards beyond the Colosseum there is the Basilica of San Clemente, called after Pope St Clement, archaeologically one of the most interesting in modern Rome, rather drab on the outside, and so old that the street on the outside is now several feet higher than the floor of the church. For more than 300 years

it has been in the hands of the Irish Dominicans, and in excavations under the church, carried out by Fr Joseph Mulooly in a
search, in 1867, for the relics of St Clement, they found the original
4th century church underneath the present 12th century one.
Digging still deeper they discovered the remains of a first century
house, 60 feet below the present street level. This house, or
palazzo to use the Roman word, was there before the Colosseum
was built. It belonged to the Clemente family, and was a meeting
place for Christians. If you go down into one of its rooms you
can say with almost certainty, that you are in a place where St
Peter offered up the sacrifice of the Mass. Like the Mass rocks in
Ireland, this was a place where persecuted Christians came
together to renew their commitment and courage, to draw
comfort from receiving the Eucharist.

Kingdoms have come and gone since then, the Roman
Empire and Colosseum are things of the past, but at San
Clemente, both in the church above and palazzo below, people
still come together to remember the Lord, and by remembering,
to make him present in their midst once again. Here there is a
living and enduring tradition. Those early Roman Christians,
our own forebears around their Mass rocks in Penal days, these
were all prepared to risk their lives for their faith. We at least
must also find a place in our lives for the worship of God, for
prayer to God, for listening to the voice of God addressing us
interiorly through his Holy Spirit.

We must never allow our faith become mere routine, or
indeed simply a superstitious fear of God. Such a mentality is
illustrated in the reaction of the unclean spirit in the gospel reading. 'What do you want with us, Jesus of Nazareth? Have you
come to destroy us?' Christ however came, not to destroy, but to
save. He is saying to us, 'Learn of me, for I am gentle and humble of heart' (Mt 11:29). In other words, he is not a destroyer. We
are part of a long tradition that says Christ is the same today,
yesterday and forever. And he abides with us, especially in his
word and in the Eucharist which in the tradition of those early
Christians at San Clemente we are celebrating now.

FIFTH SUNDAY OF THE YEAR
Job 7:1-4, 6-7; 1 Cor 9:16-19, 22-23; Mk 1:29-39

To be constantly on the move, being engrossed in earthly affairs, has always been regarded as one of the great obstacles to contemplation of God, recognising him at work in our lives, and entering into close communion with him. Hence the reason why people became hermits and lived in solitude. But, surprisingly, the last chapter of the Letter to the Hebrews tells us that to know God means to be constantly on the move, but on a different plane. 'Here we have no lasting city', it says, but we look for one in the life to come. In other words, the search for God is something that goes on and on, a continual seeking after a new and more profound understanding of who God is, what we are, and what the meaning is of life here on earth.

For the people of the Old Testament, who as yet did not believe in a general resurrection, the virtuous person was held to be rewarded in this world with prosperity, health and long life; whereas the sinner was punished by poverty, sickness and untimely death. Such was the theory, but in reality it did not always work out like that. The Book of Job set out to try and find a reason as to why God, who is the God of justice, could allow a good person to suffer. Job was a virtuous man who trusted in God, believed in God's goodness and power; and here he was, robbed of his family, stripped of all his possessions, and a prey to extreme bodily affliction. Moreover, the suffering of his body is matched by the torture of his soul, as he struggles to discover why this should be.

Such was his anguish that, instead of showing what is commonly referred to as the 'patience of Job', he cursed the day he was born, and in a rage hurled protests at God. Gripped by a spirit of bitter fatalism, he saw man as being condemned to a daily drudgery, the slave seeking rest in the shade of a palm tree, the paid workman concerned solely with the amount of his wages. Job undergoing this interior struggle really stands for each of us. What is the purpose of my life, I this solitary person who thinks and loves, remembers and hopes, lives and dies? His wife urged Job to curse God, but this he refused. What Job learns in the end is that God is beyond all human scrutiny, understanding or argument, and that never is he under any obligation to human beings however upright their lives may be. Realising that he has no ground for arguing with God, Job retracts his harsh words, repents, and humbles himself before his Creator.

The mystery of suffering, however, remains unanswered, even as it is in the Bible as a whole. 'Whoever does not bear his own cross, and come after me, cannot be my disciple' (Lk 14:27). What is certain is that suffering can reduce to despair the person without faith, but for those with faith suffering can be faced in the knowledge that they are in God's hands, that God works with those who love him, and turns everything to their good (Rom 8:28). In marked contrast to Job, St Paul accepts gladly whatever hardship each day may bring, in order to have the opportunity of sharing with others the blessings God has granted him. It is Paul who gives us the only saying of Jesus not recorded in the gospels: 'There is more happiness in giving than in receiving' (Acts 20:35).

The gospel reading today shows Christ giving of himself, of his time, his energy, in the mission his Father has entrusted to him. So complete was the cure from fever of Peter's mother-in-law that she was able to prepare a meal for them. Then after sunset, crowds came with their sick ones to have them also cured. But Jesus flees the crowds, and is found early next morning at prayer by himself elsewhere. This was a clear indication that Jesus regarded the performance of miracles as being a subordinate feature of his ministry. His principal objective was to preach, to pass on a greater understanding of God, and the meaning of life on earth.

To call him the 'Holy One of God', simply on the evidence of his miracles, as did those possessed by evil spirits, Jesus regarded as being dangerously misleading, and so the demons were warned to be silent. At the foot of the cross, the centurion was right in confessing Jesus to be the Son of God, because he saw in him, not the miracle-worker, but the crucified One. Miracles of healing were advance signs of the greatest act of healing, that which took place as a result of Christ's death on Calvary, and his glorious resurrection two days later. The merits that accrue from what took place then continue to be applied to all who have faith in Christ, especially when celebrating the Eucharist.

SIXTH SUNDAY OF THE YEAR
Lev 13:1-2, 44-46; 1 Cor 10:31-11:1; Mk 1:40-45

With two of the three readings today touching on the subject of
leprosy, it is obvious that the Church wants to direct our attention to something deeper than a purely physical disease. We
find confirmation of this in the Responsorial Psalm, which tells
of the inner joy which comes to those who candidly confess their
sins before God, and experience his forgiveness. Sin, then, we
might say is a kind of leprosy of the soul. The only way the ancient
world used to combat physical leprosy was to isolate the afflicted
ones, make them live outside the camp or town, and have them
cry aloud, 'Unclean, unclean', by way of warning to anyone who
would approach them. If anybody were even to touch a leper,
that person also would be regarded as unclean, and would be
excluded from the community.

Christians are members of a community as well, that community which is the Church, the visible presence of God's Holy
Spirit which bonds together all believers in Jesus Christ. A sin
committed by a member of this spiritual community is never a
purely private affair, but a rejection, in varying degree, of this
Holy Spirit as well as the standards which the members have
pledged to uphold. We might go so far as to say that sin is a kind
of idolatry, an attempt to put self at the centre of one's world, to
satisfy one's own urgings and cravings, without due regard for
God who is love, without caring for the consequences to oneself
or to others. A truly critical stage is reached when one utterly
rejects the promptings of Christ's Holy Spirit; and this can come
about through a definite decision made in a single moment, or
more often as a result of a gradual moral and spiritual decline.
Having lapsed thus far, one has reached the stage of rejection of
God, in other words the stage of mortal sin, and this by one's
own deliberate choice.

One of the most disturbing sayings of Christ in the gospels
was his reference to Judas when he prayed for the Apostles at
the Last Supper: 'Not one of them is lost, except the one who
chose to be lost' (Jn 17:12). As John Donne, the English 17th century poet wrote, 'I do nothing upon myself, and yet I am mine
own executioner' (Devotions). Hardly ever can it be said that a
leper is responsible for his disease, but the collapse of all that
inner striving, for what is pure and holy and sanctifying and

loving, is the sinner's own choice. And no less than leprosy, its effect is to isolate that individual from the community. Not only has he become unloving, but he becomes utterly incapable of responding to love, whether from others or from God. 'I am he in whom there is no love', the devil once said to St Catherine of Genoa.

There was an air of humility and resignation also in the leper's request to Jesus, 'If you want to, you can cure me.' And his appeal was met with compassion by Jesus, who, as St Mark tells us, was moved with pity. He reacted further, to the extent of stretching out his hand and touching the leper, thus, strictly speaking according to the law, making himself unclean. This may well be what Mark had in mind, when he tells us that Jesus could no longer go openly into any town, but had to stay outside in places where nobody lived. But this compassion for suffering humanity resulted in more and more people coming to him, and even today the outstretched arms on the cross of God's only Son are a never-ending invitation to the sinner to seek refuge within them also. No longer was the leper, when cured, forced to live apart. After showing himself to the priest he was accepted once more as a member of the community. Likewise, the sinner is reunited to God by means of reconciliation with the community, which is the Church, and which Christ has made the visible source on earth of his forgiveness.

What in the past was called penance or confession, is now referred to as the sacrament of reconciliation, and just as mortal sin is not an isolated act, but rather the culmination of a whole series of minor lapses, so reconciliation is a gradual return to God over a period of time, with the reception of the sacrament as the high point, a time to celebrate our joy and gratitude in being at one with God again. This conversion, this newly-found commitment to the Lord is a thing which has to be constantly renewed. Hence the enduring need for the sacrament of reconciliation, if we want to love God with our whole strength, and our neighbour as ourselves. This clearly is the task Christ has set each of us when he said, 'This do, and you will live' (Lk 10:2).

SEVENTH SUNDAY OF THE YEAR
Is 43:18-19, 21-21, 24-25; 2 Cor 1:18-22; Mk 2:1-12

During his earthly life Jesus normally performed the duties of a
pious Jew. He prayed frequently, he went up to the Temple in
Jerusalem for the great festivals, he attended the synagogue on
the Sabbath. But on the other hand he broke with the Jewish
interpretation of the Sabbath commandments, of the laws of
fasting, of the laws about washing before meals. Above all he
shared meals with sinners and publicans. In complete contrast
to the attitude of the Pharisees towards sinners, he laid great
stress on God's love for them. 'I tell you', he said to the Scribes
and Pharisees, 'there will be more rejoicing in heaven over one
repentant sinner, than over ninety-nine virtuous people who
have no need of repentance' (Lk 15:7).

So striking was his approach towards these religious outcasts
that, from quite early on, a satirical saying that added spice to
the gossip about him, became common knowledge. It branded
him 'a glutton and a drunkard, a friend of tax-collectors and
malefactors'. This behaviour of Jesus, which aroused so much
anger, was not purely social concern for the downtrodden – in
no sense were the tax-collectors downtrodden, but rather collab-
orators with the Romans in exacting the greatest possible
amount of money in taxes from the people.

To understand the action of Jesus in sitting down to eat with
such people, we must remember that in ancient times the sharing
of a meal with others had a special significance, that of fellowship before God. At the meal the master of the house said a
blessing over a whole loaf, and having broken it, shared it with
all those present. And so, each person who received a portion,
received also a share in the blessing spoken over it.

You will easily see the quite definite connection between this
custom, as well as its interpretation, and our Eucharist which
stems in large measure from it. Jesus then by taking sinners and
publicans into fellowship with him, was taking them into fellowship with God. By so doing he was ignoring the reasons for
their being the outcasts of society; in other words he was forgiving their sins. As it is only God who can forgive sin, Jesus in all
this was asserting that he is someone who stands in the place of
God; that in and through him God reaches out to those who are
without hope, and brings consolation and direction to those

who have lost sight of the one thing necessary – the firm belief that no matter what we have done or failed to do, God still continues to love us.

'I am he', the first reading in effect is saying, 'who for my own sake blots out your transgressions, and I will not remember your sins. I will not hold them against you. I will regard them as if they had never been committed.' If one is right with God, if one's conscience is at peace before him, then simply nothing can disturb the serenity which settles upon the soul of such a person. All this stems from faith, from the firm conviction that God is working in one, that he is looking for obedience to the demands of Christ and the gospel.

We see from today's gospel how Jesus put faith first, that he never set out systematically to heal all the sick, and drive out all the demons. He simply intended these isolated signs to convey some deeper religious significance. We might feel inclined to ask why did Jesus raise the issue of sin, why did he enter into an argument with the Scribes and keep the paralytic lying helplessly before him in expectation of a cure? Because, firstly, in Christ's mission the healing of souls took pride of place, and rejection of sin was a clear indication that one had accepted his gospel message. To this day, it is acceptance of this message that leads to life eternal, and indeed what does it profit a person to gain all the world can offer, and hereafter suffer the loss of that life?

Secondly, because even greater than the miracle of bodily healing is the miracle of the remission of sins, the bestowal by God of a new life of grace on the soul – a life which transcends every aspect of the natural, however desirable. Thirdly, because the signs worked by Jesus were intended to give a mental jolt to the onlookers, to make them wonder, 'what is taking place here?' The Scribes, however, with their closed minds were incapable of doing this. They could only see blasphemy in the words of Jesus, and not the hand of God in what he was doing. It was left to the ordinary simple folk to be made aware of that. 'We have never seen anything like this', they said, and they praised God.

EIGHTH SUNDAY OF THE YEAR
Hos 2:16-17, 21-22 2; Cor 3:1-6; Mk 2:18-22

One of the truly great theologians of the nineteenth century was
John Henry Newman, the Anglican divine of Oxford, who in
1845 at the age of 44 became a convert to the Catholic Church.
Shortly after he had been ordained a minister in the Anglican
faith he wrote, 'I have the responsibility of souls on me to the
day of my death.' And so he began a systematic study of the
writings of the Fathers of the early Church, as well as the heresies
which then prevailed, so that he might present to his parishioners in St Mary's Church, a few miles outside Oxford, the
Christian faith in all its purity. He became one of the founders of
the Oxford Movement which set out to renew and revive the
Church of England. He had a profound influence on many
committed Anglicans, but many others, including Catholics of
the day, saw him as a threat. Yet when he died in 1890, he was a
cardinal of the Catholic Church, and his epitaph was, 'Out of the
darkness and shadows into the truth.'

The more Newman studied, the more he searched, the more
surely it dawned on him that truth must be sought by the heart
as well as by the head. Christian revelation addresses itself to
our hearts, to our love of truth and goodness and virtue, to our
fear of sinning, to our desire to gain God's favour, to our longing
to advance in his love and friendship. He became more and
more convinced of what St Paul is telling us in today's readings,
that mere adherence to written laws brings death, but that it is
God's Holy Spirit working within people which gives life.

It is the Spirit who leads, is the admission that Newman
makes, in the hymn which he wrote while struggling with his
doubts about the Anglican Church, 'Lead kindly Light, lead
thou me on.' In the past, he tells us in that hymn, he loved to
choose and see his path, to map things out for himself, to have
all the Christian truths slotted into nice doctrinal compartments.
But now he was entering into a new and intimate relationship
with God, wherein however the Spirit would show the way.

'I am setting my face absolutely towards the wilderness', he
wrote to an Anglican friend, a confession which strikingly
parallels Hosea's words today about God resolving to lead the
unfaithful Israel out into the wilderness, and speak there to her
heart. Today's gospel reading also reminds us that the season of

Lent which begins shortly is a call to us, not just to modify our way of life, to make slight changes, changes very often lasting only for the duration of the Lenten season, but rather to bring about a complete conversion of life, a fundamental change of heart in order to be open to the doctrines of Christ, and the guidance of the Spirit he has left with us. New wine must not be put into old wineskins, which burst in the fermentation process.

Let us make this season in particular a time of prayer, for when one ceases to pray, it is a clear-cut indication that one is no longer walking with Christ, no longer open to the voice of the Holy Spirit, whose temples we became after being cleansed in the waters of baptism. 'Pray without ceasing', St Paul wrote to the Thessalonians, 'and in all things give thanks'. To the Philippians he said, 'Have no anxiety about anything, but in everything, by prayer and supplication with thanksgiving, let your requests be made known to God'. And his last word of advice to the people of Ephesus was, 'Pray at all times, in the Spirit.' All this brings home to us very clearly how important it is to persevere in prayer, and how in particular we should pray, not only for ourselves but for others as well. If we keep on doing this, then gradually prayer will undoubtedly change our lives, and the Spirit of Christ will be with us, interceding for us before the Father with sighs too deep for words.

But we should bear in mind that Christian living is not a matter of warm feelings and sensible consolations. It is rather a venture of faith, a journey very often into the unknown, that calls for abandonment and trust in our relationship with God. This was even demanded of those closest to Jesus, his Apostles. Outwardly they saw in him a man like themselves, a man who had to satisfy his hunger and thirst like themselves, who fished with them, slept beside them on the shore around the same campfire. Only for a brief moment was the veil that covered his divine nature drawn back, and they saw him as he really was, a man possessed by God, a divine person with two natures, that of God and that of man.

FIRST SUNDAY OF LENT
Gen 9:8-15; 1 Pet 3:18-22; Mk 1:12-15

About forty years ago there began a movement away from popular devotions, a movement even more widespread among the
clergy and religious than among the laity. 'We ought to be more
liturgical in our worship', it was maintained, and practices like
Benediction were quietly dropped on a wide scale. 'We should
be more scriptural in our prayer life', we were urged, and out
went devotions like the public recitation of the Rosary. In recent
times we have seen a partial return to these traditional ways of
bringing God into our lives, because the human spirit needs
popular devotions. All this gives rise to the question whether we
are going through the same 'yes-no' approach to Lenten penitential
exercises.

One thing we can say is that to turn our backs on the practice
of self-imposed penance would be to cast aside a genuinely
Christian tradition, stemming from the example of Christ himself, from his prayer to the Father, which in a number of recorded
instances continued throughout the whole night, from the intense
way in which he prepared for the important events of his life,
such as how he marked the beginning of his public ministry
with a period of forty days spent fasting in the wilderness, the
theme of today's gospel reading. In this isolated spot, somewhere near the Dead Sea, Jesus came face to face with evil,
personified in Satan, a name which means adversary or enemy.
He was tempted in a very real way to turn aside from the path
which his eternal Father had mapped out for him, at the end of
which would be a resurrection in glory, but a glory not to be
attained without the terrible agony of Calvary.

We see how Jesus by prayer acquired the strength never at
any moment to waver from the demands being made upon him,
because God can never be overpowered by evil. We should keep
in mind also that never, before his final suffering, did Jesus practice that type of awesome bodily mortification which was a feature
of the lives of so many saints. Perhaps it was because of this that
his enemies proclaimed him a glutton and a drunkard (Mt 11:19)
when, as he says of himself, 'the Son of Man came eating and
drinking'. But if we weigh his actions in the light of the purpose
of all self-denial, which is to hold in check our selfish and oftentimes evil tendencies, then we begin to see that from the very

outset of his public life Jesus had attained that spiritual goal. And what took place during his fast of forty days in the desert gives confirmation of this.

Of course temptations did occur while he was there, and they would come again later on, urging him to take pride in his sense of achievement, his own glorification, his going along on the crest of a wave of popular acclaim. But Jesus set his face firmly against all these, and chose that road alone, along which the Father wanted him to travel, as evidenced from remarks he himself made. 'My aim is to do, not my own will, but the will of Him who sent me' (Jn 5:3). 'What I was to say, what I had to speak, was commanded by the Father who sent me' (12:49). 'It is the Father living in me, who is doing this work. You must believe me when I say that I am in the Father, and the Father is in me' (14:10). Moreover, his outward demeanour bore distinct evidence to this inner accord with the Father's will. 'Can anyone of you convict me of sin?' he openly challenged the hostile Jews (Jn 8:46), and no one could. And as to the non-Jews who encountered him, St Mark (7:37) tells us, 'Their admiration was unbounded. "He has done all things well," they said, "he makes the deaf hear and the dumb speak".'

The devil's tactics had been to try and divert Jesus by persuasion from setting out on that course which would ensure our salvation. We see how the devil failed in this at the beginning of Christ's public life. But he would renew his attack once more in a much more vicious way at Gethsemane and Calvary, when the end of Christ's mission was near. Christ's victory this time was even more emphatic, and he has taught us as well how to triumph with him over the power of sin. By baptism we have become sharers in Christ's victory, but he is saying to us also that we must make our own contribution to this, especially by prayer and fasting. Our aim during Lent, and indeed throughout our whole lives, should be to try to be faithful to God's wishes as revealed to us by the Spirit, to have the same mind that was also in Christ Jesus, and in so far as in us lies, to do all things well, as the Lord Jesus has shown us.

SECOND SUNDAY OF LENT
Gen 22:1-2, 9-13, 15-18; Rom 8:31-34; Mk 9:2-10

'If your eye should cause you to sin, tear it out and throw it
away. It is better to enter into life with one eye, than to have two
eyes and be thrown into the hell of fire.' This is part of Christ's
discourse on the Church, as recorded by St Matthew (18:9). It is
an intense condemnation of anything which may prove a moral
stumbling-block for us, but of course does not commend self-
mutilation as a means of avoiding it. It was deliberately couched
in this disturbing language to make the message stick in people's
minds, and it does. But the 'hell of fire' is not precisely what
Matthew wrote, but rather the 'Gehenna of fire'. The Hebrew
word Gehenna meant the 'Valley of Hinnom', a gorge which lies
on the south side of the Temple Mount. It was a place regarded
as being under a curse. For it was there that the pagan
Canaanites, the predecessors of the Israelites, sacrificed children
to their god Moloch, by throwing them into a fire.

Some renegade Jews followed the same custom until the idol
was finally destroyed in the 7th century BC. The horror of the
place, however, survived, and it became the refuse dump of
Jerusalem, a place of continual flames and smoke from burning
rubbish. In the public mind it became synonymous with hell, a
visible image of what that place must be. From then on there
was no place for child-sacrifice in Jewish worship of God, and
devout Jews would claim there never was. And they saw
confirmation of this in the actions of Abraham, their father in
faith, how God stayed his hand as he was about to sacrifice his
son Isaac. God's original demand that he be sacrificed seemed to
contradict utterly his promise that the boy would guarantee the
continuation of Abraham's stock. It was a test of Abraham, and
no greater proof of his faith and obedience could be demanded.
His heart was pierced to the quick by the innocent question of
the boy, 'Father, here are the fire and the wood, but where is the
lamb for the burnt offering?'

Finding it impossible to reveal openly to his son the identity
of the intended victim Abraham replied, 'God himself will provide the lamb'. The evangelist John may well have this episode in
mind when he wrote, 'God loved the world so much that he gave
his only Son' (3:16). Arising out of this story there are several
mysteries. For instance, why did God ask Abraham to sacrifice

his son? Why did Abraham set out to obey? Indeed why did God allow his own divine Son to be sacrificed? For it is obvious that there is a definite similarity between Isaac and Jesus. Isaac here prefigured Jesus in that he was the only son born to Abraham and Sara. He was to be sacrificed on a hill. He carried the wood of sacrifice on his shoulder to the place of sacrifice, and he was not defeated by death. Jesus, however, was to conquer death by his resurrection. But there the likeness ends.

Isaac was the least outstanding of all the patriarchs, one with no great achievement to his name. In contrast, Jesus at the Transfiguration was revealed to his three Apostles, not only as a figure of miraculous glory, but as being really God's Son, his specially chosen messenger to the world. Despite the enthusiasm of the Apostles, their faith like that of Abraham was to be tested later on, and this revelation of the divine nature in the person of Christ was by way of preparation for the time the same three would be watching him in Gethsemane sweating blood at the prospect of what awaited him next day. For Christ, in whom the Father is well pleased would come to his messiahship through suffering. God had spared the son of Abraham and showered blessings on him, yet his own Son he did not spare, but gave him into the hands of his enemies for the sake of our redemption. Unlike Isaac, Jesus knew what lay ahead. 'There is a baptism I must still receive', he had said, 'and how impatient am I until it is accomplished' (Lk 12:50). Just six days before the Transfiguration, when he had told the disciples that he was to suffer in Jerusalem, Peter prayed that God would not allow such a thing to happen.

The response of Jesus was instant and severe, 'Get behind me, Satan. You are thinking not as God does, but as humans do' (Mk 8:33). In dealing with God we must have faith and trust. On the cellar wall of a bombed-out house in Cologne an unknown fugitive, obviously a Jew, left a testimony of his trust, that only came to light when the rubble was being cleared away after World War II. It read: 'I believe in the sun even when it is not shining. I believe in love even when I do not feel it. I believe in God even when he is silent.' That is the kind of faith we should have as well.

THIRD SUNDAY OF LENT
Ex 20:1-17; 1 Cor 1:22-25; Jn 2:13-25

In early biblical times the vast majority of people were unable to
read or write, but they possessed powers of memory to a far
greater degree than is common nowadays. The events and traditions of the past were stamped irrevocably on their minds, and
many hundreds of years were to elapse before these were committed to writing in the form that we know them. As we read the
account of what transpired after the Exodus from Egypt, one
thing should surely strike us. How could it possibly happen that
a band of mainly ex-slaves, fleeing from their masters, with no
organisation, no education, and no apparent skills for survival
in a desert, were responsible for changing the tide of history, a
change which to this day affects the majority of nations in the
world?

This is precisely what Moses and some refugee followers
brought about in the middle of the 13th century BC, and the
explanation offered by the Book of Exodus is direct and to the
point. It says that this nomadic group encountered God at the
foot of a mountain in the Sinai desert. They formed a covenant,
or pact, with God. God promised to watch over them, and they
in turn promised total allegiance to him, especially by their
observance of the commandments transmitted to them through
Moses. This rather rag-tag group became a nation not like the
nations all around it, but rather as a divinely-led community
formed by God himself. In ancient times other religions evolved
from worship of the things of nature, but that of Israel sprang
from the historical events leading up to Sinai, making it truly
unique. With the exception of Christianity and Islam which
derive in part from Israel, no other religion began quite like that.
The Law given by God to Moses was uncompromising in its
rejection of sin. No way would it tolerate evil.

Every year a Day of Atonement – in Hebrew, Yom Kippur –
was set aside to seek forgiveness for sin. In the beginning what is
referred to as the scapegoat ceremony took place on that day,
when the High Priest would place his hands on a goat's head and
confess over it the sins of the people, after which it was driven
out into the wilderness. St Paul writing to the Church in Rome
declared that the Law had come to an end with Christ (10:4).
Since the Law had come from God, it was in itself good and just

and holy. But of itself, in no way did it help people put it into practice. Indeed, Paul says, it made matters worse by stating clearly everything that is sinful and contrary to the will of God. But worse still, it laid a curse on all who did not observe it. We might compare it to a wonderfully skilled medical doctor, who could diagnose every possible disease, but having no medicines whatsoever to bring about a single cure.

At first sight all this seems to be at variance with the teaching of Christ who said, 'Do not imagine that I have come to set aside the Law and the Prophets. I have come not to abolish them, but to bring them to perfection' (Mt 5:17). 'The Law and the Prophets' was a phrase often used to describe the entire teaching of the OT, and Jesus' saying that he is to bring them to perfection is what we must remember. Indeed Jesus sometimes demanded a deeper adherence to these than advocated by the Scribes and Pharisees. For example the Law said one must not commit adultery, but Jesus said it is possible by looks alone to be guilty of adultery, adultery in the heart. The OT maxim was 'an eye for an eye, and tooth for tooth', but the Christian response should be to offer no resistance to the wicked, to turn the other cheek. The fifth commandment says, 'You must not kill', but according to Christ you must not even be angry with or harbour ill-will towards your neighbour.

Indeed all the commandments from the fourth onwards can be summed up in a single command, 'You must love your neighbour as yourself.' This is why we can say that to love is to keep the Law in all its perfection. It is this finished, perfected Law that endures, not the Law of Moses with its numerous oral additions from a later period, explaining the Law. In the gospel account of the Transfiguration of Christ read out last Sunday we had Jesus in discussion with Moses representing the Law, and Elijah the great prophet. Luke tells us (9:31) that they were speaking about his passing which he would accomplish in Jerusalem. And indeed it is only by the grace that comes to us from his death and resurrection that we can ultimately be pleasing to God in what we do.

FOURTH SUNDAY OF LENT
2 Chr 36:14-16, 19-23; Eph 2:4-10; Jn 3:14-21

The word Lent is derived from an Old English term, 'lencten', meaning 'spring'. And just as spring is a period when nature prepares to clothe itself in a mantle of fresh growth, a wonderful flowering of new life, in the same way Lent is meant to bring about a renewal in our understanding of the events of Calvary, events which led to a new life, a glorious existence, for Jesus Christ, our Saviour. In order to begin to comprehend the significance for us of those events, we must first try and understand the meaning of our own lives and of our destiny as well.

In the account given to us by St John of all that happened in the lead-up to the crucifixion of Jesus, there is one strange interlude, a brief period of quiet, away from the shouting of the mob, and their leaders crying out for the blood of our divine Lord. It tells us how Pilate confronted Jesus inside his governor's palace, while the Jews remained outside for fear of defiling themselves by entering the dwelling of a gentile. Pilate began to wonder at this man whose life had been placed in his hands. He wanted to know what precisely the mission of Jesus was, a mission that could arouse such passion and opposition among his own people. Pilate perhaps was interested from a political viewpoint, but Jesus tried to draw him on, to set him thinking along different lines, to bring him to look at his own life and its set of values also. 'I was born and came into the world for this one purpose', Jesus said, 'to speak about the truth. Whoever belongs to the truth listens to me'. 'And what is truth?', Pilate asked.

But, sadly, it seems that Pilate was reluctant to be confronted with any answer to this query, and so, turning his back on Jesus, he went out straightaway to speak to the Jews in the courtyard. Pilate did not have the courage to face up to the truth, or listen to anything Jesus might say about it. And today's gospel reading tells us why. Everybody who does wrong, it says, hates the light of truth and shuns it. Elsewhere in the New Testament, it is clearly stated that God wants everyone to repent and come to know the truth, so that they may escape from the snare of the devil by which they are held captive and subject to his will (2 Tim 2:25f). Deep in the heart of Pilate there was a wistful longing. Into his life had come Jesus, and suddenly in this mysterious figure he saw something which was lacking in himself. Standing before Pilate Jesus seemed like the one being judged, but in fact it was quite the opposite.

Although Jesus had said that he had not come to judge anyone, those who came in contact with him passed judgment on themselves according as they accepted or rejected him. The Jews also passed judgment on themselves when they shouted, 'We have no king but Caesar', for this was a complete rejection of all that Judaism stood for, namely that God is the one supreme being. But despite God having sent messenger after messenger to his people, as the first reading pointed out, they had met with nothing but ridicule, mockery and persecution.

We see in our own time a growing concern about material things, and a corresponding neglect of the spiritual aspirations of human nature. But each of us can say, there will come a moment in my life when all that will matter is myself and God, and then I will have to face the truth about myself, how I have allowed God prepare me for eternity. For therein lies salvation. St John tells us that eternal life can only be gained in one way, that is by the merits of the Cross of Christ, and that those who turn away from Christ, who close their minds to him, have already chosen their own condemnation.

Change will only come through grace. It has been said that to grow is to change, and to be perfect is to change often. We should of course bear in mind that in matters of grace God always takes the initiative. To each of us at baptism he gives the light of Christ, signified by the baptismal candle. In return, just like the Israelites at Mount Sinai, we take on ourselves certain obligations. Following their example we make the same promise they made, 'You will be our God, and we will be your people.' At every Mass that is celebrated we come into the presence of God, and we are asked to renew those promises made on our behalf at baptism. At the beginning of this Mass we have begged forgiveness for our sins. Let us promise to follow God where he would lead us by the faith which we now profess in the Creed.

FIFTH SUNDAY OF LENT
Jer 31:31-34; Heb 5:7-9; Jn 12:20-30

The last book in the Christian Bible is the Book of Revelation, or
the Apocalypse as it is otherwise known; and, in the first chapters
of it, the author sends a letter in the name of the risen Christ to
each of seven Christian communities, in different cities throughout Asia Minor. There are criticisms and some praise for all of
them except that in Laodicea, a wealthy city about a hundred
miles inland from the Mediterranean coast. Some distance from
it there was a place renowned for its hot springs, and the writer
states rather sarcastically about the Christians, 'I know all about
you, how you are neither hot nor cold. I wish you were one or
the other, but since you are neither, but only lukewarm, I will
spit you out of my mouth' (Rev 3:15+). Laodicea's wealth came
in part from a famous medical centre there, renowned for its
ointments for people going blind or deaf. The letter scornfully
points out that the Christian community itself is both blind to its
spiritual poverty, and deaf to the voice of Christ which is saying,
'Behold I stand at the door and knock … if anyone has ears to
hear, let him listen to what the spirit is saying to the Churches.'
    Such a method of calling sinners to repentance may well
have been copied from the prophet Jeremiah in the Old
Testament, where he poses the question, 'Is there any balm' –
meaning any ointment – 'in Gilead, to cure the deep-rooted
moral sickness of the Jewish people?' Jeremiah is regarded as
the most human of the prophets, a man whose life in many ways
prefigures that of Christ. In his writing he allows us look into the
inner anguish and torment of his soul, rather as St Augustine
does in his 'Confessions'. The tragedy of his people's ills, and
indeed of much of Jeremiah's own reaction to them, stemmed
from what he calls 'a sickness unto death', which lay within, in
people's hearts. The people put their trust in externals, in institutions like the Law, the Ark of the covenant, the sacrifices, the
Temple itself.
    We are reminded too of the account of Jesus looking down on
Jerusalem in all its glory, a glory which its people thought
would endure forever, and saying, 'Jerusalem, Jerusalem, you
that kill the prophets and stone whose who are sent to you …
your house will be left to you desolate.' God will abandon
Jerusalem, even the very Temple. All these had become mere

empty symbols for people whose minds were hardened by their love of pleasure, by their uncaring attitudes towards the weak and defenceless ones in society, by their blind nationalism.

The seat of all these ills – so much like those of our own time – lay within, as Jeremiah said, in the heart. Jeremiah looks forward to the time when God will put a new heart in his people and on it write his law. When they are in doubt as to what is right, people will no longer have to ask questions of others, or consult the books of the Law. They will gaze into their hearts. They will hear God speak quite plainly to them in their consciences, and they will make a personal response to God's messages. 'If anyone has ears to hear, let him listen to what the Spirit is saying.' If you do something because the law demands it, you are being an obedient person. If you do it because your conscience demands it, you are a moral person, making your own moral judgment. 'Then there will be no need for neighbour to try and teach neighbour', as the reading today puts it. This prophetic utterance, more than anything else that Jeremiah said, made a lasting impression on the religious tradition of Israel. Here also we have the only mention in the Old Testament of a 'new covenant'. 'I will make a new covenant with the house of Israel.'

Because covenant and testament mean the same thing, it is from this chapter of Jeremiah that the Christian section of the Bible derives its name – the New Testament. The beginning of Jeremiah's prophecy, 'Behold the days are coming, says the Lord, when I will make a new covenant with the House of Israel', points to an event in the future, which will be the work of God and give people hope. Christ, who in today's gospel speaks of the grain of wheat dying in the ground – a reference to the shedding of his blood – in order to bring forth a rich harvest, recalled those words of Jeremiah at the Last Supper, as we do at every Mass, 'This cup is the new covenant in my blood.' Let us then pray to the Lord, during this commemoration of the Last Supper, that deep in our hearts forever, he may implant his word, his law, his own most Holy Spirit.

ST PATRICK'S DAY
Jer 1:4-9; Acts 13:46-49; Lk 10:1-12, 17-20

'I have made you a light for the nations, so that my salvation
may reach the ends of the earth.' (Is 49:6) This solemn promise
was first made by God to the Suffering Servant of the Lord. We
find St Paul and St Barnabas using it to justify their mission to
the gentiles, and our own national apostle, St Patrick, quotes it in
his Confession as the reason he came to preach the gospel of
Christ among the Irish, and that despite having undergone at
their hands six years of harsh captivity as a slave. Out of suffering and evil God can bring good, and Patrick never ceased
thanking God for the way his ordeals reshaped his character and
gave him a new purpose in life. It was the Holy Spirit especially
who enabled him to survive those six years without bitterness or
feeling of revenge towards his captors. 'There I sought him', he
wrote, 'and there I found him. I am convinced that he kept me
from all evil, because of his Spirit who lives in me and works in
me to this very day'. This conviction led to a far deeper reverence
and love for God, which manifested itself especially in his
prayer-life.

In the course of a day he would say as many as a hundred
prayers, and almost as many at night; and whether there was
snow, frost or rain he would rise before dawn to commune with
God. This in turn led to mystical experiences, a number of which
are recalled in the Confession. For example he received messages
in his sleep from God, telling him that he would shortly return
to his own country, and later again he was urged to set off
because a ship was ready to bring him there. Then there is the
well documented account of how he heard in the night the voices
of people in Ireland calling out to him, and beseeching him to
'come and walk once more among them'. There was especially
an extraordinary experience of his where he, as it were, saw a
person praying within him. 'I was, as it seemed, inside my own
body', he wrote, 'and I heard him over me, that is over the inner
man. There he was, praying with great fervour. All the while I
was in a state of wonder as to who could possibly be praying
inside me. He spoke, however, when his prayer had ended,
telling me he was the Spirit'.

The only explanation Patrick could think of, for this supernatural experience, came from his recollection of St Paul's words

(Rom 8:26), 'The Spirit also helps us in our weakness. For when we are unable to pray as we ought, the Spirit himself pleads for us in a way that could never be put into words.' The courage displayed by Patrick in returning to Ireland, where he would face many difficulties, persecutions, insults, even contrived opposition to his appointment as bishop, was mainly due to the influential role in his life played by the Holy Spirit. Particularly disturbing was the action of a once dear friend of his who tried to discredit him by circulating a defamatory document setting out details of a boyhood misdemeanour confided to him by Patrick, who at the time was barely fifteen years old. What it was we do not know, but the whole thing was blown up out of all proportion, in order to bring disgrace on Patrick, then an old man.

God, however, did not abandon him, but reassured him in a vision saying, 'We have seen with disapproval the face of the chosen one deprived of his good name.' True to character, Patrick did not yield to bitterness towards his accusers, but rather had deep-felt sorrow for the man to whom, in his own words, he had confided his very soul, a man he continued to describe as his dearest friend. Although he could not condone his treachery, pardon him he did. Today, we the spiritual off-spring of St Patrick are confronted with various problems in our own era. For there is a marked drift away from a religious under-standing of life, and towards a purely materialistic concept of what our earthly goals should be, something which accompanied the collapse of many a great civilisation in history.

With growing problems of alcohol and drug abuse, violence – in particular against the defenceless and elderly – increased suicide among young men, the enforced subservience, akin to slavery, of so many to crime bosses, the collapse of marriage and family ties, it is hardly any wonder that there is talk of a near breakdown of society in many quarters, especially among the underprivileged. To counter such we could well copy St Patrick's belief in the power of prayer, a belief that brought him such inner freedom, dedication to the call of God, and such trust in the active presence of the Holy Spirit. For by these he once opened a door before us which no one can ever close.

PASSION SUNDAY
Is 50:4-7; Phil 2:6-11; Mk 14:1 - 15:47

However exemplary it may be to spend a year fasting on bread
and water, or visit all the holy places in Jerusalem, St Augustine
once said, it is still worth far more in the sight of God to shed a
single tear in remembrance of the Passion of his Son, our Lord
Jesus Christ. On the last night of his life on earth, Christ had celebrated the Passover meal with the Apostles, and at the end of it
he established the Holy Eucharist as his most precious parting
gift to them. Then all, with the exception of Judas, went down
from the upper city area into the Kidron valley, past the southern end of the Temple enclosure, and along its eastern wall until
they reached the Garden of Gethsemane near the foot of the
Mount of Olives. It was a place where Jesus often went to pray,
but this night's visit had a special urgency about it. Being in the
full vigour of his manhood, he did not want to die when there
was so much to be set right in the world, and he the only one to
bring it about. But as against this he had to accept that the path
of nonresistance to the powers of evil was the surest way of
defeating them, and that God was asking him to go down that
path. The terrible agony that acceptance of this would entail was
clearly present in minutest detail to the mind of him who could
see into the secret depths of the hearts of others.

For a while he pleaded with God to let this cup pass him by,
but gradually he stifled this natural weakness within him to the
point where he accepted the role of self-immolation with his
plea to the Father, 'Not my will but yours be done.' Being in
such an agony as to cause him to sweat blood, he prayed the
longer. Divine help in the form of an angel came to strengthen
him, whereas the special three, chosen to be near him, Peter,
James and John, had fallen asleep. 'Rise up, let us go', he told
them, 'my betrayer is near at hand'. But very soon all the disciples deserted him and fled away into the darkness, although
Peter followed at a safe distance to see what the end would be.
In the trial of Jesus that ensued, the Sanhedrin, or Supreme
Court of the Jews, broke all its own laws. The trial should have
been within the Temple precincts; it wasn't. The trial should not
take place at night: it did. Witnesses' evidence should be in agreement; it wasn't. A whole night should elapse before a verdict of
death was carried out. Christ was put to death on the very same

day. When nothing concrete was issuing from the actual trial, the High Priest took matters into his own hands.

He asked a question that was completely forbidden by the law, which strictly required that no question be put to the accused that might make him incriminate himself. It was put in such a way that Christ was forced to answer. 'I put you on oath by the living God', Caiaphas said solemnly, 'to tell us if you are the Christ, the Son of God'. Jesus replied without hesitation that he was. Then the High Priest tore his robes claiming that this was blasphemy, an insult against God that merited the death penalty, and they all agreed. This meeting, which began as a court of justice, now lost all semblance of legality. For it ended in a frenzy of venom and hatred, with these custodians of the law spitting upon the face of Jesus, blindfolding him, hitting him, and taunting him to say who hit him.

But there was one obstacle to be cleared. They might pronounce the death penalty, but only the Romans could carry it out, and Roman policy was not to become involved in religious quarrels. So the charge of blasphemy was changed to one of sedition, Jesus claiming to be king and discouraging payment of taxes to Caesar. Pilate knew full well that these were trumped up charges, but being scared at the possibility of violence by the mob he tried various means of escaping his dilemma. He tried to make Herod responsible for condemning Jesus, but failed. He offered them a choice between releasing Jesus and a notorious criminal Barabbas, but the mob chose Barabbas. He tried to arouse a spark of sympathy in them by having Jesus scourged and bringing him before them with a crown of thorns on his head and a purple robe thrown round him. But the thirst for blood of those present would not be denied. So Pilate, whose responsibility it was to dispense Roman justice, after the futile gesture of washing his hands, delivered Jesus to be crucified. The crucifixion of Christ was to be thereafter a stumbling block to the Jews, to the gentiles foolishness. But the only person to openly admit Christ's true identity in what took place on Calvary was a gentile, the Roman centurion in charge of the soldiers present. 'Truly this man was the Son of God.'

EASTER SUNDAY
Acts 10:34, 37-43; Col 3:1-4 or 1 Cor 5:6-9; Jn 20:1-9

It is hardly surprising that all religions, by their very nature, tend to be conservative, in other words they are always striving to preserve faithfully the truths and spiritual way of life which have been handed on to them. Even Christ himself said that he had come 'not to destroy but to fulfil'. We could well ask ourselves then, why did the early Christians, who were mostly Jews, abandon the sacred tradition of their forefathers, and make Sunday, rather than Saturday, their day of weekly worship. And the fact that their reason for so doing was also regarded by the educated Greeks as 'foolishness', must make us wonder all the more – their reason being the firm conviction that on the Sunday after his death, God raised Jesus Christ from the grave. Their faith in this stupendous event defied all human thinking, but, notwithstanding, it survives to this very day.

Each and every Sunday, as it comes around, is another link binding all of us with that event, something which of itself is a further proof of the resurrection. And at the end of every Sunday, all who recite the Divine Office say the following prayer, which concludes the hour called 'Night Prayer': 'God our Father, as we have celebrated today the mystery of the Lord's resurrection … free us from all harm, that we may sleep in peace and rise in joy to sing your praise.' Every Sunday Mass is a reaffirmation of our faith in the resurrection of Christ. We do not seek him among the dead, as Mary Magdalene did on that first Easter morn, because he is living, he is with us, he becomes part of us in Holy Communion, or rather we become part of him.

Without the resurrection of Jesus we would not be observing this day as that which is holy to the Lord. Furthermore, without the resurrection we would not have a Christian Church, or a Christian way of life, or even any such sacred writing as the new Testament. For, the Church herself, the Lord's day, and the new Testament are three great witnesses to the truth of the resurrection. Without the message of the resurrection there would be no gospel, no letters in the New Testament, no Christian community or Eucharist to hold it together. There would be no faith, no hope beyond this life, no worship of God in Spirit and in truth, no prayer in Christendom. 'If Christ has not been raised', St Paul wrote (1 Cor 15:17), 'your faith is futile, and you are still in your sins'. If Christ has not risen, we have been deceived, and are deceiving you. We are liars and the enemies of God, who could not be the inspiration of such teaching. We might as well cast off this unreal Christianity, and return to the ranks of those who have as their watchword, 'Let us eat, drink and be merry, for tomorrow we die' (cf. 1 Cor 15:32) – a watchword which outwardly is so cheerful and appealing to many people, but when pursued begets only a feeling of hopeless and despairing resignation.

Against this virtual cataract of awful consequences for his listeners, in the event of the resurrection being untrue, Paul sets the single truth, challenging in its simplicity, 'But in fact, Christ has been raised from the dead, the first-fruits of those who have fallen asleep' (1 Cor 15:20). In the gospels, because there were men and women who could state openly, and with utter conviction, 'We have seen the Lord' – men and women whose whole lives were transformed by that belief – a living tradition of faith began, which stretches down through two millennia to our own time, and now touches and challenges the minds of all of us here this morning. Let us then open our 'eyes of faith' to the fullness of the divine event we are recalling, that Jesus who was truly dead came to life again, not merely as some kind of pale disembodied spectre that gibbered in his stead, but in the full richness of his warm and loving and tender personality.

This is clearly shown in his appearance at first light beside the Sea of Galilee, where some of the disappointed disciples had taken to their fishing again. 'Have you caught anything friends?' he called out to them. He then goes on to advise them as to what they should do to succeed. When their efforts were rewarded so miraculously they came ashore and saw that he had even prepared breakfast for them on a charcoal fire, at which they could warm themselves after their cold and fruitless night on the lake. What tenderness and consideration coming from the risen glorified Son of God! Like the Apostles, let us too rejoice and be glad this day, for the Lord has truly risen. Alleluia!

SECOND SUNDAY OF EASTER
Acts 4:32-35; 1 Jn 5:1-6; Jn 20:19-31

Close on two hundred years ago there began what is now referred to as the Age of Enlightenment, an age so called because it was believed that every material aspect of this world – its origin, its function – could be explained by a process of scientific reasoning from cause and effect. If there is anything that exists, that lives, that moves, that can be grasped by the senses, all such must have a cause, and the true apostles of the Enlightenment believed that science would discover and explain that cause. The last century, however, has seen a rather strange intimacy evolving between science and religion. Most astronomers today accept the theory that the universe had a moment of creation – that it came about 15 to 20 billion years ago as the result of a massive nuclear explosion, now known as the Big Bang. For a million years afterwards everything was shrouded in a dense fog of radiation, and this period, as well as that which preceded the Big Bang, remain as concealed from scientists as is the face of God.

Moreover the Big Bang cannot begin to explain the billions of galaxies of stars unless assumptions are made, the most important assumption being that much, or perhaps nearly all, of the universe is made of something called dark matter, or antimatter, substances which cannot be seen but only inferred. It is a matter of debate as to whether this, as well as many of the theories about the nature of subatomic particles, can be classed as real discoveries or just inventions of the human mind. Science nowadays is seeking answers so fundamental that they border on theology, the why of existence, for example, as opposed to the how of it. Why is there something instead of nothing? Science therefore cannot even begin to say anything definite about the cause leading up to the biggest effect of all, the birth of our universe. As far as science can say it came from nothing. We might even say that between science and religion there is here a meeting of minds, because the first chapter of Genesis has been claiming all along that the universe began in a single flashing act of creation, when God willed all things into being out of nothing.

Indeed we could reflect on three separate and unique creations – direct interventions – by God, the first being that creation, or birth, of the universe from nothing. The second creation was that of the glorified body of the resurrected Christ, a body which was visible only to select witnesses, which could suddenly appear to people locked behind closed doors, which seemed able to transcend time and space, which changed utterly those privileged to see it. Here was a totally new birth. Jesus was the first born from the dead. And by way of extension to this there is a third creation, a third birth. Through baptism we have become adopted as children of God, and in Christ heirs to the kingdom of heaven. We have confirmation of this in sacred scripture which says, 'Whoever believes that Jesus is the Christ has been begotten by God' (1 Jn 5). The word 'begotten' derives from the word 'beget', which means to produce, give birth to. And Christ said (Jn 3:5), 'Truly I say to you, no one can enter the kingdom of God without being born of water and the Holy Spirit', that is without being baptised.

The greater our faith in God's promises, the more it will become a source of grace welling up within us. 'Repent, turn to God', Peter said to his listeners, 'so that your sins may be wiped away'. This however requires perseverance and dedication on our part. The pathway to God is never accompanied by resounding successes and deeds which astonish the onlookers. We see how the great expectations of the Apostles were shattered by the death of Jesus on a gibbet – the most ignoble end for a man at that time.

Indeed the successes of Jesus were with little groups – with Mary and Joseph, with Peter, James and John, with the Samaritan woman at the well, with the Roman centurion, with Nicodemus the man who came to him by night. It is what we term the little things in our lives that determine the quality of our Christian commitment, the good turns we do for others, the moments when we turn our thoughts to God, the conquering of our fears in times of difficulty, and trusting in God, the forgetting of ourselves and of the 'I must have this' complex fostered in us by the kind of world we live in. These may be little things, yes, but as St Augustine used to say to his followers, 'To be faithful in little things is itself a very great and rewarding thing.'

THIRD SUNDAY OF EASTER
Acts 3:13-15, 17-19; 1 Jn 2:1-5; Lk 24:35-48

'You see how it is written that the Christ would suffer, and on the third day rise from the dead, and that, in his name, repentance for the forgiveness of sins would be preached to all the nations.' This is the risen Christ speaking to us from out the gospel. And his words are echoed by Peter in the first reading, 'Now you must repent and turn to God, so that your sins may be wiped out.' Even in the second reading, the apostle John urges his readers to stop sinning, and if they have sinned they should seek forgiveness in Christ who by his sacrifice has taken our sins away. Most people who are living in sin, without thought of God or regard for his commandments, silence their consciences if ever they trouble them, with the promise of repenting some future day. But is it possible that a change of heart can be brought about in a single day? Can we possibly alter our tastes, our will, our character and habits without any difficulty in a brief period of time?

Alas, the sad fact is that holiness and justice are never acquired in a day, but are rather the result of much patient and enduring attempts at changing our hearts and minds. In other words they are normally the work of a lifetime. Of course we cannot set limits to God's mercy, which can sometimes effect miraculous and sudden repentance, especially if a person is destined by God to play a particular role in his plan of salvation for souls. The conversion of St Paul is one such which comes to mind. But as a general rule it is only practice which can train our faculties to distinguish between good and evil (Heb 5:14). And practice must be accompanied with perseverance.

There is a solemn and rather disturbing warning in the New Testament against all who fail to persevere but rather give up religious practice altogether. 'How can those who abandon their faith be brought back to repent again?' it asks. 'They were once brought into the light. They tasted the gift from heaven, and have shared in the Holy Spirit. They had come to appreciate the value of God's message and the powers of the age to come. Yet in spite of all this they have abandoned their faith. To repent a second time is impossible for them, since they are wilfully crucifying once more the Son of God, and openly mocking him' (Heb 6:4-6).

There are but few, thank God, who renounce entirely their Christian faith, but unfortunately there are always some who would have to admit that the fulfilment of their pledges to God has been an exercise of routine, in which the heart has had but little part. 'And if it is hard even for a good person to be saved', St Peter warns us, 'what will happen to the wicked and to sinners?' (1 Pet 4:18). We should not then be content with anything less than perfection, which can only be attained by growing daily in the grace and knowledge of almighty God. The call to repent, to change, to be converted, was the primary message of Christ's teaching. St John, in the second reading, reaffirms this clearly, and he states categorically that anyone who claims to be without stain of sin is a liar. But, however sinful we are, there is a remedy at hand, because Christ through his passion and death has obtained forgiveness for us.

Considering this we might be inclined to sit back and say, 'Why all the fuss if everyone is a sinner, and forgiveness is easily got?' But John issues a solemn warning, 'We can be sure that we know God only by keeping his commandments.' To know is one of those terms which had a special meaning in sacred scripture. It had almost nothing to do with intellectual understanding. To know God meant to abide in God, to have a close and personal relationship with him. And this is only possible if we live in imitation of Christ, if we put on Christ, as St Paul says. Christianity, it is true, gives us great privileges, but it also makes great demands on us. For we cannot be like Christ unless we are pure in heart.

There is a story of a poor and simple man who regularly visited a certain church, and would always pray on his knees before a large crucifix. He was once asked why his lips never moved while in this attitude of prayer before the image of Christ crucified. His reply was, 'I look at him, and he looks at me.' For him words had given way to contemplation. And truly, those who look long enough at Christ, whether before a representation of Christ, or just mentally, will finally become like Christ, and that for all eternity, because of the vision of him as he really is.

FOURTH SUNDAY OF EASTER
Acts 4:8-12; 1 Jn 3:1-2; Jn 10:11-18

One of the great achievements by a Socialist government in
Britain was the setting up of the National Health Scheme. It was
hailed as a sure and certain way of eliminating the anxiety and
worry that goes with illness, and of easing the suffering associated
with entry into this world as well as departure from it. But what
was extraordinary with regard to this efficient and for the most
part smoothly running structure, at the outset, was that side by
side with it there should exist the need and even the demand for
such places as the Cheshire Homes. And we have them here in
Ireland as well. It is well known that at least in Britain these very
often were just poorly equipped and ramshackle buildings
where old people and those suffering from incurable diseases
preferred to spend their last days on earth, the reason generally
speaking being the care and attention lavished on them from
those who ran them.

All this points to the need within such people, and indeed
within each and every one of us, to be loved, to have someone to
care, not only for them, but about them. Those who are longtime
suffering or wholly dependent on others are in a very special
way children of God, in Christ Jesus our Lord. But we might ask
this morning, how does God show his fatherhood, how does he
lavish his love on them as St John tells us. The answer is that
Christ is the visible sign of God's love, and that the risen Christ
continues his work among the weak and suffering of this world,
but that it is through human agencies he now does it.

This is the clear message of the first reading, in which Peter
tells us that it was by the name of Jesus that the cripple, encountered by himself and John, had been restored to health. The
gospel reading points to the continuing love of God for his people in terms of well-known Old Testament imagery, that of a
shepherd's care for his flock. In Palestine a shepherd led his
flock; he did not drive them as shepherds elsewhere did. And at
daybreak, after several flocks had been together for the whole
night in the one sheepfold, each shepherd would call his own
flock, and they would recognise his voice and follow him forth
to the pastures. The good shepherd was even prepared to lay
down his life for his flock.

All this is an image of what God has done for us in Jesus, and of what he wants in the present age to continue doing through us, the members of his Church, the visible evidence and means of the risen Christ's continuing mission of mercy in the world to this day. This is the reason why this Sunday has been designated Vocations' Sunday. A vocation is a way of life in which we become involved within our immediate community or family circle, in working for the good of others, rather than for purely selfish reasons. It is a way of allowing ourselves become instruments of God's love, of allowing Christ, through us, draw near to all who have need of his healing presence, and of the peace which he alone can bring to their souls.

The duty of fostering priestly and religious vocations falls on the whole Christian community, and they discharge it by living full Christian lives. The greatest contribution is made by families which have within them a deep spirit of faith, of piety, of the love of God, and by parishes pervaded by Christian virtue and idealism. If parents pray with their children, and are seen praying by their children, then they are most certainly sowing the seeds of those vocations which will be needed to minister full-time to the spiritual needs of the future.

But it is not only families, it is everyone who should become involved in this task. For a community which is poor in vocations makes the whole Church poorer, but a community rich in vocations, makes the entire Church richer. We should also remember how the Virgin Mary was concerned for the infant Church after the Ascension of her divine Son, how she stayed with the Apostolic group and prayed with them in the Upper Room. This role is one she pursues to this very day. We commend to her care the needs of our missionaries, the needs of religious engaged in teaching, nursing, looking after the disabled and orphaned, the need for more dedicated souls to live lives of faith and love within the cloister, praying for the salvation of the whole world. Above all we pray that there may be generous men and women who are willing to carry on such works of service within the Church, and so give witness to the continuing presence on earth of the risen Lord Jesus Christ.

FIFTH SUNDAY OF EASTER
Acts 9:26-31; 1 Jn 3:18-24; Jn 15:1-8

It is extraordinary the fascination which the history of ancient Egypt and its Pharaohs has for people of modern times, and this not only by reason of the wonderful edifices and sculptures they left behind, but also from the social and religious point of view. For here we had a whole people organised for one purpose, to secure the continuation of the Pharaoh in the next world. They surrounded the burial of their ruler with a set of customs, of laws, of ritual ceremonies, the purpose of which was to create the impression that the Pharaoh was still alive. They even placed food in the tomb for him, together with his favourite furniture, chariots, games and weapons. But the thing that strikes us about mummies, whether they be royal or not, is that they are very, very dead indeed.

The lesson from all this is that religion which has degenerated into code and cult, into a matter of laws to be kept, and ceremonies or rites to be carried out, that such a religion will in time become dry and musty, and like the mummies utterly without life. I recall a person on a TV religious programme being asked about the effect of religion on his life, whether he would be happier without it, and he said, 'Yes, sometimes, but then it is always a guide to help one get through life.' In other words for him religion was a code to regulate his conduct. But whereas people of that mind do not want their consciences being upset or disturbed, neither very often do they want their freedom restricted. They want religion to be mummified, to be static in their lives. But, if it means anything, Christianity has got to be a living, a vibrant force in one's life. Not only does Christ live on in the community of believers, he also, through them, carries on his mission of ministering to souls who are in need of his mercy and love.

In those who spread the words of the gospel to others, whether in the mission fields, in the parish, in our schools, we have the fulfilment of Jesus' prayer at the Last Supper, 'That they may know the one true God, and Jesus Christ whom you have sent.' In every instruction in the faith, given and received, we have a figure of Christ restoring his sight to the poor man, who at first beheld people dimly, as if they were trees, and then came to see clearly. In every sinner who comes to repentance we see, as it were, Lazarus raised once more from the dead, casting off the shroud of sin that enveloped him. In every coming to-gether around the Table of the Eucharist, we, like the Apostles are witnesses before the whole world to the task, entrusted to us by Christ, of proclaiming his death and resurrection until he comes at the end of time. Christianity is not, and never should be, mere code or mere cult.

If you see Christianity as a code – 'you must do this, you must avoid that, you must be present at this Mass' – is one very often heard – then it is possible to begin to credit your account before God by claiming, 'I attend Mass, I observe this law, I have progressed so much on the way you require of me.' It is possible to reach the stage where you begin to see yourself as being perfect, with no further need of a saviour. But, alas, such an assessment of one's standing before God is precisely that of the Pharisees, of whom Christ said to his listeners, 'I tell you, if your virtue goes no deeper than that of the Scribes and Pharisees, you will never enter the kingdom of heaven' (Mt 5:20). True Christianity is the vision of ourselves as being encompassed by God's love, that despite our faults, God loves us to the point of foolishness, to the point of death on a cross. If we believe in Christ, God is ready to regard us as his children and friends. Friends do not ask for literal commands, but from their personal acquaintance with the one that loves them, they try and under-stand his half-words. From love of him they try and anticipate his wishes.

If we see our lives as a response to the immense love God has for us, then there will no longer be constraint. Rather will reli-gion have a liberating effect in our lives. We will enjoy what scripture describes as 'the liberty of the children of God'. But then again, so great is the love of God for us that we will see our efforts at responding to that love as always falling short of what we desire. The trouble with those who see their lives as blame-less is that they have limited vision. They do not raise their eyes above themselves. Why should we continue to strive after some-thing which seems beyond us? The answer from St Augustine is that we must do so because we have an inbuilt need for God, and nothing short of him will ever satisfy that inner seeking which is with us all our lives.

SIXTH SUNDAY OF EASTER
Acts 10:25-26, 34-35, 44-48; 1 Jn 4:7-10; Jn 15:9-17

Two of today's readings are from the Apostle St John, whose gospel is seen by commentators from the beginning of the Christian era as having pride of place in the whole of sacred scripture, principally because of its insistence on grace, on the love of God, on eternal redemption being purely and freely a gift to us from God. Tradition has it that John lived to a great age, such that he had to be carried each Sunday into the place where the Christian community at Ephesus gathered to celebrate the Blessed Eucharist. Because of the veneration in which he was held, he was invariably asked to address the little congregation, and invariably he spoke about the love of God, to the extent that even these devout and committed early Christians grew a little weary of the same recurring theme. John, however, took little heed of their requests for a change of subject. He persisted in his refusal to speak about anything else, because for him the central theme of all the Christian message was enshrined in the love of God. 'We believe in love', was the motto of those who were in full agreement with John.

This could easily have become an empty slogan, were it not that John had stated clearly what he meant by love, and our attention is drawn to it in today's second reading. 'This is the love I mean: not our love for God, but God's love for us, when he sent his Son to be the sacrifice that takes our sins away.' The tremendous truth about God is not that he loves us or that he is a loving or lovable being, but rather that, in himself, he is the very act itself of love. This means, moreover, that God by his very nature gives and shares of his inner self. It also means that those who receive the gift of God's love must mirror God's sharing also. God's love was such as to impel him to give his only Son so that we might have life through him. And God shows no partiality or preference in the way he loves. The merits of his Son are available to all without distinction of any kind, provided they have faith and really desire to be of one mind with Jesus.

At first Israel was chosen by God, not for its own sake, but that it might bring before all people the revelation of the love of God, especially as shown in the person of his divine Son. Likewise we have been chosen and commissioned, so that we might 'go out and bear fruit, fruit that will last' (Jn 15:16). Each of us can truly say: God's love brought me into being, it sustains me, it will never let me down. God is concerned about me. He reads my thoughts, my emotions, my desires. He knows my joys, my sorrows, my weaknesses, my strengths. He is close to me in times of laughter or of tears, in illness or in health.

I am quite incapable of loving myself to the same degree that God loves me. God is even closer to me than I am to myself. Through the prophet Isaiah (49:16) God addresses to me the consoling words, 'See upon the palm of my hand I have written your name.' Indeed, in the person of Jesus, God, as it were, reaches out to us with two hands – the one extended in forgiveness which saves us from being engulfed here and now in our evil ways, the other casting a ray of light beyond the portals of death, reminding us that as God raised Christ from the dead, so he will redeem us too, when we have completed our earthly existence. That we are able to grasp those hands of God extended to us, that we are able to cling to them steadfastly, is more a gift of God's grace that our own accomplishment. No amount of self-pruning, of teeth-gritting human striving, will bring us any closer to God.

But if we try and go through life in the steady conviction that God's loving care is drawing us, watching over us, then we will cease to worry about our own happiness, about what we even regard as perfection, what we would like ourselves to be when we come before God. Strange as it may seem, faith in God's love for us frees us from all kinds of inner striving and pressure, and yet at the same time brings us to a closer and more complete commitment to God. If, day after day, we know ourselves as loved by God, then all that will matter will be his love, his will, God himself.

'There are three things that last', St Paul tells us, 'faith, hope and love; and the greatest of these is love' (1 Cor 13:13). For coming into the presence of God, faith will give way to vision, hope will be replaced by attainment, but love will continue to be bestowed and cherished for all eternity.

ASCENSION OF THE LORD
Acts 1:1-11; Eph 1:17-23 or Eph 4:1-13; Mk 16:15-20

The Feast of the Ascension is one which we should always celebrate with joy and thanksgiving, because Christ according to the
Apostles has ascended to the right hand of God, and there
makes intercession for us. Why should this, you may ask, be a
special source of gladness for us? Because not only has he gone
there to prepare a place also for us, but, as St John assures us in
his First Letter (2:1-2), 'if any of us should sin, we have one who
pleads for us with the Father, Jesus Christ who is just, and, by
his sacrifice, makes atonement for our sins'. While on earth,
Jesus had become what we are, in order to change us into what
he is. And he continues this task even now that he is in heaven. It
is thus not only with a feeling of gratitude that we recall all that
Christ has done for us, but also with a sense of wonder and awe.
For the bodily presence of Jesus, which the Apostles were privileged to see and touch, is no longer here. It is in heaven, and this
is confirmation for us when we think of heaven, not merely as a
state of happiness and bliss – which it is – but also as a definite
fixed place.

We are, however, as yet not privileged to see into that secret
shrine, where Christ now is. Not until the day of eternity breaks
for us, and the shadows which hide it from us melt away, and
we are found worthy to enter there. Christ at the Last Supper
surprised the Apostles by saying, 'It is to your advantage that I
go away, for if I do not go away, the Paraclete will not come to
you; but if I go, I will send him to you' (Jn 16:7). By his
Resurrection and Ascension, Jesus now lives wholly and for
ever with God. But mention of his being taken up into heaven
does not mean that he is at a distance from this world, and far
removed from us. No, Christ still continues to be with us, for his
last words to his disciples, as recorded by St Matthew, were, 'I
am with you always to the end of time' (Mt 28:20).

He has not therefore left us orphans, but is with us in a new
way, a new mode of being, since he is no longer visible to our
human eyes. He continues with us through his Holy Spirit. This
feast is a source of great consolation to us, because as St Paul
says, it keeps us in mind of the rich glories that God has
promised as a lasting reward to the saints, that is the faithful –
those who put their trust in Christ. It is a feast which rekindles

our hope. In a wonderful passage St John recalls for us the promise of Christ in his discourse at the Last Supper: 'I am going now to prepare a place for you, and after I have gone and prepared you a place, I shall return to take you with me, so that where I am, you too may be.' In those words, 'I shall return to take you with me', there is a wonderfully consoling description of what will happen to the devout soul when the moment arrives for its departure from this world for ever.

It is furthermore a consolation to remember that in his exalted position Jesus intercedes for us with the Father, and that he possesses the power to draw all people to himself. To be convinced of this we need only think of the unlikely people who have been converted to the cause of Christ, such as Mary Magdalene out of whom he cast seven devils, yet who was the first to see him after his resurrection; like the publican Matthew who became an Apostle and evangelist; like Paul, the persecutor of the infant Church, whose conversion the Apostles themselves could not accept as being genuine for some time.

For us and for the present era in the Church, the Ascension has a two-fold significance. (i) This power of drawing people, which in a special way characterised Christ, is passed on to his Church by the presence of the Holy Spirit in our midst today, and (ii) each and every Christian has the task of bearing witness to Christ, by responding to his/her experience of the Holy Spirit. It has been said that the modern person no longer wants to know if Christianity is true, but rather what it means, what it's significance is, what effect it has on those who profess it.

It begets especially the firm conviction that 'blessed are they who have not seen, and yet have believed'. We do not then wish for sight, but rather enjoy the privilege granted us; and this is the victory that enables us overcome the world, namely our faith. For we are certain that 'neither death, nor life, nor angels, nor rulers, nor things present, nor things to come, nor powers, nor height, nor depth, nor anything else in all creation, will ever be able to separate us from the love of God in Christ Jesus, our Lord' (Rom 8:38).

PENTECOST SUNDAY
Acts 2:1-11; Gal 5:16-15; Jn 15:26-27, 16:12-15

St Luke tells us in his gospel (Lk 24:52) that after the Ascension
into heaven of Jesus, his disciples returned to Jerusalem with
great joy. But surprisingly at the Last Supper, the same disciples
were deeply troubled when Jesus told them that he would be
leaving them shortly and going to the Father. So we find Jesus
consoling them and telling them that he will return to them
again; and this he will do, not only in the Easter apparitions, but
more permanently, and in a completely spiritual way, by an
inward vision of faith to each one of them. All of this, he says,
will be the work of the Holy Spirit, who is a separate person
from Jesus himself. 'I will ask the Father, and he will give you
another Advocate to be with you forever', Jesus had told them.
The Advocate, or Paraclete, or to give him other names, the
Comforter or Holy Spirit, will give counsel, help, protection,
support, to the disciples, to prepare them for the opposition they
will encounter from the one Jesus refers to as the Prince of this
World, in other words the devil, who has no truth in him at all,
but is a liar and the father of lies, the arch dissimulator in the
area of spirituality.

In his debates with the Scribes and Pharisees, Jesus made the
rather scarifying accusation that those plotting to kill him, and
attempting to destroy his message, were the offspring of the
devil, the devil who loves falsehood and hates whatever is good,
pure, honourable and holy; the devil who murders peace of
mind, happiness and love. Those who follow the devil are incapable of receiving the Holy Spirit, because they are incapable of
seeing or knowing him. But to the disciples at the Last Supper,
Jesus made the solemn promise, 'The Father will give you the
Paraclete to dwell with you forever, … and he will be in you'
(Jn 14:16f). And that word 'forever' means that we too are included in this promise – we, as Scripture says, 'who have been
chosen by God in Christ to be holy and spotless, and to live
through love in his presence' (Ep1:4), love here meaning that
love, primarily, which God has for us. St Paul ended his Letters
to the people of Corinth with this blessing, 'The grace of our
Lord Jesus Christ, and the love of God, and the fellowship of the
Holy Spirit be with you all', words we so often use at the beginning of Mass.

The word 'fellowship' comes from a Greek word (*koinonia*), the meaning of which is very hard to put into English. Paul is praying that the people of Corinth may partake of, or be in communion with, in fellowship with, the Holy Spirit. This Holy Spirit, with whom we too are in communion, bestows on us spiritual gifts, such as those we learned about in our Catechism days, wisdom, understanding, counsel, knowledge, fortitude, piety and the fear of the Lord. But all of these are begotten of faith, and sustained by faith. In his conversation with Nicodemus – the Pharisee who came to him by night for counsel – Jesus himself emphatically said, 'Unless a man is born of water and the Spirit, he cannot enter the kingdom of God.' Being born of water is a reference to baptism. But, you may ask, what does it mean to be 'born of the Spirit'?

Essentially it signifies being born to a new life which is a life of faith that leads to a new way of living and acting. It is the Holy Spirit alone who can bring about this change in us. We should also remember that, in the early Church, a person was baptised and confirmed on the same day, thus highlighting the special role of the Holy Spirit from the moment one became a member of the Church. The Spirit begets in us a deeper understanding of the teaching of Christ, and assists us in living up to the demands of that teaching. But the Spirit does not coerce or dominate our lives through fear. He is rather God's gracious gift to us, enabling us to become God's children with the privilege of addressing the Almighty and Eternal God as 'our Father'.

The Holy Spirit wants – we might even go so far as to say begs – to be allowed enter into the heart of each of us this day. With the risen Christ he says, 'Behold I stand at the door and knock; if you hear me calling, and open the door, I will come in to you, and eat with you, and you with me.' There has never been another religion in which the god being worshipped first seeks out his worshippers. Coming from the one through whom all things were created, what marvellous respect is here shown for the free-will our God has graciously granted us. 'Let anyone who has ears to hear, listen to what the Spirit is saying.' (Rev 3: 20, 22).

TRINITY SUNDAY
Deut 4:32-34, 39-40; Rom 8:14-17; Mt 28:16-20

The doctrine of the Holy Trinity is the supreme truth from which flows every article of our faith, and so our celebration today is an expression of our belief in God as Father, Son and Holy Spirit, three persons, but one God. No human person has ever gone to heaven and returned to earth with a description of the Trinity. Our information has come solely from the teaching of the divine person, Jesus Christ our Redeemer, and it states emphatically that the Father Almighty is truly and by himself God, that the Eternal Son is truly and by himself God, and that the Holy Spirit is truly and by himself God, and yet there are not three Gods, but rather one God, one God in three divine persons. This is the most mysterious, fundamental and essential teaching in the list of the dogmas of our faith. In practically all of the feasts of the Church calendar year, we beseech God to bestow graces and blessings on us.

But today we forget ourselves, and with reverence and joy we praise and bless the mysterious wonders of God's inner nature, which, however, will remain beyond our understanding until, hopefully one day, we will come before him face to face. Of the three great religions which had their origin in Israel, the Jewish religion, Islam, and Christianity, the first two are Unitarian, that is, God is held to be one person only. But the central doctrine in the Christian religion, we might say the very core of what it teaches, is Trinitarian. In other words, it consists in the veneration of God as Father, Son and Holy Spirit, as well as the belief that this most Holy Trinity in an active way has come into our lives.

The clear message of Christianity is that we can know, love, and serve this Triune God here on earth, as well as see and enjoy him for ever hereafter in heaven. In truth, without the Trinity there would be no heaven, for heaven consists in being drawn into, even becoming part of, the inner life of the Blessed Trinity. And even now, here on earth, we are called to be temples of the most Holy Trinity. 'If anyone loves me', says the Lord, 'he will keep my word, and my Father will love him, and we will come to him, and make our home with him' (Jn 14:23). But it might be said that the Apostle Philip spoke for the majority of us, when he said to Christ at the Last Supper, 'Lord, show us the Father, and then we shall be satisfied'. Philip, as yet, did not grasp that in Jesus Christ he was being confronted with the greatest revelation the human race had ever received concerning the inner, intimate life of God. 'Have I been with you so long, Philip', Christ solemnly said, 'and you still do not know me? To have seen me is to have seen the Father' (Jn 14:8-9).

Earlier on, Jesus had said to the Jews, 'I and the Father are one' (Jn 10:30), and that they did not miss the implication of this, is shown by the fact that on hearing it, they attempted to stone him, stoning to death being the punishment for what the Jews regarded as blasphemy. Later on at the Last Supper, when his Apostles became sad at heart at the prospect of his departure from this world, Jesus assured them that his going would be to their advantage, because unless he went, the Advocate, the Spirit of truth, who proceeds from the Father, would not come to them. The Holy Spirit, moreover, is the Spirit of Christ, who is really within us, who thereby sets us apart, and anoints us, and by his indwelling raises us up as other Christs, to the glory of God the Father.

The common factor in the Christian lives of all the Saints was the degree to which they allowed the Blessed Trinity to become part of their existence – to shape their lives. The prayer and worship, the whole life of the Saint is directed towards God as Father. And this is so because of the close union between every saintly person and Jesus, who is the way to God – and whose entire earthly career, in turn, was an upward movement of love towards the Father. But the saint for his living and striving, his praying, worshipping and loving, depends also on the Holy Spirit. As St Paul says, no one can come to God, nor can anyone say that Jesus is Lord, except by the inspiration of the Holy Spirit. We are baptised into the Church in the name of the Father, the Son and the Holy Spirit. We begin and end most of our prayers with reference to it, and in this name the Church bids each Christian soul, at the end of its life, to go forth from its earthly dwelling to see God face to face for all eternity. We beseech the one God in three divine Persons, this day, that such may be our privilege as well.

THE BODY AND BLOOD OF CHRIST
Ex 24:3-8; Heb 9:11-15; Mk 14:12-16, 22-26

In St Mark's gospel, the thing that strikes one as rather strange about the account of the Last Supper is, that while most of it is concerned with the preparations, relatively little is said about the actual meal itself. And the explanation is, that what Jesus said and did at the Last Supper, had already become part of the liturgy of the Mass, in Mark's Church, when his gospel was being written. It was something that Christians were already quite familiar with through their celebration of the Eucharist. Because of their familiarity with the liturgy and sacrifices of the Old Testament, what took place in the Upper Room on Holy Thursday night was also more readily grasped and more meaningful for those early Christians than it is for us.

As we celebrate the Feast of the Body and Blood of Christ, we should then, with the assistance of the Holy Spirit, try and set right this imbalance, and keep on seeking a deeper understanding and appreciation of the marvellous gift of the Eucharist which Christ has left us; for no other sacrament contributes more to our salvation. Setting aside Penance, it is the one we receive most often, and is also the mainstay of our relationship with God. The Holy Eucharist, first of all, from the viewpoint of the Old Testament, is both a covenant meal and a sacrificial meal. You might ask what does covenant mean.

But you should be quite familiar with that word because at every Mass it is used at the consecration of the chalice – 'This is my blood, the blood of the new and everlasting covenant.' In ancient times entering into a covenant was a very common, but also very important, method of maintaining peace and order. There was as yet no such thing as a police force, and so the idea of covenant, or pact, between cities, or tribes, or nations, was a protective measure in every-day life. But a covenant between God and man, as mentioned in the first reading, was something unique which originated with the Chosen People. This was a covenant between unequals, whereby the people solemnly promised to abide by the commandments and be faithful to God, in return for his protection of them. The making of a covenant was always sealed with a sacrifice. Since the slaying of the sacrificial victim was a once-for-all action which could not be revoked, so the offering of sacrifice was a sign of total, and absolute commitment to the terms of the covenant. Further-more, the people identified with the sacrifice by eating portion of the victim being offered. Meal-sharing was regarded as very sacred in antiquity. One did not sit down to eat with an enemy. But, by eating, one signified acceptance of, and respect for the person providing the meal.

The old covenant between God and the Israelites was renewed several times. But it was superseded by the 'new and everlasting covenant' signified by the sacrifice of Jesus Christ on Calvary. The Eucharist is the continuation and making present of this new covenant, and as the old covenants were inaugurated by eating of the sacrificial victim, so our participation in the Eucharist, the covenant meal of the New Testament, is not really complete without receiving Holy Communion. Some modern theologians would even go so far as to regard attendance at Mass, without receiving, as being of doubtful spiritual value.

By partaking of the divine victim we identify with him and with one another, and so the Eucharist becomes a community meal. In the Third Eucharistic Prayer we say, 'Grant that we, who are nourished by his body and blood, may be filled with his Holy Spirit, and become one Body, one Spirit, in Christ.' When, during the Mass, the priest says, 'The Body of Christ' to each one who receives Holy Communion, the answer 'Amen' means 'Yes, I believe this is Christ's body, I want to be identified with it, I want to be a true member of the believing community who wish to be united in it. I want, after the example of Christ, to be made over completely to the will of the Father. I want to be part of the everlasting covenant with the Father, which is guaranteed by the Mass.' If we really mean all this, then the Blessed Eucharist will truly become for us the pledge of our resurrection to glory. Each one will truly be able to say with St Paul, 'I live now not with my own life but with the life of Christ who lives with me. The life I now live in this body I live in faith; faith in the Son of God who loved me and sacrificed himself for me' (Gal 2:20f).

NINTH SUNDAY OF THE YEAR
Deut 5:12-15; 2 Cor 4:6-11; Mk 2:23-3:6

'The sabbath was made for man, not man for the sabbath; so the Son of Man is master even of the sabbath.' In this saying of Christ in today's gospel reading, we are being told that it was for the benefit of humankind that God ordained the sabbath. The full statement was intended to be a reaction to the false under-standing of the sabbath, in particular by the Pharisees, in the Old Testament era, who surrounded it with all kinds of regulations that required something akin to a slavish observance of it. Christ here is stating very clearly that the sabbath was God's gift to his chosen people, as of course is Sunday which for Christians has replaced the Saturday observation of it among the Jews. It was meant to be a day of leisure, a day of celebration, a day for reflect-ion on the wonders of creation and the hope of eternal happiness held out to us because of his own passion and resurrection. Indeed the word Sabbath is the anglicised version of the Hebrew word Shabbath, which means repose.

The fact that Christ defended his disciples, when they were accused by the Pharisees of breaking the sabbath laws, tells us a lot about Christ and his understanding of the sabbath. He was against the numerous restrictions and human laws which had come to surround it, and which did not take into consideration human needs and immediate requirements. Blind obedience to a whole code of regulations, as demanded by the Pharisees, can have the effect of restricting God's love and mercy, while ignoring his command to love one another and share our bread willingly. Religion that is sincere and authentic should be a liberating influence in our lives.

Yet how true it is that God's will is regarded by so many peo-ple as a threat to their freedom, something involving coercion, disappointment, even suffering. That attitude will surely prevail when Sunday observance is given mere lip service, such as regarding attendance at Mass as something we have to do. Strict observance of the Lord's day must of course allow provision for basic human requirements. The sick must be taken care of, meals must be served, trains, buses, planes must operate. We must never regard Sunday as being there for the benefit of God. Rather is it we ourselves who are meant to benefit from it. Celebrating it in a loving and thoughtful way should have the effect of making us more human, and more in the image of the God who brought us into being.

When life is pleasant and serene how rarely we attribute this to a benevolent God, but in times of adversity we complain, 'Why does God allow this to happen to me?' Whenever we begin to regard religious practice as being our entitlement to the good things of this world, it will undoubtedly cease to be a liberating factor in our lives. It will instead become an oppressor, not a servant. However, God's will for us is always nothing other than his love. To accept God's will is to accept his love. Hence the acceptance of God's will is for ever the only basis of our true welfare and happiness, and should be recognised by us as such.

Indeed if we try by every means at our disposal to reshape God's love into a form that fits into our narrow vision of him, if, in other words, we try and manipulate God, then we are no better than the hypocrites and pagans that Jesus spoke of. At all times we have to try and follow the example of Christ, who was always ready to accept God the Father as he is in himself. 'Not my will, but thine be done', was his prayer. In one sentence, which at first sight is rather confusing, St Augustine summed up what our approach to God should be, 'To please God', he wrote, 'is to be pleased with God'. That phrase, 'to be pleased with God', means to be filled with the firm conviction that there is nothing more precious, in this whole wide world, than God. 'Pray with all your heart', Augustine used to tell his congregation, 'and love God without looking for any gain. Then your prayer will reach God whom you have come to love unselfishly'.

This kind of prayer can be defined simply as 'a desire for God', and if this desire, this longing for God, becomes part of our inner being and is discernible deep within us every time we look into ourselves, then our life has become one continuous prayer. We have reached the stage where we are fulfilling Christ's own precept that we should pray always. We might say that each day of our life will then have become one long Sunday, one continuous Lord's day.

TENTH SUNDAY OF THE YEAR
Gen 3:9-15; 2 Cor 4:13 - 5:1; Mk 3:20-35

If you read the gospels carefully, one of the questions you are
bound to come up against is, why did Jesus so readily forgive
even the greatest sinners. To err is human, to forgive divine.
Never once do we find him condemning any of them – and yet,
at the same time, he had extremely harsh things to say about the
Scribes and Pharisees, regarded by many of their contemporaries
as the religious elite of the day. The answer, possibly, is that the
greatest evil, in the eyes of God, is not to be imperfect, but rather
to deny before the world that one is imperfect, to refuse to admit
that each one has within him or her, an area of darkness, that
cries out for the healing touch of God's tender mercy, without
which we are helpless. Indeed the greatest proof of the existence
of the devil lies in the immoral behaviour, the senseless cruelty,
envy and jealousy, the acts of racism and genocide, the unrelenting
search for wealth and power so common in the world of which
we are part.

In the twentieth century, which held out so much promise for
freedom and equality, we think of the concentration camps and
prisons, where the torturers were very good husbands, tender
fathers, obliging neighbours, who said they were carrying out
orders. We think of so many professions and businesses where
deals are often negotiated through bribes, commissions and
what we refer to as influence or pull. We think of a world where
famine is combined with over-production, where one-third of
the population is over-fed, and the other two-thirds suffer from
malnutrition or even starvation. And all this is not because of
deliberate wickedness, or hatred, or oppression. It is the result of
circumstances which individuals often seem incapable of avoiding. All of us, unless we are deceiving ourselves like the
Pharisees, have felt from time to time the insidious power of evil
at work within us, even to the extent of gaining control over our
wills. The devil of course never appears in person before us, but,
as Cardinal Newman once said, a little money and luxury, a little
selfish gratification, a little honour, is enough for him to hold us
helpless in his grasp.

However, the great message of redemption, foretold in the
words of God to the serpent in the garden of Eden, is that evil
will be overcome, that there exists a redemption even after the

worst moral collapse. 'The offspring of the woman will crush your head, and you will lie in wait for its heel.' The offspring referred to here is Christ, the promised Redeemer. A great saint once said that the devil is the one in whom there is no love; and the one thing he fears is love. Our victory over evil is achieved by the love that comes from God and cures us of ourselves, begetting a return of love for God, love for goodness, for truth, for justice, for mercy. We should not imagine that God shows us his love only if we are keeping all the commandments and living good lives. No, God's love for us does not depend on our goodness.

Even when enmeshed in the trawls of sin, God still loves us, as we know from the example of Jesus Christ his Son. While on earth, he was called the friend of sinners – sinners like Mary Magdalene, out of whom he had cast seven devils, like Zaccheus, the despised tax-collector, like the adulterous woman who was about to be stoned, like the good thief on the cross. No matter what our failures are, they can never separate us from the tremendous love of God for us. There is difficulty in reconciling this with the saying in the gospel reading today, that those who blaspheme against the Holy Spirit will never have forgiveness. These are the people who were once followers of Christ and shared in his Spirit, but now spurn and even mock him. Such souls, being guilty of apostasy and deliberate rejection of God's grace, are no longer capable of repenting.

But remember God does not want us to live in fear. St Gertrude, a German Benedictine nun of the 13th century, who was a forerunner of devotion to the Sacred Heart of Jesus, was told by the Sacred Heart in a vision, 'Some people tie the bandage of their own unworthiness so tightly about their eyes, that they cannot see me and my love.' Almost a thousand years earlier we find St Augustine declaring the same idea. 'I ask myself', he says, 'whether the fear of punishment hanging over a person does not make that person worse rather than better'. Let us then rejoice and be glad, for sinners though we are, the Lord truly loves us and will save us, if we but trust in him.

ELEVENTH SUNDAY OF THE YEAR
Ezk 17:22-24; 2 Cor 5:6-10; Mk 4:26-34

Jesus said to the crowd: 'This is what the kingdom of God is like.' Nowhere, however, does Jesus tell us in so many words what the kingdom of God is. He only tells us what it is like, or that it is near. Moreover, it is with great difficulty that we can arrive at any understanding of its original meaning. The Pharisees equated it with total and absolute observance of the Mosaic Law; the Zealots saw it as a political state established by force of arms with God as supreme ruler; the Essenes despairing of the society of their day imagined it as heralding the end of the world, and so they withdrew to Qumran and elsewhere, in the Dead Sea wilderness, to await its coming. Even through the centuries, among Christians, it has been interpreted in various ways.

Nevertheless there is no doubt but that the heart of Jesus' message about the kingdom is summed up in his first recorded words in Mark's gospel (1:15), 'Repent and believe in the good news.' The word 'repent' has a deeper meaning than just being sorry. 'Repent, for the kingdom of heaven is close at hand' (Mt 3:2), John the Baptist told those who went out into the desert to listen to him. And Peter preaching to the crowd after the first Pentecost said 'You must repent, and every one of you must be baptised in the name of Jesus Christ' (Acts 2:38). Repent is a translation of a Greek word (*metanoia*), which means 'a change of mind'. Thus the Baptist and Peter were urging their listeners to reform their lives, to undergo a conversion that touched their inner being. Conversion here does not mean a change of religion, nor making a special effort to keep the commandments, although these can be part of it. Conversion is a total and utter change of mind and heart.

This is what St Paul was trying to get the Ephesians to do when he told them, 'Your mind must be renewed by a spiritual revolution' (4:23). The kingdom of God becomes for people a search for peace, freedom, justice, a meaning to life itself. Left to one's own resources a person is incapable of acquiring these. But they can be attained by faith, by trusting absolutely in God, and seeing him as a loving Father. In the gospels God is called Father no less than 170 times. In the Old Testament, God was described as Father also, but Jesus introduced something unique. Not only did he speak of God as Father; he addressed him as Father. God is near, Jesus proclaimed, and he accepted people no matter what they had done. God's kindness and loving care knows no limits: it extends even to such insignificant creatures as sparrows. 'Can you not buy five sparrows for two pennies. And yet not one is forgotten in God's sight' (Lk 12:6).

The coming of the kingdom is the revelation that God is in love – in love with all his creatures. But this does not mean that human beings are merely called to bask in this love. Rather is the call to us, repent, change your mind, change it utterly, trust in God, believe in Christ's message. This is the challenge the Christian is confronted with. Our response in faith becomes our reply to God's love, and is at the same time love for God and love for our neighbour. Christ in his preaching of the kingdom promises the fulfilment of all human hopes, expectations and longings for a transformation of the world. The blind are to see, the lame walk, the deaf hear, the dead to be raised up and the poor to have the good news preached to them. Those whom Christ calls blessed are not the propertied, but rather the poor, the hungry, the mourners, the despised and persecuted.

This does not imply that Christ had in mind a programme for social reform. He was a realist. 'The poor you always have with you', he said (Mk 14:7). He shows no hatred towards the rich, but receives and accepts their invitations. His poor are those who have nothing to expect from the world, but expect everything from God. They have been driven to the limits of endurance, and are beggars before God. Only from God can they expect help. And God, in the person of Christ, did not distance himself from such, people like the despised tax-collectors, the lepers , the harlots, the public sinners who were held up to public contempt as being godless.

But God is love, and the coming of God's kingdom means that salvation is at hand for everyone. For, as evidenced in the person of Christ, love is stronger than hatred, than persecution, than injustice, stronger even than death. Love is the only thing which lasts for ever, and what is done out of love endures for ever.

TWELFTH SUNDAY OF THE YEAR
Job 38:1, 8-11; 2 Cor 5:14-17; Mk 4:35-41

Those of us who studied apologetics in our school days will
remember the proofs of the existence of God, and how the proof
from order was one of them. The argument that the order in our
universe came about by chance, we were told, was as impossible
to maintain as the proposition that the parts of a watch came
together accidentally. Nowadays, the proofs of the existence of
God seem to have been forgotten by theologians, but oddly
enough they appear, at least in part, to be in the process of re-
habilitation by none other than scientists. A very interesting article,
recently, had this to say: 'Many scientists now find the laws of
nature and the structure, order, complexity and beauty of the
universe difficult to explain in the absence of a creator.' Indeed,
so complex and finely proportioned are the requirements for the
emergence of living beings in this universe, that those who regard
it as the outcome of chance are forced into claiming the existence
of an infinite number of universes, one of which would inevitably have the right conditions for this to take place. If belief
in God requires faith, which of course is true, belief in the non-
existence of God, the article says, may even require greater faith.

   One thing is certain, that for everyone, whether in the past or
here and now, God remains the great unknowable. Indeed,
according to St Augustine, we can state more about what God is
not, than what God is. However – and this is the point of today's
gospel – we can experience God. We can experience him in
moments of great joy and elation, experience him in moments of
sorrow and loneliness, when we sense his sustaining hand,
experience him in moments of fear and anxiety, as did the disciples in that storm-tossed boat in today's gospel story. 'Who can
this be', they found themselves wondering, after what happened,
'that even the winds and the sea obey him?' – something that
modern science, despite all its advances, is incapable of when
confronted with monsoons and tornados.

   In the broad sense, of course, we have in this story an image
of the Church, which has been so often referred to as the barque
of Peter, the church invoking the assistance of Christ in the
storms which beset it on its pilgrim way towards God. But here
we have symbolised also the life of each one of us. For life seems,
so often, a series of storms, of minor crises, with a major one

thrown in now and again. We see ample illustration of this in the inspired writings God has given to guide us. We see it in great spiritual leaders, like Moses complaining, 'Why Oh Lord, do you treat me so badly, that you load on me the weight of all this people, and say, "Carry them in your bosom", like a nurse with a baby at the breast?' (Num 11:19); like Elijah, the fearless opponent of idolatry fleeing for refuge into the desert, and then wishing he was dead; like Jeremiah, specially chosen by God to call the people he loved to repent, but cursing the day he was born; like Paul, the man who never lacked courage, but being dismayed and alarmed by the hostility and abuse he received at the hands of the Jewish community in Corinth, to the extent that he gave up trying to convert them and instead turned to the gentiles.

Few of us are called to bear this type of witness, but at times of difficulty in our own lives we should take comfort and courage from their example, and the fact that they remained faithful to the very end. While Paul, for example, was in this disturbed state of mind, the Lord said to him one night, in a vision: 'Do not be afraid to speak out ... I am with you. I have so many people on my side in this city that no one will even attempt to hurt you' (Acts 18:9f). And Paul found courage to remain preaching the word of God in Corinth for a full 18 months. St Peter, no stranger to suffering either, wrote: 'Cast all your worries on the Lord, for he cares about you. You may for a short time be plagued with all sorts of trials, so that your faith may be tested and proved like gold' (1 Pet 5:7).

But if you remain steadfast these hardships are not to be compared with the glory, which will one day be yours. As a certain modern writer has put it: 'Fear tells us, as nothing else can, that we cannot save ourselves', that we need God. The story of Christ's death and resurrection reveals to us that darkness is habitable, not only the darkness of storms, but the deeper darkness of death, because God inhabits it – God in the person of his Son, Jesus, has endured death before us, has conquered it, and so shall we if we but have faith and trust in Christ.

THIRTEENTH SUNDAY OF THE YEAR
Wis 1:13-15, 2:23-24; 2 Cor 8:7, 9, 13-15; Mk 5:21-43

When we consider the appearance, the outlook of people we come in contact with, their talents, their behaviour, their values, there is one thing that must surely strike us, and that is how unique each person is. How often does one meet twins who are identical in every physical way, and yet are totally different, mentally and characterwise. But there is one thing which we all have in common. In every one of us there is a flaw, an imperfection, call it the result of upbringing, of environment, or in religious terms the product of original sin. We used to describe this as the predominant fault, and it can be the result of pride, greed, lust, anger, envy, gluttony, or laziness. And the sad thing is how the lives of even good people can become dominated by some inordinate, uncontrollable craving or passion, to the extent that they want only this – live only for this.

The Bible tells us that 'it is a terrible thing to fall into the hands of the living God', because, as the great French writer, Jacques Maritain, said 'those loving hands always give us what we want', what we set before us as the goal to be striven for. Hell is there for our free preferring, or heaven is there for our taking, together with every help needed to attain it. And the real horror of the state of hell lies in the fact that the soul in hell, although well aware that it is still loved with an infinite love by God, is no longer able to fulfil itself by returning that love. It is completely introverted, with no room, no consideration for others.

In today's complete gospel, we have the story of two cures, seemingly different on the outside, but actually closely related. The first, which is omitted from the short gospel, is about the woman with the issue of blood. For the Jews blood was the principle of life, and for this woman the slow loss of blood probably made her feel that life was slipping away from her. The second story tells how the breath of life was restored to a child who had already lost it. The first cure was brought about because of the faith of the woman herself; the second through the faith of the father and friends. In both there is the utter and sincere conviction that Jesus, and only Jesus can cure, that Jesus really wishes life for people. The question is, what is this life which Jesus wishes for us?

Obviously Christ did not come to remove physical death; it

still remains the destiny of each of us, although the Easter Jesus has removed the sting of death. Rather is the life which Christ offers us a moral, a spiritual, an enduring life with God. 'God formed people to be imperishable', the first reading tells us, 'God does not rejoice in the destruction of the living.' When the Book of Wisdom mentions death being repelled by the power of God, we must remember that this book was written before belief in a life hereafter emerged. What the author has in mind is not physical death, but rather spiritual collapse – eternal separation from God. In the Book of Revelation this spiritual death is called the 'second death'. Those who undergo this death must abandon hope, for there is no possibility of a new resurrection.

Revelation states it very graphically. 'But as for cowards, the faithless, perverts, murderers, fornicators, sorcerers, idolaters, and all liars, the place for them is the lake that burns with fire and sulphur, which is the second death' (21:8). The fire and sulphur mentioned are of course symbolic. The devil would alienate us from God, and make us die the second death, the death of the spirit, but Christ by assuming our humanity, can bring us back to God. Physical death, as it appears in today's gospel story, is a symbol of the destruction of this spiritual life; it is the ultimate sign of man's alienation from God. Just as the little girl in the gospel was completely unable to help herself, so are those persons who say, 'I will not serve', people who, like alcoholics, drug addicts and such, become utterly self-centred, spending all their time and energy trying to satisfy their selfish desires.

Whether we are dragging our feet in our pursuit of this spiritual life, which Christ wishes for us, or whether we have attempted to turn our backs completely on it, we must become convinced that Jesus and Jesus only can help us. Let us then renew our faith in our Saviour until it becomes a faith that will move mountains. Let each of us take away and ponder over this thought today – 'God wants me to love him not because God needs it, but because I need it.'

FOURTEENTH SUNDAY OF THE YEAR
Ezk 2:2-5; 2 Cor 12:7-10; Mk 6:1-6

As Christians, it is a good thing now and again to ask ourselves the question, how does it happen that our vision of Christ, our divine Saviour, can be so superficial, and our understanding of the message of salvation, especially in the gospels, can be so vague. The answer surely must be because we have not grown accustomed to meditating in a sincere and earnest way on Christ. Such meditation, it must be said, does not come easily without putting effort into it. We can find it irksome, and our thoughts are prone to switch to other things very quickly. But, come to think of it, if Christ regarded our salvation as being so important that he suffered immensely, yet voluntarily, to bring it about, shouldn't we in turn regard that salvation worth the slight sacrifice of learning to meditate on the one who gave his life to achieve it. It is only by slow degrees that our reflection on Christ and all he went through can begin to melt our cold hearts. Doing so once or twice will not bring about this result. It is by meditating on Christ regularly that, little by little, we grow to appreciate what he has done for us, and a feeling of warmth, and love, and light, develops deep down within us. Without being aware of it we are changing gradually, even as leaves and vegetation emerge in early summer.

We begin to appreciate the depth of the riches, the wisdom, the knowledge of God, the mystery of his decisions and ways, the wonderful changes he can effect in our thinking, in our minds. 'Do not model yourselves on the behaviour of the world around you', St Paul tells us, 'but let your way of behaving be guided by your new mind. Then you will be able to discover the will of God, and know what is good, what is pleasing to him, and the perfect thing to do' (Rom 12:2). This willingness to change we find sadly lacking among the Jews of what was at the time the small town of Nazareth, when Jesus paid a visit to his home place for the first time after the commencement of his public mission. Luke records for us how they even tried to throw him over the cliff outside their town, so great was their rejection of him, and of his preaching elsewhere throughout Galilee and Judaea. Their lack of faith was such that Jesus could not work a single miracle among them, the only place we find this mentioned in the gospels. But even though people are 'defiant and obstinate of heart', as the prophet Ezekiel points out, even though they deliberately close their minds to God's message, nevertheless God does not stop sending his prophets, his witnesses, to proclaim his message to them, whether they listen or not. Ezekiel, Jesus, Paul, each was destined to leave a trail of glory behind him, but the pattern of their mission was a hard slog of daily confrontation with the stony unbelief which by and large greeted their efforts – the insults, hardships, persecutions which the second reading today mentions. Jesus, however, showed complete disinterest in men's judgment of him.

To his contemporaries, even to his disciples he remained an enigma, an unknown quantity, which yielded up some of its secrets only in the light of their post-resurrection faith, and demands on this faith were being made continually. And so, Christ today calls us to renew our faith also, a faith which God will bring to fruition in us despite our weaknesses. 'I have opened a door in front of you', the Book of Revelation (3:8) tells us, 'a door that nobody will be able to close'. We see in the gospels (Mt 16) how Jesus rebuked the Pharisees, because while they could read the face of the sky and thus forecast the weather, they could not read the signs of the times. They could not see the significance of the events taking place before their very eyes; they could not see the door into the kingdom of God, which Jesus was opening.

All of us here this morning have this one thing in common, we are baptised into the one true faith. And as such, each of us is called by God, after the example of Christ, to be his prophet, his messenger, the bearer of some aspect of the gospel, which we give witness to by the kind of lives we lead. Like the great prophets, like the saints, each of us can be a sign, perhaps of unselfishness, of zeal for the spiritual welfare of others, of forbearance in suffering. But if we cease being a sign, then, as some theologians maintain, we can easily become a scandal. We can even be the cause of creating atheism by professing a gospel we do not believe in, by mouthing words which we do not put into practice. We should then this day begin to live for God with mind and faith renewed.

FIFTEENTH SUNDAY OF THE YEAR
Amos 7:12-15; Eph 1:3-14; Mk 6:7-13

I sometimes think that it is a cultural loss to our young generation that it has been more or less cut adrift from the classical literatures that marked the beginning of western civilisation. We look back to the time when the only education available to Irish Catholics was that provided by the hedge schools, and how an Irish poet, Eoghan Rua Ó Súilleabháin, for example who was a product of one of these, could write a poem filled with references drawn from Greek and Roman literature. Among the outstanding literary works of Europe, written by its first great poet, Homer, was the Iliad, mainly mythology, which dealt in part with the siege of Troy. It relates how Cassandra, daughter of the king of Troy, was granted by the god Apollo the gift of being able to foretell events which to everyone else lay hidden in the future. But because she offended him, he decreed also that nobody would believe her predictions. And so the more vehemently she warned against future disasters, the more her prophecies were ignored by the people. They were not prepared to accept, on her word, that their behaviour, their actions, could in any way have tragic consequences.

We are dealing here with legend, but this story paraphrases for us the reactions, in true life, of the people of the Northern Kingdom of Israel to the warnings of the prophet Amos, in today's first reading. It was a time in the history of the Northern Kingdom when there was a superabundance of court prophets, and without offence to our national advisers, one might refer to them as the spin-doctors of that age. They were kept and paid for by the king, and their task was to put before the people, as being the will of God, what really were the secret ambitions and policies of the king himself. Amos refused to be one of these professional prophets, and in turn they banded against him and told him to go home to his own countrymen in the Southern Kingdom of Judah. 'Go away', they said, 'we want no more of your style of prophesying'. Indeed it was Amos alone, who had been given an authentic message by God for the people.

He tried to get them to change, especially in the field of social justice. And it was also Amos who saw that while, outwardly, Israel seemed thriving and healthy, inwardly, it was stricken with a malignant cancer. For not only was it guilty of social injustices, it was also reneging on its call to be in a special way God's people. There would be no more special privileges for Israel, but only disaster. He delivered this warning from God, 'Behold the eyes of the Lord God are upon this sinful kingdom, and I will wipe it off the face of the earth.' God scorned those who tried to bribe him by burning incense in the shrine at Bethel one day in the week, while on the other six days defrauding the poverty-stricken of the nation. But like the warnings of Cassandra, Amos' words fell on deaf ears. Much of his message could be applied to our own age, for he criticised the inequalities amongst the people of that era of so much prosperity, the luxurious dwellings and life-style of the wealthy, their selfish and greedy exploitation of the poor, their lack of concern for justice in the community, the way in which the courts were used to evade the law and perpetuate abuses.

Yes, the people displayed all the outward trappings of religion, but in their hearts there was no place for God. God had sent them warnings through his prophets, but he did not force them to comply with his demands. And so it was that Israel slithered down the slope to its own destruction by the Assyrians, never again to attain the status of an independent kingdom. We see all this re-enacted in the person of Christ and his warnings also. But in Christ's time it was not wealth which was the obstacle, but rather a narrow-minded nationalism, which within a generation later would lead to the final destruction of Jerusalem and the Temple itself. In the light of this we might try and see what is the predominant failing of our own lives, our own society. Is it the greed which confronted the prophet Amos so long ago?

In the gospel, Christ warned his Apostles that people will refuse to listen to them, even as he himself had been ignored; but their message should not be forced on the people. Indeed the odd thing about Jesus' discourses to the Twelve is that he never tells them what to say to people; rather does he stress the kind of lives they themselves should lead. They must give witness to their own faith by what they do, what they hold precious, thus by their example leading others to change too, to accept freely the kingdom of God.

SIXTEENTH SUNDAY OF THE YEAR
Jer 23:1-6; Eph 2:13-18; Mk 6:30-34

Prayer has been defined as a raising up of our minds and thoughts to God, and the greatest difficulty with it, I suppose, is that the person we are addressing remains so unknown to us, and indeed so unknowable. The closer the great mystics came to God, the more they felt themselves surrounded by what they described as impenetrable darkness – what St John of the Cross called 'the dark night of the soul'. The nearest glimpse of God, most of us ordinary people get, comes through contemplating the Incarnation of God on earth, in the person of Christ Jesus our Lord, when we read about him and meditate on him, in the gospel accounts of his public life. St Peter urges us to cast all our worries before Christ, because he cares about us (1 Pet 5:7).

This care is manifested in a very touching way in today's gospel reading that describes the return of the Apostles, tired and wearied out after their first missionary endeavours. 'You must come away to some lonely place, all by yourselves, and rest for awhile', is how Christ greets them, since with all the crowds thronging round and following him, they would not even have time to eat in peace. And yet he refuses to send away these throngs; rather does he welcome them, listen to them, give advice to them, provide the very food they needed. If Christ was like this while on earth, will he not be the same towards us now after his resurrection?

All of this is in stark contrast to the behaviour of the lazy shepherds mentioned in the reading from the prophet Jeremiah. These lazy shepherds were primarily the Jewish kings who allowed themselves to be swayed by personal ambition and greed rather than attempt to cure the social ills of their day. But in this category also we might include all those who exploit others in the society of which they are part, rather than serve them as they were meant to – all of us indeed, who should be helping each other in solidarity and brotherhood, yet through our own selfishness, fail in the role which God has allotted us. The worst sin against others, it has been pointed out, springs not from hatred but from indifference (G. B. Shaw).

This is in stark contrast as well to God, who said to the people of Israel through the prophet Jeremiah, 'I have loved you with an everlasting love, and am constant in my affection for you' (31:3).

Christ pitied the people because they were like sheep without a shepherd. Today we see how people become frightened, shattered, lost, all because of the way society is organised, because of their disenchantment with declining standards of behaviour. Secularists, industrialists, trade unionists and others, indeed to a certain extent all of us, quite often pursue a policy of living for ourselves, of taking all that we can from our environment without thought for the less favoured or for future generations. People are striving, if sometimes unwittingly, for the maximum return for their own efforts, while regardless of the cost to others. If we follow these selfish trends in unthinking fashion, the tragedy is that life will cease to have meaning; there will be no genuine goal to aim at that will beget a feeling of self-fulfilment.

A modern philosopher has put it this way: 'Humanity's sickness is that it has nothing to believe in ..., people cannot live without a sense of significance'. Humans can never be satisfied if they are regarded merely as economic factors, or cogs in a giant industrial wheel. Let us, for our part, consider this day that people have a spiritual side to them also, and that apart from their material aspirations, they seek, like St Augustine did for twenty years, to acquire spiritual fulfilment as well. Christ, as we see in the gospel, was above all the man for others. He emptied himself of his divine glory and became the servant of the servants of God. But of course, as St Augustine said, 'God who made us without our consent, will not save us without our consent.' We must be of one mind with him. Furthermore, our consent must not be mere words; it must be accompanied by actions. 'My mother and my brothers,' Christ told the people, 'are those who hear the word of God, and put it into practice' (Lk 8:21).

We can be certain that by striving to do this we can become an influence for good in the community of which we are part. Somebody has said that it is better to light a single candle than curse the darkness. If Christianity could but capture once again the idea of service, that Christ gave us, it would restore once more the meaning of life, and the significance for others of the work we find ourselves doing.

SEVENTEENTH SUNDAY OF THE YEAR
2 Kgs 4:42-44; Eph 4:1-6; Jn 6:1-15
'Though the mills of God grind slowly, they grind exceedingly
small', is a Greek saying that comes from ancient times. It is a
good thing to go back in time and reflect on the providence of
God preparing, in gradual and unexpected ways, the ground of
the faith we profess. The cradle of civilisation linked with urban-
based society was Mesopotamia, the land of the rivers Tigris and
Euphrates of modern Iraq. This civilisation flourished centuries
before that of Egypt, and instead of being nomadic, its people
began to live in cities, something which required enterprise,
organisation, and new codes of law. It was over-run about 3,500
BC by an Asiatic race, the Sumerians, who were responsible for
some brilliant changes – irrigation by a network of canals, huge
building projects such as walled cities and towering ziggurats to
honour their gods – the tower of Babel derived from these – and
above all the development of a system of writing, called
cuneiform, wedge-shaped marks on clay tablets that formed an
alphabet. One of their cities was Ur, the birthplace of Abraham,
the father in faith of the Jewish people and of all of us Christians
too.

It was a giant step forward, demanding courage and trust,
for Abraham to abandon the gods his people worshipped, to
forsake his own relatives, leave his native country, and come to
believe in, and worship the one true God whom his successors
adore to this day. An interesting thing about the Sumerian
language is that the word for slave was foreigner, and the
descendants of Abraham who had sought refuge from famine in
Egypt, because they were foreigners, in time were subjected to
slavery, especially in the building projects of the Pharaohs.

The economy of most historic nations in ancient times was
sustained by slavery. For example, a fourth century BC census of
Attica, a province of Greece, listed 400,000 slaves, half the total
population. Slaves were regarded as low-grade human beings,
and their masters had the power of life and death over them.
When Moses led the chosen people out of Egypt and into the
Sinai wilderness to escape this slavery, they soon discovered
that freedom in the desert was a somewhat poor substitute for
slavery back in Egypt. Existence in this barren region was pre-
carious, water was scarce, and they sighed after the fleshpots of
Egypt, and the bread and vegetables they could eat there to their

hearts' content. The result was a lack of faith in God, and rebellion against Moses. 'Is the Lord with us or not?' they complained. They quickly tired of the manna and quails God sent them as food. The complaint of God through the prophet Jeremiah much later applied then also, 'They did not listen, they did not pay attention; they followed the dictates of their own evil hearts, and turned their backs on me' (7:24).

This hardness of heart was shown towards Jesus, God's own divine Son as well. People could not bring themselves to admit that there was anything special about him, so ordinary did he appear. In our own time some Christians seem to be posing the question, 'Is the Lord with us or not?', by their attitude to the Eucharistic species. But unless we firmly believe that Christ is truly present under the appearance of bread and wine, after the words of consecration have been said over them, we are not true followers of Christ. For where a handful of Christians, however few, come together to celebrate the Eucharist, there is Christ in the midst of them (Mt 18:20). In other words, the Eucharist in the Church bears enduring witness before all ages that Christ has risen from the dead, that he is really present, at this very moment in his Church.

The gospel story of the miraculous feeding of the multitude is a unique sign to us that Christ is the one who sustains us, not only by his living word, but with the gift of his very self in the bread of the Eucharist. During the first World War a saintly priest in France (Pere Lamy) was given three reasons by our Lord as to why that conflict began. These were blasphemy, the desecration of marriage, and working on Sunday. We don't have to turn to Europe to find evidence of the continued existence of these three sinful habits. Sad to say they are increasingly becoming part of our Irish way of life today, and the precious Christian heritage which has been entrusted to us will be slowly eroded unless we make room for Christ in our lives, and in particular by our love for the sacrifice of the Mass keep the Lord's Day holy.

EIGHTEENTH SUNDAY OF THE YEAR
Ex 16:2-4, 12-15; Eph 4:17, 20-24; Jn 6:24-35

One of the truly great masterpieces of fiction was the satirical story of Don Quixote, by the Spanish writer Cervantes. In it we read how the absurdly chivalrous hero, followed by his squire Sancho Panza, set out to find adventure, to perform deeds of bravery and win the admiration of all those close to him. He had such an open mind in this quest that he decided to go wherever his horse Rosinante would lead him. But the horse, finding itself given free rein, naturally returned to the place it knew best, its own stable. Too often perhaps, we humans find ourselves going the same way, doing the same thing, returning to the same sinful habits again and again, sometimes also drifting aimlessly, sometimes lured on by the novelty of sensationalism, sometimes a prey to the enticements of others, or carried away by the latest fashion in religion.

St Paul, in today's second reading, is quite adamant in his condemnation of that kind of haphazard behaviour. 'I want to urge you in the name of the Lord', he says, 'not to go on living the aimless kind of life that pagans live'. The inner life of pagans was one in which human weakness led to countless moral failures, and the pursuit of a career of indecency of every kind, very often culminating in permanent spiritual collapse. However, 'if we live by the truth and in love, we shall grow in all ways into Christ, who is the head by whom the whole body is fitted and joined together, until it has built itself up, in love' (4:15f). In other words, Christ must be seen before the whole world to be a living influence in the lives of all his true followers.

But as against this, if people concern themselves only with immoral things, their understanding will be darkened, and, worst of all, their hearts will be petrified, that is to say they become like stone. This lapsing into sin is quite discernible to others. There is a certain mystery attached to sin, but we can say for certain that nobody becomes a sinner all at once. When people first become aware by the light of their conscience that they have fallen into sin, they regard the action, which led to this, with horror and regret. But if they ignore this, if they continue with their sinful ways, there will inevitably come a time when they will lose all sense of wrongdoing, when they will even commit the most shameful actions without any feeling of guilt whatsoever.

At that stage the conscience will have become petrified, a dead thing incapable of discerning right from wrong.

In the gospel story of the people who followed Jesus all along the shore of the lake which, after the miraculous multiplication of the loaves and fishes, he had crossed by boat, we have the example of people who were concerned solely with satisfying their bodily needs. They were so enthusiastic about this sudden abundance of food that they decided to ensure its continuation. And so they wanted to make Jesus a king. The were totally blind to the spiritual content of the miracle, and the message Jesus wanted them to draw from it. 'Do not work for food that cannot last', Jesus warned them, 'but work for food that endures to eternal life, the kind of food the Son of Man is offering you'.

With us too, it so often happens that we are willing to follow Christ – even to seek him out with a certain kind of zeal – but on our own conditions, namely, that he should solve our immediate problems, and grant us the requests we make of him. If we feel he has let us down, we sometimes go so far as to contemplate turning our backs on him. But never on such conditions will Christ draw near to us. We must seek him for himself, and not for what we can get from him. The bread come down from heaven referred to by Jesus is the Blessed Eucharist, and the proper reception of this requires that we open ourselves to God's love which comes to us in the person of Jesus. Furthermore it demands of us acceptance of others as well. Unlike those who abandoned Jesus when no more bread was forthcoming, we must keep on trying to be his faithful followers.

This will most certainly be achieved if we place our trust firmly in his divine help which is there for the asking. 'Work for your salvation in fear and trembling', the New Testament urges us, and then goes on to reassure us, 'It is God who gives you both the will and the ability to act, and thus achieve his own purpose' (Phil 2:12f). It is a further consolation and encouragement to us that we could not begin to seek God, if he had not already found us.

NINETEENTH SUNDAY OF THE YEAR
1 Kgs 19:4-8; Eph 4:30 - 5:2; Jn 6:41-51

A common excuse, often given by people who do not go to church or practise their religion publicly, is: 'I don't want to have any thing to do with institutionalised religion. I seek God in my own private way.' Sadly, however, such an attempt to break away from the Church, from every kind of religious bond with others, can result in isolating oneself in what an eminent East European writer and politician has described as 'a foxhole of purely material existence'. Of course it is only God who can see into the motives and actions of each one of us; it is God who leads each of us by paths we are often not even aware of, that is, provided we are really willing in our submission to his will for us. But of this we can be certain, that, ordinarily, we place our eternal salvation at risk if we ignore the common channels of grace which Christ has left to us, especially if we cut ourselves off from the sacramental life of the Church which Christ founded on the Apostles.

Jesus brings this home to us in his parable of the rich man and Lazarus. The rich man in Hades implored Abraham to send Lazarus back from the dead to his five brothers on earth, to warn them to change their lives and so escape the torments he himself was enduring. But the reply of Abraham was, 'They have Moses and the prophets; let them listen to them.' In other words the rich man's brothers should avail of the ordinary means of salvation open to all the chosen people.

The pilgrimage of the prophet Elijah to Mount Sinai has a lesson for us also. For we too are members of a pilgrim Church on its way to the God who transcends this world. Like Elijah we too are in need of refreshment and strength to face the difficulties and perils that we encounter on our journey. We are in perpetual need of reform, of being renewed again in spirit, even as the Church herself is. The question is where do we seek this renewal. The immediate answer must be in the sacraments, which are the visible and effective signs of Christ's continued presence on earth; and it is only through the intervention of Christ that we can be raised to a new level spiritually.

You may have noticed the recurring theme of the Eucharist in the readings of the past three Sundays. The danger is always there, that we can become indifferent to the sense of the presence of Christ in our Church, even in the sacraments. This is something we cannot afford to do, especially when we celebrate the Mass. We must keep reminding ourselves, that in the Mass we are commemorating Christ's Last Supper in the upper room, his death on the cross, and his resurrection from the dead. In the Mass Christ becomes truly and efficaciously present here among us; and he becomes present in a closely personal and intimate way in each of us when we receive Holy Communion. In the words of the Second Vatican Council, 'every liturgical celebration, because it is an action of Christ, the High Priest, and of his Body, the Church, is a sacred action, surpassing all private acts of worship or prayer'.

To repeat, the Council is, in fact, saying that every celebration of the liturgy – and this especially applies to the Mass – is far more pleasing to God than any private prayers or worship, and the two agents which give rise to it are Christ and the Church. In particular, in the Eucharistic celebration, we are taken up into communion with Christ, and with one another. For the Eucharist is a sacrament of love, a sign of unity, a bond of charity, drawing us together into the one Body which is Christ. And this sacred action is something that proceeds without interruption. For the sacrifice of Christ never ceases. He is forever being immolated on the altar, and forever a victim in the tabernacle of every church. Moreover, Christ assures us , 'where two or three meet together in my name, I will be there with them'.

But if we choose to isolate ourselves from the believing community, carve out for ourselves the 'foxholes of purely material existence', which were referred to already, then Christ will inevitably pass us by. As the English poet John Donne said, 'No man is an Island, entire of itself; every man is a piece of the Continent, a part of the main' (Devotions). Whether in the world of every day life, or in the spiritual sphere, we need each other. We need the example, the encouragement, the prayers of others, so that, with them, we may answer the call of Christ's Spirit to form in him and through him, one family, one People of God.

TWENTIETH SUNDAY OF THE YEAR
Prov 9:1-6; Eph 5:15-20; Jn 6:51-58

From time to time, it is a good and very necessary thing that each of us should ask the question, 'Has my life got a goal, a purpose? What in particular am I striving for? Does existence in this world have a meaning for me?' This striving to understand the purpose of life on earth was a common feature of the ancient civilisations in the Middle-East, in the centuries before Christ, and it gave rise to what is called 'Wisdom literature' in Sacred Scripture. The concept of wisdom is one which defies exact definition, for it was concerned, not so much with philosophical thought as with the practical living out of one's life. We could say that wisdom was the legacy about life and living that parents transmitted, as a most precious heritage, to their children. It consisted primarily of practical advice to the young on how to attain a good and successful life; but as well it tried to provide answers to people's anguish about the meaning of life and death. Thus it was that the home served as the focal point in the education of youth, wherein sayings and maxims such as those we find in the Book of Proverbs were passed on.

For Israel, especially, real wisdom began with the fear of God, and so a spiritual element came to the fore. 'What does the Lord your God ask of you? Only this: to fear the Lord your God, to follow all his ways, to love him, to serve the Lord your God with all your heart and all your soul' (Deut 10:12). Life was more than eating and drinking people agreed, and this was echoed in the New Testament. 'Do not drug yourselves with wine', St Paul warns in the Second Reading, 'this is simply dissipation'. 'Leave your folly and you will live; walk in the ways of perception', the First Reading advises us. 'Walk in the ways of perception.' This is a call to reflect on the meaning of life, and what we do perceive, most of us can truly say, is that each of us has a longing, an inner craving for happiness and security. And since we are God's creatures, theologians stress that this longing must have been implanted in us by God.

However, by and large, we tend to have two entirely separate concepts of what constitutes true happiness. On the one hand we might identify it with such things as good health, prosperity, friendships, success in the here and now. Or, taking a long-term view, we could take it to mean attainment, when we die, to that eternal bliss which we call heaven. But it is an illusion to view happiness here and now and the happiness of heaven as two entirely distinct states. For our only true and perfect happiness, both on earth and in heaven, consists in the possession of God. This is the kernel of Jesus' message. 'As I ... myself draw life from the Father, so whoever eats me will draw life from me.'

While Jesus was still a little child, Mary and Joseph had begun to learn that the coming of the promised Saviour did not, for them, mean comfort, or wealth, or freedom from the hostility of officialdom. We must not base our faith and trust in God on what he does for us, but rather simply on what he is. For as well as being our God, we must come to accept him, to love him as our Father. The only thing God expects of us is that we desire him alone, a desire to be expressed in him alone. We must abandon ourselves completely to his fatherly care, his providence and love for us.

Moreover, the Christian life we are asked to live should never be one of gloom, or rigidity, or harshness. That would be a return to the false creed of Jansenism, which in essence came to regard human nature as being radically corrupt and depraved. Of course Christ had promised his Apostles at the Last Supper, 'If you keep my commandments you will remain in my love.' But keeping the commandments was never meant to be a thankless task. For Christ went on to say, 'I have told you this so that my own joy may be in you, and that your joy may be complete' (Jn 15:10f). To see this in practice we should ponder as well the words of St Paul, where he says to go on singing to the Lord in our hearts while giving thanks to God, who is our Father, in the name of the Lord Jesus.

'Rejoice in the Lord always', he told the Philippians. 'Again I say to you rejoice. Let your good sense be obvious to everybody. The Lord is very near. Never worry about anything; but reveal to God all your desires of every kind in prayer and petition with thanksgiving, and the peace of God which passes all understanding will keep your hearts and minds in Christ Jesus ... Then the God of peace will be with you' (Phil 4:4f).

THE ASSUMPTION OF THE BVM

Vigil: 1 Chron 15:3-4, 15-16, 16: 1-2; 1 Cor 15:54-57; Lk 11:27-28
Feast: Apoc 11:19, 12:1-6, 10; 1 Cor 15:20-27; Lk 1:39-56

One of the tragedies of the present age, it has been said, is the loss of zest for life, the absence of love and respect for life. This disregard for the value and preciousness of human existence on earth arises in part from a lost vision of the future; and the feast we are celebrating today asks us to look forward to life hereafter in the company of Christ, his Blessed Mother, and the entire body of saints for all eternity. The liturgy confronts us with three great mysteries that surround the person of Mary. There is her sinlessness from the first moment of her conception, her extraordinary privilege of being the mother of God, and the fact that after her death God raised her and she was taken up body and soul into heaven. The first reading about the woman clothed with the sun, and the moon at her feet, is a piece of scripture which had a very deep significance for the Church of the Middle Ages. It is, by the way, one of the most difficult passages, in the whole of the New Testament, to try and unravel what the author meant when writing it.

Some commentators hold that the birth of the Messiah referred to is not the nativity of Jesus in Bethlehem, but rather his birth to a new existence on Easter Sunday morning. The birth pangs referred to then become the sufferings he endured on the Cross. In actual fact the birth of Jesus at Bethlehem, many maintain, was virginal and therefore painless. The dragon mentioned is Satan, who represents the powers of evil which are forever hostile to God and his people. Because theologians in the Middle Ages, nevertheless, recognised the Assumption of the Virgin Mother of God as being in some way signified in the woman clothed with the sun, it made people look forward with hope, and even longing, to their own future beyond the grave.

In this feast the Church gives all of us a pledge of resurrection to a new life hereafter. We shall be like Christ, it keeps telling us, and it puts before us what happened to Mary's body after death, as a pledge of the truth of what it is claiming. Mary, a purely human person, has been taken up, body and soul, to be forever with her Divine Son. But the Assumption into heaven, or the glorification of Mary, to give it another name, does not mean that Mary has abandoned everyone living still on this earth, that

she is in the special abode of the sanctified, far removed from all
of us. Rather is it true, that by it, Mary has come all the more personally close to us. Her loving gaze is fixed forever on her risen
Son, but also on his brothers and sisters, who are still here on
earth. Her whole glorified existence is one of praise to God, is
one of thanks to God, is one of intercession with God for each
and every one of us. For what she is, she is through Christ, and
what she does, she does through Christ. Her Son of course is a
divine person, and Mary, while remaining a human person,
reflects the person of Jesus in a manner more perfect than any
other human being could possibly do.

Mary's great privilege and prerogative is that she has been,
and continues to be in a most unique way, the instrument of
God's mercy, God's plan for our redemption. His plan depended
on her 'fiat', her saying, 'Be it done unto me, according to your
word.' Her response to God's call was complete and utterly
unselfish, and so she was to become the new ark of the covenant,
the dwelling-place of the divine One on earth. It follows that
Mary is a sign of the Church also, the Church which now brings
Christ to mankind as Mary brought him into this world, and, by
the merits of her divine Son, Mary assists the Church in raising
us up to be sons and daughters of God. In order to enter into this
close relationship with God, we too must say 'yes' to God. But
Mary's 'yes' was different to ours; for hers was absolute; it was an
acceptance of the cross which was the lot of all closely associated
with Christ – seeing Christ rejected, contradicted, vilified, crucified
before her very eyes. Mary's 'yes' was an acceptance of the
sword of ultimate sorrow which would pierce her heart.

Thus it was fitting that she, whose response to God was so
complete, should be rewarded in a very special way, and become
united, soul and body, with her maker after death. Much of the
Bible can be summed up in one word, 'remember', that helped
keep the faith alive in Israel. Our faith also can be vitalised by
reflection on God's plan of salvation in Jesus and Mary, Jesus'
mother and ours. Let us rejoice then with Mary this day, let us
take hope, let us remember that we also have a glorious future.

TWENTY-FIRST SUNDAY OF THE YEAR
Josh 24:1-2, 15-18; Eph 5:25-32; Jn 6:60-69

We sometimes think how fortunate the disciples and close followers of Christ were, how easy it must have been for them to
live holy and virtuous lives, since they had Jesus, the source of
all grace, as their constant companion. But today's gospel reading, which describes the conclusion, according to St John, of the
long discourse of our Lord on the Eucharist, shows us the same
followers of Jesus at a time of great crisis, faced as they were
with a most difficult doctrine, that of the Eucharistic presence of
Christ. 'I tell you most solemnly', Christ had said earlier on
(6:53), 'if you do not eat the flesh of the Son of Man, and drink
his blood, you will not have life in you'.

Many of those who were listeners to Jesus, or followers of
his, deemed it unreasonable, even intolerable on the part of
Christ to put this doctrine before them for their acceptance, and
several of his chosen disciples turned back and walked no more
with him. This was their choice, but Jesus did not go back on
anything he had said. Many of you will recall how in the past
parishioners were divided into sodalities, and received Holy
Communion once a month on their sodality Sunday. Many outside the sodalities would receive once or twice in the year. It is
quite possible that we have gone to the opposite extreme
nowadays, in that we receive almost in a casual fashion without
fully realising what we are doing. We have to ask ourselves
what does reception of the Eucharist mean in our lives. Because
it should not be receiving his body that alone matters but rather
being his body, becoming other Christs in what we do and what
we are.

We can see how appropriately the First Reading fits into the
picture. 'Choose today whom you will serve', Joshua had said to
the assembled tribes. And this is paralleled by the question of
Jesus to the Twelve, 'What about you, do you want to go away
too?' We can see a comparison between the response of the
Israelites, 'We have no intention of deserting the Lord', and the
reply of Peter, 'Lord, to whom shall we go, for you have the
words of eternal life?' Those who make a decision for Christ,
those who say 'yes' to the doctrines of Christ, enter into a special
friendship with Christ, which bears quite a similarity to the relationship between man and wife in marriage. This is the message

underlying the Second Reading, Here St Paul sees the marriage relationship, not as one in which the wife is subjected to the husband without qualification, but as one in which the husband devotes himself unreservedly to the love of his wife. The old Jewish household code is turned upside down; the emphasis rests no longer on the duty of the wife to the husband, but on the husband's love for his wife. The union of two people in marriage should be inspired by, and indeed be an image of, the love of Jesus Christ for each member of his Church. The more married people, through their experience and knowledge of the way Christ comes to them in the sacraments, reflect on the relation between Christ and his Church, the more they will understand the mystery of their own relationship. And just as a marital relationship, which does not rise above the purely natural level, is bound to run into difficulties, in the same way to approach the teaching of Christ, from a purely human perspective, is to rob it of all spiritual value.

From this arises the tragedy of our own times, the lapse of those who have turned their backs on the Church and cancelled their baptismal pledges, because they claim that the Church is irrelevant in our modern world, too dogmatic, not sufficiently involved in social activities, and so on. 'The flesh has nothing to offer', Christ warns us, and by flesh he means the purely natural principle in people, which cannot bring eternal life. Rather is it the spirit which gives life. A mere outward acceptance of Christ then is not sufficient; we must accept his spirit, his outlook, his devotion to all he came in contact with, his concern for all people no matter who they were. He is asking us to open our hearts today, and say with the chosen people: 'We too will serve the Lord, for he is our God.'

For Peter obviously there was something about Jesus which made him willing to give his life for him. To be a Christian is not to accept a philosophy, nor to devote oneself to public or social reform. Christianity is the allegiance and love which generous people give to God because their hearts will not allow them to do anything else. God grant that we may always have the courage to respond to Christ Jesus in that way.

TWENTY-SECOND SUNDAY OF THE YEAR
Deut 4:1-2, 6-8; Jm 1:17-18, 21-22, 27; Mk 7:1-8, 14-15, 21-23

It has ever been somewhat of a mystery why burial, in ancient times, was rarely, if ever, permitted within the walls of a city, while one of the commonest places for tombs was by the side of public roads. You can still, to this day, see a great number of these latter, still bearing their inscriptions, after close on 2,000 years, just outside Rome, along the Via Appia, the Appian Way. At one time in particular, in Palestine, just before the Feast of Passover, the roads to Jerusalem were thronged with pilgrims coming to celebrate this great annual feast. But, according to the Mosaic Law, anyone who touched a dead body, or came into contact with a tomb, became automatically unclean, and was thereby debarred from attending the ceremonies of Passover in Jerusalem. To prevent the occurrence of such a disaster it became a Jewish custom to whitewash all wayside tombs in advance of the Feast, so that they became more conspicuous. Thus in the Spring sunshine these tombs stood out, sparkling white, and almost lovely, although within they were full of decaying bodies or bones, whose touch would defile.

That, according to Jesus, was the precise picture of what the Pharisees were, whited sepulchres, men who seemed intensely religious in their every outward action, and yet could look down with sinful contempt on those they regarded as sinners. The name Pharisees put into English means 'separated ones', – separated because they distanced themselves from gentiles, sinners, and even Jews whom they deemed less observant of the Law than themselves. With haughty arrogance they dismissed all such people as being 'a rabble that knew not the Law'. In today's gospel reading we see how the Scribes and Pharisees had come to listen to Jesus, but instead of pondering on what he had to say they began to pass judgment on the behaviour of his disciples. It was the age-old tactic of lowering a man's credibility by disparaging his adherents.

The charge they laid against the disciples was that they were eating without having first washed their hands, and so were to be deemed in contravention of the traditions of the elders. This typified the air of self-righteousness of the Pharisees, which derived not from any interior, or personal, relationship with God, but from observing purely human customs. This is not to say that all the Pharisees were bad. Some, like Nicodemus, were sincere searchers for the truth. But there is nothing harder than for a good man not to know that he is good, and once he sees himself as good, pride intervenes, and his goodness is tarnished, no matter how sincere the image he outwardly projects before others. However, there was always the possibility that the Pharisee in attempting to fulfil every little detail of the Law could end up as a bigoted legalist, or indeed as a man of burning devotion to God. This is not simply a Christian verdict on the Pharisees, but rather that of the Jews themselves. For the Talmud, which is the Jewish written code of civil and canon Law, cites seven different types of Pharisee, only one of which was seen as being good. Thus when Jesus condemned the Pharisees as being whited sepulchres, many of those listening would have agreed with him.

The words of Jesus in today's reading, however, have a message also for each of us. They are asking us to look inwards into the depths of our own souls. Deep within us God has written his Law, and it is our honour and obligation to obey it, as God unfolds it to our conscience. We will be judged according to the way we have acted, based on what we, in our hearts, have believed to be right and true and proper. 'It is from within', Jesus is saying to us today, 'that evil arises'. He is calling upon us to look beyond the troubled situations, the confrontations, the problems of our own time, and strive for greater personal spiritual purity of heart. Steer clear of stupid conflicts and sterile slavery to mere human customs and taboos, he is bidding us. Instead open up to the Holy Spirit's word of life, which unknown to us, is fashioning a new world in our time.

What we should be aiming for, striving for, is summed up in the words of sacred scripture (Ps 51): 'A new heart create for me, Oh God, and put a steadfast spirit within me.' This is God's work, not something we can achieve of ourselves. 'Without me', Christ told his disciples, 'you can do nothing' (Jn 15:5). But with him, we are assured, all things are possible for those who love him.

TWENTY-THIRD SUNDAY OF THE YEAR
Is 34:4-7; Jm 2:1-5; Mk 7:31-37

When Jesus had cured the deaf-mute he gave the onlookers a
rather strange command. He ordered them to tell no one about
this miraculous happening. But the more he told them to keep it
secret, the more widely they published it. Their admiration was
unbounded. We might well ponder as to why Christ gave them
that command at all. It was surely not because of humility, since
humility is about revealing the truth, and there was no denying
that a miracle had taken place. Nor was the occurrence meant to
be something private between Jesus and the man cured, because
all the events of Jesus' life had a purpose, which was to draw all
people to a greater awareness of the providence of God, and of
the role Christ was to play in it. 'He does all things well', the
people said, 'he makes the deaf hear and the dumb speak'. They
were astounded by the physical cures and the things Christ
could do, to such an extent that by spreading word of these
more and more people flocked to Jesus out of curiosity. They
wanted simply to witness these sensational happenings.

That kind of reaction was precisely the opposite of what
Jesus wanted. The primary purpose of his miracles was to draw
the attention of people to the presence of the divine among
them, of God's message of eternal salvation being unfolded
through these supernatural happenings. While the people wanted
more miracles, more wonderful cures, what Jesus wanted was
that they should hear the word of God and keep it. Indeed the
question might be put, do miracles bring about an increase in
people's faith or not?

It should truly be a source of wonder to us that the people of
both the Old and New Testaments should have seen so many
miraculous happenings, the laws of nature being set aside, thousands fed in a way that defied explanation, dead people restored
to life. And yet despite all these they did not in any way obey
God better than people then or nowadays who have never witnessed any miracles. Angels were sent by God as messengers,
and prophets who for the most part lived saintly lives preached
repentance. God even sent his only begotten Son, Jesus, who did
more wonderful things than any person whatsoever who had
gone before him. How did people respond to these supernatural
happenings? It is a reflection on the obstinacy of those who were

privileged to witness all these supernatural events that messages were mostly ignored, prophets very often were slain, and
as to the reaction of the majority to Jesus, St John describes it
very graphically in a few short sentences.

'The chief priests and Pharisees called a meeting. "Here is
this man working all these signs", they said, 'and what action
are we taking? If we let him go on this way, everybody will believe
in him.' So, from that day on they plotted how to kill him'
(Jn 11:47, 53). Hard as it is to understand them, miracles, generally
speaking, do not make people any better. We find confirmation
of this not only from the reaction of Moses' followers in the
desert, but also from the multitude Jesus had fed by the miraculous multiplication of the loaves and fishes. These latter, as Jesus
pointed out, were thinking purely of their own interests, and
were set on placing him in a position of authority so that a
plentiful supply of food would be forthcoming thereafter at no
cost to themselves.

Some would say that the Jews were stiff-necked and hard-
hearted, but the question is, would we have responded any differently? Would a miracle teach us anything about God that we
do not already have enshrined in the deposit of our faith, and
which we acknowledge every time we say the Creed? You might
argue that witnessing a miracle would startle people and have a
lasting effect on them. But being startled is not the same as being
converted to God, just as people who are startled by witnessing
terrible accidents, are more inclined to blame God for not pre-
venting them than to become more deeply moved spiritually as
a result of witnessing them. As Jesus himself made clear to the
Apostle Thomas, who was reluctant to believe in his resurrection, 'You believe because you can see me. Blessed are those who
have not seen and yet believe' (Jn 20:29). 'He makes the deaf
hear and the dumb speak' (Mk 7:37), the crowd earlier on had
said of Jesus. Taken in a spiritual sense this is saying to us that if
we but listen to the gospel message of Christ, we can by our
actions become living witnesses to Christian values before the
whole world.

TWENTY-FOURTH SUNDAY OF THE YEAR
Num 21:4-9; Phil 2:6-11; Jn 3:13-17

The gospel reading you have just heard represents a kind of watershed, or turning-point, in the public life of Jesus. He had brought his chosen disciples to Caesarea Philippi, a place remote from everything that was Jewish, to discover what understanding each of them had of his person and mission. Having done that, Jesus, according to Mark, began to teach his disciples that he, the very person they looked to as the promised Messiah, was destined to suffer grievously, to be rejected, and to be put to death. 'Teach' is the important word here. Jesus did not simply tell them all this, he had to teach them, to re-educate them in the meaning of his messiahship, because in their traditional understanding of what the Messiah should be there was no room for the cross, and little room either for suffering.

The statement of Jesus that his destiny was to be one of suffering and death was to the disciples both incredible and incomprehensible, and it was left to Peter to voice their revulsion at the idea, to take Jesus aside and remonstrate with him. But Jesus, who normally used harsh language only in his condemnation of hypocrisy, especially that of the Pharisees, responded to Peter with a most stern rebuke. 'Get behind me, Satan. The way you think is not God's way but man's.' And Jesus went on to emphasise that the true disciple of his must take up his cross also and follow him.

Again and again, throughout the rest of St Mark's gospel we find the disciples trying to come to terms with this saying of Jesus, being afraid to ask him to clarify it further, and eventually showing that they had failed to grasp its meaning, when they abandoned him on his arrest in Gethsemane. All this raises the question, 'Why does God, who is loving, compassionate, just and forgiving, allow suffering to enter into the lives of even good and holy people?' We, all of us, at some time or other, find ourselves confronted with this dilemma, and it is one of the most difficult to answer to the satisfaction of everyone. We might approach the problem in a concrete way, by examining how the saints reacted to the cross in their lives, since saints give a witness to Christian virtue, a witness approved of by the Church in their canonisation. St John of the Cross, for example, in the final years of his short life, asked God for three favours:

not to die as a superior of any Carmelite friary; to die in a place where he was unknown; and to die after having suffered much. All these requests were granted in their entirety.

In the last years of his life – he died at the age of 49 – he was stripped of all office by his superiors, and some even attempted to have him expelled from the Order which he himself had helped found. He was sent to a house where nobody knew him, where the superior disliked him, installed him in the worst cell in the friary and complained bitterly of the expense to the community caused by his ill-health. Finally, the suffering of the saint worsened as his legs and back became ulcerated. Realising that death was near, John, instead of seeking medical care, called for the prior, and begged his pardon for all the trouble and expense he had caused him. The prior in turn was moved to ask forgiveness and left the cell in tears, a changed man, so much so that he was later to die in the odour of sanctity. That same night, without agony or struggle, John yielded up his spirit to his Creator.

All of this does not immediately answer the question, 'Why does God permit suffering?' Perhaps we could begin to see its meaning if we framed the question differently. 'Would John of the Cross, whose example has changed the lives of hundreds of thousands of people in the 400 years since his death, would John have had the same influence on Christianity if the cross had never come into his life?' The answer has to be no, because suffering is something sacred; it confers upon all whom it touches the most intimate resemblance to the suffering Christ, whose cross saves the world.

Indeed we could go so far as to say that the suffering of all who have faith in Christ can become the suffering of Christ himself; that in them the passion of Christ, even now, is being continued, and that, by the merits thereby gained, souls are being won for God. And we have the words of Sacred Scripture to confirm it. 'It makes me happy to suffer for you, as I am suffering now', St Paul wrote to the Colossians, 'and in my own body to do what I can to make up all that has still to be undergone by Christ for the sake of his body, the Church' (1:24). Would that we also may be ready to embrace the cross in our lives, and so play our part in building up the body which is Christ.

TWENTY-FIFTH SUNDAY OF THE YEAR
Wis 2:12, 17-20; Jm 3:16 - 4:3; Mk 9:30-37

'After leaving the mountain Jesus and his disciples made their way through Galilee.' The mountain there referred to, at the beginning of today's gospel reading, was Mt Tabor, where Jesus was transfigured before the gaze of Peter, James and John, and where the prophets Moses and Elijah were seen speaking to him. And when all this wonderful vision had faded away, the Apostles, as it were, came down to earth again. 'They looked around', the gospel tells us, 'and they saw no one with them any more, only Jesus'. What wouldn't we give to get a glimpse of Jesus face to face, for just a moment, and yet those words, 'they saw only Jesus', indicate that, for the Apostles, Jesus had become commonplace, taken for granted. Do we also take for granted the people we live with – those we worship and pray with? As the old saying puts it: 'To live above with the Saints we love, that is the purest glory; to live below with the saints we know, that is a different story.'

It is with the eyes of faith that we can detect the wonders of divine love at work in the seemingly weak and commonplace people around us. And this vision must encompass the Mass and the Sacraments as well. For if the Sacraments – and especially the Mass, the public and most important prayer of the Church – cease to be for us the means of encountering Jesus, coming face to face with him, then they will have become practically useless. The first Eucharistic Prayer begins with the words, 'We come to you, Father, with praise and thanksgiving through Jesus Christ your Son.' Now thanksgiving is not just saying 'thank you' to God for some particular favour he has granted, while deep down within us there is the attitude which says, 'I can manage on my own – thank you – most of the time.' On the contrary, thanksgiving should be a constant attitude, an enduring disposition towards God which says, 'I am totally dependent on you, Lord, and at all times.' We read how the Apostles with Mary and several women, after the Ascension of Christ, joined in continuous prayer.

The Eucharist is Christ's sacrifice, the absolute surrender of his life, his whole being to God. And our joining in the Eucharist will become sincere and meaningful only if we begin to live our whole lives in a perpetual offering of praise and thanksgiving to

God, as did Jesus. It was Jesus who said that in a child are to be seen those characteristics which should be present too in our striving for the kingdom of God. There is the child's dependence. In all its needs it turns instinctively to its parents – abandoning itself to their care and love. There is the child's trust, that this care and love will be readily forthcoming. There is the child's humility, which makes it shy away from public attention – makes it regard all its elders with a feeling of awe and wonder. In this humility lies the basis of what the attitude of the Christian should be towards other human beings. Because, since the human soul is made in God's likeness, there is something of the wonder of God in every one of us, no matter how lacking in divine virtue we may be. And many of those for whom Jesus, while on earth, showed his love, in a very special way, were indeed sorely lacking in virtue.

Furthermore, the child's sense of dependence and trust towards those whom it knows characterises the attitude of the true follower of Christ towards God, the Father of all, who re-assures us solemnly in these words from sacred scripture, 'Can a mother forget the child she has borne and nourished? Yet if she should, never will I forget you' (Is 49:15). If our reliance on God should be moulded on that of the child on its parents, this does not imply that we should always remain childish in our thinking and behaviour. On the contrary, scripture also has this to say, 'See that you go on growing in the Lord, and become strong and vigorous in the truth. Let your lives overflow with joy and thanksgiving for all that he has done' (Col 2:6f). Our need for spiritual maturity and courage is every bit as great as that shown by the twelve Apostles in the gospel reading.

There we have Jesus telling them plainly what lay in store for him in Jerusalem, and yet they were dreaming about his king-dom in earthly terms. There is something heart-breaking in the picture of Jesus going to his death on the cross, while his follow-ers argued among themselves as to which of them should be the greatest in the earthly kingdom they were convinced he was about to establish. But Christ had come, not to wield power over others, but to be their servant before God.

TWENTY-SIXTH SUNDAY OF THE YEAR
Num 11:25-29; Jm 5:1-6; Mk 9:38-43, 45, 47-48

'There is nothing new under the sun', the Book of Ecclesiastes
tells us (1:9), and this is very true of human nature, as we see in
the readings from the Old and New Testament for this Sunday.
We find a close parallel between the first reading from the Book
of Numbers and the gospel reading from Mark. In the first of
these we are told how two men who, despite not being among the
seventy elders chosen to assist Moses, had, nevertheless, received
a share in Moses' gift of prophecy, and how Joshua, the one
specially chosen by Moses to be his successor, tried to have them
silenced. In close parallel with this we find John, the beloved disciple, who misunderstands completely the universal character
of Jesus' mission, and tries to prevent two men from casting out
devils in Jesus' name.

We should of course make allowance for the difficulties in
the situation from John's point of view. How could a non-disciple
use Jesus' name and his spiritual powers, when not instructed or
commissioned by Jesus? However, the reaction of John was as
yet lacking in openness and understanding of the way God works,
how God's love reaches out to everyone without exception. God
does not confine the gift of his Spirit to institutional or author-
ised channels. His work, even today, is often carried on by many
who appear to be beyond the community of those who profess
to be followers of Christ. Even in the increasingly pluralist age in
which we live, we are so easily inclined to form our own little
spiritual aristocracy, while looking down on anyone who differs
from us in faith, or persuasion, or religious practice.

Thus we Catholics in the South are inclined to look on the
Northern Presbyterians with an air of aloof tolerance tinged
with pity. It is also true that Victorian Anglicans, in England
during the 19th century, when society was very class-conscious,
regarded Catholic churches as places frequented by the lower
classes and the servants – very often Irish – working in the houses
of the rich. No respectable and true minded English person
would ever be seen frequenting such places of worship. Such
attitudes of course are totally contrary to the true Christian spirit
which should unite all those who claim to be followers of Christ.
As such we all stand before God on the same level, self con-
fessed sinners seeking redemption from his Son Jesus Christ. We

are all God's children. He leads each of us by a different way, and for anyone to put an obstacle between Christ and somebody of simple faith can have drastic consequences for that trouble maker, more drastic even, the gospel tells us, than being weighed down to the bottom of the sea by a millstone tied round the neck. From time to time we must scrutinise our lives to see whether they reflect the gospel values we profess to believe in.

Sadly there are many who are caught up in the rat-race of modern life, who are afraid to take a long and critical look at themselves, afraid of the senselessness and emptiness of their lives. The great Swiss psychiatrist, Carl Jung, founder of analytical psychology, stated that there was not a single one of the many patients, over the age of 35, that he had treated, whose problem in the last resort was not that of finding a religious outlook on life, and that none of them was really healed without regaining this religious outlook. If we wish to renew our faith we should recall, first of all that God is love, and that Jesus is the living, and full expression of that love.

We should be convinced that God really loves each one of us, as we really are, regardless of whether we are sinners or his dedicated followers, and that in his providence he watches over each of us. Our response to God, moreover, must be manifested outwardly in our love for our fellow human beings. St John tells us, 'We know that we have passed from death to life, because we love one another. Whoever does not love remains in death' (1 Jn 3:14). Life on this earth will finally become meaningful for us only if we see God as our destiny. We are members of a pilgrim Church being directed towards our heavenly home through the action of the Spirit of Christ within us. A certain long-distance swimmer (Florence Chadwick), who because of fog had failed in her attempt to cross the English Channel said afterwards, 'If I could have seen the shore, I would have made it.' We should keep ever in mind that eternal shore where Christ has gone ahead to prepare a place for us, and that thought will give us courage to cope with whatever obstacles we may encounter on the way.

TWENTY-SEVENTH SUNDAY OF THE YEAR
Gen 2:18-24; Heb 2:9-11; Mk 10:2-16

When Jesus wanted to change the moral attitudes and behaviour of his listeners, he did not address them in abstract terms, or make an appeal to them with logical arguments. Instead he spoke to them in parables; in other words, he told them stories. For an audience with little or no access to the written word, it was an excellent way of remembering what he had said. For example a dissertation on the love of God for us would be quickly forgotten, whereas the parable of the prodigal son, which deals with the same subject, remains fixed in our minds. By employing such methods, Jesus was being faithful to a tradition that went back to the earliest times among the Jewish people. We find an example of this in the first reading today, where the author of the Book of Genesis sets out to explain why there is an attraction between man and woman, why they leave their childhood surroundings, and become joined together, so as to form, as it were, a single entity. To describe this attraction of the sexes, the author makes use of metaphorical language, the rib story, which is meant to bring home to people that man and woman share a common human nature.

The word rib, as used, is not certain in meaning, and may perhaps have come from a foreign Sumerian word which meant life. Being blessed with life by God, they are complementary to each other, they need each other, and neither is complete without the other. Man who has lost his rib feels incomplete until he gets his rib back, until he is united with a woman, and likewise the woman yearns for the man from whom she, the rib, was taken. Remember that these are terms symbolising the abstract idea of mutual attraction. It is because God made them for each other from the beginning that man and woman will set aside all other ties, and in marriage join together as one.

A greater person than the author of Genesis, namely Jesus, in today's gospel reading puts it in clearer terms. 'For this reason a man shall leave his father and mother, and be joined to his wife, and the two shall become one flesh. They are no longer two therefore, but one body. So then, what God has joined together, let no human being separate.' At the Last Supper, Jesus out of love for his disciples said, 'This is my body, which will be given up for you' (Lk 22:19), and this promise was fulfilled on Calvary.

All Christians must consciously or subconsciously, in some way, make a similar commitment. Priests and religious, by their vows of celibacy, do so before God's people and for God's people, and God receives this offering, blesses it and makes it fruitful. By their marriage vow, a man and woman also dedicate themselves to one another. And this dedication, as well, God receives, blesses and makes fruitful. 'This is why a man leaves his father and mother, and joins himself to his wife, and they become one body.'

Marriage, Christ says, is made in heaven. Fundamentally it is the work of God. A happy and successful marriage is based primarily on the ideal of fidelity. It demands that the husband and wife be true to themselves, loyal to one another, and constant in their observance of the wishes of God's Holy Spirit, for without this last, the bond of union between them becomes unstable. However it also is true that despite being a sacrament, and so enjoying the graces that flow from this, the marriage of Catholics, no less than that of all other couples, has to contend with the reality of human frailty, shortcomings, quarrels, and sin. The second reading, however, has a message of hope in coping with these, when it says, 'It was fitting that God should make perfect through suffering the leader (a reference to Jesus) who would take many children to their salvation.' Christ suffered for love of us, and this confirms that at the heart of all loving is the Cross, that love and suffering are inseparably linked.

Thus whereas most marriages are reasonably happy, none however are without problems at some time or other, problems that can lead to suffering, worry and pain. A happy marriage does not occur all at once without an on-going commitment by both spouses to making it such. It has to be created, worked at, and often requires great effort and self-sacrifice. It begins to crumble when wife and husband ignore each other, and live for self alone. Jesus out of compassion worked his first miracle at a wedding feast. By his self-giving may he help all married couples to mature and grow in the fullness of love. 'Husbands love your wives as Christ loved the Church' (Eph 5:25), and this should be absolute and enduring.

TWENTY-EIGHTH SUNDAY OF THE YEAR
Wis 7:7-11; Heb 4:12-13; Mk 10:17-30

In the light of that gospel reading we might recall briefly one of
the most dramatic events recorded in the Acts of the Apostles,
that which occurred on the road from Jerusalem to Damascus,
when Saul, the fanatical persecutor of the infant Church, was
thrown from his horse onto the ground, and heard a voice saying,
'Saul, Saul, why are you persecuting me?' When told that this
was Jesus of Nazareth addressing him, Saul put the question,
'Lord, what will you have me to do?' And even though there
was no immediate reply, this question, 'What will you have me
to do?', marked an about turn in Saul's life, one on which there
was to be no going back. For the question itself is the very voice
of self-surrender, with which Saul responded, and led to his
becoming Paul, the great Apostle to the gentiles. As a result of
this vision, Paul forever afterwards became convinced of what
for him were two great certainties, that Jesus had truly risen
from the dead, and furthermore, following on that question,
'Saul, Saul, why are you persecuting me?', that Jesus was truly
present in those Christians whom he had been persecuting.
Furthermore, that presence continues to this very day, and will
be so until the end of time.

By way of contrast, in today's gospel reading we have a
young man putting the same question to Jesus, 'What must I
do?', and when told to renounce all his riches, as St Mark so
superbly and succinctly describes his reaction, his face fell, and
he went away sad, for he was a man of great wealth. So many
people come to God, wishing to be saved, but in their own way,
wishing to surrender but on their own terms. 'If you love me,
keep my commandments', says the Lord, but there are so many
of us who see the commandments as so many regulations and
rules laid down by a capricious God, to be observed under the
threat of punishment hanging over us. So many people, even
some who are regarded as being very religious people, have
their hearts set on the world, and are only restrained by rules,
while outwardly paying mere lip-service to the claims of God.

But God is not an inflexible law-giver, not a harsh and exacting judge, as we so often imagine. God is a God of compassion
and love; he does not force himself upon us; he treats each soul
after the manner of Jesus, who is God come down in human

nature among us. And the gospel tells us how Jesus looked steadily at the young man and loved him. There are many passages throughout the Sacred Scriptures which underline this consideration of God for our freedom of choice. For example the Book of Revelation has Jesus saying, 'Behold I stand at the door and knock; if anyone hears my voice and opens the door, I will come in to him, and will sup with him, and he with me' (Rev 3:20). But Jesus does not, and will not, force open that door. 'God', we are also told, 'has sent the Spirit of his divine Son into our hearts'. But for this to come about we must make room in our hearts for God's Spirit.

In Old Testament times God repeatedly asked his people to renounce the false gods they were tempted to worship. The false gods of our own times have their own devotees as well. They are, of course, more deceptive, but no less real. By their fruits you will recognise them. Very often their presence is denoted by a grasping ambition which sets some individuals on the road to succeed, to rise in life, to amass riches, to gain power, an intense, restless, never-wearied, never-satisfied pursuit of their own interests, coupled with complete disregard for all that is spiritual, all that is holy, all that is calm and reverent.

We all of course do not tread this extreme path, but there is a more subtle course which may draw us on. As Cardinal Newman wrote over a hundred years ago, 'a smooth and easy life, an uninterrupted enjoyment of the goods of providence, full meals, soft garments, well furnished homes, the pleasures of sense, the feeling of security, the consciousness of wealth – these and the like, if we are not careful, choke up all the avenues of the soul, through which the light and breath of heaven might come to us'. But the true Christian has neither hope nor fear about this world. He can own in God's sight that he wants nothing, that he is full and abounds, that God has given him all the things that he needs. The thought that he could possess more holiness, more gratitude, more of heaven, is not a thought of sadness but of joy, of joy in the belief that he is being cared for by a truly benevolent, and concerned, and loving God.

TWENTY-NINTH SUNDAY OF THE YEAR
Joel 3:1-5 (2:28-32); Acts 1:3-8; Mt 5:13-16

In the Bible we have the inspired word of God. This means that God so employed the writers of sacred scripture that, while remaining true authors, they committed to writing all those things and only those things which God wanted to have recorded. The inspired authors remained truly human, using their own personal talents, and indeed retaining their own particular foibles as well. In fact we, have an example of this latter in the gospel for today, where Mark recalls how the apostles James and John, who were brothers, asked Jesus as a favour to allow them sit one at his right, the other on his left, in his glory, in other words his kingdom. But Matthew's gospel states it was their mother who made that request.

It has been suggested that Matthew, writing a number of years after Mark, when James and John had become important figures in the infant Church, did not wish to accuse them of being over-ambitious for power. Matthew was reacting in a very human way. It is of course possible that, since their family and that of Jesus were closely related, their mother, at some time or other, had made the same request as the sons. What is certain is that the apostles were as yet ignorant of the purpose of Christ's mission. He had warned them not to be like pagan rulers who lord it over their subjects, but rather to be the slaves of all. John, long afterwards, saw the Cross as being the glory of Christ. That message had begun to form in his mind while being the sole apostle to remain near the Cross during the final stage of Christ's passion.

At the last supper, Jesus had prayed for his disciples: 'I pray for them; I am not praying for the world' (Jn 17:9). This last remark is rather puzzling, especially in view of the fact that Christ had said to Nicodemus, the man who came to him at night, 'God so loved the world that he gave his only Son, so that everyone who believes in him may not perish but may have eternal life' (Jn 3:16). Why, then, did Jesus not pray for the world which the Father so loved? The explanation lies in the term 'world', which for John meant that part of society which had cut itself off from God its Creator. Jesus prayed especially that his disciples might be pro-tected from the power of the devil, and from the hatred of those who would oppose them. He looked into the future, and prayed 'for those who will believe in me', he said. His prayer would reach out to future generations, ours included. His request to the Father was that this same bond of unity might be the predominant feature of his Church, and that its members might observe this faithfully, so as to share with him in that glory which would be his.

We might this day, seriously reflect on the extent to which our life-style, our attitudes are moulded by the 'world', by those who have distanced themselves from God, those who stand in such stark contrast to the kind of community envisaged in Jesus' priestly prayer. Christ was concerned in a very special way about the preservation of unity among his followers. 'May they all be one. Father may they be one in us as you are in me and I am in you' (Jn 17:21). The Christian community, therefore, which he had in mind, was one which would be characterised by the presence of the Holy Spirit binding its members closely together in the love of Christ. If we make it our aim to achieve this, there is one thing we should bear in mind. We are not alone. Christ even now continues to intercede for us, and were we to reflect on the indescribable dignity, the infinite holiness of the one thus praying for us, we would set about seeking this unity with more enthusiasm. It is a sad reflection on the human race that even two thousand years after Christ the ranks of those who claim to be his followers are split by dissensions, disharmony and divisions. Christ stands in complete contrast to all disharmony, for he identified with mankind by assuming a human nature like ours, and made himself one with suffering humanity by undergoing a most cruel death.

The Eucharist we are celebrating is a sign of the unity which God wants between his Son and human beings, a sign of the unity which should exist in a special way between the members of Christ's Church, a sign and promise of that unity already existing between God and those faithful souls who have gone to their eternal reward. As the early Christians used to do, we should keep in mind the Christ, the one who guarantees these things by recalling his promise: 'I shall indeed be with you soon.' And our response like theirs should be, 'Amen, come Lord Jesus'.

MISSION SUNDAY
Joel 3:1-5 (2:28-32); Acts 1:3-8; Mt 5:13-16

In our modern age the construction of motorways, and rapid movement from one place to another in ever faster cars and aeroplanes seem to be good things, until one starts trying to pin down the precise human value of speed and mobility. Are we really better people because of them? We pride ourselves on the lines of communication opened up between peoples and nations; but to what purpose are they used? At the level of the human spirit, what, if anything, is being communicated?

On this Mission Sunday we might ponder on the secret of the first Apostles and disciples of Christ, the thousands of miles they travelled mainly on foot, and what great communicators they were. Despite the difficulties besetting them in journeying, in peril from robbers, in peril from false brethren, in peril at sea, in preaching to great gatherings, in overcoming barriers of language, the message which had wrought such a change in their own lives soon spread to so many countries. Again and again we are confronted and challenged by their deep belief that Jesus Christ had risen from the dead, and was constituted Lord, and their sense of urgency in trying to communicate this faith to as many as possible.

We sense that urgency in the advice of St Paul to the Romans (10:13+) – 'Everyone who calls on the name of the Lord will be saved. But how are people to call on him unless they believe in him; and how are they to believe in him unless they have heard of him; and how are they to hear of him unless someone preaches to them; and how can persons preach unless they are sent? ... Faith comes from what is preached, and what is preached comes from the word of Christ.'

That phrase 'unless they are sent' is associated with the concept of mission and missionaries. Indeed the name Apostle, although initially associated with the Twelve, little by little came to signify all those sent, or commissioned, by the Churches to spread the gospel, those who were envoys or messengers (2 Cor 8:23) from the small Christian communities, which inspired and supported them in their task. Recently, the significance of foreign missions has changed quite noticeably. We are beginning to accept that, to be a missionary, you do not necessarily have to travel, nor do you have to carry the message out from a

Christian land. Every Christian can, and should, be a missionary wherever he or she is. This, however, should not close our eyes to the courage, and spirit of dedication, and the needs of the chosen few, the envoys of Christ's Church on earth, who nowadays set out to bring the news of eternal salvation and the divine Sacraments to those who have never known Christ – and these latter, alas, still form a majority in our world.

The task of today's missionary is beset by new problems and new difficulties. Gone are the days when the missionary worked in the wake of a conquering army, or under the umbrella of a colonial power structure. Now he is allowed into a strange country on sufferance; his position and future are insecure; he must adapt to the ways, customs and language of the people he serves. His is a demanding and lonely existence, and oftentimes (as in Africa and South America) one that is even fraught with danger. Consider then today in what ways you can contribute to the work and endeavour of this front line corps of the Church in its battle for the souls of humankind. You can offer an extra Mass, a Communion, a Rosary, spend some time before the Blessed Sacrament, make a contribution to the mission funds.

From time to time you might offer in prayer those words of Christ at the Last Supper, words which Pope John XXIII kept repeating on his death-bed (Whit Monday, June 3rd, 1963), 'Father, may they all be one. May they be one in us, as you are in me, and I am in you.' The dying Pope was beseeching God to grant not only unity of belief between Christians and non-Christians but also harmony among the many differing Christian groupings as well. The continued existence of these latter in today's world is truly a scandal. If from time to time we offer up a similar prayer to that of Christ and Pope John, we will be helping to prolong the mission of Jesus on earth until he comes. We will be sharers in the tradition of the first Christians, whose love for their new-found faith was such that not only did they pray for the success of its full-time preachers, they some-times spent their lives assisting them.

ALL SAINTS
Apoc 7:2-4, 9-14; 1 Jn 3:1-3; Mt 5:1-12

In the second quarter of the 20th century, most primary pupils in Ireland were familiar with the story of High Brasil, the Isle of the Blest, an imaginary haven of contentment, happiness and peace, which fascinated them. But this idea was not peculiar to Celtic mythology only. The ancient Greeks always called the island of Cyprus 'he Makaria', meaning 'The Happy or Blessed Isle'. The Greek word they used – *makarios* – was a very special word, which in particular they applied to the serene existence of the gods, their untouchability, their complete independence of all the changes, the ups and downs of life. This word 'makarios', or blessed, is the precise word used in each of the Beatitudes set out by Christ at the beginning of the Sermon on the Mount. What in effect the Beatitudes are saying is that the person who is a true and sincere follower of Christ will find an inner calm and serenity, an attitude of mind that can never be disturbed by the worries and troubles of this life. 'I will see you again', Christ had promised the Apostles at the Last Supper, 'and your hearts will be full of joy, and that joy no one will take from you' (Jn 16:22).

At the very beginning of his public preaching then, we find Christ, in today's gospel account of the Beatitudes, emphasising that his message is not a thing of gloom and doom, of strict adherence to regulations and laws, coupled with a kind of Stoic indifference to the hardships that life may bring. How could we ever see the Beatitudes as a list of things to be observed, when their very language is a statement of what the joyous thrill, the radiant happiness of the Christian life should be. 'Oh! the wonder of being a Christian!' – they are saying – 'the sheer bliss of being a follower of Christ and accepting him as Guide and Saviour'. This is the lesson, above all, which we should learn today from the celebration of the Feast of all Saints, as we rejoice with those whose lives on earth were specially marked by holiness and love for God. We rejoice because God has done great things in them, and they are calling on us to follow in their footsteps.

There are two further considerations we might bear in mind. Firstly, God want us also to be saints. 'You must therefore be perfect just as your heavenly Father is perfect', Jesus told his disciples (Mt 5:48). We cannot, however, conjure up sanctity within ourselves by our own endeavours. The comment of St Teresa of

Avila on certain persons, who regarded themselves as being holy was, 'They frightened me more than anything in this world', and St Teresa, as anyone who has studied her life will readily admit, was a person not easily frightened.

Holiness as the first Beatitude indicates, begins with the realisation of one's own utter helplessness, one's need for God, and the necessity of placing all one's trust in God, who has made this promise, 'The mountains may depart, the hills be shaken, but my love for you will never leave you, and my pledge of peace with you will never be shaken' (Is 54:10). Holiness is a gradual and barely perceptible day-by-day process of filling one's mind with 'whatever is true, whatever is honourable, whatever is just, whatever is pure, whatever is lovely, whatever is gracious', as St Paul urged the Christians in Philippi (Phil 4:8).

The second consideration is the example of all the Saints themselves. It is indeed regrettable that books on the lives of the Saints have gone almost completely out of fashion in our time. For we are all human; we tend easily to grow discouraged. And there can be no greater stimulus to our striving for perfection than to reflect on the example of saintly souls. Let us then rejoice with the Saints today, and ask them to assist us. Let us also be convinced that God is never outdone in generosity. For 'eye has not seen, nor ear heard, neither has it entered into the heart of man what God has prepared for those who love him' (1 Cor 2:9). In heaven the reward of the least of all the saints is far greater than all the honours a person in this world could have bestowed on him or her. Such has been the revelation of God through the Holy Spirit.

It comes as a surprise that in early times Christianity would, in this celebration, include even those still alive. For in the scriptures 'all the saints' meant 'all the faithful'. The very last line of the Christian Bible says, 'The grace of the Lord Jesus be with all the saints'. And since the blessed in heaven do not stand in need of grace any more, this little prayer is for all the living faithful, ourselves included.

THIRTIETH SUNDAY OF THE YEAR
Jer 31:7-9; Heb 5:1-6; Mk 10:46-52

One thing stands out in the gospel story today about Bartimaeus, the central figure in it, and that is the sheer desperate persistence of this blind man from Jericho. He was determined to draw Jesus' attention, and nothing was going to stop him. He just refused to be restrained, to be silenced by the demands of others. And when at last he had secured the attention of Jesus, he made that earnest plea, 'Lord, that I may see.' We can sense the passionate, intense longing welling up from the very depths of the heart of Bartimaeus. If people want a miracle, that is the spirit with which they must make their request. And Christ did not disappoint Bartimaeus.

The Christians of the New Testament times, as a rule, adhered to the Jewish tradition which saw human beings as living under constant threat from evil, malevolent powers, from disease, from sin, death, wicked spirits, even the law. And although in the present time, we are inclined to think of ourselves as enjoying a new age of liberation from such a view of life, the fact, nevertheless, is that we too are as much menaced as ever by most of these. They are still with us despite the new forms they have taken on, despite attempts to gloss over them, to disregard their very existence. Advertisements in the media, and indeed many popular TV programmes, love to portray men and women as being predominantly young, healthy and beautiful. Rarely do they reveal to us the anguish, the feelings of anxiety, which beset people when they are confronted with trouble ahead, with old age, sickness, decay, death, and the consideration of what lies beyond the portals of death.

All too often our modern person is powerless in trying to cope with such things as drug addiction, with greed for material possessions, with irrepressible compulsions and obsessions. The peoples of the Bible saw themselves as engaged in a continuous battle with evil spirits, but such forces are no less with us today, however different the forms they assume. We need only glance through the newspapers to find daily evidence of uncontrollable greed, jealousy, fear, on a national and international scale, exploitation of groups and peoples for economic gain, injustices built into legal systems and institutions, revenge attacks and terrorism. The 20th century may not have had graven images of silver and gold, but it viewed as sacred such things as National Security, nuclear deterrents, the Gross National Product, the demands of capitalism or state-run economies. One could go on adding to this list.

What it tells us is that when people turn from God to their own inventions, to what human nature without God sets its heart upon, the result is oppressive bondage rather than true freedom. As St Paul puts it: 'It is death to limit oneself to what is unspiritual' (Rom 8:6). In other words, to allow the things of the world to dominate one's life completely tends to a sort of inner extinction that, if unchecked, can end in spiritual death – complete alienation from God. The remedy for the evils of our time begins with a plea for understanding – 'Lord that I may see'. It begins with the conviction that there is something deeply wrong within human beings, that calls for the healing power of the divine physician, a remedy such as we find in the Book of Psalms: 'A new heart create for me, Oh God, and put a steadfast spirit within me' (Ps 51:10). And the inspiration for this new inner creation will come, not from the fear of what God may do to us, but rather from the thought of all that God has done for us, in Christ Jesus, our Lord. 'Master let me see again', Bartimaeus had said, and Jesus responded with the words, 'Go; your faith has saved you.'

We should take note that faith came before his cure, and that afterwards Bartimaeus immediately followed Jesus. The old saying, 'Seeing is believing', has been turned around, and in this miracle the opposite is what happens, namely 'Believing is seeing'. A certain amount of praise is due to the Apostle Thomas who insisted on first seeing the risen Jesus, and then professing his faith in what had taken place on the first Easter Sunday. But Bartimaeus merits greater praise, because he believed before being able to see. The lesson to be drawn from this is that faith begets healing, especially inner healing, and that this healing leads on to the following of Christ along the road he would have us tread in order to draw near to God.

THIRTY-FIRST SUNDAY OF THE YEAR
Deut 6:2-6; Heb 7:23-28; Mk 12:28-34

At first sight, today's gospel seems to be direct and simple; it contains nothing new or startling that was not already known by the Jews of the Old Testament. Indeed the words, 'You shall love the Lord your God with all your heart, with all your soul, with all your strength and with all your mind', were words written on the heart of every Jew, and to this day they form part of the daily prayer a devout Jew is required to say. This prayer is referred to as the Shema, because it begins with the Hebrew words, 'Shema Yisrael', meaning 'Listen Israel'. 'Listen Israel, the Lord our God is the one Lord', and it continues with the words just quoted. And yet, there is a certain paradox about today's gospel reading, in that it tells us that love of God is realised by our love for each other.

In other words, love of God is an illusion if it stops short with God, if it does not manifest itself outwardly in our love for each other, for our every neighbour without exception, even for our enemies. But then, a word of caution, love of neighbour, if it is divorced from love of God, can very well become refined self-love. For one can easily end up loving others purely for the response one gets from those loved, for the feeling of satisfaction and self-gratification one derives from being generous and kind to them. A Jewish Rabbi, named Hillel, a renowned scholar, a spiritual and ethical leader of his generation, who had a great following just before the birth of Christ, when asked, 'Which is the greatest commandment?', gave the famous reply, 'What you hate for yourself, do not do to your neighbour. This is the whole law; the rest is commentary.'

Jesus, however, stated that love of God linked with love of neighbour jointly form the greatest commandment. Commenting on that, the advice of St Augustine was, 'Love God first, and then do what you will', meaning that if we love God with all our heart, soul, strength and mind, then we cannot but be obedient to his will, which wants others to share in that love. St John, the evangelist, who saw all the events of Christ's life on earth in terms of love, and kept preaching about this virtue to the early Christians, to the extent that they became wearied of it, and asked him to talk about something else, St John in his first letter puts it very forcibly like this, 'Anyone who says, "I love God", and hates his brother, is a liar, for how can a man who does not love the brother that he can see, love God whom he has never seen. So this is the commandment that he has given us, that anyone who loves God must also love his brother' (1 Jn 4:20f).

If we embrace this commandment, if we try and put it into practice, as did the saints, then we will be doing something which is truly radical, which to the non-Christian outsider will often be seen as odd, a seeming contradiction, difficult to understand. These seeming contradictions abound in our faith. For we believe that life comes from death, that gain comes from loss, that receiving comes from giving, and that Christ had to die and come to life again that we might share a new life with him in heaven. We profess to be followers of Christ, who made a complete offering of himself to the Father – 'Not my will but thine be done' – who gave his life, his energies, his time in the service of others, who returned to his Father devoid of any earthly goods – the very clothes he had worn ceasing to be his before he yielded up his spirit, having being made over by lots into the possession of his executioners.

All this does not imply that we have to tread exactly the same path as Christ. What it does indicate, however, is that our surrender to God does not mean that we retreat into a paradise of unreal spirituality. It means that if we love God, then we have to concern ourselves with others, with the members of our family and community. It means that we must rise above ourselves, and our own interests, and become convinced from the words of Christ that St Paul has given us, that 'there is greater happiness in giving than in receiving' (Acts 20:35).

'The world is too much with us', the poet Wordsworth wrote, 'late and soon, getting and spending, we lay waste our powers'. We pass this way but once, and while we are on our way let us do as much good as we possibly can with our God-given powers, the gifts that each of us has, in serving God and others. But always keep in mind as well the promise of Jesus (Jn 15:5), 'Whoever remains in me, with me in him, bears fruit in plenty', and because of the presence of Jesus, this fruit will last.

THIRTY-SECOND SUNDAY OF THE YEAR
Ex 47:1-2, 8-9, 12; 1 Cor 3:9-11, 16-17; Jn 2:13-22

The two stories in today's liturgy readings, about the generosity of two poor widows, bring to mind two separate sayings elsewhere in the New Testament: one which recalls the words of the Lord Jesus, who himself said, 'There is more happiness in giving than in receiving' (Acts 20:35); the other, a word of caution, 'If I give away all that I possess, piece by piece, and if I even let them take my body to burn it, but am without love, it will do me no good whatever' (1 Cor 13:3). Indeed it is quite possible to give, and give lavishly, without having any love, as evidenced in the lives of some of the world's richest people, even though little spiritual benefit comes from such giving. But on the other hand we can also be certain that it is impossible to love without giving. We see this exemplified in a supreme way in Christ, who loved us and gave himself up for us.

Giving on a purely human level, moreover, should not be thought of in terms of quantity alone. There is a far greater giving exemplified in the person who gives a little cheerfully, than in one who gives much, but with a grudging air. The great difference, for example, between the reception of benefit from an institutional source, such as the state, and true Christian charity, is the personal interest which should always be evidenced in the latter. Here, all the things St Paul mentions about love, are also applicable. For love is not mere emotion, a warm feeling in the heart. Love is rather being patient and kind, and avoiding anything that is rude or selfish, or boastful, or conceited, or jealous. Love is not taking offence, not being resentful, not taking pleasure at the shortcomings of others, but rather taking delight in the truth, being ready to excuse, to trust, and to endure, come what may.

There is a beautiful saying of St Irenaeus, who was a pupil of St Polycarp, who in turn learned his spirituality from the Apostle St John. Irenaeus states that Christian joy is 'the echo of God's life in us'. It is by doing things joyfully that we begin to love God with all our heart, with all our soul, with all our mind, with all our strength, and our neighbour as ourselves, as Holy Scripture bids us do. It is far better to be simple, even less well educated – as long as we remain close to God through love – than to appear wise and gifted, and at the same time blaspheme our divine Maker. Despite living at a time of appalling violence, exploitation, disregard for the rights and needs of others, the desire of every human being, now as in the past, is to be happy. Yet in our pursuit of contentment and happiness we seldom steer clear of paths which are beset by contradictions. If the question were put to one, 'What would you prefer to have most of all?' – the answer frequently would be, 'Lots of money'. If you probe further and ask, 'To what purpose all this money?' – quite often you will find that it is to be spent on luxuries which merely give the owners the opportunity to be more dissatisfied, more unhappy, but on a higher level than before. People keep asking God for many favours, and this is as it should be. But nine times out of ten their requests are for useless things which have little bearing on their eternal salvation.

Early in the last century, a French priest (Pere Lamy) who will probably be canonised one day, never tired of telling his people that the profanation of Sunday leads to a decline in moral values. The first thing Catholics must do, he said, is to come together to observe the sanctification of Sunday. The same decline is becoming more and more evident in our own time here in Ireland. Most of us abhor violence, and yet to entertain ourselves we purchase costly video equipment, and spend hours watching the most obscenely violent films. We shy away from breaking bad news to anybody, and yet in our search for news we listen in daily, on TV and radio, to a veritable litany of the latest disasters, scandals, self-seeking and cruelty worldwide. Hardly ever do we hear mention of the many unselfish and generous good people, who are striving to live the life Jesus preached. The giving of a few coppers by a poor widow to a deserving cause would never, ever, make the headlines. Yet the Son of God noticed it; it will be recorded in the book of life; it will be rewarded. Even such a seemingly trivial act as a cup of cold water, given in the name of Christ, will be good news for all eternity. To live in accordance with the teaching of Christ is the only true road to joy, that Christian joy which is 'the echo of God's life within us', and our wish and prayer should be never to deviate from that road.

THIRTY-THIRD SUNDAY OF THE YEAR
Dan 12:1-13; Heb 10:11-14, 18; Mk 13:24-32

In the Bible we find very many passages which deal with what
the future holds in store, in so far as the eternal destiny of each
and every human being is concerned, references to death, judgment, heaven, hell, the second coming of Christ, and, as in
today's gospel, the signs by which the return of Christ will be
known. Many Christians, regrettably, are tempted to read and
interpret such statements as if they were eyewitness accounts,
detailed advance descriptions, of what lies ahead of us when we
depart this life. This gives rise to all kinds of fears and difficulties about how literally we should take these scripture passages,
difficulties which, objectively speaking, we should be able to
avoid. For statements about what we describe as the last things,
from the very nature of human thinking and its limitations, are
conclusions drawn from the experience of the present. They are
in no way an advance report of what is to take place later. For
any attempt to reach ahead, to grasp the future and bring it into
the here and now, is beyond the powers of the human mind.

But, strangely enough, the here and now also becomes meaningful only is so far as it is seen, against the future, as gradually
bringing nearer a real union – in grace and in Jesus Christ – with
God our Father, a union which we believe, in a dark and mysterious way, underlies all the events of our present every-day
existence, and which will only be fully grasped when we have
departed this life. We might then ask, what is the significance,
for the present moment, of today's gospel reading, with its
fantastic prophecy, which year after year intones its note of
doom for humankind, and frightens us with its predictions. We
might answer by saying, first of all, that the hereafter will not
simply be a continuation of all the good things of this life, with
the unpleasant things cut out. The gospel mention of the sun
being darkened, the moon failing to give its light, the stars
falling from the heavens, is a purely dramatic way of impressing
upon us that at death everything will be changed.

The human race often cherishes lofty dreams of how its
knowledge is going to reconstruct the world, as it were to complete creation and master the universe. But, as the liturgical year
draws to a close, the Church reminds us that this world also will
pass away, as well as each and every individual person, who is

but a fragile, insignificant part of it. And when Jesus Christ says that we, who are faithful, shall sit at table with him in the kingdom of heaven, he is making use of imagery, as is St Paul, when he says that Christ will come again amidst the sound of the trumpets of the archangels, as are the synoptic gospels, when they tell us that everyone will be gathered together by the angels, and split into two groups, the sheep and the goats, the good and the wicked. To be saved is to be in the closest union with God; to be lost is to be in a state where one is closed in on oneself utterly, without contact with others or with God, a condition which Sacred Scripture again uses terrifying words to describe, like darkness, gnashing of teeth, fire.

If we find all this impossible to reconcile with the love of God, then we should remember the advice of our Lord Jesus, who, when asked about the number of the damned, did not answer directly, but urged his followers, in the most solemn manner, to follow the narrow way which leads to life. If we do, then we may be sure of St Paul's promise that we shall be with the Lord, that we shall be filled with the joy of the marriage feast, that we shall partake for all eternity of the great Supper, which the Lord spoke of. But as to life after death, let us always bear in mind that here and now we do not have, nor indeed can we have, definite knowledge about what God has prepared for those who love him. The reason, as St John tells us, is that the faithful departed shall become like God, because they shall see him as he really is. And until then everything associated with God remains beyond our comprehension.

Of one thing, however, we can be sure, and we have it from the mouth of Jesus himself. 'Heaven and earth will pass away, but my words will not pass away. But as for that day or hour, nobody knows it, neither the angels of heaven, nor the Son; no one but the Father' (Mk 13:31f), and the Father, moreover, reassures us in these words, 'Look I am going to create new heavens and a new earth, and the past will not be remembered, and will come no more to people's minds' (Is 65:17).

OUR LORD JESUS CHRIST, UNIVERSAL KING
Dan 7:13-14; Apoc 1:5-8; Jn 18:33-37

Before becoming a Catholic, Cardinal Newman spent 15 years as Vicar to St Mary's, the Oxford University Anglican Church. Here he preached his famous sermons, and although, nowadays, we find them rather dry they kept his congregation of mainly young dons and undergraduates spellbound. One student wrote of those sermons: 'They spoke of God, as no man, I think, could speak, unless God were with him. It was to many of us as if God had spoken to us for the first time.' Newman's appeal to them was that of a prophet, a kind of John the Baptist. But this enthusiasm aroused jealousy and hostility among other staff members at Oriel College to which Newman was attached. They tried every means to reduce his influence; they jockeyed him out of university posts, even changed mealtimes on Sundays, so as to keep undergraduates in residence away from attending his sermons, but all in vain. The young men were drawn by his deep faith, his commitment to his pastoral duties, his disregard for advancement in this world, his life of prayer and fasting. The example of Newman, in some small way, mirrors the extraordinary fascination that Jesus held for those who witnessed him in person.

We can plainly see from today's gospel how even Pilate was deeply impressed by Jesus. It is obvious that he did not believe in the accusation that Jesus claimed to be king of the Jews. He knew a political revolutionary when he saw one, and in no way was Jesus such an individual. In any case his own secret intelligence agents would have kept him informed of any plotting in the country. But Jesus he could not fit into any other category either. There was an air of mystery about him. Pilate, in some way, sensed the power of Jesus, but was afraid to allow it to influence him, afraid to submit to it.

Throughout his public life, and during the events leading up to Calvary, whether he was speaking to those assembled or remaining silent in the face of accusation, Jesus was in command at all times. To all those who try and follow what the Holy Spirit is telling them, Christ is truly the visible presence of the hidden God. 'May your spiritual growth become richer', the New Testament says, 'as you see more fully God's great secret, Christ himself. For it is in him, and in him alone, that people will find all the treasures of wisdom and understanding' (Col 2:2). Although Pilate acknowledged the innocence of Jesus, when he told the Jews, 'I find no crime in him', he did not set Jesus free; and this because he had turned his back on the truth. He was blind to the mysterious presence of God in Christ.

To those, however, who see God at work in the person, words, and actions of Jesus, and who seriously endeavour to respond to what God, through Jesus, is asking of them, to such committed souls Jesus becomes Lord of their lives. He becomes truly their king. The title 'king' presents us with some difficulties, because in the past earthly kings as a rule were prone to lord it over their subjects. But the kingship of Christ is far removed from any kind of earthly domineering. 'My kingdom is not of this world', he told Pilate. Christ is chiefly concerned, not about domination, but rather the spiritual liberation of the weak and the oppressed. It was this objective he was surely pursuing wherever the gospel describes him as having pity on the multitudes.

In his own town synagogue of Nazareth, he likened his mission to that of the Suffering Servant in Isaiah: 'He has sent me to proclaim the good news to the poor, to proclaim liberty to captives, and to the blind new sight, to set the downtrodden free, to proclaim the Lord's year of favour' (Lk 4:18f). Here we have the blueprint set out by Christ for his kingly role. All those things which Jesus once did throughout Judaea and Galilee he continues to do in the world today. In him those who were blind to the truth about themselves and about God have new sight given them; in him those who were deaf to the voice of conscience and of the Holy Spirit have begun to listen; in him those who were dead and powerless in sin are restored to vitality and a new happiness in life; in him the poorest and the despised of this world inherit the immeasurable riches of the love of God. In all this Christ shows that he truly watches over us, that for us today, this is how he is still king. It is only by faith that we can come to recognise him as the chosen One of God, and the true and universal King.

Year C

'The believers who were scattered went from place to place preaching the good news. Philip went down to a Samaritan city and proclaimed the Christ to them. The people with one accord eagerly listened to the message he preached to them.'
(Acts 8:4-6)

FIRST SUNDAY OF ADVENT
Jer 33:14-16; 1 Thess 3:12-4:2; Lk 21:25-28, 34-36

We are in what has been described as the time of year when frost
or rain regularly herald each day, when the breath of morning is
damp and worshippers are fewer. It is also the beginning of the
season when the familiar words of the Church's Advent liturgy
warn us to awake from out our spiritual lethargy, in order to
welcome him who comes in the name of the Lord, and also to be
prepared for that final awakening, when each human soul will
be called from this world to stand before the God who created it.
The word Advent, which means coming or arrival, can refer to
the first or second coming of Christ. The first coming took place
when Jesus the Son of the eternal God was born of the Virgin
Mary, and became a member of the human race.

He clearly manifested his divine power and wisdom before
the world, and some who witnessed this saw in him God's Holy
Spirit at work, while others hated him because they saw in him a
threat to established beliefs, customs and institutions. 'It is better
for one man to die for the people, than for the whole nation to be
destroyed', these latter argued (Jn 11:50), and so they crucified
him. But, among his followers, the firm belief grew in the
promise of Christ, that at the end of time he will come on the
clouds of heaven with great power and glory, and that all flesh
will see the salvation of our God. We shall all have to stand
before the judgment seat of Christ, the New Testament says,
where we will 'all be seen for what we are, so that each of us may
receive what we deserve, whether good or bad, according to
what we did in the body' (2 Cor 5:10).

This second coming of Christ gave rise to such an intense
spirit of expectancy among the early Christians, that, when they
met, they greeted each other with the Aramaic words 'Marana tha',
meaning 'Lord, come' (1 Cor 16:22). It is a wish which, at the
beginning of the liturgical year, we, who are followers of Christ
also, should try to capture and make our own in some small
measure. 'Stay awake, praying at all times for the strength to
survive all that is going to happen, and to stand with confidence
before the Son of Man', the gospel urges us. And the Lord, we
are assured, will confirm our hearts in holiness, so that we may
be blameless in the sight of God our Father, when our Lord Jesus
Christ comes with all his saints. The first coming of Christ has
taken place in the past; the second coming lies in the future.

But St Bernard, the great Cistercian Abbot of Clairvaux and friend of Saint Malachy, bishop of Armagh, spoke of a third coming of Christ, a secret one which is taking place here and now. Even though this coming is hidden from us, it is nonetheless very real, as Christ himself in the words of scripture tells us, 'I will not leave you orphans; I will come to you … If anyone loves me he will keep my word, and my Father will love him, and we shall come to him and make our home with him' (Jn 14: 18, 23). Of course, Christ does not now reveal himself to us in any physical or concrete way. Nevertheless, St Paul says that 'now we see him as in a mirror dimly' – and we should remember that mirrors in Paul's time were just made of polished bronze – 'but then' – meaning in the next life – 'we shall see him face to face' (1 Cor 13:12).

Christ then did not leave us orphans. When he became one of us as a little baby, he was coming to remain with us for ever. 'The Virgin will conceive and give birth to a son, and they will call him Emmanuel, a name which means "God-is-with-us".' Thus St Matthew wrote in the first chapter of his gospel; and St Paul put the following challenge to the Christians at Corinth, roughly 24 years after the Crucifixion: 'Examine yourselves to make sure you are in the faith; test yourselves. Do you acknowledge that Jesus Christ is really in you? If not you have failed the test' (2 Cor 13:5). We speak about putting Christ back into Christmas, but we should begin by prayer and especially by the Eucharist to make his presence within each one of us more real, more lasting.

The English Jesuit poet, Robert Southwell, who at the age of 34 was martyred at Tyburn for the faith in 1595 wrote:
'God is my gift, himself he freely gave me.
God's gift am I, and none but God shall have me.'

May our prayer this Advent be that of the first Christians: 'Marana tha' – Come, Lord Jesus, come.

SECOND SUNDAY OF ADVENT
Bar 5:1-9; Phil 1:3-6, 8-11; Lk 3:1-6

In this Advent season, the Church in a special way brings home to us that we are at a stage of our existence when God for us remains the great unknown, that God is hidden from us. We are also told that this period will come to an end unexpectedly; and the last few Sunday Readings have been warning us to be prepared, to be on guard, to make sure that we do not shut ourselves up in a restricted and closed routine of day-to-day activity, but to watch for this coming of the Lord. But when all is said and done, we might well begin to wonder why the words they speak have not yet come to pass. This reminds us of the episode in the gospels where Christ was speaking to the Apostles about the Father, and Philip showed the same kind of impatience. 'Show us the Father', he said, 'and we shall be satisfied'. And Jesus answered, 'Have I been with you all this time, Philip, and you still do not know me. To have seen me is to have seen the Father' (Jn 14:8f). The vision being demanded of Philip was a vision of faith; and we also, especially at this time, must have faith. We must 'put on the armour of light' (Rom 13:12), as St Paul vividly describes it, and become children of the day. Thus we are made citizens of the kingdom of God and his divine Son, and freed from the empire of darkness.

Before we sit in judgment on Philip for his demand to be shown the Father, we should take an honest look at our own attitudes when we ask God to reveal himself, especially to reveal his divine power. Quite frequently, when we do this, we are not even thinking of God, or of other human beings, but purely of ourselves. How often do we appeal to God, as some kind of sovereign magician, to wave his wand and give us an easy life, get rid of all the suffering, and the torment, and the anxiety that we encounter as part of the human condition. If we were to reflect deeply on such an approach to God, we should find that it is not at all God's presence we are seeking, but rather a kind of heaven on earth. It is an attempt to idealise our present life, to fix ourselves in it forever, to be rid of all that bothers us, and be surrounded with all the creature comforts that appeal to us.

But God is not that kind of benevolent provider. God is the Creator who will fashion a new heaven and a new earth, and, in the process, this world, as we know it, will completely disappear.

That is not to say, however, that God does not have regard for our worries, that he is some kind of impersonal, remote looker-on. For, in the person of Jesus Christ, God showed how he cares for, and loves each and every one of us. In and through Jesus, God shared in the sorrow of Martha and Mary for their brother Lazarus, he wept over the city of Jerusalem and all its inhabitants, he sacrificed himself on the Cross for all our sakes.

To-day, in the first reading, he addresses to us the words he spoke to his chosen people through the prophet Baruch: 'Jerusalem, put aside your garments of sorrow and distress; put on the beauty of the glory of God forever.' We should, then, try and drop the self-seeking attitude which so frequently prompts us to ask, 'What is there in all of this for me? What can I gain from this?' Even our earthly friends would sense this selfishness, were it to be the only reason for our friendship with them. We should rather try and learn from the example of the Patron Saint of the Missions, whose feast-day we celebrate at this time, St Francis Xavier (1506-1552), who was, what one might describe as, the St Paul of the second Christian millennium, who travelled through India, Malaysia, China and Japan, in order to spread the good news of Christ's coming. His prayer was, 'I love you Lord, not because I hope for heaven thereby. I love you, and will love, solely because you are my Lord'. Loving God purely for his own sake will give a new direction to our lives.

The English saint, Richard of Chichester, was wont to state this way what the desire of a truly Christian soul should be, 'Lord Jesus, as we begin this new year in the Church, help us to see you more clearly, to love your more dearly, and to follow you more nearly'. Following in the footsteps of Christ is what matters. In this season therefore, we should, as Scripture urges us, give special thanks to God for having loved us, and beseech him to fill us with a pure and disinterested holiness, to fill us with love for all our neighbours, to fill us with a joyful expectancy that, at the end of our sojourn on earth, Christ may meet us, and take us to be with him in God's new creation for ever.

THE IMMACULATE CONCEPTION OF THE BVM
Gen 3:9-15, 20; Eph 1:3-6, 11-12; Lk 1:26-38

I remember one evening walking along a street in a certain town, where scaffolding had just been erected in front of one of the houses. There I came across a blind man who had been trying to make his way to a chemist's shop close by, using one of those metal canes to tap out what had, from practice, become for him familiar landmarks along the route. But because of the scaffolding which covered the whole sidewalk, he told me that he had become completely confused. After I had helped him to negotiate his way past the scaffolding it suddenly struck me, that here he was trusting wholly in the disembodied voice of a complete stranger, whom he could not see. To have faith is, like that blind man, to take a step into the dark because of an implicit trust in somebody beyond one's immediate awareness.

If, on this feast of the Immaculate Conception, we were to ask the question, 'What was the greatest virtue in Mary', the answer must surely be her faith. The Fathers of the Church used to express it this way, 'Mary first believed, and in her faith conceived', or as St Augustine wrote, 'Mary conceived Jesus in her heart, before conceiving him in her womb'. To have faith, it has been said, is to remain faithful in darkness to what has been grasped for a brief moment in light. In the life of the Blessed Virgin Mary, as unfolded by sacred scripture, we find only one such moment of light, one apparition, the Annunciation, and this was enough to convince Mary for ever thereafter that God was calling her, in a very special way, to be part of his plan for the salvation of all mankind. Despite the risks Mary must have been aware her consent would lead to, her faith was such that no further apparitions were needed.

But what was revealed in that moment of light was something which, instead of making her complacent, caused her rather to be filled with apprehension and wonder. 'Hail, full of grace', the Angel had said, a more exact translation being, 'Rejoice, Oh highly favoured one', and this note of wonder and praise would be re-echoed in the greeting of Mary's cousin Elizabeth, 'Of all women you are the most blessed'. Mary being deeply disturbed by the words of the Angel is reassured by him, 'Mary, do not be afraid: you have won God's favour'.

Hence it is that on this day we recall with honour, the central

privilege in the outpouring of God's favour on Mary, her absolute sinlessness from the moment of her conception. Not only
was she freed from original sin, by a singular grace and privilege
of almighty God, acquired from the merits of the Son to whom,
one day, she would give birth, but also by cooperation with the
Holy Spirit's gifts of faith, hope and love, she was to remain
until her very last breath sinless and holy. Within the Church,
this doctrine of the absolute sinlessness of Mary, we might add,
was first set forth by St Augustine.

Mary's election as Mother of Jesus would bring with it so
high a degree of union with God that, right from the very moment
of her conception, she was preserved completely free from the
least stain of original sin. In the same way her unique closeness
to Christ in his fight against sin and death would also bring her
a share in the victor's spoils, something which became manifest
to the whole world in her glorious Assumption, body and soul,
into heaven. It is extraordinary, however, that Mary, who, by
the word of her Son on the Cross, was designated Mother of the
Apostles, never preached, nor did she carry on any public apost-
olate. But her task lay elsewhere – to communicate the true
presence of God to the world. For thirty years she had never
gone away from her home, until her divine Son began his public
mission.

But then one day, after Christ had ascended into heaven, his
closest followers would gather around her. They were to keep
vigil with her and pray with her until the day of Pentecost. For,
in so far as it is humanly possible, she was the one who could see
deepest into the mind of Christ, being the Virgin most prudent
and preserved from the least fault or stain of evil. Each of us too
has the same incredible vocation which Mary had, namely, to be
so united with the Holy Spirit as to give life to God in the world,
to make God alive in the world. May we, too, keep vigil with
Mary, as did the first members of the Church; and let us keep on
asking her to pray for and assist us, both now and at the hour of
our death. Amen.

THIRD SUNDAY OF ADVENT
Zeph 3:14-18; Phil 4:4-7; Lk 3:10-18

The liturgy of this Third Sunday in Advent is full of reassurance and comfort for us. In the past it was known as 'Gaudete Sunday', the Latin word 'gaudete' meaning 'rejoice'. The liturgy then tells us to be happy, not to worry, that the Lord is near. And if we want the peace of God to be in our hearts, and in our thoughts – our hearts which are always seeking to possess the things of this world – our thoughts which are so often filled not only with fears, worries and anxieties about our present circumstances, but moreover about our future – then, that peace will be ours, if we simply and trustfully ask God for it. Scripture tells us to do precisely this where it says, 'There is no need to worry; but if there is anything you need, pray for it, asking God for it with prayer and thanksgiving' (Phil 4:6). Note as well that it tells us not to wait until after God grants our requests before thanking him. Even as we ask, we should be giving thanks. One of the things we should thank God for at the end of this year has been the Christian witness given by so many good people in our time.

Wherever there is evil, God will ensure that resolute and saintly souls will rise up to combat it. Such was the call, the prophetic witness associated with the person of St John the Baptist, as described in the readings for this Christmas preparation period. People were prepared to walk all the way from Jerusalem down to the vicinity of Jericho in the deep Jordan valley, on the edge of the desert – all of fifteen miles each way – in order to see John, this charismatic figure who till then had lived the life of a recluse in the wilderness around the Dead Sea. Having seen him, many moreover wanted to stay and listen to his message and be baptised by him. But the reaction also of many of them to John was one of uncertainty, that uncertainty which surfaces in all of us when we take time to cast a critical eye on the kind of life we are leading.

'What must we do?', they asked him. And John spelt out the answer for them in no uncertain terms. While their seeking for guidance showed their willingness to change, it also showed that they were lacking in the Holy Spirit, in that fire with which, according to the Baptist, Christ when he comes will baptise. For not only does the Holy Spirit guide us, he pleads for us with sighs too deep for words. 'Love and do what you will', was to be the motto of St Augustine, meaning that if people have total inner commitment to God, then they will be incapable of doing wrong, they will know instinctively what is right from the promptings of the Spirit within them.

John the Baptist, however, attempted to effect this inner change in his listeners' hearts by telling them not to be grasping, not to exact from others more than a just return for their services, but rather to help those in need. 'If anyone has two cloaks, he must share with the man who has none.' 'Give your blood', the ancient monks in the desert used to say, 'and you will possess the Spirit'. The society to which John was addressing himself – as indeed Jesus did later– was to collapse within a generation – was to collapse, because of its lack of spiritual depth, its over concern with externals, as evidenced by the Pharisees, its pursuit of a narrow-minded nationalism, as seen in the Zealots who were willing to resort to violence and assassination in their hatred of the Romans.

The greatest danger to the continuation of any society becomes a reality when most of its members become motivated by selfish concerns, greed and covetousness. The message which our own society invariably highlights is not, alas, that of sharing cloaks, but of acquiring outfits which are better, more comfortable, more in keeping with the size of one's pay differential. The sad thing is that all this unbridled seeking for earthly comforts, this concern with the cares of life, pulls us further and further away from the yearning for himself, which God has placed within all of us. It turns us away from the things of the Spirit, and from the pursuit of religious idealism. Prayerfully then, and in the presence of God, let us give thanks to the Father in this Mass, for the gift of his divine Son, who in its celebration makes us one with himself. Let us ask for the peace of God, as Sacred scripture urges us, for that abiding peace which is so much greater than we can ever understand, so much greater than anything this world can ever offer us. And we can be assured that for all who faithfully do this the reward will be everlasting.

FOURTH SUNDAY OF ADVENT
Mic 5:2-5; Heb 10:5-10; Lk 1:39-45

No matter how we regard ourselves, one thing is certain, and that is that the life of each one of us has a unique purpose in the designs of God. Sad to say, however, instead of allowing God to direct us, very often we want to dictate to God. It has been said of our age that it is the age, not of the obedient child, but of the obedient parent. Small wonder then if we, who should see ourselves as children of God – for that is what we are – find ourselves trying to make God an obedient God, one who will bring about the things we are seeking in this life, while warding off all the undesirable things. We would like to use God for our own purposes, instead of seeing ourselves as the instruments of God's will.

The story is told about a famous operatic singer, who had given a public performance, and who, after being applauded rapturously by his audience, returned to his dressing room, where he thanked God for making his concert such a success. But, it could well be that if we were to reflect critically on the action of this man, we might find that he was not thanking God at all. Indeed he could, very possibly, have blamed God, accused God of letting him down, had his audience booed his performance instead of clapping him.

In contrast to such a concept of God is the message that we have today in the second reading, which puts into Christ's mouth the words, 'God here I am. I have come to do your will'. The real value of Christ's life, of Christ's teaching for us, lies in this conformity to the intention, the purpose, the will of God the Father. In St John's gospel, Christ expresses the same sentiment in his own words: 'I seek, not my own will, but the will of him who sent me' (6:38). And when, in the Garden of Gethsemane, he found himself being broken in the hands of God, and confronted with the terrors of death, he still prayed: 'Father, not my will, but thine, be done'. He made this motto the very meaning of his sonship, and the way through which we also become children of God. 'Whoever does the will of my Father in heaven is my brother and sister, and mother' (Mt 12:50), he said, meaning that the claims of physical ties are less important than those of spiritual relationships. By forming a close spiritual bond with God, by submitting ourselves completely to the Father, we, as it were, become other Christs; we bring Christ into the world again, so that people looking at us, can say there is Christ. St Francis of Assisi said, 'We beget Christ when, through divine love and a pure and sincere conscience, we carry him in our hearts and bodies. We bring him forth through deeds which are a shining example to others'.

We find confirmation of this in the works of St Bernard of Clairvaux, the learned and devout theologian, who had such a great devotion to Our Lady. Like Mary, he argues, it is necessary that we must, in a spiritual manner, conceive in ourselves and bring forth in ourselves the risen and glorified Christ. 'The one who has created us,' he writes, 'is born in us'. Since the time when the Blessed Virgin Mary first conceived him, Jesus, as it were, still continues to be conceived in each one of us by faith, day by day, according to the graces God has given each of us. And the Christian soul, if it is to bring forth Christ, the Son of God, must have the Blessed Virgin Mary as its model, and try to imitate her always.

During the week we celebrated the feast of St John of the Cross, one of the truly great saints who suffered much during his life. St Teresa of Avilla who was his co-worker in reforming the Carmelite Order had a great sense of humour and openness with God. While complaining in her prayers about the sufferings of St John she said, 'Lord, no wonder you have so few friends, since you have such a strange way of dealing with them'. The Blessed Virgin herself was granted the extraordinary blessing of being the Mother of the Son of God. Her heart was filled with a wondering, tremulous joy at receiving so great a privilege. Yet that privilege was to be a sword to pierce her very heart, for it meant that one day she would see her Son hanging on a Cross. Jesus came on earth, not to make life easy, but rather to make people great.

No matter what crosses come our way, we should have the courage to say with Mary, 'My soul glorifies the Lord, and my spirit rejoices in God my Saviour'. Joy, tranquillity, peace, these are the blessings that we associate with the holy season of Christmas. They are the echo of God's life within us.

THE NATIVITY OF OUR LORD
Vigil: Is 62:1-5; Acts 13:16-17, 22-25; Mt 1:1-25
Midnight: Is 9:1-6; Tit 2:11-14; Lk 2:1-14
Dawn: Is 62:11-12; Tit 3:11-14; Lk 2:15-20
Day: Is 52:7-10; Heb 1:1-6; Jn 1:1-18

'The glory of the Lord shone round the shepherds, and they were terrified'. A little knowledge, it has been said, is a dangerous thing, because it can give rise to doubt and a tendency to question everything. But there is no doubting the effects on a person of a little faith, or a little religion. For, if we allow the light of God's Holy Spirit, even in a little way, to illuminate our consciences, the darkness – if we might so describe it – or the shortcomings, the defects, which are lurking within, become all the more visible. 'The glory of the Lord shone round them, and they were terrified.' It is extraordinary that, as with the shepherds on the first Christmas night, for us too the glory of God can be a source of alarm.

When confronted with the perfect holiness of God, God's call to us to be perfect as he is perfect, the difficulty of keeping his commandments, the lessons of divine revelation contained in God's holy and inspired word, in the face of all these the superficial believer can be filled with apprehension and fear. And often when the world sees a person so afraid, it thinks that religion has thus reformed him, whereas he may not be religious at all, but simply conscience-stricken. On the other hand religion which is true, far from filling us with alarm and terror and apprehension, says to us in the words of the Angel on Christmas night, 'Fear not' – don't be afraid – 'for behold I bring you tidings of great joy, a joy to be shared by all. To-day a Saviour has been born to you; he is Christ the Lord'. However, lest they should be lulled into a false sense of new-found security, the Angel tells the shepherds – and indeed all of us – 'Here is a sign for you. You will find a baby wrapped in swaddling clothes and lying in a manger'. The shepherds, we are told, 'came with haste, and they found Mary and Joseph and the infant'. They 'found' implies effort on their part; the shepherds had to search.

To those, however, who, from the outset, were closest to this event at Bethlehem, there was nothing outwardly which struck them as marvellous. The angels and angelic choirs were seen and heard some miles away. God came anonymously into our world, and most people passed him by. The shepherds came because they had witnessed a sign. Sacred Scripture is full of descriptions of people asking God for signs, miraculous portents that would confirm their beliefs. We ourselves are all familiar with the sign of the Cross, and this sign, given by the Angel to the shepherds, is a sign for us too, and every Christmas we should make an earnest effort to understand its message.

The Son of the Almighty God assuming the form of a helpless infant is surely a sign that is intended to pierce our hearts, to call us to conversion, a sign that he, who was rich, had become poor for our sakes, that he, who was great, had become little; and the sad thing is that this sign of the baby in the manger can also be interpreted as a sign of rejection. 'There was no room for him in the inn'. He came to his own people and his own received him not. And how many there are throughout the world who look into their Christmas cribs and see nothing.

They fail to recognise in the tiny and helpless figure of the infant lying in the manger the human features of the God who created us, who, when we fell from grace did not abandon us, but assumed our lowly human nature, in order to free us from our sinfulness, to make us his own people, to make us his children. What we must remember is that the first Christmas was only the beginning of God's coming. He is still in the process of coming for each one of us; he is still trying to gain entrance into our hearts. 'Behold I stand at the door and knock' (Rev 3:20). It is only when we open our hearts to God's Holy Spirit, pointing the way to us from within our conscious being, that peace and happiness will be ours.

For true joy, lasting joy, is begotten of God's life within us. And in the Eucharist, which we are about to celebrate together, let us not forget to thank God for the precious gift of his own divine Son, our Lord, Jesus Christ. Let us also rejoice and be glad, for this day a Saviour has been born for us, a Son given to us, and this is the name given to him, Wonder-Counsellor, Mighty-God, Eternal-Father, Prince-of-Peace. This gift of Christ's peace and love and true joy – this is the most precious gift we can receive at Christmas, and we pray that, for our spiritual nourishment, we and all the members of Christ's Church may be granted it.

FEAST OF THE HOLY FAMILY
1 Sam 1:20-22, 24-28; 1 Jn 3:1-2, 21-24; Lk 2:41-52

It is very true to say that many of the structures that under-pinned Irish society in the past are nowadays being challenged, and none more so than the traditional family. We have more and more one parent families, couples who have children without sealing their union with marriage vows, and homosexual couples – perhaps more outside than in this country – who demand the right to have children and live as a normal family. While society and the State are putting forward a different understanding of family, the Church in this feast urges us to look to the Holy Family of Jesus, Mary and Joseph as a model to be upheld and copied. What message does this model have for normal modern families and for all of us in general? Before giving an answer, we must bear in mind that the Holy Family was far from being a normal family. Mary, the wife, was a mother while remaining a virgin; Joseph, in the eyes of others the father, was a celibate husband; and the only child was the Son of God. Far from being normal, this family was absolutely unique. God certainly works in devious ways, and yet he obviously wanted the stability, we might even say anonymity, of everyday family life for his Son while he was growing up.

To neighbours, Jesus was simply the son of Joseph, the carpenter, and living under his authority while helping him at his trade. After the manner of any other family of that time, and perhaps even more so, the Holy Family had problems and wor-ries: the discovery by Joseph that Mary was with child before they had come together, the birth of Jesus in circumstances of extreme poverty away from home and neighbours, the threats from Herod and flight into Egypt, the task of finding a new home in Nazareth far away from Mary's friends and parental home. Then in today's gospel reading we have the disappear-ance of Jesus during the celebration of Passover in Jerusalem, something which left Mary and Joseph in a state of shock and apprehension. Furthermore, Jesus' response, 'Why were you looking for me? Did you not know that I must be busy with my Father's affairs?' was an explanation that left them dumbfounded, for it seemed to imply that their worry was of their own making. This single insight into the normal activity of the Holy Family shows us that, just as within any other family, there were tensions, differences of opinion, and even pain and misunderstanding.

But it is not because this family had no differences and up-sets, but precisely because it had, that it is a model for others. Its members were able to cope with, and overcome, anything that threatened to create lasting divisions within it. We are told that Jesus lived under the authority of his parents, and furthermore that he increased in wisdom, stature, and favour with God and those around him. It was not easy for the parents, and Mary especially stored up all these things in her heart. She pondered over them for a long time afterwards, before learning their meaning. That learning comes from listening was something Mary and Joseph were familiar with. At the Annunciation Mary had listened to the angel, as did Joseph when told in a dream to take Mary as his wife. And Jesus later, when complemented by one of a crowd, said, 'Still happier those who hear the word of God and keep it' (Lk 11:28).

In like fashion, the members of a family must listen in order to acquire the skills to cope with conflict within it. In an atmos-phere of mutual respect virtue will flourish as will acceptance of one another, even when at fault or misunderstood. Christ in Nazareth also listened, and was taught by the Holy Spirit in a manner no one else was, so that he came to see himself as the Son of God in a way unique to him alone. The mystery of Nazareth was the mystery of the hiddeness of God, and how the Holy Family sought to understand Him.

How beneficial it would be if the members of every family, every now and again, were to sit down together, let God speak in their hearts, let the gospel confront their lives, and engage, not in heated emotional discussions, but in prayerful listening together. They would then learn how to act, not out of their con-victions, which can so often be mere prejudice, but out of their experience of being moved interiorly by God. Always remember that the Spirit speaks, not in a whirlwind, but, as the prophet Elijah discovered, from out a gentle breeze. The voice of God is heard in moments of listening, in stillness, in an atmosphere of prayer.

MARY, MOTHER OF GOD
Num 6:22-27; Gal 4:4-7; Lk 2:16-21

To-day marks an ending and a beginning. It is a time for evaluating the past year, and for setting targets, by way of resolutions, for the coming one; a time when we reflect on God's promise of a Redeemer, who has come, and look forward to the promise of an eternal reward in heaven which, God willing, will come. In doing all this our thoughts should inevitably be brought to dwell upon the one whose feast we are celebrating this day, the feast of the Blessed Virgin Mary, who is both Mother of God and Queen of heaven. The title, Mother of God, is one which above all others we should have thought impossible for any creature to possess. Yet we cannot refuse this title to Mary, for to do so would be to deny the sublime truth at the heart of our faith, namely, that the divine Son of God took on a human nature like ours.

When, in 1854, Pope Pius IX proclaimed the dogma of the Immaculate Conception, he also stated that Mary was granted such perfection that nothing greater than she can be imagined apart from God. By the redeeming action of her own Son, which we recall every time we celebrate Mass, Mary was kept free from the least imperfection or sin, in such a way that she personifies the redemption gained by Jesus in the greatest possible manner. All this does not mean that Mary suffered life's pains and troubles in any way different from ours. In the Litany in her honour we refer to her as the Queen of Sorrows. But she knew how to accept all the crosses that she encountered in such a way that the virtue bestowed on her by God was proved to be genuine and even enhanced by these. When we reflect on the perfection which was Mary's, we can say that more important than Mary's virginity was her motherhood.

As virgin, Mary was consecrated to God; as Mother she was possessed by God; she became the spouse of God in a way much more real than that recorded in the lives of several saints where mystical espousals to God are mentioned. And Mary is not only the Mother of God's divine Son, she is also the Mother of the whole human race, which is made up of the sisters and brothers of Jesus. In Jesus we find a great deal of what is in Mary. She is reproduced in Jesus. And yet Jesus, who is so close to her, because he is her child, is ever so distant from her, for he also is the only-begotten Son of the Father from all eternity.

We have then the unique situation, by which Mary, on the one hand, begets the eternal Son in time, and, on the other hand, is herself begotten in that Son from all eternity, since through him, with him, in him, all things were made by God. What amazes us is the delicacy, the sensitivity, with which God called Mary to play so essential a role in the eternal salvation of the human race. At the Annunciation the eternal destiny of all of us, depended on the free choice of a girl, no more than 14 years old. And when she said 'Yes', she was answering for us all. This, however, entailed more than a mere word; for it meant the broadening of the scope of her motherhood to include all God's family. In other words Mary, in a very special way, became our Mother also.

We find confirmation of this in St John's account of the Passion, where Jesus seeing his mother, and also the disciple whom he loved, said to his mother, 'Woman, this is your son'. He did not say, 'He will take the place of your Son, or he will be like another son to you.' His solemn words were, 'This is your son.' What Christ was saying was that in the beloved disciple Christ himself would live on, and with him, moreover, Mary's role as mother would also endure. In a symbolic way that disciple represented each one of us.

When St Paul speaks of 'living now, not with his own life, but with the life of Christ living in him' (Gal 2:20), we begin to understand how Mary's motherhood extends to all generations of believers, you and I included, and this because we all form one Body, one Spirit in Christ. To-day, as we celebrate the Feast of the Mother of God, and our Mother too, let us begin again, in a much deeper, more meaningful way to say 'Yes', as did Mary, to God's plans involving both Mother and Son, for our eternal redemption. St Luke tells us, in his gospel, how Mary treasured in her heart and pondered over all the events surrounding the birth of Christ. Here she set an example for us to follow, so that, in a spiritual sense, Christ may be born in us too.

SECOND SUNDAY AFTER CHRISTMAS
Sir 24:1-4; Eph 1:3-6, 15-18; Jn 1:1-18

In the Bible account of the Exodus (33:19+) there is a strange and intriguing passage where the Lord God tells Moses that he will let his splendour pass in front of him on Mount Sinai. But, 'you cannot see my face', God warned him, 'for man cannot see me and live'. 'I will put you in a cleft of the rock', the Lord promised, 'and shield you with my hand while I pass by. Then I will take my hand away and you shall see the back of me; but my face is not to be seen'. This attitude of reverential fear before God, which we find throughout the whole of the Old Testament, gives way to something profoundly different with the coming of Christ. 'The Word was made flesh; he lived among us, and we saw his glory', St John says at the end of today's gospel reading.

Here we have a sublime statement of the visible aspect of God in the Incarnation; and this visible aspect is even more emphasised by John in his First Letter, where he speaks of Christ as the Word, that 'which has existed from the beginning, which we have heard, and have seen with our own eyes, which we have watched, and touched with our hands, – the Word, who is life'. But let us not assume from this that the privilege enjoyed by the people around Jesus, of seeing him face to face, made it any easier for them to recognise in him God's holy presence among them. The majority of his own townsfolk in Nazareth saw him only as the 'son of the carpenter'. God indeed had become man, but for all but three years of his life, while living with Mary and Joseph until the latter's death, we have the mystery of the concealment of his divinity. Even after his resurrection, when he made himself visible to some of his closest followers, we are told for example by St Luke how at first 'their eyes were kept from recognising him' (Lk 24:13-16). It is in the light of all this that we begin to grasp the necessity of faith, the need to be able to understand and perceive what is revealed', the need to have the eyes of our hearts fully enlightened bringing us to a more complete knowledge of our Redeemer, as St Paul prayed for the Ephesians (in today's Second Reading).

We find this happening in St Luke's story of the two disciples on the road to Emmaus, after the Resurrection. At first they saw Christ, but did not know him. So walking by their side he explained the scriptures that were about himself. Then, at the end of the evening, when he sat at table with them, he took the bread and said the blessing, broke the bread and gave it to them. At this the scales fell from their eyes; but by the time they had recognised him, he had already vanished from their sight. As Cardinal Newman once said, the risen Lord had gone from the hiding-place of being seen without being known, to that of being known without being seen. God is Spirit, and can only be apprehended by the spiritual part of the human being, who is both body and spirit. The disciples' eyes were opened and they recognised him; but he had already vanished from their sight. Recognition came when vision was lost. Far from looking at this event as a once-and-for-all occurrence, we too are confronted with just such a daily apparition, as often as we celebrate the Eucharist.

At every Mass we too listen to the scriptures, and we should ask ourselves, 'do they enlighten the eyes of our hearts? Did our hearts burn within us, as the scriptures were being explained to us?' At every Mass we witness the breaking of the Eucharistic bread, but do we therein recognise the presence of Christ? For truly present he is, in a mysterious but very real way. And when we receive Holy Communion, we are united, not with the Christ living two thousand years ago, but with the risen, glorified Christ, now living with the Father for ever. If the Eucharist was the great means of bringing the two disciples, and the Apostles also, to believe in the risen Christ, God grant that it may be the centre of our faith-life also during the New Year before us.

When St Paul had crossed from Asia Minor to Greece, to evangelise Europeans for the first time, he preached to the people of Athens. But their response was, 'We will listen to you some other time'; and, neglecting the grace offered them, they never did until much later. The future is something we cannot be sure of; the past we cannot change. The present moment, the here and now, is the only part of our lives we can really grasp. May we then, this very day, make use of the opportunities which are now granted to us, and begin to serve our God anew.

THE EPIPHANY OF THE LORD
Is 60:1-6; Eph 3:2-3, 5-6; Mt 2:1-12

The word 'Epiphany' means manifestation or showing forth.
And after the showing forth of the newly-born Saviour, our
Lord Jesus Christ, to the Jews through the medium of the shepherds, we have in today's feast his manifestation to the gentiles
represented by the Magi. The Magi were good, holy, and
learned men who originally formed the priestly caste in Persia.
They were skilled in philosophy, medicine, natural science and
astrology, and played a great part in educating the Persian
kings. It was only later that their skills degenerated into magic,
fortune telling and sorcery. It may seem remarkable to us that
the wise men, or Magi, should come out of the East in search of a
king, whose star they claimed to have seen in its rising. But more
remarkable still, just about the time Jesus was born, there was an
extraordinary expectation that a special ruler was about to
come. And we find this evidenced even in the writings of pagan
historians of the period (like Tacitus and Suetonius, as well as by
the Jew Josephus, who courted the Romans).

Among the Jews, at the time of Jesus' birth, there were four
religious groups; the Pharisees who believed in a life hereafter
that could be attained only by strict adherence to the Law, both
written and oral; the Sadducees or priestly caste who rejected
oral Law and did not believe in life after death; the Zealots who
were fanatical nationalists; and the party never mentioned in the
New Testament, the Essenes (Or Pious Ones), who looked on
society at the time as being corrupt and beyond redemption.
Accordingly these last withdrew into the Judaean wilderness
along the western shores of the Dead Sea, where they formed
communities of men women and children, and faced an unrelenting struggle for survival in the sweltering heat and barren
landscape 1,300 ft. below sea-level. After their daily work they
would assemble each night for prayer study and reading. These
were the people responsible for the writing of the Dead Sea
Scrolls at the settlement of Qumran. They deserve special mention because what helped them endure was their belief – a much
firmer one than that of the other parties – that the expected day
of the Lord was at hand, and that this would be marked by the
coming of a messiah who would ensure the victory of the Sons
of Light over the Sons of Darkness.

Nowadays some scholars regard John the Baptist as a part-product of their way of life. He was an ascetic and saw his task as that of preparing the way for the Lord. When Jesus began his public life, John sent two of his disciples to ask him, 'Are you the one who is to come, or are we to look for another?' One of the OT passages which had especial significance for the Essenes, who devoted so much of their time to the study of Scripture, was the prophecy of Balaam (Num 24:17): 'I see him – but not in the present; I behold him – but not close at hand. A star from Jacob takes the leadership, a sceptre arises from Israel.' Herein lay the origin of the Star of David symbol, cherished to this day by the Jews as their national emblem. And perhaps this prophecy is the reason also why the Magi came out of the East in search of a king, whose star they claimed to have seen in its rising. People everywhere then seemed to be waiting for God, and the desire for God was in their hearts, as the quest of the Magi bears witness.

But no sooner did God come on earth in the person of Jesus than people reacted in different ways. (1) Some like King Herod saw him as a possible threat to their power over people, and sought by every means possible to destroy him. (2) Others reacted with almost complete indifference. His birth meant nothing to them. Later they would set conditions before accepting him – let him cure their sick, provide them with bread, come down from the Cross. The lack of faith of even his own townspeople would amaze Jesus. (3) And then we have the reaction of the wise men, that of adoring worship, offering precious and symbolic gifts, gold, frankincense and myrrh.

In the Magi paying homage to the new-born Jesus, today's liturgy is saying, let all the nations worship the Creator of this universe, who lowered himself to the point of sharing in the nature of his own creatures, by becoming man. In them is fulfilled the saying of Isaiah, 'The people that walked in darkness has seen a great light; on those who live in a land of deep shadow a light has shone' (9:1). May this star shine for ever for each of us, and show us also the way to Jesus the Son of God.

THE BAPTISM OF THE LORD
Is 40:1-5, 9-11; Tit 2:11-14, 3:4-7; Lk 3:15-16, 21-22

Because we have completed a whole series of major liturgical
feasts to end the old year and begin the new, we may be inclined
to regard today's feast of the 'Baptism of the Lord' as being of
minor importance. But to do so would be a very great mistake
indeed. We should never forget that Christianity is something
which originated in the East, and that in the first thousand years
of its existence the Eastern tradition, with its emphasis on mysti-
cism and spirituality, was perhaps richer than Western tradition,
which placed more emphasis on humanity and material things.
We have just celebrated the Epiphany, but, in the East, the life of
Christ was regarded as a whole series of epiphanies or manifest-
ations, that is God making himself known to the world through
the person of Christ; and the first of these, which occurred in the
public life of the God-man, the Baptism of Christ, we commemorate today. To show this we might put the question: 'What was
the first truly significant happening, in all the events which the
Apostles witnessed, that brought them to believe in Christ?'

We find the answer if we examine the conditions laid down
by the Apostles, when they came to select a successor to Judas
Iscariot after he had killed himself, so that the original group
might number twelve once more. 'We must choose someone',
they decided, 'who has been with us the whole time that the
Lord Jesus was travelling round with us, someone who was
with us right from the time of the baptism by John until the day
when he was taken up from us; and he can act with us as a
witness to his resurrection'. The baptism of Christ then was of
paramount importance, because it was the significant event
which led the disciples present to believe in him. It marked the
beginning of a new era, when God would fulfil his Old
Testament promise to pour out his Spirit on all flesh. For as St
Peter says, 'God anointed Christ with the Holy Spirit and with
power'. And John the Baptist declared, 'I saw the Spirit coming
down on him from heaven like a dove, and resting on him. I am
the witness that he is the chosen one of God, the one who is
going to baptise with the Holy Spirit'.

Christmas is the time when we recall the Incarnation, the
physical birth of Christ; today we celebrate another birthday for
Christ, his spiritual birth in the Holy Spirit. We must always

remember, however, that Christ received the Holy Spirit, not for himself – for the Spirit was his, and his to bestow – but for the sake of the human nature, which he had taken upon himself. In his person he was consecrating once more that human nature, which he shares with each and every one of us. In the Epiphany we celebrated the presentation of the child Jesus to the Magi by his Mother. To-day we commemorate the presentation of Christ to the whole world by his Father, who says solemnly to us, 'This is my Beloved Son; in him I am well pleased.'

We think of our own baptism in a special way this day, for by it we too are marked with the seal of God, we become especially chosen members of his people, we are set apart, as was Christ, for a particular divine purpose. And in the degree that we are faithful to this call we become pleasing to God. If God has chosen us for a special purpose, we should ask ourselves today what we have chosen as the purpose of our lives. What are we looking for? We read in St John's gospel how on the day after Christ's baptism, John the Baptist was with two of his disciples, one of whom was Andrew, the brother of Peter, when Jesus again came by, and the two disciples got up and followed Jesus. And Jesus turning around asked them, 'What are you looking for?' A very simple question it seems on the surface, but in reality the most profound question anyone can ask another. Sooner or later God will ask each of us this question too, and we will not be able to give a proper answer, unless we have tried to see life with the eyes of Christ, and made him always the goal of our seeking and searching, on our pilgrim way through life.

Through our baptism we share in the mission of Christ. For most of us this simply entails being faithful in the ordinary things associated with our state of life, the demands it makes of us. When we try and respond to the voice of our conscience pointing the way we should follow, then we can be assured that Christ is in our lives, that we have become the bearers of his message to those who do not know him, and that on us too God's favour will rest even as it did on Christ.

SECOND SUNDAY OF THE YEAR
Is 62:1-5; 1 Cor 12:4-11; Jn 2:1-11

'Like a young man marrying a virgin, so will the one who built you marry you, and as the bridegroom rejoices in his bride, so will your God rejoice in you.' This marriage imagery at the end of the First Reading, imagery which is so frequently found in the Old Testament, is something we must also keep in mind if we are to understand the gospel account of the miracle at Cana. This account is one of the most difficult passages in the whole of St John's gospel if we are trying to discover what the writer had in mind in writing it. Many scripture commentators today maintain that here we do not have a straightforward description of a marriage at Cana nor a simple account of Jesus' first miracle. Even St Augustine was aware of this when he said, 'When one has understood everything that is entirely clear in the gospel, only then will the mysteries which lie hidden in this miracle come to light'.

The first thing which strikes us as strange is the fact that the bridegroom is mentioned only once, the bride and the guests never, but that Jesus and Mary appear to be the principal characters. There is further the problem of Jesus addressing his mother as 'Woman', and then appearing to refuse her request. Yet he turns water into a huge amount of wine, from seven to eight hundred litres in quantity, despite the fact that the guests had already plenty to drink. Moreover, the chief steward should surely have resented Christ giving orders directly to the employees, who nevertheless respond in perfect obedience. St John says that this miracle was the beginning of the signs given by Jesus, and to unravel its meaning one must bear in mind that John's gospel is full of symbolism, and so too is every part of this Cana account.

'We are all called to the spiritual wedding feast, where Jesus Christ is the Bridegroom', St Bernard once wrote; and in the Cana story that is what Christ really is. If Christ is the Bridegroom in the nuptials here symbolised, who is the Bride? She has to be a specific person, and in John's vision she is, symbolically speaking, Mary, who also is the one referred to by the prophets as 'Daughter of Zion', 'Mother Zion', 'Virgin Israel'. Hence the reason why Jesus addresses her as 'Woman'. In Mary, and through Mary, Christ is espoused to the chosen people Israel, and as well to the Church, which has now taken on the visible role of Mary on earth. Mary says, 'They have no wine'. Jesus replies, 'What is this for me and for you?', meaning that while Mary is thinking of ordinary wine, he sees the shortage of wine as the absence of God's Holy Spirit from the life of the Jewish people ever since the age of the prophets ceased. Mary seems to be making a suggestion, but most likely did not ask for a miracle.

The symbolism of what Jesus does in response should not escape us. For he takes the water that was used for purification under the Old Law, and turns it into the choice wine of the New Law. St Augustine sees in this choice wine a symbol of the gospel of Christ, his message for the whole world. Mary's last words in the gospels are, 'Do whatever he (meaning Christ) tells you', and she addresses them to the servants, whom John refers to by a Greek word that means 'ministers' or 'helpers' (The word is 'diakonois' from which we get the word deacons). In their role these servants are figures of the Apostles and disciples, who assist in bringing the choice wine of the gospel to the world.

To these, as well as to each of us, is addressed Mary's invitation to heed what Jesus is saying. What is the significance of all this for us here and now? We might return again to the conclusion of the First Reading, '… as the bridegroom rejoices in his bride, so will your God rejoice in you'. God, in the person of Christ, celebrates his taking on the role of Bridegroom to his chosen people with a symbolic feast. A new covenant, a unique bond is set up between God and his elect, a union which is made manifest in the Church. We speak of it as our holy Mother the Church which gives birth to us, its members. As such we should love it always.

Mary continues to be the image of the Church and the mother of all believers, in each of whom she wants her son to be born again. And as she prayed with the disciples in the upper room after the Ascension, so she is willing, here and now, to point out our needs to her divine Son, for in the order of grace she looks on each one of us with a mother's special concern and love.

A TIME TO SPEAK

THIRD SUNDAY OF THE YEAR
Neh 8:2-6, 8-10; 1 Cor 12:12-30; Lk 1:1-4, 4:14-21

In the First Reading and the gospel today we have the seeds of an argument which, in the early Church, was to scandalise the Jews and even some Christians, and become the reason why St Paul's journeying was everywhere dogged with controversy and hostility. On the one hand we have the famous priest and scribe, Ezra, who led a contingent of Jews back from exile about the year 400 BC, setting out to revive the Mosaic Law, translating and explaining it to the people, and these in turn showing their veneration for the Law. On the other hand we have Christ, in his hometown of Nazareth, saying that part of his mission is to bring the good news to the poor and proclaim liberty to captives.

What St Paul, from the very beginning, regarded as his most essential task was to help people understand Christ's teaching, and so attain this liberty, which he regarded as freedom from enslavement to the Old Law. 'Now we are rid of the Law', he wrote to the Romans (7:6), 'freed by death (meaning the death of Christ) from our imprisonment, free to serve in the new spiritual way and not the old way of a written law'. No wonder the Jews took offence, for they imagined that the Law by itself conferred life, that one's religion consisted in knowing perfectly the Mosaic code of written laws, as well as the thousands upon thousands of oral laws and regulations added on by the rabbis to explain the code. And yet the Law seems to have failed the Jews: in spite of it they, like everyone else, were sinners. The Law gave information; without it, Paul says, he should not have known what sin is. But the Law did not give spiritual strength. For a law as such, Paul contended, even if it proposed the loftiest ideals, can never transform a being of flesh into a spiritual being, capable of living the very life of God. It is not the Law, but grace, which keeps the virtuous person from being dominated by sin.

Religion for a Christian, Paul would say, is a question of knowing a person, Christ, and of loving and following him. For if sin has lost its control over a person's life, it is due to something radically different from the Old Law, what we might refer to as the law of the Spirit, a law which is no longer part of a written code, but rather a new spiritual force acting from within. 'And where the Spirit of the Lord is, there is freedom' (2 Cor 3:17). The gift of the Holy Spirit is what the Christian 'receives under the guise of a law' (Card. Seripando). Indeed the whole of the Old Law could be fulfilled in one word: 'You must love your neighbour as yourself' (Gal 5:14). 'The only thing you should owe to anyone is love for one another, for to love the other person is to fulfil the law. All these: You shall not commit adultery, you shall not kill, you shall not steal, you shall not covet, and all other commandments, are summed up in this single phrase, You must love your neighbour as yourself' (Rom 13:8-10).

The spiritual person will almost instinctively avoid offending God or others. But whoever avoids evil because it is against a law has not attained the freedom Paul spoke about. That person alone is free who avoids sin because sin is wrong in itself. Of course Christianity does contain commandments, moral precepts, the teachings of faith. But these are intended purely to avoid moral collapse. Thus, as long as Christians in the first centuries after Christ received frequent Holy Communion, the Church never obliged them to receive once a year. But when fervour decreased, in order to remind them that one cannot possess divine life without being nourished by the Body and Blood of Christ, the Church laid down the law of Easter duty. This law, however, is not aimed at the fervent, because those who are fervent are guided by the prompting of the Holy Spirit within them, and observe the law without thinking about it. Nevertheless, commandments, such as we find in the Catechism, are something that even the just require from time to time, for we all carry the treasure of God's grace in frail vessels.

Our consciences can be led astray, and the interior call of the Spirit may be drowned out by the urgings of sinful nature. When in doubt we could do no better than follow the advice given to his followers by Fr Charles de Foucauld, the French army officer who, after conversion, became a hermit in the Sahara desert: 'Ask yourself in all instances: "What would our Lord have done?", and then imitate him. This is your only rule, but it is your absolute rule.'

FOURTH SUNDAY OF THE YEAR
Jer 1:4-5, 17-19; 1 Cor 12:31 - 13:13; Lk 4:21-30

'I tell you solemnly, no prophet is ever accepted in his own country.' If this was true of Elijah and Elisha, as Christ rightly pointed out, then we can say that it was equally, if not more, true of the author of today's first reading, the prophet Jeremiah. We are told elsewhere in the gospel of St Luke that on the first Easter Sunday, when the risen Christ wanted to reveal his identity to the two unbelieving disciples on the road to Emmaus, he went 'through all the prophets and explained to them all the passages that were about himself' (Lk 24:27). He must surely therefore have mentioned Jeremiah. And what we can say for certain is that, in his very life and person and God-given mission, Jeremiah in many ways paralleled Jesus. But it was not so much by what Jeremiah said, as by the demands God made on him, the kind of opposition and rejection he encountered, that this resemblance arises. We know more about Jeremiah personally, his life, his God-given vocation, his inner feelings, than we do about any other OT person. He lived during the break-up of the Judaean monarchy centred in Jerusalem, and was still a young man when God gave him the task of calling upon his own people, whom he sincerely loved, to amend their ways.

At the best of times this is a thankless job, but for a man like Jeremiah, with a gentle and affectionate nature, it became an absolute torture. He describes his task as one to 'tear up and knock down, to destroy and to overthrow, to be a man of strife and division for all the land'. Few people have suffered so deeply as he did, to the extent that in the darkness and agony of his soul he cursed the day he was born. His faith had brought him to the brink of despair. But God revealed that Jeremiah him-self needed to repent, to have a new heart put within him, and be guided by God's Spirit speaking to him internally. Only then would he grasp the meaning of God's promise: 'I am with you to deliver you.' We remember that Christ too was 'set for the rise and fall of many in the house of Israel', as Simeon prophesied at the Presentation in the Temple; he would be a sign to be contra-dicted; he would sweat blood in Gethsemane at the thought of what people would do to him. Jeremiah met with opposition on all sides because people did not want to listen to the truth about themselves. They said, they had the Temple and the Ark of the

Covenant, the sacrifices and the Law. They saw themselves as being justified before God, whereas Jeremiah maintained that one could walk the streets of Jerusalem and not find a single man 'who does right and seeks the truth'. The truth was so bitter that Jeremiah was branded a false prophet, a public enemy, even a traitor. This charge was levelled at him especially by the princes who saw the power they wielded under a weak king being snatched away from them if, as Jeremiah pleaded, no resistance was offered to the invading Babylonian army, who were so vastly superior to the defenders of Jerusalem. So he was put in prison several times, even thrown down a deep well by the princes, and left to die in the mud at the bottom. He was rescued at the last minute by a friend in the king's palace – ironically an Egyptian. His enemies did not stop there, and after the destruction, by the Babylonians, of Jerusalem and the monarchy a small group fled to Egypt forcing Jeremiah to accompany them. Although the Bible does not tell us anything further about him, there is a Christian tradition that says he was stoned to death in Egypt.

The Church honours John the Baptist, an OT figure, as a saint, and we can say with certainty that Jeremiah was one of the truly great saints of the OT also. The similarity between him and Christ is striking. If we let this man go on working miracles and winning over people, the Pharisees and Priests said of Christ, 'the Romans will come and destroy our holy place and our nation'. Their hearts were closed to his message; he was a threat to their power, and Caiaphas, the high priest, saw the solution. 'It is better for you that one man should die for the people', he said, 'rather than that the whole nation should perish' (Jn 11:48+). And so they plotted his downfall. The only way some people have of blotting out the truth about themselves, of trying to oppose spiritual values, is by using physical violence. This was tried with Jeremiah, this was attempted against Christ, it was pursued against the people of our own country for several centuries. But truth cannot be stopped in that way. It is the task of each one of us to cherish divine truth, and also to hand it on. We are all called by God to imitate Christ and be witnesses to him, each of us in his/her own way.

FIFTH SUNDAY OF THE YEAR
Jer 17:5-8; 1 Cor 15:12, 16-20; Lk 6:17, 20-26

'What a wretched state I am in! I am lost, for I am a man of unclean lips', Isaiah states in today's readings. 'Leave me Lord, for
I am a sinful man', St Peter says. And St Paul is so full of remorse
for his former religious bigotry against Christians that he makes
this confession, 'I am the least of all the apostles; in fact, since I
persecuted the Church of God, I hardly deserve the name apostle.'
In these anguished cries we have a description of the reactions of
three very different people, when God made himself known to
them in a very clear and special way. And it is evident from
what they are saying that their response was one of intense
humility in the presence of God, that humility which is the clear
attitude of the creature as he/she stands before the all-holy and
incomprehensible God.

This awe when faced with the supernatural is exemplified
still further when we celebrate the feast of Our Lady of Lourdes.
For we see it present in the humble obedience of the child
Bernadette, how she scraped the ground until water began to
flow, and then, when told to wash herself in this dirty little pool,
and even drink from it, she complied with this demand, showing no regard for what others, who witnessed this behaviour,
thought. Hence it is that ever since, millions of people have been
drawn to follow the example of Bernadette, and thus show their
trust in the claim of a little girl of fourteen years that God's own
Mother appeared in that grotto. As we read through the Bible,
we see how God's gift of faith to people was accompanied by a
deep perception of his holiness. For to say that God is holy
means first of all, according to sacred scripture that 'he is God
and not man' (Hos 11:9).

Throughout the Old Testament, there is this idea of the
transcendence, the separateness of God from people, the in-
accessibility of God to people, the awe-inspiring manner in
which God is beyond everything we can associate with people.
And this holiness of God communicates itself to everything in
God's vicinity. We are told in the Book of Exodus (34:30) that
after Moses had spoken with God his face became so radiant
that his followers would not venture near him until he had covered his face with a veil. When we are gathered together in the
Church we should always remain mindful of the words of Jacob,

'The Lord is in this place, and I never knew it. How awe-inspiring is this place. This is nothing less than a house of God; this is a gate of heaven' (Gen 28:16f).

We should keep in mind also the warning given to Moses from out the burning bush, 'Come no nearer; take off your shoes, for the place on which you stand is holy ground' (Ex 3:5). But the greater our awareness of the wonder, the glory, and the holiness of God, the more overwhelmed we are with the sense of our own unworthiness, like Isaiah, 'What a wretched state I am in! I am lost, for I am a man of unclean lips' – like St Peter, 'Depart from me, for I am a sinful man, Oh Lord' – or like St Paul, 'I am the least of all the Apostles. I hardly deserve the name apostle, since I persecuted the Church of God.' If we open our minds to the clear light of the presence of God, as did Isaiah, Peter and Paul, then we too will become aware of the existence within us of dark areas from which we try and shut out God, aware of our refusal to allow ourselves be guided, in all that we do, by God's Holy Spirit, which really is being aware of the tendency to evil in all of us, that is the legacy of original sin.

But all this should not discourage us. Let us rather think of God's promise to the prophet Jeremiah, while he was in the depths of despair, 'I am with you to save you and deliver you.' It is only when we are prepared to acknowledge sincerely all our imperfections that we begin to see our need for a redeemer, our helplessness without God's saving grace. And this is essential for everyone on the road to sanctity, just as it was for Isaiah, and for Peter, and for Paul, from whose example we should take courage as we set out on the road where God's Spirit would lead us.

For Isaiah offered to be God's messenger, Peter who had denied Christ became the vicar of all who would live according to Christ's teaching, and Paul, the arch-persecutor of the first members of the Church, was the one above all who spelt out clearly the heart of Christ's teaching and carried it to the gentiles. 'When you call to me ... I will listen to you. When you seek me you shall find me', God says to us by way of encouragement (Jer 29:13), 'provided you seek me with all your heart'.

SIXTH SUNDAY OF THE YEAR
Jer 17:5-8; 1 Cor 15:12, 16-20; Lk 6:17, 20-26

Anyone who has been to the Holy Land, and who has seen the
rocky landscape and barren yellow soil of the southern part of it in
particular, would regard a description of it as a 'land flowing with
milk and honey' (Num 13:27) as being rather an exaggeration. Yet
such was the report received by Moses from the twelve spies he
had sent ahead to explore the country, when he and his followers first arrived at its borders. We must of course make allow-
ances for the enthusiasm of the spies, considering that, since
they had left Egypt, they had been wandering in the wilderness
of the Sinai desert, which was even less hospitable. The truth is
that the Promised Land of ancient times was a place of two
extremes – the wilderness of much of Judaea in the south, where
few living things could survive, and the extraordinary fertility
of Galilee in the north, with its thriving population. And this
familiarity with the two extremes in nature was one which perhaps coloured the Israelites' thinking when it came to describing
their own response to God's call.

We find ample illustration of this in Moses' last discourse to
his followers (Deut 30:15): 'See, today I set before you life and
prosperity, death and disaster. If you obey the commandments
of the Lord your God, he will bless you; but if you refuse to listen … if your heart strays, you will most certainly perish … I set
before you life or death, blessing or curse. Choose life', he urged
them, 'that you may live in the love of the Lord, your God, obeying him, clinging to him'.

Here we have the concept of 'The Two Ways' – one good, one
evil – a concept which figured prominently in the moral teaching of the early Church. It appears also in the gospel reading
today, with its four beatitudes and four woes, and in particular
in the first reading from Jeremiah, where the prophet links it
symbolically with the extremes of nature found in Israel. A curse
on the one who trusts only in human resources – he will be like
the dry scrub in the parched areas of the wilderness. But a blessing on the one who places his trust in the Lord. He is like the tree
planted near water, which never fades, never ceases to bear
fruit.

If you open the Book of Psalms, you will find the same idea
of the 'two ways' – almost the same words – in the very first

Psalm, which forms today's Responsorial Psalm, and which is a kind of preface to the entire Book, and indeed summarises the whole moral teaching there. The strange thing about today's gospel sermon by Jesus is that it is addressed, not to the crowds, but to the disciples – 'Then, fixing his eyes on the disciples, he said,' – implying that the sermon is meant for those who have already decided to follow Christ. Jesus warns them not to allow themselves be harnessed to the things of the world.

The same warning was issued many times by the prophets: 'Woe to those who add house to house, and join field to field, until everything belongs to them' – in other words, woe to the speculators and those who seek a monopoly of the world's resources. 'Woe to those who from early morning chase after strong drink, and stay up late at night inflamed with wine' – that is those who are pleasure seekers. 'Woe to those who call evil good, and good evil, who substitute darkness for light' – that is those who subvert morality and seek to lead others astray. 'Woe to those who for a bribe acquit the guilty and cheat the good man of his due' – that is those who lack all sense of justice and honesty in dealing with others. Human nature does not change. All these are just as relevant today as when the prophets first proclaimed them (Is 5:8-23).

But as for the people with no lofty aspirations, the poor and destitute, those burdened with sorrows, those persecuted for trying to pursue the ideals of Christ – the only refuge for all these is to place their trust in divine providence; and Jesus says, happy are these people when they do so, because their confidence will be surely rewarded by God. Here Christ has turned upside down accepted worldly standards. If you set out with all your energy to acquire the things which the world regards as valuable, you will in all probability get them. But that will be your sole reward, he says. Whereas, if you set out to be loyal to God and true to the message of Christ, you may be mocked and insulted by the world, but your reward is still to come. And that reward will be joy eternal, and no one will take it from you.

SEVENTH SUNDAY OF THE YEAR
1 Sam 26:2, 7-9, 12-13, 22-23; 1 Cor 15:45-49; Lk 6:27-38

There is a famous passage in the OT which says, 'See the days
are coming – it is the Lord who speaks – when I will make a new
covenant with the house of Israel'. And then it continues, 'Deep
within them I will plant my Law, writing it on their hearts. Then
I will be their God, and they shall be my people... There will be
no further need to teach one another, or say to one another,
'Know the Lord'. No they will all know me from the least to the
greatest'. You will find this passage in the Book of Jeremiah,
chapter 31, verse 31. The important message contained in it is
that people should look into the centre of their being, their heart,
in order to discover God, what God wants them to do. One of
the great saints who, very likely, was influenced by Jeremiah's
concept of a new inner covenant with God was St Augustine,
who was to make it the basis of his spiritual life. 'Do not go outside', he wrote, 'but enter into yourself; for truth dwells in the
interior person'. In his Confessions he tells how he experienced
it. 'I entered, and with the eye of my soul I saw the Light that
never changes lighting up my soul, my mind.' From there on he
was to put into practice what was revealed to Jeremiah, beginning at chapter 31, verse 31.

It is by extraordinary coincidence that the conversion of
Augustine came about originally by his reading of the Epistle to
the Romans, beginning at chapter 13, verse 13. This was a most
earnest challenge by St Paul to everyone who professed to be a
follower of Christ. 'Let us live decently as in the day', Paul
urged, 'not in carousing and drunkenness, not in debauchery
and licentiousness, not in quarrelling and jealousy. Instead put
on the Lord Jesus Christ, and stop pandering to your sinful
nature, and satisfying its desires'. This is down-to-earth and very
concrete advice, a kind of corollary to be taken in conjunction
with the idea of interior being in Jeremiah. The acid test of inner
holiness is whether or not it is accompanied by good works, the
opposite of all the sins mentioned by Paul.

We must remember that the New Testament was written in
Greek, and 'carousing' (*komos*) in Greek was used to describe a
noisy band of revellers who rampaged through the city streets at
night, demeaning themselves and being a nuisance to others. It
sounds familiar today also. Even to the pagan Greeks, drunkenness was a particular disgrace. Although they were a wine-

drinking people – they did not have tea or coffee in those days – drunkenness was considered especially shameful, for the wine they drank was much diluted, and was only taken because water was scarce, and moreover dangerous, on account of possible contamination, something which is true to this day in very warm climates. Drunkenness, then, was a vice which not only a Christian but any respectable pagan would condemn. Today, the last Sunday before the beginning of Lent, has been designated Temperance Sunday throughout the country. Temperance does not mean total abstinence but rather moderation in indulging our apetites.

In the 19th century, inordinate craving for strong drink was seen as a kind of curse on the Irish, a glaring weakness in our national character. People resorted to drink, during periods of great deprivation and misery, to try and escape their troubles. Nowadays it is by and large an unbridled seeking for earthly pleasure. And while the simple pleasures of life are something we should be grateful to God for, what we must impress upon our minds is that pleasure unlimited and Christianity simply cannot co-exist. 'Unless you deny yourself, take up your cross daily and follow me, you cannot be my disciple', Christ is saying to us as we begin our Lenten preparation for the celebration of Easter. What he is asking of us is not so much total abstinence, but rather temperance, restraint, self-control, virtues which are gifts of the Holy Spirit.

Over-indulgence in alcohol is never a means of escaping life's problems. It merely adds to them. It can lead to break-up in marriages, the disruption of personal relationships, the danger of alcohol-related diseases which after heart disease and cancer is the third most likely cause of premature death among Irish people. The over-riding reason why we should exercise restraint in drinking is that temperance is a virtue. Temperance is not only a duty; it is a test as to whether we are true disciples of Christ or not. On this Temperance Sunday we should pray that we, and others, may cherish this virtue of temperance, and always respond to the warning of John the Baptist, 'Be sober and watch. The Lord is near.'

EIGHTH SUNDAY OF THE YEAR
Sir 27:4-7; 1 Cor 15:54-58; Lk 6:39-45

In the first part of the Book of Revelation, the Risen Jesus sends a message or revelation to each one of seven churches in Asia Minor. The last of these messages was addressed to the Church in the city of Laodicea. This city stood astride the great road East from the port of Ephesus on the Mediterranean coast, the ancient trade-route to the heart of what is now Turkey and countries beyond. Laodicea was renowned as a financial centre, for its commercial enterprise, for its medical discoveries, and especially for its wealth. It was so rich that it did not even need God, and the Christian Church there had the grim distinction of being the only one of the seven Churches about which the Risen Christ had not a single good thing to say. These were his words: 'I know all about you; how you are neither cold nor hot. I wish you were one or the other, but since you are neither, but only luke-warm, I will spit you out of my mouth' (Rev 7:15f). Such an awful pronouncement of Jesus contains a very apt message for the world today also; for the spiritual state of much of modern society can be summed up as religious indifference – something which has been described as the least conspicuous yet, the most radical form, of atheism.

Like the citizens of Laodicea, millions of modern people are neither hot nor cold; they experience no religious stirrings what-soever, nor do they see why they should trouble themselves about religion (GS 19). They lapse into a form of spiritual stagnation, which is quite remote from both energetic faith and energetic atheism alike, and without the support of the believing com-munity spurring them on to seek Christ, without the guidance that comes from the word of God in Scripture, without the grace that follows from reception of the Sacraments, they become stuck in the rut of their own indifference. Their attitude has become predictable, static, whereas to grow in a spiritual rela-tionship with God demands change, and, as Cardinal Newman wrote in his famous *Apologia,* to grow is to change and to be perfect is to change often.

Nevertheless, indifference need not continue throughout the whole of one's life. For the human mind deep down is constantly being drawn by God's Spirit, and this being so, it is never quite totally cut adrift from reflecting on the meaning of life, and death, and eternity. When an attempt is made to convert a person who has fallen away from the practice of religion, we can say that the grace of God has been there ahead of that very attempt, and conversion is not so much passing on spiritual truths as awakening something within, which has been really present all along. For this purpose God makes use of human agents.

Nowhere do we see a clearer example of this than in the first chapter of John's gospel, where the call of the first disciples of Christ is described. We read how John the Baptist was with two of his disciples when Jesus passed by. John said, 'Look, there is the Lamb of God', and this simple remark was sufficient to make the two become followers of Jesus. One was Andrew, and he was instrumental in making his brother Peter a disciple as well, when he said, 'We have found the Messiah'. Next day Philip was added to the group, because Jesus had said to him, 'Follow me'. Philip then met up with Nathanael, known also as Bartholomew, and told him of his belief that Jesus was the one promised by Moses and the prophets. When Nathanael dismissed this claim as being ludicrous, Philip said, 'Come and see'. The brief conversation with Jesus that followed was enough to make Nathanael change his mind completely. In each case a few simple words brought about a life-long commitment.

We are told that when Jesus came to select the twelve Apostles he spent the whole night beforehand in prayer to the Father, as it were to discover the Father's wishes. At the Last Supper, Jesus in his priestly prayer to the Father referred again and again to the Apostles as those whom the Father had given him. The seeds of their vocation had been already sown in them by the Holy Spirit, and Jesus' task had been to call them. Jesus was the agent, who with a few brief words would cause those seeds to germinate and take on new life. God has great plans for each one of us too, if only we remain receptive to his call. And the advice of the Risen Christ to us is that in the conclusion of his message to every one in turn of the seven Churches in the Book of Revelation, 'If anyone has ears to hear, let him listen to what the Spirit is saying.'

NINTH SUNDAY OF THE YEAR
1 Kgs 8:41-43; Gal 1:1-2, 6-10; Lk 7:1-10

'Lord, I am not worthy to receive you, but only say the word and I shall be healed.' This confession which we all make before receiving Holy Communion is based on today's gospel story about the Roman centurion. 'Lord, I am not worthy to receive you under my roof, but only say the word and my servant shall be healed.' This was what the centurion had said, and the fact that this man – a foreigner or gentile, and an army officer – was given the highest commendation by Jesus – 'Nowhere in Israel have I found faith like this' – all this must have really infuriated the critics of Jesus, who were listening on. We might even add that hardly anywhere in the Roman Empire could one find an official so concerned about his personal slave as this man. For example a highly respected Roman statesman and moralist (Cato) in ancient times, writing on farm management, strongly advised land-owners that each year they should examine their farming implements and get rid of all those which were faulty or old, and that they should do the same with any of their slaves who were old or sickly. It was the accepted practice in those days that when a slave was past his usefulness he was thrown out to die.

In the light of such indifference to human suffering we should view the action of the centurion in the gospel story. His slave was very dear to him and he was prepared to try every-thing to save his life. He was a deeply religious man, and we know that he donated some of his modest income towards building a synagogue for Jewish worship in Capernaum, at a time when most Romans regarded the Jewish faith as barbarous superstition. He was, moreover, a humble man; he would not even come to Jesus himself. And finally he was a man of faith; even before Jesus performed the miracle, his attitude was 'I know you can cure my servant, you need only say the word and he will be healed.'

The Jews, on the other hand, who had witnessed Jesus perform even more miracles, persisted in ascribing all of these to the power of the devil. Surprisingly, however, with few exceptions, we can say that as far as those who witness miracles are concerned, nothing lasting seems to be gained, that apart from creating a short-lived sense of wonder, they do not appear to make people better as regards their religious views, or principles, or habits. You might say that a miracle would startle you, but being startled is not conversion, any more than religious knowledge is the same as religious practice.

God offers his grace to us in several other ways, and if these make no impression, the likelihood is that, as in the case of the Jews, miracles will not convert us either. We might ask then, what is the real reason why we do not seek God with all our hearts, and devote ourselves to serving him? Why do people, even after witnessing miraculous happenings, continue to ignore the voice of God that speaks to everyone from within? Sacred Scripture gives us part of the answer when it says, 'Take care brothers (and sisters) that there is not in any of you a heart so evil and unbelieving as to turn away from the living God'. In other words, we do not serve God, precisely because we lack the heart, the will, and the desire to serve him. We prefer anything to religion as did the Jews at the foot of Mount Sinai, when they grew tired of waiting for Moses to come down from the mountain. They proceeded to erect and adore a golden calf, and afterwards amuse themselves.

Alas, we are no better. How often do we allow ourselves to be seduced by the glitter and attractions of this passing world? We turn aside from the promptings of God's divine Spirit because of our lack of fervour and love in serving him. Oh yes, we keep hoping that we will be converted to God, but at some future date, like the people of Athens whose response to Paul's teaching was, 'We would like to hear you talk about this another time', or the young Augustine who prayed, 'Make me pure Lord, but not yet'. We should keep reminding ourselves of the warning of Psalm 94, recited daily by all who say the Divine Office, 'Oh, that today you would listen to his voice. Harden not your hearts.' 'Listen' is a key-word in the Bible. It appears 1,100 times in the OT and 445 in the NT. In our prayer to God, especially when celebrating the Mass, not only do we speak to God, but God, in turn speaks to us, provided we listen to the voice of his Holy Spirit within us, and not allow ourselves to be wilfully distracted.

FIRST SUNDAY OF LENT
Deut 26:4-10; Rom 10:8-13; Lk 4:1-13

If you were to visit the only remaining part of the Temple in Jerusalem, the Wailing Wall, you would find rows of Jews praying there every day, their heads nodding up and down, and most of them with their prayer shawls draped over their shoulders. These shawls have their origin in the larger robes with fringes ending in tassels which all devout Jews wore in ancient times. We know that Jesus himself wore one of these, because when the woman, who for twelve years had suffered from a haemorrhage, came seeking a cure, we are told that she touched the tassel of his robe. She was overjoyed to find herself cured, but grew alarmed when Christ wanted to know who had touched him. His disciples were very down to earth in their response, 'Look at the crowds crushing you on every side. What's the point of saying, "Who touched me?"' But then came the rather puzzling remark of Jesus, 'Someone has touched me, for I know that power has gone out of me.' This self-awareness of Jesus lies behind today's gospel account of his Temptation in the wilderness, an event which, following on God's approval of him at his baptism in the Jordan by John, marked his preparation for his public mission throughout the next three years.

The Temptation narrative is the most sacred of stories, for, as he was alone throughout his forty days in the wilderness, no one other than Jesus himself could have revealed it to his disciples; and it tells us clearly that Christ, even before he had commenced preaching, was conscious of having this quite exceptional power. The whole point of the Temptation story is that in telling it he was revealing to those close to him how he struggled within himself to find the most effective way of using this marvellous power. We ordinary humans are never tempted to try turning stones into bread, for the simple reason that such a thing is quite impossible for us. It could only be a temptation for a man with the unique power of being able to do it. We see then how Jesus, in the first temptation, toyed with the possibility of winning followers by providing a miraculous and limitless supply of free bread for people, but then saw this as akin to the offering of bribes which would inevitably fail since spiritual commitment does not necessarily follow from material gain. On the contrary, material wealth can easily lead to an erosion of religious values, as he was to say later.

Next, being taken up to the top of a mountain and shown all the kingdoms of the world in a moment of time – meaning that this was a vision – the temptation for Christ was to become a secular messiah, one who would use political means to make people turn to God. Again Jesus dismisses this, being convinced that people will enter into a spiritual union with God, if, and only if, they are drawn by God's Holy Spirit. The third and final temptation was to become a messiah of the spectacular, the sensational, the kind that so many people wanted – those who throughout his public life kept asking for signs. What if he were to throw himself from off the pinnacle of the Temple and emerge unscathed! But Jesus saw quite clearly that by such performances he could well end up being a nine days' wonder, and quickly forgotten once he had passed on. 'You must not put the Lord your God to the test', he said, perhaps as a warning to himself not to be rash, not to experiment with the power God had given him.

The conviction formed in his mind that the hard way of service to mankind, the only one which would endure, would take the form of suffering and the Cross, and only after the Cross would come the crown. Without the crucifixion Christ would long since be forgotten. In every event of Christ's earthly life, God is saying something to us too. The story of the Temptations is surely a warning to us not to allow purely selfish considerations to govern our lives. We must try and be guided by the Holy Spirit, who continues to speak to us in our conscience throughout our stay on this earth. Imitate Christ by taking up the Cross every day, not with an air of gloomy resignation, but with a cheerful acceptance of what the daily round may bring. Try and make Jesus a dominating influence in our lives, reflect upon his words and actions with reverence and affection, so as to bring about an inner purification of our minds and wills.

Our prayer during this Lenten season might well be summed up in the words of the Psalmist (51:8): 'A new heart create for me, Oh God, and put a steadfast spirit within me. Do not cast me away from your presence, nor deprive me of your Holy Spirit.'

SECOND SUNDAY OF LENT
Gen 15:5-12; Phil 3:17-4:1; Lk 9:28-36

'Our young people today love luxury. They have bad manners, contempt for authority, disrespect for the elderly. Children nowadays are domineering. They contradict their parents, gobble their food, and tyrannise their teachers.' How many of us, older people, would see this as a true assessment of modern behaviour, as compared to that of our own young days? But – and here is the catch – these words were written by the famous Greek philosopher, Socrates, one of the wisest men who ever lived, and ironically condemned to death in 399 BC, for supposedly corrupting the morals of young people and preaching religious heresy. Perhaps it is a question of human nature not changing, being the same yesterday and today.

What we can say with certainty, however, about the present age is that it is, in some ways, a time of extraordinary change. We seem to be thrilled by change; and yet the older we grow, the more we protest against change, even change for the better (John Steinbech). But we cannot get away from the fact that we are unable to experience the unchanging fullness of life here and now. Only God is capable of this. 'Change and decay in all around I see. Oh thou who changest not, abide with me', the well-known hymn 'Abide with me' says. Once, and once only, for 33 years, God lowered himself to become like us a being subject to change, when in the person of his only begotten Son, he was born of the Virgin Mary into this material world. And God in doing this had a special purpose in mind. It was that in the person of Jesus Christ he might show human beings the way forward they should pursue, in a changing universe.

Of course God did not neglect previous generations. For example, in the person of Abraham, our father in faith, we see somebody who was called to follow such a way, called to leave his home, his own people, to give up the gods he had so far worshipped, to change from the settled ways of city-dweller (in Ur) to the uncertain existence of nomadic tribesman in the mountainous regions of central Palestine – and all this surely in order to safeguard the new relationship between him and God, a relationship so personal that Abraham was later to be remembered as 'the friend of God' (Is 41:8, 'El Khalil' among Arabs). In return for Abraham's venture of faith, God made a covenant with him.

This was a form of treaty entered into by individuals or groups of people in ancient times. According to the terms of this, God promised that Abraham would be the father of a great people – something most unlikely at the time, since he and Sara were as yet childless. Yet the faith of each of us here, and that of the countless people who have professed it through the ages, bears witness to the fulfilment of that promise.

Because of Abraham's acceptance of God's word, nothing would ever be the same again. And what the second reading and the gospel are saying is that death, which will usher in a new existence for each of us, will not be simply a continuation of the pleasant things of this life. Rather will it herald the most profound change of all – the beginning of a completely new existence of which the three Apostles on Mt Tabor had a premonition, a fleeting glance, in the person of Christ transfigured before them. Christ was about to enter this new state as the first-fruits of God's plan of redemption. And in so doing he would make it possible for all true believers to enter after him. For, as St Paul assures us, our true home is in heaven, and if we manifest a willingness to be changed under the influence of God's grace, he will transform these poor lowly bodies of ours, also, into copies of Christ's glorious, risen body. In the meantime, 'life passes, riches fly away, popularity comes and goes, the senses decay, the world changes, friends die. One alone is constant; one alone is true to us, one alone can be all things to us' (Newman), and this is God.

If one's abiding trust is in him, then after the fever of life is over, after the set-backs and illnesses, the strivings and failures, the changes and uncertainties of this troubled earthly existence, there will come the ultimate change, that which will usher all those, who have persevered in Jesus Christ, through the darkness of death, into the enduring brilliance of the beatific vision of God. Then in the presence of the Father of all light, St James tells us, there will be no more change, nor shadow of alteration. God grant that this may be our destiny as well.

THIRD SUNDAY OF LENT
Ex 3:1-8, 13-15; 1 Cor 10:1-6, 10-12; Lk 13:1-9

A very popular retreat giver and writer on present-day spiritual-ity (Fr David Knight, *His Way*, p. 94) has some rather striking things to say about religious practice in America. 'As a priest' he wrote, 'I seldom encounter real conversion in confession. Most people who come to confession are not repenting; they are just showing concern about their faults. And sometimes they are not even concerned about their faults, but rather about the conse-quences of those faults.' For example a normally good-living man believes from the outset that it is an evil thing to take intox-icating drink to excess, but despite this he gets drunk repeatedly. He feels sorry afterwards, but quite often it is really being sorry for himself – perhaps because people have begun to gossip about his failing – because he is losing his self-respect – or because he is spending too much. Yet by no means do these reactions denote conversion or repentance, because there is no real change of heart. Conversion is not even a matter of changing behaviour, but rather a complete inner spiritual revolution, which renews one's mind, and gives it an entirely new outlook. Sacred Scripture says, 'Your hearts and minds must be made completely new, and you must put on the new self, which is created in God's likeness and reveals itself in the true life that is upright and holy' (Eph 4:23).

The parable of the fig-tree brings home to us that, if things in the natural world are of no value whatsoever, they are destined for extinction. The most searching question God can put to us humans, when we come face to face with him hereafter will be, 'What purpose was served by your existence in the world?' Just as the fig-tree was given a reprieve, a second chance, it can be said that, time after time, all of us without exception are given the opportunity to redeem ourselves, to change. But it is obvious that a time will come when the chance offered us will be final, and by our own choice we will cut ourselves off from God, or become united for ever with Christ our Redeemer.

For all of us conversion is our response to the call of God deep down within us – a response made possible only by the grace of God. Behind the story of Moses and the 'burning bush' there is a conversion. In the loneliness of the mountain slopes of Horeb, or Sinai, Moses reflecting on the plight of his people, began to see the events of the recent past in a new light. Life for the Israelites, he realised, had become that of slavery and bondage. And Moses felt that God, in making all this clear to him, was also calling on him to make a decision, to accept a role of responsibility in the deliverance of his people – a personal responsibility so demanding on all his energy and powers, that later on, in the desert, he was to beseech God to kill him rather than that he should be shouldered with this burden any longer (Num 11:15). The call to conversion, then, is more than a call to amend our lives, or fulfil our moral duties.

To be converted is to reject all those enslaving influences which keep the soul chained in the grip of evil; it is to rise above the twin obsessions of people since life began – namely the hunger for life, and the fear of death; and it is the entrusting of oneself, from now on, to God, a willingness to travel along that unexpected, unchartered way into the future which God has chosen for each of us. Some conversions have been clearly marked by dramatic happenings, such as those of Mary Magdalene, Paul, Augustine, Ignatius Loyola, Matt Talbot, but more often the pilgrimage of a soul to God is gradual and hidden. Conversion, in other words, is not a once-off occurrence, but rather an on-going experience. We must be constantly renewing our commitment to the following of Christ, grasping the opportunity presented now, and not being complacent in the fond hope that salvation is always available. For we know not the day nor the hour when we will stand before God's judgment seat.

This is the gospel message today, the lesson of the fig tree that no longer yielded fruit; and it sounds a warning to every one of us. The one who thinks he is safe must take heed lest he fall. And we must not wait until to-morrow to do something about it. Death-bed conversions are rare. As God said to the Israelites through Joshua, when they entered the Promised Land, 'Choose today whom you wish to serve' (Josh 24:15), even so he is now likewise saying clearly to us. 'Behold, now is the acceptable time; now is the day of salvation' (2 Cor 6:2).

ST PATRICK'S DAY
Jer 1:4-9; Acts 13:46-49; Lk 10:1-12, 17-20

One day when Jesus was alone with his disciples, on the southern slopes of the Golan heights, he suddenly asked them the
question, 'Who do people say that I am?' And from their reply
we see how divided people were in their attempts at identifying
Jesus. Some saw him as John the Baptist returned to life; others
said Elijah, others Jeremiah or one of the prophets. And even
though the disciples seemed united behind Peter when he took
it upon himself to answer on their behalf, 'You are the Christ',
we might ask what did this mean to them? We find, in the New
Testament itself, a whole series of varying interpretations of
Jesus, that go right back to the very first local communities of
Christians. What then, if any, is the factor which brings all these
different understandings together? The answer has to be a
Christian spiritual experience, a community experience which
points to the one figure of Christ.

The great legacy of the gospel is the living Christian community which lives out, and puts into practice, the message of
our Saviour, Jesus Christ, a community which makes Christ still
visibly present in the world. From the number of people who
daily come into this church to pray, to visit our divine Lord in
the Blessed Sacrament, we see confirmation, here and now, of
the remarkable words of St Paul to the Christian community at
Corinth: 'You yourselves are an open letter from Christ, a letter
written not on tablets of stone, but on tablets of human hearts'
(2 Cor 3:2f). In other words there is a living, community tradition stretching back from us, here and now, to Christ and his
first disciples; and what we are celebrating today is the fact that
the people of this land were drawn into this tradition, that the
heart of this nation took on the imprint of a letter from Christ,
mainly through the efforts of one man, St Patrick, our national
apostle. Patrick was Christ's chosen courier to the Irish people,
bringing, not so much written blueprints for conversion, but
rather a living testimony to the following of Christ enshrined in
his very own person.

Faith does not simply come from knowledge about Christ,
his teachings and the teaching of the Church, however important these are. Faith comes from the awareness of Christ's Spirit
within oneself and how one responds to that presence. Enslaved

and cut off at the age of sixteen from the intimate and loving environment of his family, the boy Patrick discovered that he was not alone. As he prayed on the slopes of Slieve Mish, where he herded his master's flocks, he came to the knowledge that he was a member of another family, that of the Blessed Trinity, the Father whose love embraced him, the Son whose example encouraged and sustained him, the Holy Spirit who prayed in him. His love of the Holy Trinity was to colour his spirituality for ever afterwards. 'I bind unto myself today the strong name of the Trinity, by invocation of the same, the three in one and one in three.'

The example of St Patrick brings home to us that spreading the faith has more to do with the inner, spiritual growth of a missionary's own self than with geographical travelling, although Patrick did not spare himself in that respect either. Much of the secret of Patrick's success arose from his deep humility – 'I am Patrick, the sinner', he wrote, 'the most unlearned of men' – from his trust in God – 'It is many a time I prayed, one hundred times a day, and as often at night' – from his courage and generosity – 'I am most willing to spend my life ceaselessly and gladly for Christ's name, and continue on that path until my dying day' – from his urgent sense of mission, his feeling, after his escape, that those who had held him captive were themselves crying out to him for deliverance, that God was calling him 'to deliver all those, who through fear of death were themselves subject to life-long bondage'.

Patrick was to identify utterly with the people whose eternal salvation he was convinced God had entrusted to his missionary zeal. He refers to the great graces the Lord conferred on him in the land of his captivity, to the extent that he would say 'My enemies are those who think that being Irish is a cause for shame'. Let each of us on this feast-day, reflect on what Patrick did to wipe out any stigma associated with being Irish in his time, and on the ways we can do the same in ours. Let us so bear ourselves that we too will be a letter from Christ not only to our contemporaries but also to all the generations which will succeed us.

FOURTH SUNDAY OF LENT
Jos 5:9-12 2; Cor 5:17-21; Lk 15:1-3, 11-32

'If you are bringing your offering to the altar, and there remember that your brother has something against you, leave your offering there before the altar, go and be reconciled with your brother first, and then come back and present your offering' (Mt 5:24). This is the warning given by Jesus himself in his Sermon on the Mount, and it is one that every Christian should ponder over, especially before celebrating the Blessed Eucharist. Before we can hope, in any meaningful way, to experience the presence of God, we must first endeavour, not only to be at peace with God, but also be reconciled with members of the community of which we are part. This theme of reconciliation, and of the joy that arises from it, is something which is highlighted in all the readings today.

There is the joy of the Israelites eating the first Passover meal in the Promised Land, after the often bitter quarrels which marked their sojourn in the desert; there is the joy of the Christians realising that they, however unworthy, are ambassadors for Christ; and above all there is the tremendous joy of the father in the gospel story that describes the return of his prodigal son, despite everything that son had done. We might say that in all this we are being urged to reflect on the necessity of repentance in our lives, and especially on our attitude towards the sacrament of reconciliation, the sacrament of penance. We keep on referring to this sacrament as confession; but the greatest and most essential part of the sacrament is not confessing all our sins, or even being sorry for them, however necessary these may be. No, the greatest and most wonderful thing is that God forgives our sin, and the sacrament is meant to be a celebration of our restoration to friendship with God.

This is depicted for us in a most wonderful way by St Luke, in what we refer to as the parable of the Prodigal Son, but which should more rightly be called the parable of the Loving Father, a father who lavishes love and forgiveness on his erring son, and rejoices and celebrates at his son's return. This was a son who had sunk to desperate depths. Having squandered in sinful living the share of the family inheritance due to him, he was reduced to looking after swine – animals abhorred in Jewish tradition as being unclean – and he even joined with them in eating the same

food. 'When he came to himself', Jesus says, he decides to return
to his father's house, meaning that a person is not truly himself/
herself while trying to keep God at a distance. In his joy at his
son's return, the father almost forgets the dignified bearing of a
Jewish parent, the filial respect commanded by a father in those
times. We need only think of the young man, elsewhere in the
gospel, whom Jesus invited to be his disciple, and who wanted
to delay making his decision. 'Let me first go and bury my father',
he said. Jesus' reply, 'Let the dead bury their dead', sounds
harsh to us, rather like a refusal to allow him attend his own
father's funeral, but what the young man really asked was that
he be allowed stay in the family home until after his father's
death whenever in the future that should take place, a custom in
the Middle-East still followed even in the beginning of the last
century. The father in the parable, however, does not stand on
his parental dignity. He runs out to meet his son, he doesn't
allow him finish what he had intended to ask, namely, to be
treated as a hired servant. He puts a robe on him as a sign that he
is being reinstated as a member of the family, a ring on his finger
to indicate that he will have authority within the home once
more, and sandals on his feet to show that he is no longer a
slave. A feast is made that all may rejoice at his return, for this
son was dead and has come back to life, was lost and is found.

What Jesus is telling us in all this is that God the Father likewise rejoices when a sinner seeks reconciliation with him once
more. In the actions of the elder brother we see typified the outlook of the Pharisees, who had lost the vision of themselves as
being children of God. Indeed the elder brother, by choice, was
more of a hired servant that a son. 'All these years I have slaved
for you', he said to his father, 'and never once disobeyed you'.
There was little love in his life, but rather a soul-destroying bitterness towards his father for welcoming home his brother. Do
we bear a grudge towards such a loving God, who in Christ
loved us even unto death on a Cross, when instead our attitude
should surely be, 'What can I render to God, for all that he has
done for me?'

FIFTH SUNDAY OF LENT
Is 43:16-21; Phil 3:8-14; Jn 8:1-11

If you read the Bible carefully and reflect on the events described in it, you can gain extraordinary insights into the character and outlook of some of the people whose memory is enshrined for ever in its pages. Recently we celebrated the feast of St Joseph, and the gospel describes for us his reaction to the discovery that Mary was with child before their marriage was consummated. Joseph being a just man, wanting to spare Mary from public disgrace and shame, decided to separate from her secretly, as the Law permitted. But being warned in a dream, he refrained from doing this.

What a stark contrast there is between the reaction of Joseph and that of the Pharisees in today's gospel story. These latter brought the woman taken in adultery into the Temple precincts, a place much frequented by all kinds of people, and made her stand before everyone in as public a manner as possible. In such cases they insisted that the penalty to be exacted should be strictly in accord with the full rigour of the Mosaic Law, namely death by stoning. But the Pharisees here were not so much motivated by zeal for the Law, as in using the woman merely as a pawn, in a scheme of theirs to discredit Jesus. If, for example, in response to their query, 'What have you to say?' Jesus were to reply, 'Let the woman go free', then they would feel justified in accusing him of breaking the Mosaic Law as well as condoning adultery. If, however, he were to say, 'Let her be stoned to death', then not only could it be claimed that he was lacking in mercy, but also he could be accused of going against the legal restrictions of the Roman authorities, who at this time reserved for themselves alone the right to impose the death penalty. But Jesus saw through their plotting and made them withdraw in confusion.

The intriguing question is what did Jesus write with his finger on the ground. The account of St John gives us a possible clue. He does not use the normal Greek word for 'write' (*graphein*), but rather one (*katagraphein*) which means to draw up a list against someone. From this some have suggested that Christ listed on the ground the sins of each of the woman's accusers, and so his challenge that the one without sin should cast the first stone met with no response. Although Jesus did not condemn the woman, neither did he condone what she had done. 'Don't sin any more', was his invitation and warning to her.

In the case of the Pharisees, as we see, and indeed in the case of most of us, there is the subtle danger of creating God in our own image and likeness, imagining him to be a stern and demanding God, who takes revenge, who loves to punish, who can be persuaded to forgive only after we have made a great show of repentance. Such of course is a mere caricature of God. At best this kind of religion can be cold and loveless. At worst, as St Paul says in the Second Reading, trying to form a right relationship with God by mere adherence to the Law and all its ways can be as worthless as the rubbish one throws away. It is only when we allow the love of God, as seen in Christ, to encompass our lives, to change our inner being, that we begin to understand Christianity.

Contrary to the thinking of the Pharisees, we must get rid of the tendency to regard ourselves as better than others, no matter what commandments we keep; nor must we judge and condemn others. Rather should we be generous, forgiving and loving towards others. From the gospel story we see that the worst of the seven deadly sins is not lust as so many think. Indeed, Christ's harshest condemnation was reserved for those who, like the Pharisees, in their pride and self-righteousness shut themselves off from God, who felt no need to ask God for help and grace. We cannot be true followers of Christ unless we acknowledge our frailty, our sinfulness, our need for his help which alone can save us. When we do fall we gain a deeper understanding of the extraordinary mercy God is prepared to extend to the sinner. For our sins make no difference to God's enduring love for us.

St Paul says that all things work together for the good of those who love God (Rom 8:28), and St Augustine adds, 'Yes, even sin'. And St Augustine, from bitter personal experience, knew all about the false allure of sin, how difficult it is very often to break away from it, and how God's love alone can help us conquer it.

PASSION SUNDAY
Is 50:4-7; Phil 2:6-11; Lk 22:14-23, 56

Looking back on what happened on the first Good Friday, it strikes us that there is nothing so terrible, so soul-destroying for the truly sincere person, who wishes to help those in need of conversion, than to be met with rejection and injury. To-day we recall how such was the fate of Jesus Christ, God's own beloved Son. During his earthly life Christ had worked, preached, striven without sparing himself, in order to deliver people from the burden of their sins and from the fear of death, only to be met, for the most part, with a cynical indifference, and finally to be condemned out of hand to a most cruel death. Long before this, Nicodemus – the one who came to Jesus by night – had foreseen this impending tragedy.

He had tried to reason with the chief priests and Pharisees, 'Surely the Law does not allow us to pass judgment on a man without giving him a hearing, and discovering what he is about' (Jn 7:50). But the answer he got was the harsh one of prejudice and bigotry. 'Are you a Galilean too?' they mocked at him. 'Examine and see for yourself that prophets do not come from Galilee.' In other words they were fixed in their mistaken belief that God would never show his saving power except within the limits of their own little closed group. The thought of these hardened hearts, of the many who would turn away from his gospel message of self-commitment to the Father, of the existence of treachery, even in the ranks of his specially chosen Twelve, these were some of the things that kept crowding in on Christ's troubled mind in the darkness of Gethsemane, a darkness that reflected the dark night of his soul. His human nature rebelled at the seeming futility of his endeavours, at the inevitability of his being delivered by the Temple authorities into the hands of the Romans, and at the thought of the terrible penalty that would be exacted should this be so.

In the struggle to overcome his natural fears and revulsion, we are told how the perspiration poured down his face and became as large drops of blood falling to the ground. But the greater his suffering, the more intense became his prayer, and in his prayer of utter abandonment to God he summoned up courage to face whatever lay before him. 'Father, if it is your will, take this cup away from me; yet not my will, but yours be done.' He had gone into Gethsemane in an agony; he came out with a victory won, and with peace in his soul, because he had talked with God. Throughout the several mock trials that ensued, that calm never left him. Not once, before the high priest and his council, did he offer a single word in defence of himself, even when they deliberately employed false witnesses to try and make their trumped-up accusations stick. But the witnesses contradicted each other; the case against Jesus was in disarray. At last the high priest asked of Jesus the kind of question which was strictly forbidden by the Law, a leading question, whereby the accused would be condemned by his own evidence. He asked it upon oath, so that an answer had to be given. 'I put you on oath, by the living God, that you tell us whether you are the Promised one, the Son of God.' When Jesus answered 'yes' the charge became blasphemy, and the cross an inescapable certainty.

But since blasphemy cut no ice with Pilate, further mention of it was dropped, and the charge against Jesus before the Roman court was turned into a political one, that of claiming to be king and telling people not to pay taxes. Fearing civil disorder, Pilate, although certain the charge was a false one, yielded to the mob baying for Jesus' blood, in preference even to that of the renegade Barabbas. Having failed to win their sympathy by having Jesus scourged, crowned with thorns, mocked as a king, Pilate handed him over to be crucified. Triumphant now the crowd followed their victim on his dolorous way to Calvary, mouthing blasphemies, insults, mockery and derision, until death gave him merciful release. 'Come down from the cross', they taunted Christ, 'and we will believe in you'. But it is precisely because he did not come down, that today we continue to believe in him. For, whereas the Jews turned their backs on God because he did not reveal himself as a figure of power, Jesus has shown, for all time, that God is sacrificial love. From the Father he begged forgiveness for his executioners. 'A man can have no greater love than to lay down his life for his friends', he had said at the Last Supper, but the one who would do so for his enemies had to be of divine origin. Never should we forget the sacrificial offering of himself for us by God's own divine Son.

EASTER SUNDAY
Acts 10:34, 37-43; Col 3:1-4 or 1 Cor 5:6-9; Jn 20:1-9

After a week of sombre reflection on the Passion of our Lord Jesus Christ, the Church in her liturgy today cannot contain the feeling of joy which breaks forth repeatedly into glad Alleluias. This joyful liturgical enthusiasm, evoked when recalling the resurrection of our Saviour, has a great deal to do with faith, for indeed in the light of what today's feast signifies, a sad Christian is truly not an authentic Christian. From the very beginning, the Resurrection has been the supreme feast in the calendar of Mother Church, giving substance and meaning to people's beliefs, lighting up the way ahead, reassuring them of the certainty of the continued presence of Christ's Holy Spirit with them. The Resurrection is the one glorious fact on which all our worship, all our spiritual strivings are founded.

If we turn to the gospels, we see how the common life in fellowship and companionship, which brought the disciples so close to the earthly Jesus, ended so abruptly in the space of a few days. The feeling uppermost in their minds, at first, was one of stark tragedy, a sense of final separation, heightened by the thought that on his last day on earth, they – his very own disciples – had utterly failed Jesus, by their abandonment of him in the hour of his Passion and death. Then, to add to their sorrow, they discovered that his body was missing. Were they even to be deprived of this most precious relic? This too is the impression we get from the tearful and earnest request of Mary Magdalene, later on, to the one she supposed to be the gardener: 'Sir, if you have taken him away, tell me where you have put him, and I will go and remove him'. She had not considered how impossible it would be for her to remove the body without help from others. Her primary concern was to find it. Indeed, in today's gospel reading, there is not even thought of Jesus' resurrection. It states quite bluntly: 'As yet they did not know the scripture, that he must rise again from the dead.' After carefully examining the tomb, Peter and the others returned home again, as though nothing had really happened.

But then, after Jesus had graciously appeared to them in a whole series of visions, the disciples were electrified by the dawning conviction which they expressed in words like, 'Jesus is here, he is alive, he is risen.' Although, at the exact moment of resurrection, nobody was present as witness, something which they could not explain had taken place, which had this tangible result, namely, that it brought the select group of disciples of Christ, comprising both men and women, who had been closest to Jesus before the events of Good Friday, together once more into a present and living companionship with him. 'Why seek among the dead, for someone who is alive?', the angel asked. The tomb is no longer a place of death, but the spot where new life has begun.

But the cardinal point is that the resurrection of Christ does not mean a resumption by him of his former existence, nor must it be thought of as a kind of reanimation of a body, as for instance in the story of Lazarus. Lazarus would die again, but as to the risen Christ, 'death has no power over him any more' (Rom 6:9). The physical body which was placed in the tomb is raised a spiritual body (1 Cor 15:42f), incorruptible, immortal, glorious. On this, the most wonderful of feast-days, let us submit to the radiant power of the risen Lord, and allow him draw us more completely into that living community, held together by faith in his living presence with us, even with us now in this very church, as we recall, and celebrate, both his death and his resurrection.

Through the merits Christ has won for us by that same death and resurrection, may we, when we have departed from these earthly bodies of ours, be found worthy to share in the glorious resurrection of Christ, our Redeemer, and be with him for ever in paradise. In the New Testament there is a beautiful and reassuring passage which gives substance to that wish. 'Through our faith and through Jesus', it says, 'we have gained access to this state of grace where we can rejoice in our hope of sharing in God's glory. More than that, we can rejoice in the midst of our sufferings, knowing that suffering produces endurance, and endurance produces character, and character produces hope, and hope does not deceive us, because God's love has been poured into our heart by the Holy Spirit, which has been given us' (Rom 5:2-5).

SECOND SUNDAY OF EASTER
Acts 5:12-16; Apoc 1:9-13, 17-19; Jn 20:19-31

'You believe because you have seen me. Blessed are those who
have not seen and yet believe.' The lack of faith in the resurrection of Christ by the apostle Thomas has given him a certain
character in the minds of people ever since the events of today's
gospel. The phrase, 'a doubting Thomas', has become part of
everyday language right up to this very day. But the truth is that
the reaction of Thomas to what took place on that first Easter
day was not very much different from that of the other apostles.
They all, more or less, became disillusioned about Christ when
they saw him being led away to be crucified. When he was
buried in the tomb their hopes were buried with him, and when
the news broke that he was risen again, they all disbelieved it.
The last ten verses of St Mark's gospel tell us quite clearly that
such was the case.

When Mary Magdalene hurried back from the tomb with the
news that Jesus was alive, and that she herself had seen him,
they did not believe her. When the two disciples, who had seen
him while journeying to Emmaus, returned to Jerusalem and
related what had befallen them, neither were they believed.
They were all unprepared for the marvellous Easter morning
happenings, and were caught completely unawares by them. St
John, in his gospel, recounts how he and Peter ran to the tomb,
when first they heard that the body of Jesus was no longer in it.
John arriving first looked in, but did not enter until Peter also
had reached it. For the moment, the reaction of Peter to the
empty tomb was solely one of astonishment, 'for as yet they did
not realise the meaning of scripture that Jesus should rise from
the dead', John says. Nevertheless, things began to happen in
John's mind.

If the body had been stolen, why did the robbers leave
behind the grave-cloths in which it was enwrapped? Moreover,
these cloths were not thrown aside in a heap. They were lying in
a regular arrangement, still folded, as if the body of Jesus had
simply evaporated from within them. Slowly the significance of
what he saw in the tomb began to dawn on John's mind, and to
quote his own words, 'he believed'. Love is blind, it has been
said, but it was Mary Magdalene, who loved Jesus so much, who
was the first at the tomb, the first to see the risen Jesus, the first

to be convinced that what she saw was a living being and not a ghost. As well, it was John, the disciple whom Jesus loved and who loved Jesus in return, who was the first apostle to believe in the Resurrection of Jesus. But as to the others, we find, in those verses of St Mark, how Jesus rebuked them for their obstinacy and incredulity in the face of the Easter Sunday occurrences.

When finally they believed in the resurrection and their doubts had been resolved, those of Thomas nevertheless continued unabated. Thomas had made the mistake of withdrawing by himself, remaining apart from the community of Christ's followers, and so he was not present when the others received the grace of faith once more. It is a warning to all of us, here and now, that we should never withdraw from the worshipping Christian community. Otherwise, God's grace may well pass us by too. The response of Thomas, when confronted with the risen Jesus, has a message for us also. When Christ allowed himself to be touched, and the wounds on his body to be probed, the doubts of Thomas melted away, and his heart was so full of love and emotion that all he could say was 'My Lord and my God', words that signified not only his belief in the Resurrection but also his being convinced of the divinity of the risen One.

God grant that every time we come together to worship and pray, we may find ourselves strengthened in our faith and union with our risen Saviour, even as Thomas was. Strange as it may seem, we should be grateful that Thomas and the other apostles were so reluctant to believe in Christ's resurrection. Such had been their familiarity with him, that despite all the miracles they had witnessed they could not bring themselves, before his death, to accept fully that he was by nature a truly divine person. Indeed his death seemed to offer proof of their estimation of him. It took impressive evidence to make them change their minds on this. The fact that they were slow to do so, that they were fearful of being deluded, makes the basis of our belief in the resurrection that much stronger. For what happened on the first Easter morning was, and still remains, a pledge of our own resurrection as well.

THIRD SUNDAY OF EASTER
Acts 5:27-32, 40-41; Apoc 5:11-14; Jn 21:1-19

'The true Christian's entire life is a holy longing', St Augustine used to say. The true Christian is continually on the move, not so much physically however, but inwardly, in the heart. In today's gospel reading, we find that after the events of the first Easter Sunday, although the small group of Apostles had moved back to Capernaum and to their fishing in the Sea of Galilee, their hearts were not fully in what they were doing. Their days were spent in a holy longing, and in expectation too, on account of what Jesus had said to the women when they were returning from the empty tomb, 'Go and tell my brothers that they must leave for Galilee; there they will see me.' And then, when they must have been utterly disheartened with their work – they had laboured all night, we are told, and caught nothing – at a moment when they least expected him, there Jesus was standing on the shore waiting for them, in the half-light of the early morning.

It is a reminder also to us that, in moments of desperation, Christ is ever close at hand, for he has promised to be with us always to the end of time. The night's labour by the disciples is suddenly rewarded with a huge haul of fish, something so extra-ordinary that John realises it must be the Lord who caused it. Throughout the long night prior to this they had been toiling in vain, and in the space of a few minutes Christ brings success for them, as well as warmth and food, and a reawakening of their hopes in him. Mention of fish and bread prepared for them by Christ introduces a Eucharistic note. It calls to mind the miracle of the loaves and fishes whereby Jesus fed the multitude. This perhaps in John's gospel, in a symbolic way, supplies for the account of the institution of the Eucharist at the Last Supper, as recorded by the other three evangelists, an event which is not mentioned by John. Indeed, as a matter of interest, on the large host used in this Mass there is the outline of a fish, and the Greek word for fish, *ichthys*, is written over it.

That word was especially linked with Christ after his death by Christians of the early centuries. The five letters in it are the initials of the five Greek words that form the phrase 'Jesus Christ, Son of God, Saviour'. The account of Jesus' appearance, quite possibly, leads to an explanation as to why this strange last chapter was added on to John's gospel, either by the evangelist himself or one of his disciples. It was clearly intended to refute any claim that the appearances of the risen Christ were mere hallucinations. For no vision, or spirit, or ghost could point out a shoal of fish from the shore, or light a charcoal fire to prepare a meal. The risen Lord was clearly a real person, but a person who had conquered death and come back. The whole chapter is a reminder to us too that Christ is waiting to come to us in Holy Communion, and ready to give on a spiritual level, all he had to offer to the Apostles on that special morning.

But we must be eager to draw near to Christ, as was Peter when he waded ashore to meet him; we must be respectful to the sacrament we are celebrating, as was Peter in clothing himself before encountering Christ; and we must have faith, like St John when he said, 'It is the Lord'. The whole gospel story shows the wonderful consideration and tenderness of Jesus, as he looked after the bodily needs of the disciples, wearied and spent after their night on the lake. It is a vivid illustration that even after his resurrection Christ was still abiding by what he said while on earth, 'The Son of man came, not to be served, but to serve, and to give his life as a ransom for many' (Mk 10:4). And now from the shores of eternity Jesus stands calling us also. He has prepared an eternal banquet for us, and if we now strive to remain close to him spiritually, then when life's journey is over, we will behold him face to face, as did the Apostles.

If only we have faith meanwhile, we will be assisted on our pilgrim way by the one who walked on the waters, who rebuked the wind and the waves, who multiplied the loaves, who turned water into wine, who made the blind see and the lame walk, who entered through closed doors, and came and vanished at will. May the risen Christ remain with each of us evermore, filling our hearts with a longing for our heavenly home, until the dawn of eternity breaks and all the shadows of this earthly life melt away (Cant. of Cant. 4:6) and in the company of the angels and saints we can enjoy the vision of the glorified Christ as he really is. Amen.

FOURTH SUNDAY OF EASTER
Acts 13:14, 43-52; Apoc 7:9, 14-17; Jn 10:27-30

During this period following on the Easter celebrations, there is one thing that the liturgy readings try to impress upon us, and that is the zeal and sense of urgency the Apostles showed in preaching the good news about Christ. They disregarded every attempt on the part of the Jews to put a stop to them. Death threats did not deter them, and whether people accepted their message or not, they appeared to be driven on by an inner God-given sense of mission to hand on to everyone their faith in Jesus. This weekend every year is set aside as a time of prayer for vocations to the priesthood and the religious life, and we must bear in mind that the idea of vocations and that of handing on the faith are very closely linked. We might from time to time ponder over the question: 'Why did God create us?' The answer has to be that God is love, that God is goodness, and love and goodness are only meaningful if they are communicated to others, if there is someone else to be loved and to experience that goodness.

The Holy Spirit poured out his graces and gifts in abundance on the members of the early Church, and they in turn felt compelled to share them with others. In season and out of season, as St Paul puts it, the Apostles and those close to them preached the marvellous news about the salvation won for the world by Christ. And with the departure through death or old age, of these disciples, from the scene of this activity, there was no scarcity of people to take their place. It is this willingness on the part of chosen members of a community, to devote their whole lives to the task of spreading the gospel message, that marks the depth and the quality of the Christianity which is practised within that community. There is no doubt about the quality of missionary zeal among the first members of the early Church, nor indeed that of the Irish people during the golden age of Irish monasticism, when throughout Europe monks and missionaries from these shores spread the Christian ideals of love of God and of living together in harmony and peace.

If here and now we ourselves are found wanting in these ideals there is one thing we can and must do, and that is pray. People only pray for things they really want, such as health, success, secure employment, provision for their children's future.

But it is possible to enjoy all of these and yet be conscious of a profound emptiness in one's life, for we were intended for something greater than these passing attainments. God has created us for himself, to be the recipients of his love and goodness for all eternity. This surely is something worth praying for, as are the vocations of those God chooses as his special agents in helping people attain their destiny. Not only is it important to pray for these, to think and talk about them, but they are so vitally necessary as to urge parents to encourage sons and daughters to consider seriously the option of a vocation within the family.

It is within the context of family that most vocations are nurtured. The famous French Jesuit, scientist and philosopher, Teilhard de Chardin, once said, 'I come from a family where I became who I am. The great majority of my opinions, of my likes and dislikes, of my values and appreciations, of my judgments, my behaviour, my tastes, were moulded by the family I came from.' For this reason parents remain, and always will remain, the first and most important teachers of the faith to their children. In fulfilling this role they should strive to make prayer, daily family prayer, a natural part of life within the home. By so doing, they will most certainly be sowing the seeds of those vocations which in the providence of God will be necessary to minister to the spiritual needs of the next generation. Such vocations, however, must also be seen in the context of the whole spiritual life, the spiritual values, the spiritual aspirations of the community in which they are nurtured.

Each one of us here present can truly say, 'As God called the Israelites of the OT to be his special people, just so has he called me. Hence what I do, what I am, concerns other people to as great an extent as it does myself.' Therefore, on this special Sunday, each one should feel in duty bound to ask God's blessing, so that generous souls may not be wanting in the apostolic work of teaching and preaching to all nations. Christ's injunction to his disciples was quite explicit, 'Pray ye therefore the Lord of the harvest, that he may send labourers to his harvest' (Mt 9:37).

FIFTH SUNDAY OF EASTER
Acts 14:21-27; Apoc 21:1-5; Jn 13:31-33, 34-35

'We have all to experience many hardships before we enter the kingdom of God.' This was the warning of Paul and Barnabas to the people of Antioch. Yet, we are told earlier on that the two apostles were filled with joy when they were driven out of Antioch (Acts 13:52). If you read the very first book in the New Testament to be set down in writing, St Paul's First Letter to the Thessalonians – written, by the way, at least twelve years before Mark's gospel, and close on twenty years before the Acts of the Apostles – you will find Paul warning his Christian followers in Thessalonika about the difficulties that lie ahead. 'Affliction is bound to come our way', he warns, 'we must expect to have troubles to bear' (1 Thess 3:3f). Indeed, Paul himself was to become the persecuted confessor of Christ – a 'vessel of election', that is elected, or called, to suffer, and thus bear witness, in his own life, to the sufferings of Christ.

However, the apostles did not want their listeners to dwell on this theme of suffering in any kind of morbid way. Their purpose, at all times, was to put fresh heart into the disciples, to encourage them to persevere in the faith, just as Paul urged the Thessalonians to comfort one another, to sustain each other's hopes of the eternal vision of God. 'All things work together unto good, for those who love God', were his words of consolation, later on, to the Christians in Rome (8:28). We can always be certain that our God is the God of love, and God himself tells us, in today's gospel reading, to allow this love to give direction and shape to our lives. Indeed every single chapter in the New Testament carries a special message from him to us; and ever so often it is similar to that contained in the words of Christ to his Apostles at the Last Supper; 'Let not your hearts be troubled. Trust in God and trust in me' (Jn 14:1).

We see this exemplified, in a concrete way, in the encounter of the risen Christ with the two disciples, weighed down as they were with gloom and despondency, while walking to Emmaus, on that first Easter Sunday. 'Their eyes, as yet, were kept from recognising him', we are told. When questioned as to what they were discussing between themselves, and why they were so down-hearted, they endeavoured to explain their grief by giving an account of the tragic things that had taken place in Jerusalem, during the previous days. But their companion's amazing response to all this was by way of a simple question. 'What things?', he asked them. It is difficult for us to begin to understand this kind of innocence on the part of Christ. It belongs to the mystery of what the French dramatist, poet, and diplomat, Paul Claudel, called 'the eternal childhood of God'. For that brief question, 'What things?', conveys the impression that so perfectly has Christ passed into the freedom, and joy, and glory of his Father, that he scarcely remembers the cruel and terrible journey he had travelled in arriving there. There are no dark clouds on God's horizon, nor any sorrowful memories weighing upon the mind of God.

The disciples at Emmaus were led gradually to make an act of faith in the risen Christ. While he remained visually present to them they had failed to recognise him. When the moment of recognition did come, St Luke says that 'he had already vanished from their sight'. In other words, it was not by the sight of their eyes, but rather by the response of their hearts that Christ made himself known to them. 'Did not our hearts burn within us as he talked to us on the road', the disciples said in retrospect. When the true follower of Christ comes to celebrate the Eucharist, his/her primary purpose should not be to complain, or even to ask for graces, but rather to render thanks to God.

Yet the dialogue of the hidden Christ with the disciples of Emmaus is renewed, to a certain extent at every Mass. Like the two distraught disciples, we often find ourselves saying to our hidden Lord during the moments after Holy Communion, 'Do you not know, Jesus, what things I have been going through?' Then he amazes us with his answer, 'What things have you been going through?' And in the light of what took place on that first Holy Week, he proceeds to tell us, just as he did the two disciples, that the sufferings and anxieties of this present life are not to be compared with the glory that is to come, when God will wipe away all tears from our eyes, and death shall be no more, nor mourning nor crying shall be any more, for the former things will have passed completely away.

SIXTH SUNDAY OF EASTER
Acts 15:1-2, 22-29; Apoc 21:10-14, 22-23; Jn 14:23-29

One of the great libraries of present times is the British Library in London. If all of its books were to be arranged on one continuous shelf, that shelf would stretch approximately from Malin Head in northern Donegal to Kinsale on the south coast, and every year which goes by a further eight miles of new publications would be added on. Never has the human race had more knowledge available to it; never has it had more understanding of the universe, of the forces that govern the environment, and with advances in communication technology most of this will soon be accessible to people in their own homes at the press of a button.

Yet despite all this there is abroad also a tremendous sense of helplessness, of being at the mercy of powers outside oneself, of being monopolised by richer countries, by international business cartels, by far away centres of oftentimes bureaucratic control that can change one's way of life and of earning a living, and that with no hope of redress for those affected. Regardless of the advances in knowledge, there is a growing sense of uncertainty, even disenchantment, about where we are going, about the goals we should be striving for in life. So many people suffer from depression, isolation, lack of self-esteem, the futility of much of modern pursuits, the difficulties of just getting by, the obsessive scramble to get on in the world by fair means or foul, the sheer revulsion before the endless accounts of cruelty and horror which the media love to dwell upon.

When such a climate prevails, there is one factor being overlooked, and that is the fact of God. 'Whoever walks in darkness, and has no light shining for him, let him trust in the name of the Lord, let him lean on his God', was the remarkable advice of the prophet Isaiah (50:10) to the people of his time, and how true it is today. Lean on God, hang on to God. So-called liberals in our age, while denying the very freedom of choice they proclaim, would like to have a situation enforced whereby God would be shut up in his churches, and mention of divine principles banned in the life of society, as well as in the place where we prepare our young for society, in our schools. But, not only is God a fact of religion, he is also a fact of life, and indeed a fact of human history, since he assumed human nature. And as Scripture rightly points out (1 Cor 2:11+), the depths of a man can only be known by his own spirit, not by any other man, and in the same way the depths of God can only be known by the Spirit of God, and those whom the divine Spirit teaches.

Left to one's own natural resources, one is utterly incapable of learning anything about the Spirit of God. During this period of the liturgical year we keep on reminding ourselves that our eternal salvation has been gained through the death and resurrection of Jesus Christ. Christ is not to be sought in the realm of the dead; he is living, he is with us. And if Christ is on our side, what need we care who is against us. In its infancy, the future of the Church was very bleak indeed, for not only was its existence threatened by the Jews, but the pagan gentiles also were determined by every means to put a stop to it. We find St Paul giving his followers encouragement in words which are addressed to us as well across the centuries: 'Just as you trusted Christ to save you, trust him too for each day's problems; live in vital union with him. Let your roots grow down into him, and draw up nourishment from him. See that you go on growing in the Lord, and become strong and vigorous in the truth. Let your lives overflow with joy and thanksgiving for all he has done. Make sure that no one deceives you or takes away your freedom by some secondhand, empty, rational philosophy based on the principles of this world instead of on Christ' (Col 2:6).

In those early days people believed that the earthly scheme of things preexisted in heaven, and thus the new Jerusalem, God's new plan for the salvation of the world, would descend from heaven to earth. This work was to begin with the Annunciation to Mary by the archangel Gabriel, that God's Son would become man. And the Assumption of Mary into heaven is God's guarantee that his plan for the salvation of each of us will only be fulfilled when we too are taken up from earth to heaven. We should therefore keep our gaze ever fixed on this eternal goal, and be mindful also of the plans God has for each of us, and of the reward he has prepared for those who love him.

ASCENSION OF THE LORD
Acts 1:1-11; Eph 1:17-23; Mt 28:16-20

St Luke in his account of the Ascension into heaven of Our Lord, Jesus Christ, is attempting to put into words what in effect is beyond words, to try and describe an event which really defies description. For the Ascension, or to give it a more meaningful title the Exaltation of Christ, will always remain a mystery to us while we are in this life. We find confirmation of this from the response the Ascension evoked in Christ's closest followers. Our natural reaction to the thought of a final separation of the risen Christ from his disciples, is that for them this must surely have been the saddest of occasions. Indeed we might very well see advance confirmation of this as well in the words addressed to the apostles by Jesus, at the Last Supper, 'Now I am going to the one who sent me. Not one of you has asked, "Where are you going?" Yet you are sad at heart because I have told you this' (Jn 16:5+). However, when the last parting, at the Ascension, really does take place, amazingly, we read how the disciples returned to Jerusalem, not only with no great signs of grief, but rather as the gospel of St Luke states, 'with great joy' (24:52).

What was it, we may well ask, which made that final separation an occasion, not of sorrow, but of great spiritual rejoicing and enrichment? Of course we can say that for the apostolic group it was inevitable that the time would come when Jesus' stay on earth, in visible form, would cease. St Luke sees this occurring, not at the moment of death, nor even that of the resurrection of Christ, but with his Ascension into heaven. The days when their faith depended on the flesh and blood presence of Christ were now over. Indeed because of the appearances to them of the risen Christ, that faith was raised up to a new plane; for they were slowly convinced that Jesus was living in a mysteriously new and wonderful manner beyond the portals of death.

From here on they felt that they had entered into an entirely new union with the One who, because of his Ascension, had passed beyond the limits of time and space, and was exalted and confirmed in glory, in the presence of the Father, henceforth and for ever. Putting aside selfish considerations, the disciples rejoiced for the sake of Jesus, the suffering Servant of the Lord, rejected and put to death as he had been by his own people, but now vindicated, in this wonderful manner, by God. Thus the Ascension was a happy ending to that period of terrible self-sacrifice he had willingly taken on himself. But equally the Ascension marked a beginning also. Very soon it would usher in a new era, and the supreme indication of this would be the presence of 'God's Spirit', referred to also as the 'Spirit of Jesus'. The Holy Spirit will be both in the Church and in every individual member of the Church. Thus would be fulfilled the promise of Jesus at the Last Supper, 'I will not leave you orphans, I will come back to you' (Jn 14:18). We find Peter himself acknowledging the truth of this in the first great Pentecostal sermon he addressed to the people: 'God raised this man Jesus to life, and all of us are witnesses to that. Having been raised up to the right hand of God' – in other words, having ascended into heaven – 'he has received from the Father the Holy Spirit ... and what you see and hear is the outpouring of that Spirit' (Acts 2:32+).

The disciples then returned to Jerusalem after the Ascension, rejoicing in the knowledge that nothing, either in life or in death, 'could ever come between them and the love of God made visible in Christ Jesus, our Lord' (Rom 8:39). Christ would be the final and definitive revelation of God for the whole world thereafter. And, as it was while he was on earth, so now that he is exalted in heaven, he is still the comforting friend of all who call upon him, whether in life or in death. For to die is not to go out into the dark; it is to go to the one who up to the end of his life demonstrated his love for each and every person that he met while on earth, and even to a greater extent thereafter, right up to this present moment. Our prayer today should be that we, and all who believe in Christ, may be found worthy to follow him into the new creation of which he is the first member and guarantor, for his Ascension is our glory and our hope, the thought of which should lighten our burdens as we make our pilgrim way to the place in heaven he has gone ahead to prepare for us. And from the final page of the NT (Rev 22:12), Christ reassures us, 'Very soon, I shall be with you again, bringing to each and every one the reward they deserve '.

PENTECOST SUNDAY
Acts 2:1-11; Rom 8:8-17; Jn 14:15-16, 23-26

The wonderful feast of Pentecost is really our birthday, for it calls to mind the beginning of our role as God's chosen people, chosen not on account of any merit on our part, but by reason of God's mercy, in order that the power of God may become more manifest in our weakness. In the Book of Revelation (5:9+) a hymn is sung in praise of the Lamb of God, because by his blood he has purchased people for God from every tribe and language and nation, and made them a line of kings and priests to serve our God and rule the world. Hence as true followers of Christ we are a kingly people: in us and through us the reign of grace is made visible before the world. We are a priestly people: through us Christ continues to offer spiritual worship for the glory of God and for the salvation of all mankind. We are a prophetic people: we listen to the word of God and to the Spirit stirring within us. We are given an understanding of the faith and the grace of speech, so that the power of the gospel might shine forth in our daily lives. But we must listen, if we are to have that grace of speech.

This is precisely what the apostles and disciples did, and were granted at the first Pentecost. They listened to the Holy Spirit, who revealed to them, in a new light, all that they had experienced and learned about Jesus. This revelation became a burning force within them, compelling them to speak out about it. They became like Jeremiah, the reluctant prophet, who used to say: 'I will not think about the Lord, I will not speak in his name any more. But then there seemed to be a fire burning in my heart, imprisoned in my bones. The effort to restrain it wearied me, and I could not bear it' (Jer 20:9). Likewise, Peter and John were to say before the Sanhedrin: 'We cannot promise to stop proclaiming what we have seen and heard' (Acts 4:20). To understand the imagery of Luke's account of all this in the Acts of the Apostles, we must try and grasp his purpose. He wants to convey the idea of a new covenant being set up between God and mankind. He draws on the Exodus account of the establishment of the Sinai Covenant, when the mountain was entirely wrapped in smoke and the Lord descended on it in the form of fire. Likewise, those in the Upper Room heard what sounded like a powerful wind – wind was always associated with the presence of the Holy Spirit. Noise filled the entire house and tongues of fire appeared also. These were indications that the Chosen People of the new alliance with God had come into being.

In the gospel of today, St John's account recalls for us the story of Elijah (1 Kings 19), who was so dispirited by the opposition which he encountered in his fight against the worship of pagan gods that he wished he were dead. He was told to go to the mountain of God, Horeb or Sinai. And standing in a cave he heard a mighty wind go by, but the Lord was not in the wind. Then came the sound of an earthquake and then a fire, but neither was the Lord in these. Finally, there came the sound of a gentle breeze, and hearing it he covered his face with his cloak. And the Lord spoke to him from out the breeze, and entrusted him with a mission. The morale of Christ's apostles, at this juncture, was also very low. For fear of the Jews, they had locked themselves in the Upper Room. Then Jesus appears in their midst; he breathes upon them and they receive the Holy Spirit. As with Elijah, they also have a mission given to them. Just as the Lord had breathed the breath of life into Adam's nostrils, thus making him the first living human being of creation, so with the breathing of Jesus upon the apostles, which makes them part of a new creation. In fact the activity of the Spirit is a continuation through them of the mission of Jesus.

That very special gifts had been granted to the specially chosen followers of Jesus became very obvious to those who were not members of that group. This was necessary to show to the pagans, and unbelievers among the Jews, that the truth of the Christian religion was being confirmed by God. The event as described by John is not a once-and-for-all event. Rather does it describe an on-going process. Christian beliefs and traditions have their enemies in our own time as well. But we should not despair, for the divine presence is always ready to come to our aid. Jesus and the Father continue to communicate the Holy Spirit to all those entrusted with a mission by God to this day. We too can be drawn into the Pentecostal experience provided that we keep our hearts open to what the Spirit is telling us, and offer ourselves as willing propagators of his designs.

THE MOST HOLY TRINITY
Prov 8:22-31; Rom 5:1-5; Jn 16:12-15

'God is closer to us than we are to ourselves', is a famous saying from the early Church. Yet how true it is that quite often we feel that between us and God there is, as it were, a great gulf, which separates us, cuts us off, from our Creator. The human spirit seems to be embarked on an endless search for something more profound and lasting than the material world around us, and were we but able to analyse this quest for happiness, for security, for an assurance of life hereafter, for peace – call it what you will – we should find that it is this same Creator we yearn for with our whole being. 'You have made us for yourself, Oh Lord, and we shall not rest until we rest in you', was St Augustine's comment after years spent in seeking for meaning to earthly existence. That we should feel abandoned from time to time seems to be part of the human condition, here and now. Even Christ himself experienced it when he uttered from the Cross the forlorn cry, 'My God, my God, why have you forsaken me?' (Mk 15:34). These words form the first line of Ps 22, which Christ was apparently praying.

But that this wonderful and loving God is not always remote from us is made clear again and again throughout the scriptures, in passages such as, 'I did forsake you for a brief moment, but with great love will I take you back' – words ascribed to God by Isaiah (54:7), who elsewhere has God putting the question, 'Does a woman forget the baby at her breast, or fail to cherish the son she has borne? Even if these forget, yet will I never forget you' (Is 49:15), – a promise reaffirmed by the prophet Jeremiah, 'I have loved you with an everlasting love, and so I am unchanging in my affection for you' (31:3). God wants to communicate himself to us, or rather to lead us into partaking of the intimate unity shared by the three Divine Persons in one God, a mystery we celebrate in today's feast. But if God wishes to communicate himself, you may well ask, how do we encounter God in our lives?

To attain this we must by reflection try and see God at work in the events of our own lives as well as of those around us, for that is where God is. Here we can take Christ himself as our supreme model and exemplar, for he always sought to do not his own will but that of God. He acted thus, not because of legalistic pressure, but rather as the natural result of a truly special relationship with God. This is shown by his repeated reference to God as Father, or in the language of the day 'Abba'. This term was used purely within the family circle to denote one's earthly father, and its use by Jesus, in a perfectly natural manner in addressing God, was one which impressed itself on the memory of his disciples for ever after. Jesus never used the words 'Our Father', except once when teaching the Apostles the prayer of that name, but his use of 'My Father' occurs no less than forty-six times in the gospels.

It is clear that Christ saw himself as being Son of the Father in a unique way. 'Go to my brothers', he said to Mary Magdalene after his resurrection, 'and tell them that I am going to my Father and your Father, to my God and your God' (Jn 20:17). At his baptism in the Jordan by John, and again at the Transfiguration on Mount Tabor, the onlookers heard a voice say, 'This is my Son, the Beloved; my favour rests on him.' The Father saw him as his beloved Son, and the Son committed himself totally to carrying out the Father's will, and in this mutual giving and response we become aware of the presence of the Holy Spirit, bonding Father and Son together.

All the great Saints of the Church have been inspired by the sublime mystery of the Holy Trinity; for being children of God by adoption we too are called to become part of this intimate life of God, members of God's triune family. This is even achieved here and now, in a limited way on our part, by what St Paul refers to as 'putting on Christ', so that when the Father looks on us he sees reproduced in us the spirit of his Beloved Son, and his favour also rests on us. Christ himself said, 'If anyone loves me he will keep my word, and my Father will love him, and we shall come to him, and make our abode with him' (Jn 14:23). Note especially the use of the plural, 'we shall come to him, and make our abode with him'. Our adoption into God's family is something which, here and now, can only be experienced by faith, but our hope and prayer is that we will see the Blessed Trinity face to face in the life hereafter.

THE BODY AND BLOOD OF CHRIST
Gen 14:18-20; 1 Cor 11:23-26; Lk 9:11-17

Migration of people has been a feature of the human race from the earliest times. We read in the Book of Genesis how the patriarch Jacob was forced to leave his father's house, and travel far to the north, because of the hostility of his brother Esau. On his first night away from home, we are told how Jacob lay down to sleep with a stone for his pillow, and how a mysterious dream came to him. In it he saw a ladder stretching from earth to heaven, and angels of God ascending and descending on it. But no explanation of this dream is given by the sacred author. However, we might say that in the great cycle of feasts now ending, there was forged, in a symbolic way, a ladder by which God comes to us, and we in turn are drawn to God. From the Holy Trinity we learn that God is a family of divine persons, and for us, holiness, sanctification, salvation, consist in being drawn by the power of God's grace into membership of this divine family. If the question is raised how can this be, the answer is supplied in today's feast of Corpus Christi. For Corpus Christi, or the Body of Christ, is the ladder linking heaven and earth, enabling us to rise to a new and intimate relationship with God.

To achieve this, the disciples of Christ, we are told in the Acts of the Apostles (2:46f), 'went as a body to the Temple every day, but met in their houses for the breaking of bread'. Their meeting in the Temple was for prayer, and note they met as a body, a united group. Meeting to break bread in their houses, on the other hand, is a reference to their celebration of the Holy Eucharist. Prayer is a raising of the mind and heart to God, but Holy Communion achieves something further. For it is the source and summit of the Christian life. By it and through it we enter into the closest possible union with Christ on earth. We share in his Body and Blood, and form a single body in him (1 Cor 10:16f). Of necessity, here and now, bodily existence is sustained by partaking of food, and likewise reception of the Eucharist is vital for our being made holy, for our sanctification. 'Unless you eat the flesh of the Son of Man and drink his blood, you will not have life in you. Any one who does eat my flesh and drink my blood has eternal life, and I will raise that person up on the last day' (Jn 6:53).

The cycle of recent feasts, the Ascension, Pentecost, Holy

Trinity, tells how God, as it were, has created this ladder between heaven and earth, by which He comes to us, and we in turn can rise up to Him. The message of the feast of Holy Trinity, last Sunday, was that purification, holiness, redemption, are not achieved by one's own efforts, but rather by sharing in the life of the Holy Trinity with the help of God's grace. If we ask where, or how, this takes place, the answer is through the Body and Blood of Jesus Christ, to which we pay honour in this feast today. The feast recalls, not so much the establishment of the Eucharist, but rather the whole story of salvation, how God's only Son became man for us, and dwelt with us. And just as the Blessed Trinity came down from heaven to us in visible form in the person of the Son of God made man, thus it is in, and through, the same Son of God made man, that we can become part of the family of God. As St Paul never tires of repeating, we must put on Christ, become other Christs, and thus become children of the one Father by adoption. Since Christ is now a glorified Spirit, what we must change then is nothing external, but rather our inner being, our minds, so that the Father who knows the inner secrets of our minds and hearts, when he looks at them, sees imprinted there the image of his own divine Son. This can only happen firstly, by living out our lives according to the Word of God, and secondly by reception of the Holy Eucharist.

To-day's feast then challenges us to respond by believing sincerely that God revealed himself to his chosen people through the events of the OT, and that this self-revelation reached its culmination with Christ's coming on earth. But, furthermore, this feast reminds us that we have not been left orphans after Christ's ascension, but that in the sacramental signs of bread and wine, Christ's glorified body is still with us, and that by the reception of Holy Communion we are united with our glorified Saviour in a most intimate way, to the extent that the Father looking on us, sees and loves his Son in us, and Christ, on our behalf, returns that love, as he does in the intimacy of the Blessed Trinity. God, who is all-powerful, could not have given us a greater gift than that of his Son in the Eucharist.

TENTH SUNDAY OF THE YEAR
1 Kgs 17:17-24; Gal 1:11-19; Lk 7:11-17

The most touching story in all four gospels, is how many would describe the gospel reading for this Sunday. Luke in few words paints a masterly picture of the poignancy, helplessness, and tragedy of human life. 'He was his mother's only son, and she was a widow'. This austere, simple statement, were we to reflect on it, cannot but touch an inner chord in us. How often does it seem, that we who were created to be free, to be loved by God, to be happy, are doomed to live in a world of broken hearts, without being able to do much about it, except to try and bring comfort with our presence. 'And a large crowd from the city was with her.' There is a human helplessness which no one but God can relieve. 'When the Lord saw her, he had compassion on her', or more precisely, to give the Greek its full force, 'he was moved to the depths of his heart for her'. 'Don't cry', were the only words he spoke to her, and when the young man was restored to life, we read that Jesus 'gave him to his mother', the exact same phrase as in the Elijah story of the first reading.

'When the Lord saw her, he was moved to the depths of his heart for her.' This must have been a puzzling assertion for the ancient gentile world. Here we are speaking about God, for the title, 'Lord', was reserved by the Jews for God alone, and this is the first time in the gospel narrative where it is applied to Jesus. This idea of God being moved to sympathy for a creature was completely unacceptable to the followers of even the noblest religious cult in ancient times, the Stoics. For they maintained that the principal characteristic of God was apathy, which comes from a Greek word, *apatheia*, that means being incapable of showing affection or emotion, indifference. But the gospel message is that our God is a God of divine tenderness, reaching out to us in the person of Jesus Christ. Indeed showing compassion is the principal role that God intends to fulfil in history. And in the lives of the poor, the hungry, the sorrowful, how often do they reach a stage when they have nothing more to hope for from this human history of ours but to continue waiting expectantly on God. 'I waited, I waited for the Lord, and he stooped down to me; he heard my cry', the Psalms tell us (40:1).

But the manifestation of God's mercy in the healing power of Christ evoked a response in his onlookers quite different from what it does in us. For the people of Christ's own time, who according to their traditions saw the hand of God at work in every occurrence, the miracle was no problem. For them the real problem was that this person, Jesus, whose origins they all knew, should be working miracles at all. Some went so far as to say that his powers came from the devil. On the other hand our attention, here and now, tends to focus on the miraculous action itself. We ask the question what, if in his own day Jesus healed and helped a few, does that signify for all of us today. If on a few occasions, during his earthly life he fed thousands miraculously, what does that mean for the two-thirds of the human race who struggle to survive now?

The answer is not easily arrived at if we stick to purely human reasoning. It can only come at the level of faith, if for example we can see in the action of Jesus, at Nain, God saying 'no' to all forms of evil, of separation, of suffering, of deprivation, that lead to human suffering. That is Jesus' message throughout his public life, and it has enormous consequences. We should not expect God to wave his hand, as it were, and solve all our problems for us. Setting out, with God's help, to find solutions ourselves is what confers nobility and greatness on the human race. There comes a time when human offspring have to take on responsibility for themselves, and develop independently of their parents. Likewise with the human race and its creator, except that God continues to sustain the universe, otherwise it would cease to exist. But it is true that God helps those who help themselves.

What God is telling us through this miracle Christ worked is that evil can and will be overcome. Admittedly, despite being able to resuscitate people after near-death experiences, modern medicine has not yet conquered death. But Christ has, and the miracle at Nain is a guarantee that with faith in Christ so will we. Hence the poor, the suffering, the oppressed, in very truth all of us, have sure grounds for positive hope. Our motto should be, 'If God is with us, who can be against us?'

ELEVENTH SUNDAY OF THE YEAR
2 Sam 12:7-10, 13; Gal 2:16, 19-21; Lk 7:36 - 8:3

As we read through the gospels, one of those questions bound to arise is, why was Jesus so considerate and forgiving towards the wayward and the sinners, and yet so seemingly harsh and critical towards the Pharisees, who were regarded by many as pillars of the Jewish religion, but whom he referred to as whited sepulchres, excellent and becoming on the outside, but full of corruption within. Part of the answer must be that the Pharisees saw the goodness of a person as being that person's own creation, coming entirely from his or her own moral behaviour. There was no need for divine assistance or forgiveness. God's principal task, they maintained, was solely to watch over those who observed all the details of the Mosaic Law, and reward them, while sending punishment on all offenders against the Law. This explains their attitude towards sinners, whom they shunned and despised. They were blind to the fact that a person does not, and cannot, create his or her own goodness.

St Paul in his Letter to the Romans (7:15,21) keeps on coming to this very point, and indeed puts into words what most of us feel, on occasion, about our own conduct. 'I cannot understand my own behaviour', he says. 'I fail to carry out the things I hate, … In fact this seems to be the rule, that every single time I want to do good, it is something evil that comes about'. And he goes on to say that he can only be rescued from this dilemma, by cultivating a loving trust and faith in Jesus Christ. Be guided by the Holy Spirit, he advised others, not by the Law, and you will never yield to self-indulgence (Gal 5:17). The core of the Christian message, then, is not so much demands, and commandments, and laws. Rather is it the grace of God, the forgiveness and love of God, the Spirit of life, which Christ alone can bestow on us. For St John also, the very meaning of sin is precisely this lack of faith and trust in Jesus. And faith in Jesus is an admission of the absolute need of our whole being for Jesus, an acceptance of the claims of Jesus, a willingness to come to Jesus and throw ourselves on his mercy. This is the whole point of today's gospel reading. Love flows into our hearts from the experience of being forgiven by God.

The extraordinary English mystic of the 14th century, Dame Julian of Norwich, who lived most of her life as a recluse in a cell attached to a Church, saw the following of Christ as a succession of failures, of falling down, picking ourselves up and falling flat again. 'We need to fall', she wrote, 'and we need to see that we have done so. For if we never fell, we should not know how weak and pitiable we are in ourselves. Nor should we fully know the wonderful love of our maker'. And indeed no one, but no one, is barred from God's forgiveness. In the first reading we had the repentance of king David, and in the gospel that of a lowly and anonymous public sinner. No matter how terrible the sin, God is ready to look upon it as if it had never been committed.

The acknowledgment of our need for God's mercy and pardon will have tremendous consequences for ourselves, in that it will give birth to the love of God within us. This is made clear by the fact that today's gospel concentrates, not on the unexpected and unexplained forgiveness of the sinner, but on the sinner's response of gratitude towards Christ. The woman's sins were forgiven because she loved much, because she had faith in Jesus, because she was aware of her own shortcomings, and saw Jesus as the one who could, and would, deliver her from them. Jesus, also, was prepared to bring his message and his healing grace to the so-called good people too, like Simon, but found it harder to get through to them. We, therefore, should examine ourselves, this day, and see how much of the attitude of the Pharisees we have got. Do we regard ourselves as being in little need of forgiveness, because if so, Christ assures us, we have little love for God. 'It is the one who is forgiven little who has little love', was his rebuke to the Pharisee.

We should see this Mass we are celebrating for what it is, God's generous and loving gift of himself to us. The ones who are good for making excuses are seldom good for anything else, and we see how King David did not offer excuses for having brought about the death of Uriah after committing adultery with his wife. 'I have sinned against God', he openly admitted, and God forgave him. Let us too sincerely admit the need we have for forgiveness from such a forgiving and compassionate God.

TWELFTH SUNDAY OF THE YEAR
Zech 12:10-11, 13:1; Gal 3:26-29; Lk 9:18-24

If you find yourself anywhere in the vicinity of the Sea of Galilee, and look towards the north, you will see a very high mountain, Mt Hermon (9,233 ft. or 2,814 metres), almost three times the height of our highest mountain, and surprisingly its summit is covered with snow all year round. One day, somewhere in the southern foothills of this mountain, where Jesus had brought his disciples, to rest and pray, he asked them rather disconcertingly, 'Who do people say that I am?' It marks one of the most crucial moments in the public life of Jesus. St Luke suggests that the whole episode took place in a brief period of stillness and reflection, far withdrawn from the hectic course of events prior to it. Indeed this very chapter in Luke's gospel marks a turning point in Christ's mission, for towards the end of it we are told, 'As the time drew near for him to be taken up to heaven, he fixed his face firmly to go to Jerusalem.'

Fixing his face firmly implies an interior struggle on the part of Jesus. Was he looking ahead with apprehension to what was to be his fate in Jerusalem? The reading makes clear he knew quite well that he was going to his death there on the Cross. Or was he looking back at what he had achieved, trying to discover the kind of understanding of himself and his mission, which his disciples had acquired? By way of answer to his query, 'Who do people say that I am?', his disciples listed for him some of the popular rumours that were circulating about him, that he was John the Baptist restored to life, or a reincarnation of Elijah, one of the greatest prophets in Jewish history. Then came a breathless silence, and he put the question which meant so much to him, 'Who do you say that I am?' It is never enough to know what other people have seen in Jesus. Christianity never consists in knowing about Jesus; it always consists in knowing Jesus, and this in a more intimate and personal way. In other words, the discovery of Christ must ultimately come from a person-to-person experience between each of us and Christ, an experience moreover that matures within the Christian community that begets it and plays such a prominent part in sustaining it.

The answer of Peter to this question about the identity of Jesus is the only one recorded in the New Testament, and it is very interesting to examine the different wordings given in the three synoptic gospels. The oldest one, that of Mark, simply states, 'You are the Christ'. The title Christ, or Messiah, means 'the anointed one', and in Old Testament times only kings, priests, and prophets were anointed, and Christ was seen as all three. Luke's gospel has the slightly longer answer, 'You are the Christ of God'. The version in Matthew, written later still, is the longest, 'You are the Christ, the Son of the living God'. 'You are the Christ', 'You are the Christ of God', 'You are the Christ, the Son of the living God'. At least two of these answers, you might argue, are not exactly what Peter said. But a religious message with computerised exactness, in every detail, was never what the evangelists set out to give us.

The primary purpose of the gospels was to evoke a response of faith from everyone who listened to them or read them, in other words to draw people to believe in Christ. They are also, however, a reflection of the faith of the Christian communities out of which they grew. And what we are witnessing, in the short period between the writing of Mark's gospel and that of Matthew, is the growth in their understanding of the significance of Christ. The active faith of the first Christians was penetrating deeper and deeper into the mystery that was Christ. It was only after deep reflection on the sayings of Christ, on the miracles he worked, and especially on his post-resurrection appearances that they arrived at the conviction that he was a divine person.

The successors to the contemporaries of Jesus continued to find a more meaningful answer to that query, 'Who do you say that I am?' And Christ to this day continues to issue the same challenge to each one of us also. St Paul writing about the faith to his young companion Timothy said, 'I know whom I have believed'. Note he did not say, 'I know what I have believed'. Christianity does not mean saying 'yes' to a list of truths. It means knowing a person – not a person away out there, remote from us, but the person of Jesus Christ as he dwells by faith within us, for each of us is called to be the temple of the risen glorified Son of God.

THIRTEENTH SUNDAY OF THE YEAR
1 Kgs 19:16, 19-21; Gal 5:1, 13-18; Lk 9:51-62

It is a sad reflection on human nature that even religion can give rise to bitter and long-lasting divisions among peoples living in close proximity all their lives. We see an example of this in today's gospel reading which tells us how Jesus resolutely set out to go from Galilee to Jerusalem for the last time. The shortest route for that journey should take one through Samaria, but most Jews avoided this, because for centuries Jews and Samaritans were sworn enemies, the main reason being that the Jews worshipped in Jerusalem and the Samaritans on Mount Gerizim, close to modern-day Nablus. Jesus had hoped to find hospitality in a Samaritan village, and extend the hand of friendship to its people. But he was rebuffed, especially as he was a pilgrim on the way to the Temple in Jerusalem. Even more bitter was the reaction of James and John, who wanted to call down fire from heaven to burn up the inhabitants. It was an example of the kind of bigotry, which has become all too common today, where people are forced into a religious mould by the threat of physical violence. That the stern rebuke of Jesus had its effect is evidenced from the fact that John, who must have felt the brunt of it very keenly, was to make love the central theme of both his gospel and letters.

In contrast to all this we have the advice of Jesus to three separate people who wanted to become followers of his. Far from putting pressure on them, he even seemed to be discouraging them. The first man was advised to count the cost before setting out to follow him, as Christ had no fixed abode. His response to the second man seemed to be quite harsh. Let the spiritually dead bury their dead, the man was told, after asking that he be first allowed bury his father. The father, however, was very likely not yet dead, the custom then being that the eldest son should not leave the family home until after his father' death. The lesson is that if we are faced with an option, and do not avail of it at once, it is less likely that we will do so later. His message for the third man was uncompromising too. No one who puts his hand to the plough and looks back is the right kind of person for the kingdom of God. The wooden ploughs of that time were very fragile, and were in danger of being smashed if they struck any of the stones which were a feature of the land. Therefore the ploughman had to keep his eyes on the ground ahead at all times. The commitment to his task by the disciple of Christ should be total at all times as well.

All through our lives, God is also calling us, whether we respond or not, even as he called Abraham from his homeland, Peter from his nets, Matthew from his tax office, Elisha from his farm. But, how many of us answer the call? Referring to the Jews, Jesus said, 'Many are called but few are chosen' (Mt 22:14). The almighty God, speaking through Moses to the Israelites, seemed almost to rejoice and take delight in the small numbers who were following his call. 'It is you that the Lord your God has chosen to be his very own people out of all the peoples on the earth. If the Lord set his heart on you and chose you, it was not because you outnumbered other peoples; you were the fewest of all peoples' (Deut 7:6f).

This was again echoed by Christ before his disciples, 'Fear not little flock, for it has pleased the Father to give you the kingdom' (Lk 12:32). But the sad thing, not only in the Old Testament, but throughout the history of Christianity, is that God's generosity has been often met by a lack of gratitude, faith, holiness, truth and fidelity. It is a great mystery why one person follows the call of God and lets it give direction to his/her life, and another does not. We do not know why this happens, but we cannot blame God for it. 'As I live, says the Lord God, I take no pleasure in the death of the wicked, but rather that the wicked should turn from their evil ways and live' (Ez 33:11). 'God so loved the world that he gave his only Son so that everyone who believes in him may not be lost, but may have eternal life' (Jn 3:16). This reassures us that there is no lack of love on God's part for each and every person that ever lived. It is in the manner of their response to God's love that people are found wanting. Nor can there be room for complacency, taking our salvation for granted. Even so great a saint as the apostle St Paul said, 'I treat my body hard, and bring it into subjection, lest by any means, having preached to others, I myself should become a castaway' (1 Cor 9:16). We should always bear in mind that we are children of God, called to live in the light of Christ, and not dwell in the darkness.

FOURTEENTH SUNDAY OF THE YEAR
Is 66:10-14; Gal 6:14-18; Lk 10:1-12, 17-20

It has been said by psychologists and career guidance counsel-
lors that there is a close connection between the career a person
chooses in life and the development of the personality of that
person. People in positions of authority who become arrogant
and overbearing, and scientists who become so carried away
with their research that they become eccentric in behaviour, are
just a few examples that spring to mind. In total contradiction to
this, at a Dublin seminar on career guidance, an English professor
in this field from Leeds University stated that in his experience
many Irish people working in England identified in a minimal
way with the career tasks in which they were employed. It was a
time when emigrants from Ireland were ill-prepared for under-
taking any kind of managerial role. There was little job-satisfaction,
he said, or self-fulfilment in their work, which quite often they
looked upon as an unavoidable intrusion into what they
deemed to be their daily lives.

When they clocked off from work in the evening or at the
week-end, they resumed the threads of what they looked upon
as their normal existence, which to their way of thinking was
sharply distinguished and altogether remote from their working
hours. One would be slow to say that this evaluation is applicable generally, but what can be said is that there is a remarkable
parallel between it and the attitude some of us have towards our
Christian faith. We might well ask ourselves whether we regard
the practice of our Catholic religion as a kind of series of inter-
mittent digressions from our normal lives, whether Christianity
is something to be practised only on Sundays within a church
building, or at odd moments when we say prayers at home
throughout the week. Such an approach is far removed from the
kingdom of God which Christ wanted preached by the disciples
when spreading the gospel, far from the new Israel of God, for
which St Paul was prepared to be crucified to the world and to
bear in his body the marks of Jesus, far also from the vision, in
the reading from the prophet Isaiah, of the New Jerusalem, that
is the Church, which should be our heavenly sustenance, our
consolation, our joy, bringing peace flowing like a mighty river
into our souls.

Religion is not something we put on with our Sunday

clothes; it must enter into the very centre of our being, become a dynamic force lending purpose to our every-day existence. Membership of the Church means this: that God the Father has gathered together in one body all of us who have faith in Jesus Christ, all who see him as the one who has delivered us from the power of evil, and the fear of death, that we are called to identify with Christ in our daily lives, become one with him and with each other in harmony and peace, and furthermore, that Christ has left us the Holy Spirit to establish in each of us this sense of community and service to others. But the Church is meant to be a sacrament, a visible sign to the whole world of God's redeeming love offered to all humanity, and of humankind's response to this offer.

This sign becomes most clearly visible, when we are united to each other and to God, in truth, holiness and mutual love, and especially when we are openly gathered together, as we are at this moment, to confess our faith in Christ, and to celebrate what God has done for us in Christ. In the Blessed Eucharist, not only do we offer homage and thanks – that is the meaning of the word Eucharist – but the risen, glorified Christ becomes one with us. We, in our turn, offer to Christ our lives, and not only our Sunday lives, but also our daily lives, our regular existence with all its concerns, its heart-aches, its joys. It does not mean that we have to go so far as to stop in the middle of our work during the day to turn in prayer to God, as was the custom, for example, of the Ven Matt Talbot in the timber yard in Dublin where he was employed. Neither does it not mean that we have to do violence to our nature, but it does mean that we allow grace to build on our nature, so that in our work, in our leisure, we bear witness to Christian virtue. Let us try and see our lives, in the context of work as well as within our family circle, as lives of service to others, as Christ loving others through us. In all that we do, let us strive, like the early Christians used to phrase it, to be God to others, to let our Morning Offering give direction to our full day, so that all our thoughts, words and actions may be blessed by God, as long as we live on this earth.

FIFTEENTH SUNDAY OF THE YEAR
Deut 30:10-14; Col 1:15-20; Lk 10:25-37

One of the most prolific writers of all time, a genius blessed with a powerful brain, was the Englishman, G. K. Chesterton. In his early years he was an agnostic, with little religious belief. After leaving school at 18, he drifted into what he describes as a state of 'moral anarchy', something which only led to misery and despair. He was saved by his sense of wonder and joy at the existence of the natural world around him. 'Having stretched my brain till it bursts', he wrote, 'I have come to the belief that heresy is worse than sin'. After five years of deep spiritual reasoning, he found that his personal religious vision was for centuries present already in the Apostles' Creed of the Christian Church, although he was 48 before he finally became a Catholic.

Primarily a journalist, he was also a poet, writer of several books, radio broadcaster, public debater, and theologian. So great were the demands on his literary genius that he died at the age of 62 from heart fatigue and chronic exhaustion. Such was his contribution to emerging Catholicism in England that the cause for his beatification is being promoted within the Church there recently. He once stated that the English secularised culture of his day, which often regarded atheism as the hallmark of the intellectual, retained within itself, in spite of everything, especially its attitude to religion, many concepts which were deep-rooted in Christianity. One such concept must surely be that of the good Samaritan. In fact it was in England that the action group called 'The Samaritans' originated. The enduring impact of Jesus' parable of the 'Good Samaritan' is all the more extraordinary when we remember that for the Jews the Samaritans were anything but good. Instead they looked on them as being despicable renegades from the Jewish faith. They even accused Jesus himself of being a Samaritan and possessed by a devil (Jn 8:48).

We would do well to consider the significance of the parable for us here and now. What is certain is that Jesus used this unusual story to bring home to us in a dramatic way the most important, the most demanding, the most all-embracing quality he requires of those who would be his followers. The importance of Jesus' parable lies in its context. It is the answer to a very specific question – who is my neighbour to whom I must show as much love as to myself? The answer is brought home very forcibly to the Jewish lawyer who put the question. Everyone without exception, even such as the despised Samaritan, must be regarded as a neighbour.

But if we ponder over the whole account there are further lessons we can draw from it. Firstly, we could ask ourselves what the Samaritan had to gain personally from his act of charity. The answer, in material terms, is precisely nothing. The whole point is that love which is really and truly love, is disinterested. Indeed where is the merit in being good only to friends, who will obviously reward you in return, should the need arise? Christian love must embrace everyone. Secondly, if you do not show love to the neighbour whom you see, then no matter what commandments you keep, what ritual sacrifices you join in, as did the priest and Levite in the parable, you become incapable of loving God, whom you cannot see. This is something which St John reiterates again and again. If you want to join in the Eucharistic banquet and receive God's Son into your heart, then you must first cleanse your heart of all hatred, bitterness, ill-will, because the God we receive in this sacrament is love.

Finally, we could read a deeper meaning into the parable – that we are the very ones who have fallen among the robbers, and that these latter represent the forces of evil which have stripped us of our virtue, of our heavenly birthright. The one who comes to our rescue is Christ, the Suffering Servant of the Lord, described so graphically by the prophet Isaiah as the one despised and rejected by his own people. And he has rescued us, not by means of gold or silver, but by the sacrifice of his very life, by the shedding of his blood, which takes away our sins, and restores us to the friendship of God once more. Pressed as to why he entered the Catholic Church, Chesterton, incidentally, said it was the only Church which claimed to be able to forgive sin. Confronted then with the heroic self-sacrifice on the part of Jesus, our response is clearly indicated for us by St John in his First Letter: 'My dear people, since God has loved us so much, then we too should love one another.' (1 Jn 4:11)

SIXTEENTH SUNDAY OF THE YEAR
Gen 18:1-10; Col 1:24-28; Lk 10:38-42

'What is man that you care for him', the writer of the Psalms
asks God to explain (Ps 4:8), 'mortal man that you keep him in
mind?' It has been said that when it comes to discovering the
meaning of human life and of our existence in this world, most
of us are like pygmies, who travel on the backs of the giants who
have gone before us. In other words the number of people who
were able to stand back, as it were, and try to see human striving,
endeavour, hardship, in meaningful terms, is very small indeed.
The majority of us are willing to go along in varying degrees
with their discoveries, as they filter down to us through different channels.

The Word of God, which is the theme running through all
three readings today, comes to us in more or less the same way.
There were some chosen individuals who were able to grasp in a
wonderful way God's message for the human race, who discovered fresh insights into this message, and as a result had an
enduring influence on those who came after them. Thus the
Word of God came to Abraham. But it was not something abstract,
something which for Abraham was to be found in books; there
was no such thing as books then, but rather a wonderful oral
tradition handed on from generation to generation, and finally
committed to scrolls. Abraham's encounter with God was on a
very personal plane. He was the friend of God, the Bible says,
and his welcoming reception of the message of God is depicted
in terms of eastern nomadic hospitality.

Abraham is the supreme example, in the OT, of deep-rooted
faith and trust in God. He was called by God to leave his own
clan, to leave off worshipping their gods, to set out for an
unknown destination, and in return he would become the father
of a new and numerous people. Abraham trusted, and followed
this call, even though there seemed little hope that the promises
to him would ever be fulfilled. Then, after a long time has
elapsed, he is told that his wife, Sarah, will give birth to a son,
even though both were now very old. Again he trusts in God's
word. But later when his son Isaac was born he was asked to
sacrifice this son. How could the promise of God that he would
be the father of a people as numerous as the stars in the heavens
now come true? Nevertheless, Abraham's faith and confidence

in God never wavered, and was vindicated in the end. This faith was the means by which Abraham was justified – there was as yet no written commandments of the Law – and this faith was to endure in his children, among whom we also are privileged to be numbered.

As we saw in the gospel today, the Word of God came to Mary, the sister of Martha, and was the outcome of an even more personal and direct relationship with God in Christ. We always feel a little sorry for Martha, who was left on her own to attend to the household work, but what is brought home to us here is that our relationship with God, our attentiveness to his voice speaking to us through the Spirit must never be pushed aside, drowned out by the hustle and bustle of our everyday lives. Finally, in the reading from St Paul we are told how the Word of God, hidden from all mankind for centuries, comes to the gentiles.

What then is this Word of God, and where do we find it, you may ask. This glorious and rich secret, as St Paul says, is that Christ lives on in us, that he has conquered sin and death for us, that he calls us to share in the glory of God, if only we listen to him as did Mary, and have faith like that of Abraham. For he continues to speak to us, through the Scriptures, through the new Testament in particular, through the liturgy, through the homily, through the community in which we live, and through our own families, provided we open our eyes, our ears, our hearts. For the message of salvation is a living tradition handed down from one generation to the next, as it was in the early days of the chosen people. It is a message which is continually being revealed in new light to us by the Holy Spirit, and like the man in the gospel, who buried his master's talent, we also will be called to account if we do not cherish, preserve, and hand on this message of hope to those who will follow us.

Only one thing really matters in the hurly-burly of our modern world, that we always make space for God in our lives, that we reach out and grasp the message which God is continually presenting to us, that we make it our own, and that we allow it to guide and shape us, as we live and as we hope to die, in fulfilment of God's wishes for us.

SEVENTEENTH SUNDAY OF THE YEAR
Gen 18:20-32; Col 2:12-14; Lk 11:1-13

One of the most moving sections of the New Testament, beautifully narrated by St Luke in the Acts of the Apostles, is the account of St Paul taking leave of the Christian communities, for what he thought was the last time, and setting out for Jerusalem, where he knew he was going to be thrown into prison. It gives us graphic insights into the change which the new Christian faith had brought about in these converts from paganism, and the esteem and love they had for Paul. In the port city of Troas, on the Turkish Mediterranean coast, some ten miles from the site of ancient Troy, after first celebrating the Eucharist, they spent the whole night listening to Paul and conversing with him. It was there that a young boy, sitting on a window-sill, grew drowsy and fell backwards through the open window onto the ground below. And Paul went down, lifted him up, and restored him, still living, to his parents. Next, sailing southwards, Paul stopped at Miletus, the port serving the great city of Ephesus. The elders of the Church at Ephesus came out to hear his farewell discourse to them, and when Paul had finished we are told that he knelt down and they all joined together with him in prayer.

Paul is often regarded by us as a stern, academic, off-putting figure, but not by those who came close to him. Here we are told that his listeners broke down in tears and embraced and kissed Paul, sorrowing most of all because he had said they should see his face no more. And they all accompanied him back to his ship. After the last stop at the famous ancient port of Tyre, the disciples yet again, men, women, and children, went with him down to the quay side, and regardless of the sailors and pagan onlookers, kneeling down on the beach they joined together in prayer, and bade one another farewell. The lesson for all of us in this is the depth of faith of these first generation Christians, which can be seen from the extraordinarily rich prayer life they had already acquired.

As soon as one ceases to pray, it is a clear-cut indication that one is no longer walking with Christ, Christ who, according to Luke, went out into the hills to pray, and even spent the whole night in prayer to the Father before selecting his Apostles (Lk 6:12). This obviously was one aspect of Christ's life that made a deep impression on Paul. Time and again he reminded his converts of the need for prayer. 'Rejoice always. Pray without ceasing', he warned the Thessalonians (15:17f), and to the Philippians he wrote, 'Have no anxiety about anything, but in everything, by prayer and thanksgiving, let your requests be made known to God' (4:6). And his last word of advice to those at Ephesus was to pray at all times in the Spirit, to persevere in their prayer, and to pray for one another. Why is it then, you might ask, that our prayers, especially our prayers of petition, seem so often to go unanswered?

The fact, however, is that every prayer of petition is answered, provided it is made in faith, made with a readiness to accept God's will, and made with a heart devoid of any feeling of hatred or ill-will towards others. 'Have faith in God', Jesus said to his disciples; 'I tell you, whatever you ask for in prayer, believe that you receive it, and you will' (Mt 11:24). The problem is, do we know how to pray, and what to pray for? When Jesus said, 'believe that you receive whatever you ask for', he was telling us that above all we must have faith in God. The only place Jesus could not work miracles was his home town, Nazareth, because people did not have faith. St James, moreover, in his letter has this warning (4:2), 'You ask and do not receive, because you ask wrongly, to spend it on your passions.' We may in fact be asking for something harmful, and our heavenly Father will only give what will be for our good.

A certain man once asked a Carthusian monk how he should pray, and the reply was, 'Pray in, not up' – just four words. It is indeed true that most of the time we imagine the One we are addressing in prayer as being somewhere above or outside ourselves. But scripture tells us that we are temples of the Holy Spirit, and we should focus on God's Spirit dwelling within us. Furthermore, the Spirit pleads for us with sighs too deep for words, and intercedes for us according to the will of God. May we never leave off praying, but rather ask God daily for the gift of prayer, as did Matt Talbot, who set for us such an example of a life wholly dedicated to prayer, by day and by night, at home or at work.

EIGHTEENTH SUNDAY OF THE YEAR
Qo 1:2. 2:21-23; Col 3:1-5, 9-11; Lk 12:13-21

'What does it profit a man to have gained the whole world, and to have lost or ruined his very self?' (Lk 9:25). 'For a man's life is not made secure by what he owns, even when he has more than he needs' (Lk 12:15). Here the gospel is emphatically telling us that a real and meaningful life cannot be attained from an abundance of material possessions alone. The rich man in the gospel reading must have thought that his future was secure, and that his existence hence forward was under his own control. It must have come as quite a shock to him to be reminded that his life on earth was God's to give and God's to take away again. But it must also be admitted that in many of us there is a certain sneaking admiration and sympathy for this industrious man. For deep down in our human nature, there is in all of us, it could very well be said, a streak of greed and covetousness, whether this is linked with our innate instinct for self-preservation, or is more essentially the heritage of original sin, the result of Adam's fall from original grace before God.

It has been said that greed is a sign of a lack of love in our lives, and that to make up for this want, we proceed to amass for ourselves all kinds of possessions and to strive for things that often bring us a mere fleeting satisfaction. We need only look around to find ample evidence of this in today's world. We are surrounded on every side by the obsessive clamour of the rat-race, a scramble to get on in the world by fair means or foul, the strident demands of greater remuneration for their services by some sections of society, backed up by the threat of putting the rest to intolerable inconvenience if these demands are not met. But the message of Jesus in today's gospel reading is in complete contradiction to such self-seeking. In it he is indicating that, at some time or other, each one of us must face up to these questions – what am I seeking to attain here and now in this life, what for me is the meaning of existence in this world, and what are my hopes for the life hereafter?

As regards life here and now, we can be led astray by pursuing either of two extremes – the first a purely material one, which strives to put self first, and regards all things, even other people, as means towards achieving one's own selfish ambitions. If we adopt this approach to life, if we never consider that we have an eternal destiny also, then, Jesus is telling us, some day we are in for the grimmest of grim shocks. The other extreme is that which sees no value whatsoever in striving for material gain. Why bother working at all is the attitude. We actually find an example of this among certain communities of the first Christians, when they thought that the second coming of Christ was at hand. St Paul, whose mind seemed to be ever preoccupied with spiritual matters, was also a realist. 'If you do not work', he told them bluntly, 'then you do not eat'.

Virtues, strangely enough, theologians tell us, are the middle way between two extremes, the golden mean, the best course to follow. Our attitude towards worldly goods must pursue this approach in some way. On the one hand we have Christ's total giving of himself. He came into the world in a place used to house animals; he departed from the world possessing nothing, not even clothes to cover his nakedness. But then, on the other hand, most of us stand in need of worldly goods, especially in the kind of society we live in. The one rich by human standards, who makes use of his wealth to employ others, and thereby enables them to provide for themselves and their dependents, is a better person in the eyes of God then the one who, while professing dedication to the gospel message, refuses to use his God-given talents for the welfare of those with whom he finds himself involved.

We lay up treasure for ourselves in heaven, not only through love of God but also through concern for our neighbour. In showing his compassion for the sick, the elderly, the sinner, God makes use of human instruments. In order to partake in this task, we must be open to Christ's message, we must show deter-mination, as the second reading strongly urges us, to 'kill' the vices which are in us, especially greed which is the equivalent of worshipping a false god. There is nothing which can bring us to a more proper understanding of the value of material goods than that stark question of God in the gospel reading, 'This hoard of yours, when the moment comes to face your God, whose then shall it be?'

NINETEENTH SUNDAY OF THE YEAR
Wis 18:6-9; Heb 11:1-2, 8-19; Lk 12:32-48

The Second Reading today is from a chapter in the Letter to the Hebrews that has been described as 'the roll call of heroes of the faith', Old Testament patriarchs, and others who fulfilled a special role in salvation history, such as Abel, Noah, Abraham, Sarah, Jacob, Moses, who were commended for their trust in God, down to King David, Samuel and the prophets who acted as God's messengers to his people. These were people who took God at his word, for faith is trust in God, the acceptance of things unseen, truths that cannot be grasped with reason alone. Even for us who are members of the New Testament, it is only with the help of the Holy Spirit of God, and not by our reasoning powers, that we come to accept Jesus Christ. Intellectual giants, doctors of divinity, simple people, illiterates, we are all equally like children when trying to comprehend the mystery we call God.

To advance in the love of God is the greatest possible achievement of the human spirit. How wonderful is God's love, in that he permits us to love him without having to compel or force us to do so by commandments. Of course the first commandment states that we should love the Lord, our God with all our heart, with all our soul and with all our mind. But here the initiative is always taken by God, who draws us to love him by his grace freely given, which we are free to accept or not. The greatest exponent of this doctrine was St Francis de Sales, who died in 1622, having served as bishop of Geneva for 20 years. He was renowned for his graciousness towards penitents, and is said to have brought back into the Church some 72,000 followers of Calvin. Often people came to him just to be reassured, to draw strength from his deep faith. For the ordinary soul slips in and out of faith a hundred times a day. Yet underneath the confusion, the doubts, the loneliness, the sense of being abandoned, God is always there.

Often it is when we reach zero-point that the deepest religious experiences occur, and we are transformed by God's healing presence within us. Even at the most desperate moments, faith is ever possible, and the trusting soul will find God is close at hand. 'Fear not little flock, for it has pleased the Father to give you the kingdom' (Lk 12:32), to give you the strength to bear your burdens, the courage to shoulder your cross. At the end of World War II, in the dreaded German concentration camp at Ravensbruck, there was found on a piece of wrapping-paper, a prayer written by one the inmates there. It read: 'Oh Lord, remember not only men and women of good-will, but also those of ill-will. But do not remember all the suffering they have inflicted on us; remember the fruits we have bought, thanks to this suffering, our comradeship, our loyalty, our humility, our courage, our generosity, the greatness of heart which has grown out of all this, and when they come to judgment, let all the fruits which we have borne, be their forgiveness'. There cannot be any doubt but that the writer of this most extraordinary plea for God's mercy towards his/her persecutors, will be included in the roll-call of heroes of the faith, when the Son of God returns on judgment day.

Such heroic forgiveness proves that no matter how terrible and shattering the trials some souls undergo, they can frequently come through them with a deeper and stronger faith, so convinced are they of the abiding presence of God with them. For most of us, however, the greatest test of our faith may arise from the ordinary, humdrum, daily routines, the ups and downs of life as we go through it. And it is true that we can brood over these until they get us down, until our faith in divine providence turns sour, and we are left stranded in our misery. It is at such times that we should turn to prayer and renew our inner strength through reception of the sacraments. 'No matter what happens, keep on praying', St Paul told the first Christians who endured so much for their faith.

If we really try and respond to God's grace as they did, then our faith also will grow strong and vigorous, like that of those great figures of the Old Testament who were commended for their trust in God's word. We have all seen this take place in the lives of people we happen to know, how they often acquire great serenity in the face of acute and prolonged suffering. For although the final reward of faith in God will come hereafter in his promised kingdom, even here and now it is possible to acquire a foretaste of that eternal peace which this world cannot give.

THE ASSUMPTION OF THE BVM
Vigil: 1 Chron 15:3-4, 15-16. 16:1-2; 1 Cor 15:54-57; Lk 11:27-28
Feast: Apoc 11:19. 12:1-6, 10; 1 Cor 15:20-27; Lk 1:39-56

'God created man in his own image and likeness.' On this feast of the Assumption into heaven of the blessed Virgin Mary, God's most perfect creation apart from the humanity of Jesus Christ himself, we could profitably consider that statement from the Bible creation story, and how most of us tend to reverse the whole thrust of it, in other words how we attempt to create God in our image and likeness. Each of us tries to form his, or her, own unique and very limited concept of God. How often do we cling to the notion of an obedient God, a God who will grant us all our wishes if we but ask him in the right way; or of an indulgent God who will turn a blind eye on the double standards in our lives; or again, a vengeful, exacting God, whom we serve out of fear, and to whom we make offerings, say little prayers, in order to buy ourselves into his good graces. Admittedly these pictures are somewhat overdrawn, but to test our concept of God each of us should ask, 'Does my idea of God in any way reflect Mary's vision of God, especially when she says, in today's gospel reading, "My soul glorifies the Lord, and my spirit rejoices in God my Saviour".'

Here we see how Mary linked prayerful worship of God with joy in his presence, foreshadowing the advice later given by St Paul to the first Christians, 'Rejoice always. Pray without ceasing' (1 Thess 5:17f). In this her prayer, known as the Magnificat, Mary is not concerned about herself, she does not ask anything for herself, she is not worried about the future; she thinks only of the great things that God has done for her up to the present moment, and of the debt of gratitude owed by her people to him. Self-forgetfulness is a prerequisite for true love, and in Mary we have a supreme example of a person totally possessed by the love of God. No one apart from Mary has ever lived, suffered, died, in such simplicity, in such deep unawareness of her own dignity, a dignity placing her above the angels who enjoy God's presence in heaven.

Because she knew nothing of her dignity, she regarded herself as being the handmaid, that is the attendant or servant, of the Lord, one who, in her own thinking, had not the slightest importance before him. As a result of this self-forgetfulness she abandoned herself completely to God; she lived solely for God, and God, who can never be outdone in generosity, was to confer on Mary the fullness of grace; he blessed her in a most exceptional manner, through the merits of her Son, Jesus Christ. By his passion and resurrection, Christ conquered the powers of evil, especially through his victory over sin and death. And if Mary, who was never touched by the least stain of sin, was so intimately associated with her divine Son on Calvary in his conquest of sin, it was only proper that she should also be given a very special role to play in his victory over death. We must bear in mind, however, that just as Christ suffered death, Mary as well really died, as can be inferred from the opening prayer where it says how God 'raised' the sinless Virgin Mary, Mother of God's Son. Addressing God the Father, the Preface of the Mass says, 'You would not allow decay to touch her body, for she had given birth to your Son, the Lord of all life.' Furthermore in the divine office for the Feast (Evening Prayer 1), we read, 'When Christ ascended into heaven, he prepared there an immortal place for his most chaste Mother.'

So it is that we recall today, how shortly after her death, our Lady's body was united with her soul in anticipated resurrection, and how she was taken up, body and soul into heaven, to be enthroned above the angels and saints for ever. This is what we mean by the Assumption; this is what we do honour to, this day. Just as Jesus did not abandon us by his Ascension, but continually sends his Holy Spirit to sustain his Church, so Mary in the Assumption has not been separated from us, but remains, for each one of us, a sure sign that we too are called, like her, to share in the fullness of Christ's glory. Linked as she also is, in a most special manner, with God's Holy Spirit, Mary is the model, and indeed guarantee, of all that the Church hopes to become in heaven. She conceived the living God and, by her prayers, will help deliver our souls from death. We should pray then today that Mary may plead for us with her divine Son, so that we too may be found worthy to come to that place in heaven which God has prepared for all those who love him, and place all their trust in him.

TWENTIETH SUNDAY OF THE YEAR
Jer 38:4-6, 8-10; Heb 12:1-4; Lk 12:49-53

'Oh all you who walk by, consider and see if there is any sorrow
like unto my sorrow.' These words have often been said of Jesus,
but they were not said by Jesus. They are from the Lamentations
of the prophet Jeremiah (1:12), the one saintly figure from out
the Old Testament, whose life bears the greatest resemblance to
that of Jesus. He is often described as the antetype of Jesus. He
lived in the 6th century BC, an age of great upheaval in the
Middle East, which saw the collapse of the Assyrian empire, and
the emergence of a greater one in Babylon. Having been in
bondage to Assyria for some time, the Jewish leaders allowed
their faith in God, and worship of him, to become tainted by
pagan practice.

The task given to Jeremiah by God, was to condemn idolatry
– pagan idols were even set up in the Temple itself – and to warn
against forming an alliance against Babylon, something which
ultimately led to the end of the Jewish monarchy. The ruling
officials blocked all his efforts, and even wanted to kill him, but
in such a way as to make it appear that he died of the famine
then afflicting the country. The king, despite having very little
real power, managed to save him. Being a young man of gentle
character, Jeremiah's whole being shuddered before God's call
to him, which was 'to tear up and to knock down, to destroy and
to overthrow' (1:10). As we see from his own descriptions it was
to lead him to the verge of despair. 'Each time I speak, I have to
cry out and shout, "Violence and destruction". The word of the
Lord has brought on me insult and derision all day long' (20:8).
'I hear many muttering, "Terror is everywhere. Denounce him.
Let us denounce him"' (20:10).

Faced with such threats, the agony of Jeremiah grew deeper
and deeper. 'Woe is me my mother, that you gave birth to me, to
be a man of strife and discord for all the land' (15:10). 'Why is
my suffering endless, my wound incurable, refusing to be
healed?' (15:18). 'Cursed be the day when I was born' (20:18).
But self-concern was not allowed dominate his thoughts. 'Oh
that my head were a spring of water, and my eyes a fountain of
tears, that I might weep night and day for all the dead of my
people' (8:23). Jeremiah was going through what St John of the
Cross called 'the dark night of the soul', when the soul specially

chosen by God seems to be abandoned by him. By such suffering the heart of Jeremiah was purified, leaving it open to the wishes of God.

Instead of concentrating on externals like the Law, circumcision, sacrifice, the Temple itself, Jeremiah began to see that religion should really be inward, heartfelt, a more personal relationship with God. Deep within his people God would plant his Law, writing it on their hearts (Jer 31:33). 'Seek God within' was the motto of St Augustine as well. 'Enter into yourselves', he advised, 'for truth dwells in the interior person'. The practice of this interior religion by Jeremiah is what makes him dear to Christians. He spoke about a new covenant between God and the house of Israel, the first time such an idea is found in the OT. Incidentally the words of consecration over the chalice in every Mass refer to 'the blood of the new and everlasting covenant'. Both Jesus and Jeremiah had tremendous love for the ordinary people, and a burning desire for their welfare, and both were rejected by the powers that prevailed in their time.

Speaking of Jesus, Caiphas the high priest, at a meeting of the chief priests and Pharisees, said, 'It is better for one man to die for the people than for the whole nation to be destroyed' (Jn 11:50), and from that day they wanted to kill Jesus. But a generation later the Romans were to capture Jerusalem, wipe out all opposition, and destroy the Temple for ever. 'This fellow does not have the welfare of the people at heart, but its ruin', were the precise words of the leading men in Jerusalem about the prophet Jeremiah, who also saw clearly the disaster looming ahead for his people. We heard in the first reading, how they plotted to kill Jeremiah in such a way as to make it appear that he had died from the famine then raging in the land. He was only saved by a Cushite, i.e. an Egyptian, who raised the alarm and then helped draw him out of the muddy well into which he had been thrown. The only person to assist Jesus on his way to Calvary, Simon of Cyrene, was also a foreigner, a Libyan. The clear lesson for us also, as St Paul told his disciple Timothy, is that 'anybody who tries to live in devotion to Christ is bound to be attacked' (2 Tim 3:12).

TWENTY-FIRST SUNDAY OF THE YEAR
Is 66:18-21; Heb 12:5-7, 11-13; Lk 13:22-30

The English poet Robert Browning, describing the beauty of a
spring morning, ends by saying, 'The lark's on the wing, the
snail's on the thorn; God's in his heaven, all's right with the
world.' It is a beautiful piece of poetry, but the ending shows a
misleading concept of God, a concept which, if we were to ponder over it, most of us from time to time entertain in our minds
as well. 'God's in his heaven, all's right with the world.' How
often do we imagine God as being away up there in his heaven,
and the world going its own separate way, with the events of its
history taking place independently of God. And we think of
God intervening in human affairs, in the person of Jesus Christ,
in order to combat the evil forces let loose in the history of
mankind; and at the back of our minds there is the nagging, but
persistent suspicion that the battle against evil is not quite going
God's way.

If we go to the Old Testament, we find that this kind of
dilemma never posed any great problems for his chosen people,
Israel. For them God was not remote, away up there. They saw
God present in the events, whether good or evil, of everyday
existence. Every event in history was God's doing. For example,
the Israelites had looked upon the monarchy, the line of David,
as something which would last for ever, bringing glory to their
nation. This they regarded as a certainty, based on what the
great prophets had told them. But when the exile to Babylon of
all the leading figures among them occurred, the monarchy
itself was utterly destroyed, and was never to be restored.

This tragedy did not however destroy their trust in God's
promises. Rather, from out the ensuing suffering and shattered
hopes there emerged a purer and more spiritual vision of what
God meant their role to be. They saw their national catastrophe,
not so much as a punishment for sin – for most of the exiles were
good and devout people – but as the means God would employ
to bring salvation to the pagan nations. They saw their destiny
as still being glorious, but now purely from a spiritual perspective. As stated in Isaiah, all the nations would come to worship
the true God in Jerusalem. In other words God would bring
good out of the catastrophe they had endured, and this would
have an effect as well on nations apart from their own. In all of
this there is a lesson also for us.

As the reading from Hebrews puts it, God is treating us as his sons and daughters, but he is training us too, and suffering is part of this training. However painful, however unpleasant this suffering is, it will bear fruit, it will bring peace, it will generate goodness. Whatever the anxieties on the surface, deep down we can be utterly at peace with God as he relates to us through the events of our lives. Constantly at the back of our minds as we go through the day, we carry on, as it were, a conversation with ourselves – talking to ourselves, expressing mentally our hopes and fears, making plans. Relating to God means not leaving him on the fringe of all this consciousness, but making him part of it, discussing it with him, asking his guidance, his assistance, expressing to him our gratitude. All day long he is with you, and you can walk with God, you can talk with God, you can discern his loving purpose for you in every passing moment, you can rest in his presence, even while you go about your business. God, however, will not posses your soul unless you sincerely want him to.

But the tragedy is that so many of us remain, what Pope Paul VI called 'unconverted Christians'. We have no spiritual vision of the meaning and significance of our lives. We remain on a purely material plane, like the people in the gospel who said they ate and drank with Jesus and heard him preaching in the streets, but with never a hint that this, in any spiritual way, changed their lives. As for those who do not accept Christ in faith, God will simply pass them by. People will come from the east and west, from the north and south, and take the places at the feast in the kingdom of God, which had been promised to those who were called originally. Let us never cease asking God to enable us to enter by that narrow door, to possess the inheritance set aside for us by God, and not to be found wanting but rather persevere to the end.

TWENTY-SECOND SUNDAY OF THE YEAR
Sir 3:17-20, 28-29; Heb 12:18-19, 22-24; Lk 14:1, 7-14

Psalm 15, in the Book of Psalms contains the following message:
> 'Lord, who shall be admitted to your tent, and dwell on your holy mountain?
> He who keeps his pledge, come what may; who takes no interest on a loan,
> and accepts no bribe against the innocent. Such a one will stand firm for ever.'

It seems extraordinary to us, looking back to the era of the Middle Ages, how people then, arguing from that passage in the Psalms, also came to regard the charging of interest on a loan as being morally wrong. Even the great theologian, St Thomas Aquinas, agreed with this general view. But, however, it is clear from other passages in the OT that this condemnation was not originally a general one, but only applied where it meant making a profit from the financial misfortunes of another member of the community to which one belonged in ancient times. To quote one example, 'You may demand interest on a loan to a foreigner, but you must not demand interest from your brother' (Deut 23:21).

All this is a far cry from financial practices today, where the greater the demand for services, for money, for labour, the more we charge for these. The modern motto most certainly seems to be, 'get as much as possible for every transaction, and if there is no profit accruing from it, have nothing to do with it'. Repayment in the next life for the good deeds of this one has very little attraction for the modern business mind. And – let's face it – this attitude also has passed over into the spiritual sphere, whereby many of us, in varying degree, attempt to become masters of our own destiny. We subscribe to the great idolatry of our time – the belief that we can bring about our own salvation. We find ourselves saying things like, 'I'm saving my soul; I'm winning a place for myself in heaven'. We store up credits and merits, towards the day when we'll present them before God, and claim our reward on the basis of strict justice.

But if this in any way is a true reflection of our attitude, then we are living an illusion. The problem underlying this is one which is touched upon in the readings of today, namely the problem of pharisaism, the idea of self-sufficiency, the absence of true humility. In other words we do not understand the truth about ourselves, and how we stand in regard to God. The Pharisees in the gospel parable picked the places of honour, which they regarded as being theirs by right, because they observed the Law. We, too, fail to recognise the common lot of humankind, its complete dependence on God's mercy, freely offered and not merited. The idea of giving a party, not for our friends and relations, but for the poor and the crippled and the blind, does not particularly appeal to us.

We must, however, remember that this is a parable, and what Christ is saying is, 'Accept others; be open to others. Don't put up barriers between yourselves and others, as did the Pharisees.' Another possible interpretation is that we ourselves are the poor, the lame and the blind. And God has invited us to the heavenly banquet, precisely because, for himself, there is no possibility of gain or interest by so doing. He has invited us so that his mercy and his bountiful goodness may be shown before all the world. The only way we can deny this goodness of a merciful God is by declaring it to be unnecessary. And this we do whenever we show a lack of humility, a misunderstanding of the role God wants to play in our lives, whenever we say secretly, at the back of our minds, 'Lord, I'm a pretty good Catholic. I go to Mass every Sunday, and extra times during Lent. I contribute to every collection. I don't criticise people behind their backs, even though I know a lot of others who do. Actually, Lord, I'm getting on quite well.' But such is the very attitude Jesus condemns, because it is a violation of the truth. It fails to see that salvation cannot be deserved, cannot be claimed, that salvation is a pure gift.

Indeed, there is only one true posture for a Christian, and that is to come as a beggar before God, and make this very basic request: 'Lord, please help me'. It is being true to Christian practice to face honestly our emptiness and limitations, to realise the need we have for Christ's redeeming power in our lives, to glory in our infirmities, because the power of God is more evident when the recipient of it is weak. As St Paul himself stated it, 'I am quite content with my weaknesses and with insults, hardships, persecutions … for when I am weak, then I am strong' (2 Cor 12:9f) in Christ Jesus, my Lord.

TWENTY-THIRD SUNDAY OF THE YEAR
Wis 9:13-19; Philem 9-10, 12-17; Lk 14:25-33

The ways of God are mysterious, and our inability to understand them is stressed in the first reading from the book of
Wisdom, and were we seriously to consider the message of the
other two readings we should perhaps find ourselves asking the
question, why should St Paul, having devoted most of his life to
the spread of the gospel of Christ, end up a prisoner in chains,
with death by violence to follow. Or indeed, why should it be, as
stated in the gospel reading, that in order to be a disciple of his
Christ says we should carry a cross. Again and again, on our
journey through life, we come up against the mystery of suffering, the mystery of the path of the cross which Christ calls us to
tread.

One of the saints who suffered all her days, and despite this
led a most active life, never allowing herself to be overcome by
her troubles, was St Teresa of Avila, foundress of the Discalced
Carmelite Sisters. She was an extraordinary person, uniting
sublime and mystical holiness with practical good sense and
humour. When she heard that her close associate, St John of the
Cross, was imprisoned, and being punished as a renegade from
the Carmelite Order, she wrote, 'God has a terrible way of treating his friends, and in truth he does them no wrong, since that
was the way he treated his own Son, Jesus Christ'. If Christ then,
the all-holy Son of God, submitted to suffering and death, then
we his servants cannot expect to be treated any differently from
our Master. And this he states for us quite categorically.
'Anyone who does not carry his cross and come after me, cannot
be my disciple.'

But we should not picture God as being one who takes an
unholy delight in seeing his children suffer. If no earthly father
worthy of the name would adopt such an attitude, then how
much more so our heavenly Father, who sent his Son to show his
love for us, to the extent of sacrificing himself for us. This raises
the question, why did Christ, in compliance with the Father's
will, have to suffer? Indeed, why should any of us have to suffer? We can approach the problem differently by saying that all
sufferings, especially those associated with death, are concrete
evidence of the mystery of evil, our tendency to upset God's
purpose, in other words to commit sin. At the end of the creation

story in Genesis (1:31), we are told that 'God saw all he had made and indeed it was very good.' We can therefore say that everything is truly good in so far as it serves God's purpose. But here and now it is obvious that, both physically and morally, the world is not all good. The culprit is sin, which is not only the root of all evil, but tends to blind people's awareness of this fact.

Evil entered the world because of a human will which opposed the will of God. 'Through one man, sin came into the world', St Paul says, 'and through sin death. And thus death has spread through the whole human race because everyone has sinned' (Rom 5:12). But, he adds, our Saviour Christ Jesus, abolished death and gained life and immortality, because of his utter and absolute dedication to the will of the Father. 'If you believe in your heart that God raised him from the dead, then you will be saved' (Rom 10:9). Note Paul does not say if you believe in your mind, but if you believe in your heart. The heart we associate with emotions, love, trust, confidence. These are the things which give rise to faith, and not intellectual arguments. After the example of Christ we are called to abandon ourselves to the will of God, to take up our daily cross, and to identify with Christ suffering.

But this also means identifying with Christ loving, Christ accepting all the evil that the sinful will of mankind could subject him to. There is nothing in the gospels to suggest that Christ liked suffering. On the contrary, his prayer in Gethsemane was, 'Father if it be possible, let this chalice pass from me' (Mt 26:39). But the example of Jesus, as well as that of his sinless mother, shows us that it is impossible, even for the just and virtuous person, to avoid suffering and the effects of the evil power which humanity has unleashed on the world. When St Paul besought God three times to cure him of a certain ailment, the answer he got was, 'My grace is all you need; for my power is strongest when you are weak' (2 Cor 12:9f). Paul learned his lesson. 'It makes me happy to suffer for you ... and in my body to do what I can to make up all that has still to be undergone by Christ for the sake of his body, the Church' (Col 1:24).

TWENTY-FOURTH SUNDAY OF THE YEAR
Ex 32:7-11, 13-14; 1 Tim 1:12-17; Lk 15:1-32

I remember many years ago, on a very warm and sunny after-
noon in August, going into a public house in a tiny village away
out in the country to empty a collection box in aid of the foreign
missions. What amazed me was that, although it was just before
three o'clock, there was not a single empty space in front of the
bar. As I began to empty the box one man left his place, a little
unsteadily, and pointing to another box with a picture of St
Anthony on it, which however was not mine, he said, 'I put all
my money in there'. Having delivered himself of this consoling
message to me, he then asked me for an account of St Anthony's
life. But alas it was some time since I had read anything about
the Saint, and I found myself merely mentioning the popular
belief that the key to the recovery of lost property was a prayer
to St Anthony. Be this true or not, we have all experienced, from
time to time, the relief and the joy of finding something we have
mislaid, like the woman in today's gospel finding the lost
drachma, which was, by the way, the equivalent of a day's
wages. And a certain saint has pointed out that God also knows
the joy of finding things that have gone lost, as we learn from
today's gospel story, the joy at the return of a single soul that has
been separated from him. It is a wonderful and amazing thought
that the almighty God loves and cherishes each individual soul
in such a truly personal way.

The longer version of today's gospel forms a whole chapter,
the 15th chapter of St Luke, one of the best known and most
consoling chapters of the whole New Testament. In it there are
really three parables: the stray sheep recovered, the lost coin
found, and the prodigal son welcomed back by his father. All
three are intended by Christ to give us an insight into the attitude
of God, our Father, towards those who go astray. The sharing of
a meal with another person in ancient times was more than an
act of courtesy; it denoted acceptance of that person. And Christ,
who was God himself become man, not only welcomed sinners,
he sat down to table with them and ate with them. This was in
stark contrast to the Pharisees, who looked forward with certainty, not to the salvation, but to the annihilation of the sinner.
Indeed, instead of the promise of Christ that, 'There will be joy
in heaven over one sinner who repents', the common saying

among the strictly orthodox Jews was, 'There will be joy in heaven over one sinner who is exterminated before God'.

In the parable of the lost sheep and the joy of the shepherd who finds it, Jesus has drawn a picture of the way God deals with the sinner. For the erring person it is a thousand times easier to come back to God than to come home to the biting criticisms of humans. Abraham Lincoln, who was a deeply religious man, was once asked how he would treat the people of the Southern States when defeated and forced into union with the Northern States once more. But instead of threatening vengeance, Lincoln's reply was, 'I will treat them as if they had never been away'. It is surely the wonder of the love of God that he will not be outdone in generosity and loving kindness by a mere member of the human race. So it is that from the moment God forgives us our sins, it is as if they had never been committed. Indeed to keep on harping back to past sins is to cast doubt on God's forgiveness for them, to regard it as a favour which any moment may be revoked. To keep on harbouring such scruples is where the devil attacks and tries to capture us. Since God is love itself then God's forgiveness is not half-measure but absolute. He will never hold their sins over those he has forgiven, whether by hint, or by word, or by threat.

Finally, all three parables in the long gospel reading today are each saying something different as well. The sheep got lost through its own foolishness, and many a person would steer clear of sin if they reflected seriously on the consequences of their action. The coin was lost through no fault of its own, just as many are enticed into sin by others, and it is these latter whom God will hold accountable. Lastly, the prodigal son went astray deliberately, turning his back on his father. What today's gospel then is saying is that if we throw ourselves on the mercy of God, we will find that his love is greater than human foolishness, greater than the allure of temptation, greater even than the deliberate rebellion of the human heart. May we always find new heart, courage and inspiration in the knowledge of this forgiving love of our God for each and every one of us.

TWENTY-FIFTH SUNDAY OF THE YEAR
Amos 8:4-7; 1Tim 2:1-8; Lk 16: 1-13

It was an age when wealthy business people amassed riches by ruthlessly exploiting and cheating the poor and defenceless, when resort to fraud and swindling was the order of the day, when the law courts showed greater concern for the vested interests of the commercial classes rather than for justice, when city life became corrupt, when landowners were more concerned about the sale of their crops than the observance of the Lord's Day, and when religion had become an empty gesture without purpose, without sincerity, a mere outward compliance with social custom. No, I'm not referring to the ailments of society today, but rather to the kind of moral standards that prevailed in Israel during the time of the prophet Amos, almost 3,000 years ago.

The preaching of Amos has a clearer message for modern-day social standards than that of any other Old Testament prophet. He lived during a period when the threat of war was remote, and a cultural, social and economic revival took place in Israel. The expansion of trade and commerce brought about a steady drift from country to city, and small towns in the northern kingdom became overcrowded, just as in most countries this past century. But this prosperity was accompanied by an almost unprecedented degree of social degradation. The fall away from religion especially led to a corruption of justice, to wanton and luxurious living, and to the break-up of social unity. Amos prophesied that Israel would be punished for these crimes, that her wealth would vanish, her houses adorned with expensive ivory would be torn down, and within twenty years all this was to come true when the Northern Kingdom was overrun by the Assyrians, the most hated and feared race in the history of the Middle East.

Writing to Timothy, his disciple, St Paul quotes the proverb which says, 'The love of money is the root of all evil'. Note it does not say that money is the root of all evil, but rather the 'love of money' is. Of course money is necessary, and always was, as a means of exchanging goods in every complex organised society. But through excessive love of money a person can become its slave. Money can become a substitute for God in one's life, to the extent that in one's efforts to acquire more of it one can become, in Christ's own words, 'choked by the riches and pleasures of life and fail to reach spiritual maturity' (Lk 8:13). Life is something far more precious than the food we take, the clothes we wear, or the riches we acquire. Earthly possessions are things which are on loan to us. After a brief life-span we have to relinquish our hold on them and leave them behind. 'Naked I came from my mother's womb', Job said (1:21), 'and naked shall I return; the Lord gave, and the Lord has taken away'.

Why was the rather strange Parable of the Unjust Steward included in St Luke's gospel, you might ask. And the answer is that it was because of the Church's concern about the proper use of wealth even in the apostolic age. The parable shows us how the steward when faced with a crisis used all his astuteness and worldly craftiness to make provision for the future. A steward's salary took the form of a commission on the sale of his master's goods. This was his only salary. And so in reducing the debtors' bills the steward was not defrauding his master. He was only giving up the commission due to himself. Great wealth however is rarely acquired without some sharp practice, and so Christ refers to money as being tainted. We have to keep reminding ourselves that, by and large, our society, like that of ancient Israel, is organised, not so much for the welfare of ordinary citizens, for the common good, but rather geared towards maximum production and gain for those who invest in it.

If there is love among people, if there is civility and compassion, it is certainly not due to the systems of production in our industrial society, but in spite of them. There will be little reward for us, hereafter, if we are pleasant to others purely for self-gain, for example, to induce them to buy our goods. In our use of wealth therefore we must remain ever mindful of the words of Christ, 'Blessed are the poor in spirit, blessed are the merciful, blessed are those who strive for justice.' It is such people who will find true self-fulfilment, who, having left behind this world and all its possessions, will find the greatest reward of all, that of possessing God himself for all eternity, or should I rephrase that and say, that of being possessed by God for all eternity.

TWENTY-SIXTH SUNDAY OF THE YEAR
Amos 6:1, 4-7; 1 Tim 6:11-16; Lk 16:19-31

One of the problems that the early Church had to cope with was, strangely enough, that of the place in it which should be granted to children. At what age could they be admitted to full membership? What sacraments could they receive? We must remember that in its foundation stage the Christian community was comprised mainly of adults. In dealing with this problem the members took as their guide the attitude of Jesus towards children. Jesus had rebuked the Apostles for keeping the children away from him, and had said that unless they themselves became like little children they would never enter the kingdom of heaven (Mt 18:3). Undoubtedly, what Jesus also had in mind for us was that we all have to come before God convinced of our own weakness and insufficiency, that to gain admission into heaven we must place all our trust in him, as in a loving and gracious Father.

This, of course, was in complete contrast to the attitude of the Pharisees, who loved money and power and the things of this world, and were convinced that by the mere external observance of laws and customs, they could, by their own unaided efforts, secure a place in heaven for themselves as well. They refused to believe in Christ, and even excluded from the Jewish community those who did. 'No servant can be the slave of two masters', Christ told them. 'You cannot be the slave of both God and money.' (Lk 16:15). But the Pharisees only laughed at him. 'What is thought highly of by men is an abomination in the sight of God', was his response.

The gospel today contrasts the two attitudes, that of Lazarus, the image of the poor, the downtrodden, those left penniless by the greed of the wealthy and the tax-collectors, and whose only hope was in the mercy of God, and on the other hand that of the rich man, clothed extravagantly, and feasting magnificently every day, self-sufficient, not seeing any need whatsoever to beg for God's mercy. But deliverance is at hand for the poor, who for a short while share in Christ's sufferings so as to share in his glory. For, as St Paul tells us, 'What we suffer in this life can never be compared to the glory as yet unrevealed, which is awaiting us' (Rom 8:18). For the man, however, who stores up treasure for himself in this world instead of making himself rich in the sight of God, there comes with death the realisation that his heart cannot be satisfied with mere earthly possessions, that his spirit wants to reach out and be possessed by God, and that it cannot do so because it has become fixed in its ways. As a man lives, so shall he die. But, no matter how far we have strayed, salvation is still available. We can be converted if we but listen to the voice of God's Holy Spirit speaking to us, not only through Moses and the Prophets, namely in the Old Testament, but also through the message of Christ in the New Testament coming to us through the Church. And this Holy Spirit, who will become the dynamic force of our lives, if we but open ourselves to him, is not the Spirit of slaves bringing fear into our lives. He is the Spirit of sons and daughters who makes us turn to God and cry 'Abba, Father', the words used by Christ himself in the garden of Gethsemane. God looking on us, will see us as his children, and, with Christ, as his heirs, heirs to a place for eternity in his kingdom. For with such a trusting attitude on our part, neither poverty, nor riches, neither death nor life, nor any created thing whatsoever will be able to come between us and love of God made visible to us in Christ Jesus, our Lord (Rom 8:39).

Therefore, we should always keep our gaze fixed on our eternal home, which is heaven. How should we set about ensuring that we are on the right way to heaven? Firstly, desire it above all else. 'There is one thing I ask of the Lord; for this I long; to dwell in the house of the Lord all the days of my life' (Ps 26). Secondly, use the means God has given us, namely, frequent Mass and Communion, prayer and penance, striving to live a truly Christian life. Thirdly, bear life's crosses with patience, faith, and willingness. Fourthly, 'Use this world without becoming engrossed in it', as St Paul says, 'because the world as we know it is passing away' (1 Cor 7:31). Fifthly, persevere to the end in faith, hope and love. Take each day as it comes and live it well. The closer we live to God in our daily lives the more intense will our longing be to see him in heaven. With the Psalmist we will find ourselves saying, 'My soul thirsts for God, the God of my life. When can I enter and see the face of God' (Ps 42).

TWENTY-SEVENTH SUNDAY OF THE YEAR
Hab 1:2-3, 2:2-4; 2 Tim 1:6-8, 13-14; Lk 17:5-10

'Lord increase our faith', the apostles requested of Jesus in that gospel reading. Elsewhere they asked, 'Lord teach us how to pray' (Lk 11:1). And really these two requests were the same. For to pray is simply to think of God, and at the same time to love him, to trust him, to have faith in him. Every prayer then is an act of faith in God, and conversely every time our thoughts turn to God in faith, we are praying to him. Indeed, we can say that it is no more possible to have faith without prayer than it would be to swim without water. We must always, however, have proper motives when we pray to God. For it is possible because of emotional involvement, because of worry, or fear, or undue concern about the success of our day-to-day undertakings, that we can sometimes offer up intense prayers, but an intensity caused by our purely human concerns rather than by any thought of God.

We are often trying to win God over to our way of thinking, to have him on our side, in a scheme of things we have mapped out for ourselves. Or again we sometimes look on prayer as a kind of magical last resort, which is always worth a try. There is a story of a clergyman walking along a street with a friend who was a man of considerable scholarship. When they came to a ladder leaning over the sidewalk and against a wall which was being decorated, the friend refused to pass under it . 'Surely you don't believe in that superstition', said the clergyman. 'No, I don't exactly believe in it', was the reply he got, 'but I never throw away a chance of avoiding an accident'. Well, that describes the way some of us approach prayer. We don't exactly believe in it, but we never ignore the possibility that it may work. Sometimes it becomes a last forlorn hope. On the contrary, however, our constant plea should be, 'Lord, increase our faith. Lord, teach us how to pray'.

'When you pray for something', St James reminds us, 'and don't get it, it is because you have not prayed properly. You have prayed for something purely to satisfy your own desires' (Jas 4:3). In order to avoid such pitfalls we all need guidance, in particular the guidance of God's Holy Spirit. Prayer according to St Augustine is not a matter of informing God of our needs, but rather of God transforming our inmost thoughts and desires. Prayer is not an instruction of God, but rather the construction of a new heart within us. For true prayer has what may be called a natural effect. It elevates and spiritualises the soul. Gradually, and almost imperceptibly, the person who prays acquires a new outlook, a different set of values, a clearer understanding of what lies behind and beyond the topsy-turvy of our everyday existence. For as speech is the necessary means for entering into fellowship with other human beings, so prayer is the instrument of communing with God.

There is no greater proof of this than the example of Jesus himself. Never before did a human being pray as he did. Even in the middle of a public discourse he would turn to God and address him as Father. Early in the morning he would steal away and go out by himself onto the hillside, his favourite location for uninterrupted prayer. Apparently it was a regular custom of his also, while in Jerusalem, to pray during the night in the Garden of Gethsemane, and that his visit there on the night of his arrest was not his first one. On that particular occasion, as recorded in the gospels, we are told that 'being in anguish he prayed the longer'. We can learn much as well from his prayer that night. 'Father, if it is your will, take this cup away from me. Nevertheless, let your will, not mine be done' (Lk 22:42f). Note that the first part of that prayer was not granted, in other words God did not take away the cup, that is the suffering of a most cruel death which lay ahead. But by being open to the will of God, something even greater was to follow for Jesus, namely, his glorious resurrection. 'Unless a wheat grain falls on the ground and dies, it remains only a single grain' (Jn 12:24).

The letter to the Hebrews sums it all up this way (5:7-10): 'During his life on earth, he offered up prayer and entreaty, aloud and in silent tears, to the one who had the power to raise him from the dead, and he submitted so humbly that his prayer was heard.' And God grant that our prayers, throughout our lives, may be heard also, and that being raised from the dead through the merits of Jesus' prayers we may be united with him for ever in heaven.

TWENTY-EIGHTH SUNDAY OF THE YEAR
2 Kgs 5:14-17; 2 Tim 2:8-13; Lk 17:11-19

We, in the Western world, pride ourselves in having the highest form of democratic society in the history of mankind, a claim which indeed is very debatable. We place great stress on individual freedom and liberty, on the right to do our own thing. Yet how often do we allow ourselves to be swayed by pressure groups, and sometimes have no scruples ourselves about inflicting in-convenience, and hardship, and curtailment of their liberties on others, in order to gain our own ends. We say we do not suffer tyrants and dictators gladly, nevertheless, bearing in mind these trends of our demanding society, is it any wonder that we want to dictate to God himself also. We want him to do things our way, to acquiesce to our demands, and so, to a certain degree, enable us become masters of our own destiny. There are some who even abandon the practice of prayer because they claim that God has not granted their requests.

This in a way reflects the attitude of Naaman the leper, the army commander of the King of Syria, as shown in the passage from the Second Book of Kings which leads up to today's First Reading. Hoping to be cured of his leprosy by Elisha, the prophet, Naaman arrived from Syria, laden with gifts of silver and gold and precious garments. The prophet, however, did not even come out to meet him, but rather sent a messenger telling him to wash seven times in the river Jordan. This response left Naaman deeply offended, indignant, and he prepared to return to Syria. Why wash in this particular river, when there were so many larger rivers back home? 'Here was I thinking Elisha would be sure to come out to me, and stand there, and wave his hand over the spot, and cure the leprous part', he said, and so he set off in a rage.

Things had not gone according to what he had planned. It was only after his servants had pointed out the simplicity of the prophet's request, that he was persuaded to carry it out, and thus was cured. And come to think of it, how often do we be-have precisely in the same way! Why do I have to go to church, we say, when I can worship God out in the open air on Sundays? Why do I have to confess my sins to a priest, when I can tell them directly to God, and say I'm sorry? Why does God send me crosses and sickness, when instead of being a burden to my family and relations I could do so much good for them? We even find such attitudes among those disciples privileged to see Christ face to face and listen to his preaching. 'Why not show us the Father?' (Jn 14:8), the Apostle Philip said to him, instead of just speaking about him; and those who regarded themselves as his faithful followers complained, 'Why did he have to speak about giving us his flesh to eat and his blood to drink? This is intolerable language, and how could anyone accept it?' (Jn 6:52, 60). And they walked with him no more. This is the reaction of Naaman, all over again. It stands to Naaman's credit, however, that he returned to thank Elisha.

But the ways of human beings are not God's ways. God always does things in his own time, and in his own way. He calls us to make an act of faith in him on his conditions, not on ours. So we must be patient. We must cease regarding God as a kind of puppet that should react in the desired way when we pull the right strings. We must allow him play a central role in our lives, while accepting his will in a spirit of adoration. When we are seeking a favour, the New Testament keeps reminding us to do so with prayer and thanksgiving, because God answers every prayer for help, even though it may not be precisely in the way we would wish, since he will only grant what is for our good. We should then make it a habit, especially in every Mass to praise and thank God with all our hearts, like Naaman when he was cured, like the only one of the ten lepers who returned to express his appreciation of God's gift. There is a sadness in the failure of the other nine to say a personal 'thank you', for what Jesus had done for them.

As Shakespeare wrote in his play King Lear, 'How sharper than a serpent's tooth it is to have a thankless child.' The Eucharist we are celebrating is a reminder to us, never to forget God's greatest gift to us, that of his own divine Son. If, however, we concentrate too much on particular favours sought or received, there is a danger that we may reduce the Eucharist to the level of magical thinking, a means of procuring good turns from God. We should rather rejoice, that through it, our names, as Christ said to his Apostles, are written in heaven.

TWENTY-NINTH SUNDAY OF THE YEAR
Ex 1:8-13 2; Tim 3:14 - 4:2; Lk 18:1-8

There are two ways, and only two, in which the soul of each person on earth stands in relation to God. It can be living a life of union with God, or in effect be banishing God entirely from the pattern of its daily existence. With regard to the exclusion of God, if you were to meditate on the last six verses of chapter one of the Letter of St Paul to the Romans, there is hardly any passage in the whole Bible which shows more clearly what happens to a society, when God is completely and deliberately ignored. It is a profound judgment on pagan existence in Rome. In the passage we are given a long list of the terrible evils which ensue, evils which signify not only a loss of godliness, but a loss of true humanity as well. God had abandoned them to their own irrational ideas and to their monstrous behaviour. Nor is there exaggeration here, because what is written has been confirmed by Roman writers and historians themselves from the period concerned.

The Satires of the poet Juvenal, for example, denounced the luxury of Rome, and the moral depravity of some individuals who set out deliberately to corrupt others, to destroy any innocence and goodness which the virtuous had. Among the monstrous vices of pagans St Paul lists wickedness, by which people become absolutely self-centred and deny the rights of both God and humans; greed, the accursed love of seeking more for self, regardless of the rights of others; viciousness, the complete absence of goodness and tenderness towards others; envy, that twisted attitude which resents excellence of character in others; wrongdoing, spite, treachery, murder, all stemming from the kind of hatred that threatens violence against one's neighbours. People with such vices, Paul says, know what God's verdict is; that all who practice them deserve to die. And yet they indulge in them, and what is worse, they encourage others to do the same. We cannot say that we are above all or any of these vices, for we too are sinners, who rely on Jesus our Redeemer to rescue us from their effects. Indeed we could cite many more which are characteristic of our time, such as personal hatred of God by those who regard him as placing a barrier between them and their pleasures.

How can we be rescued from falling victim to the snares that beget such evil habits? We must always bear in mind that Christ requires our cooperation. Redemption will pass us by if we do not sincerely long to be redeemed. We must cultivate the virtues of faith, hope and love; and especially we must pray, for faith needs to be nurtured at all times by prayer. The necessity of this last is highlighted in today's gospel. I can certainly say that every time I turn to God in prayer, I am making an act of faith, of trust in him; and just as surely, if I do not pray, my faith will become weak and limp and ineffective, even as bodily muscles do, which are never exercised.

One of the Greek Fathers of the Church, St Gregory of Nyssa, in one of his sermons, has left a beautiful passage on prayer. 'The effect of prayer is union with God, and if one is united with God, then that person is separated from the enemy. Through prayer we guard our chastity, control our temper, rid ourselves of vanity. It makes us forget injuries, and overcome envy. Through prayer we obtain physical well-being, a happy home, a strong well-ordered society... Prayer is the seal of virginity and a pledge of faithfulness in marriage... It is intimacy with God, and contemplation of the invisible. It is the enjoyment of things present and the substance of the things to come.' The really important thing about praying is perseverance. 'Pray all the time', the New Testament urges us, 'asking for what you need, praying in the Spirit on every possible occasion. Never grow tired of staying awake to pray for all God's people' (Eph 6:18).

How often do we stop praying because we accuse God of not answering it. But the fact is that a prayer goes unanswered only when we stop praying, having decided that God will not answer us. And Jesus is telling us as much in the gospel story of the widow and the unjust judge. The widow's enemy, against whom she had a just complaint, was probably a rich individual, and she was too poor to offer a bribe to the unjust judge. Although the corrupt judge did not want to antagonise an influential citizen, nevertheless, because of the widow's perseverance he finally gave in to her request. She had never reached the point where she was inclined to say, 'What's the use?', and neither must we, when we pray.

MISSION SUNDAY

It has been said that miracles were a frequent occurrence among the people who thronged St Peter's Basilica for the general audiences of Pope Pius X, the last Pope to be canonised a saint. The story is told that at one of these audiences a man asked the Pope for a pair of his discarded socks. The Pope, amused and rather mystified, wanted to know why, and the man's reply was that he suffered greatly from his feet, and that by wearing the Pope's socks he hoped for a cure. And the Pope, laughingly, said, 'For years and years I have been suffering from all kinds of ailments in my feet. I suffer from corns and bunions, and never did I find that my socks were of any use in curing me'. Which goes to show that the gift of miracles is given to the saints, not for their own benefit, but for the benefit of others.

On this Mission Sunday a parallel could be drawn between this little story and the gift of the faith that God has given to each one of us. For this most precious gift was not given solely to achieve our own personal salvation, not to be kept hidden away in the depths of our inner self, like the man who buried his talent in the ground for purely selfish motives. No, we are the ones specially chosen by God to proclaim before the whole world, the gospel of Jesus Christ, the news that death does not end everything for us, that our bodies shall rise again from the grave, and that, by putting all our trust and faith in Christ, our sins will be wiped away, and we shall enjoy eternally the vision of God, face to face. Indeed, Jesus' very last message to his Apostles, as given by St Mark, was most emphatic. 'Go out to the whole world', he said, 'and proclaim the Good News to all creation. He who believes and is baptised will be saved; he who does not believe will be condemned' (Mk 16:16). The Apostles thereafter were to devote their entire lives to this mission, to the extent of shedding their very blood in their efforts to be true to Christ's last wish.

In the experience of St Paul, we have a vivid description of the effect this command of Christ had on his thoughts. 'I have preached Christ's Good News to the utmost of my capacity', he says, '…My chief concern has been to fulfil the text, 'Those who have never been told about him will see him, and those who have never heard about him will understand' (Rom 15:21). 'To make everyone perfect in Christ, it is for this I struggle wearily on, helped only by Christ's power driving me irresistibly'

(Col 1:29). Christ's last promise before his Ascension had been, 'Know that I am with you always, even to the end of time' (Mt 28:20). This promise he now fulfils not only helping us, but also by continuing his mission to the world through us. For, as St Teresa of Avila once said, 'Christ now has no visible hands, he has only our hands to do his work today; Christ has no feet, he has only our feet to guide people along his path; Christ has no lips, he has only our lips to announce him to people today; Christ has no means, he has only our help to lead people to himself. We are the only bible which people still read. We are the last message of God written in works and words.' So let us give Christ to the world, hand on the treasures of our faith to people. Let us bring the world to Christ, bring the gifts of people to Jesus, the Lord, for we are the hands and feet and lips of Jesus today. Just as goodness passes on to, and makes an impression on the beholder, so should our faith.

In the past this country responded magnificently to Christ's call to spread the gospel, The money for the missions, the prayers, the sacrifices by the people at home, the journeying, the dangers, the homesickness, the vision and enterprise of the men and women who went out foreign, the pride and caring of those at home, the interest displayed in the missionaries, many of us remember all these very vividly. But we should be aware also that such people were not isolated phenomena. They were the products of the faith of the families back home, and the believing community into which they were born. Faith is not something which is purely abstract, a mere intellectual assent to revealed truths about God. It is an acceptance of God into our daily lives, seeing him at work in us in every-day events, and placing our trust in him, our belief that all things will be for our good, if we but love him, as St Peter tells us. Faith will reach its pinnacle in us when it generates within us, a movement of our whole being towards God, and the abandonment of ourselves to his holy will. Let us pray for such faith on this Mission Sunday, and beg God, with all the fervour of our being, that the light of faith may never die in our people.

THIRTIETH SUNDAY OF THE YEAR
Sir 35:15-17, 20-22; 2 Tim 4:6-8, 16-18; Lk 18:9-14

One of the sad things about Christian believers is that they can
so often become divided, embittered and rebellious about certain
aspects of their faith, and fail to appreciate the extraordinary
about-turns in the religious thinking of humankind, which have
evolved from it. For example the supreme penalty for the sinner
under the Mosaic Law was to condemn him to death. 'Anyone
who is hanged on a tree is under God's curse', the Book of
Deuteronomy said (21:23). Strictly speaking hanging as we
understand it was never part of the Old Testament penal code.
Anyone guilty of a grave offence was stoned to death, and the
body sometimes displayed on a tree or gibbet as a deterrent to
others. And so a gibbet or cross became a sign of infamy and fear
in Old Testament times. The law was not able to do anything
about a sinner except condemn him to death. But God's Son, St
Paul points out, was made sin, made a subject to the Law, and
executed on a cross in order to redeem us from this curse of the
Law (cf. Col 2:14). Thus it is that instead of looking on the cross
with horror, Christians everywhere, especially on Good Friday,
kiss and venerate it.

Looking at today's gospel, we should remember also that the
ancient world regarded humility as a despicable quality, a thing
to be expected from a cowering, cringing, slavish person; and
yet with Christ it undergoes a marvellous reaffirmation. He puts
it forward as being one of the greatest of all the virtues. Two
men, he tells us, a Pharisee and a publican, both of them Jews,
went up to the Temple to pray. The Pharisee, in his own estimation, saw himself as the perfect example of what a true Jewish
believer should be. The publican regarded himself as a failure.
But God saw further again than either of them, and so, we are
told, because he humbled himself, the publican returned home a
better person before God, whereas the Pharisee did not. We
might say that Christians also fall into two classes: those who are
true Christians, and those who are Christian only in name, nominal Christians. But how to tell a true Christian from a nominal
one poses quite a problem. For the true Christian, however good
he, or she, may be, is not yet perfect either. You may well ask
then what, in God's sight, is the quality which distinguishes the
one from the other. Part of the answer lies in that story of the

Pharisee and the publican, which paints a picture of hypocrisy contrasted with sincerity.

A true Christian, we might say, is one with an abiding sense of God's presence, one who lives in the belief that God is present, not externally, not merely in nature or providence, but in his inmost heart, in his conscience. And this presence of God so lights his inner awareness, that he comes to accept naturally that all his thoughts, his motives, his wishes, his failings, are like an open book before almighty God; and he willingly accepts that this should be so. He enthrones God in his conscience, and when in doubt he refers to him here as to a supreme authority, without trying to argue, or reason, or make excuses, or defend himself. As scripture tells us, 'All things are open and laid bare to the eyes of the One to whom one day we must give an account of ourselves' (Heb 4:13). The nominal Christian, on the other hand, tries like the Pharisee, to have within himself an inner sanctuary, from which he would exclude even God himself. And here he attempts to make himself ruler and judge, the one with sole control over all his own actions. The Pharisee, then, did not really go to the Temple to pray. He went to tell God how well he was performing, what a good fellow he was at doing his own thing, and how confident he was that his observance of the details of the Law placed him on a level far above that of such moral outcasts as typified by the publican.

The plea of freedom of conscience, by which so many people justify their actions nowadays, is also an attempt to dispense with conscience entirely, to ignore God as lawgiver and judge, to be independent like the Pharisee, and disregard the voice of God that speaks within one. But this parable tells us unmistakably that no one who is proud can pray, no one who lifts himself or herself above other people can pray, and especially no one who despises others can pray. For before God we are all one great army of sinning, suffering humanity, and our most recurring prayer should be what is called the 'Jesus prayer', a prayer that millions of devout and sincere Christians have offered up fervently since Christianity began, 'Jesus, Son of the Living God, be merciful to me a sinner'.

ALL SAINTS DAY
Apoc 7:2-4, 9-14; 1 Jn 3:1-3; Mt 5:1-12

The first words which Jesus spoke when he had begun his public ministry in Galilee, and which were recorded by St Mark in his gospel, contain a summary of the special message that Jesus wanted to give to the whole world. 'The time has come', he said, 'and the kingdom of God is close at hand. Repent, and believe the good news' (1:15). 'The time has come', that is to say, the moment of decision is now, this very day. 'Repent'. Here the English translation fails to bring out the full significance of the Greek word used by Mark, which really is a call to change absolutely the whole pattern of one's life, and to have trust in God.

To-day we recall the numerous saintly people who took to heart these words of Christ, and allowed them to change their lives accordingly. 'The kingdom of God', we are told by St Matthew, 'is like leaven which is hid in three measures of meal, until the whole is leavened' (13:33). The kingdom of God, in other words, stems from small beginnings, from the dedication of individual men and women, who live out the message of the gospel in a truly heroic fashion. Like the leaven, or yeast, within the dough, the kingdom of heaven works from inside. People are never really changed from outside. Better housing, higher financial returns, better working conditions – all these in themselves change one's personality only on the surface. It is the task of Christianity to make new persons of us from within, and this begins when we find ourselves praying sincerely, and regularly, with the Psalmist: 'A clean heart create for me, Oh God, and put a steadfast spirit within me' (Ps 51:10). And God will respond; he will not disappoint us, as he makes clear in the words of scripture, 'I shall give you a new heart, and put a new spirit within you. I shall remove the heart of stone from your bodies, and give you a heart of flesh instead' (Ez 36:26).

The saints have been, and still are, recipients of divine grace in a wonderful way, but not solely for their own benefit. They are God's leaven within the community. As the leaven turns the dough into a bubbling and expanding mass, so the Christian ex-ample of saintly people can bring about a revolution in society. It can cause an upheaval in standards, in behaviour, in outlook, even within the family, as the gospel points out, setting a man against his father, a daughter against her mother (Mt 10:35), something impossible in Old Testament times. Small wonder that the non-Christian Jews of Thessalonika in Greece, according to the Acts of the Apostles (17:6), referred to the Christians as 'the people who have been turning the whole world upside down'.

The saints, indeed, were not always the easiest people to live with, because by the way they acted they challenged others to take stock in turn of their personal lives, even to the extent of examining their consciences; and what some individuals saw there did not, very often, flatter them. The thing which characterised all the saints, despite their different personalities, was their faith, their trust in the providential care of God, no matter what befell them. The kingdom of God was especially promised, not to the sensible and the educated, but to such as retain throughout their lives the spirit of little children, an unconcerned, almost irrational trust in God. And still each of the saints was marked by an individual and very personal sanctity, which reflects the wonderful variety of God's gifts. No two saints were ever exactly similar in the spiritual gifts which God had granted to them.

The great multitude of saintly souls down through the ages gives testimony to the perfection of God, a perfection which is infinite in its goodness, its beauty, and its variety. Even in an age with little regard for religion, people are on the look-out for men and women of God, and when they encounter souls of rare sanctity, they watch them with a mixture of curiosity and awe. Indeed it is true that just a few such souls, highly endowed with Christian virtue, will rescue the world for centuries to come, because truly committed souls, such as were the Apostles for example, can exert an influence on others which is almost irresistible. But our response to the witness of the saints, if it is not to be tainted with superstition, must be one of true inner devotion to the Holy Spirit who originally inspired those saints; for our true and real happiness consists, not in considering saintly people, but in the thought of God, and nothing short of it. As with all the saints, the human heart can only find rest in the God who made it.

THIRTY-FIRST SUNDAY OF THE YEAR
Wis 11:22-12:2; 2 Thess 1:11-2:2; Lk 19:1-10

'It is by hope that we are saved', the New Testament (Rom 8:24) tells us , a promise that reflects the faith of the psalmist who wrote, 'Hope in God, I will praise him still, my Saviour and my God'. I remember a certain man who survived a long period of depression by repeating that verse from Psalm 42 over and over again. We might even say that the reason why the people of ancient Palestine, from the time of Abraham onwards, did not succumb to despair was their wonderful hope in God. Situated as they were between Egypt to the south of them, and the numerous empires which emerged to the north of them, they were repeatedly overrun by powerful foreign armies. Yet they never despaired, but rather were convinced that God would be faithful to the promises he had given that he would watch over them as his specially chosen people.

Likewise, we ourselves should renew the hope which God holds out to us, that one day we shall all be gathered together in heaven in the company of our risen and glorified Lord, Jesus Christ. Our knowledge of God in this life is admittedly very imperfect; it is confused and partial, drawn as it is from our understanding of creation. But there will come a time when we shall see God face to face. Then the divine Word, in the humanity of Jesus, will look at us with the face of a man. The knowledge that we have now may be imperfect, but then we shall know him as fully as we are known, and we shall be able to return God's personal love, even as people on earth love one another. As scripture says, if our hope in Christ has been for this life only, then we are the most unfortunate of people. For if there is no resurrection from the dead, then Christ himself cannot have been raised, and then, as St Paul says, 'Our preaching is useless, and your believing it is useless' (1 Cor 15:14).

But we believe, from the testimony of the Apostles, that Jesus died and rose again, and that it will be the same for those who have died in Jesus. God will bring them with him and so they shall stay with the Lord for ever. With such thoughts as these, Paul urged the first Christians, we should comfort one another. And Paul himself had reason to be certain of what he preached, for in a vision that was granted him he was taken up into the third heaven, although he could not describe his experience in human terms, because, as he stated, 'no eye has seen, nor ear heard, neither has it entered into the heart of man, what God has prepared for those who love him' (1 Cor 2:9). There are three great virtues, faith, hope and love. In heaven faith and hope will be merged in the love of God for ever.

What St John, in his first Epistle, says gives further credence to this. 'My dear people', he writes, 'we are already the children of God, but what we shall be in the future has not yet been revealed; all we know is, that when it is revealed, we shall be like him, because we shall see him as he really is' (1 Jn 3:2). The vision of God, in other words, will change us utterly, and make us Godlike in our understanding of the one who created us. But this 'we shall be like him' is a change which, somehow, must begin here and now, and we who entertain the hope of bringing about this change must first purify ourselves, must try and model our lives on that of Christ. We must try and keep the commandments of God, especially that of loving one another, and this not in words and idle talk, but in a real and active way. Furthermore we have to be on our guard against the enemies of Christ and against becoming totally absorbed in purely worldly pursuits and concerns. We find acknowledgement of this in some purely secular sources. 'There is another dimension to the plight of those who belong to the 'do as you like' society, a moral dimension which we scoff at to our peril. We are now paying for the decline, over many decades, of parental influence, the erosion of family values, and the diminution of community spirit and religion. These must be rebuilt before it is too late' (*Sunday Times*, 13-7-86).

At the moment when we depart this world, we will be confronted by Christ, the complete example of what the ideal person, spiritually speaking, should be. We will say yes or no to our divine exemplar, according to whether we have, or have not, attempted to make his set of values ours as well during our life in this world. Let us ask ourselves whether we mean what we say together every Sunday at the end of the Creed, 'We look to', or more exactly, 'we eagerly await the resurrection from the dead, and the life of the world to come. Amen.'

THIRTY-SECOND SUNDAY OF THE YEAR
2 Mac 7:1-2, 9-14; 2 Thess 2:16-3:5 Lk 20:27-38

We would regard as highly foolish the one who would set out on a journey and never consider where he was going. Yet the pilgrim way we are all following through life is largely a journey into the unknown. For it is a journey of faith, and of hope in God. However, a hope which is already visible is not hope any longer; for how can one hope for what one already sees. But if we hope for what we do not see, then in patience we eagerly wait for it (Rom 8:24f). When we think about it, much of our ideas about heaven and hell stems from a section of Jewish writings, referred to as Apocalyptic literature, which does not form part of the Hebrew canon of scripture, and also from writings and paintings of the Middle Ages, for example Dante's Inferno and Michelangelo's paintings on the ceiling of the Sistine Chapel in the Vatican. The Bible tells us that heaven is the vision of God, face to face, and that hell is eternal separation from God; and, apart from that, nothing further is revealed to us. In fact, among the rabbis, heaven was another name for God. During this month of the Holy Souls, it is good to recall the sober teaching of the Church about the condition of those who have gone before us, and the kind of assistance we can render to them.

As well as emphasising the existence of Purgatory, the official teaching of the Church simply says: firstly, that for all those who die, while being truly sorrowful for the sins they committed on earth, but without having made full satisfaction for these sins by acts of penance, there is a purification available in the next life; secondly, the Church says that such souls can be helped by the prayers of the faithful who are still on earth; thirdly, the Church tells us that such help is especially available through the holy sacrifice of the Mass. And that in full, is what the Church teaches. There is nothing whatsoever said about the nature of this purification, or about its duration. It is purely popular imagination which has come to regard Purgatory as a kind of hell with a lower temperature, or with the back-door open, so that escape is ultimately possible. There is never a word about fire or any specific torments. Practically speaking, most of our talk about future existence is simply guesswork. The Curé of Ars, St John Mary Vianney, a great mystic, whose days, and even more so nights, were a continuous encounter with the preternatural, was once asked about the future and the hereafter. In reply he simply said, 'I know nothing of to-morrow, except that the love of God will rise before the sun'.

Our lack of information about what awaits us beyond the grave should not give rise to undue alarm in our hearts, and we have Christ's word for that in the promise he made to the Apostles at the Last Supper. 'Do not let your hearts be troubled. Trust in God still, and trust in me. In my Father's house there are many rooms. If it were not so I would have told you. Now I am going to prepare a place for you, and after I have gone and pre-pared a place for you, I will return again and take you with me, so that where I am you also may be' (Jn 14:1-3). Reflection on these words, however, should not make us complacent. For we are being continually challenged to make a choice between the call of God coming to us in the person and message of Christ himself on the one hand, and our own selfish cravings on the other. The only thing we must fear is our failure to rise above this self-seeking, because if we shut out God from our lives, we can become no better than Judas Iscariot who, as Jesus himself said, 'chose to be lost'. Sin does indeed bring punishment, but such punishment is self-inflicted, brought about by one's inability to love, or respond to the love which comes from God, and from others. Sinners become locked within themselves, and, cut adrift from God and the believing community, their hearts experience a sense of profound unrest and loneliness.

To repent, to turn again to God is a gradual process, even having recourse to the Sacrament of Reconciliation. If death inter-venes, the healing process of what we call Purgatory enables one to be rid of the last traces of selfishness, and thus be ready to abide for ever in the vision of God face to face. To have all one's shortcomings laid bare by being confronted with the perfection which is the glorified person of Christ can be an experience of intense anguish for the departed soul. But remember that Christ also will be there to plead for that soul. And by our prayers, almsgiving, pious works, and in particular the Mass, we too can give comfort and support to all such Holy Souls.

THIRTY-THIRD SUNDAY OF THE YEAR
Mal 3:19-20; 2 Thess 3:7-12; Lk 21:5-19

As we draw near to the end of the liturgical year – next Sunday is the last Sunday – the Church is putting this question to each of us: 'What do you see as the purpose of your life, of your existence in this world? How seriously should we take the predictions of today's gospel about the end of this world and the day of judgment?' To help us reflect on this, we should keep ever before our minds this one great certainty, that death puts an end, absolutely and beyond recall, to all our works, all our plans, all the seemingly vital concerns which lend a certain purpose to our daily involvement. Every human soul that has cast off this worldly body goes forth into the unknown like a traveller entering into unexplored territory. But, whereas that soul to the rest of mankind seems to be no more, it is only then really beginning to live, to live a new existence for all eternity, hopefully in the presence of God. Cardinal Newman, reflecting on these two lives, the one now and the other hereafter, once wrote, 'Fear not that your life shall come to an end, but rather that it shall never have a beginning'. It is at the moment that this new life begins that understanding of our former existence will be revealed to us, that God's plan for each of us, and the role we were given to play while on earth in the spread of his kingdom, will become clear to us. We might well ask ourselves, then, whether we are conscious of playing a part in building up the city of God, the kingdom of God on earth.

The readings in the liturgy of these final Sundays of the Church calendar year are meant to bring home to us the necessity of looking beyond our own immediate preoccupations, worries, troubles, interests, that are largely of selfish concern. And they do this by confronting us in a very striking manner with the thought of the four last things, namely, death, judgment, heaven, and hell. People who never look beyond this life criticise the Church for asking its members to reflect seriously on these, but there is nothing morbid about such reflection, nothing that should terrify us. For if we are exiles on this earth, then as we progress through life, we are drawing ever nearer to our true home, which is heaven, a consideration which should fill us, not with sorrow, but, as St Paul pointed out, a heightened longing 'to be dissolved and to be with Christ'.

To understand fully today's gospel we should remember that Christ, while on earth, made two distinct prophecies, one about the destruction of the Temple in Jerusalem, the other about the second coming of the Son of God at the end of time – what the early Christians referred to as the 'parousia', meaning presence or arrival. In the minds of the disciples these two prophecies became fused into one, for to a pious Jew such a catastrophe as the destruction of the Temple could only signify the end of the world. We now know that the Temple was destroyed by the Romans in 70 AD. It had been the largest and grandest of all the three temples on the site, and also the shortest lived. But it is useless speculating about the second coming of Christ, although the first Christians thought it would happen in their lifetime. However, the message for us in this whole narrative is to be watchful, to allow the thought of what is to come to influence our present behaviour, to bear in mind always that the trials endured in this life are not to be compared with the glory to come. Nor indeed should we be alarmed by the imagery of wars, earthquakes, famines, stars falling from the heavens. These are OT terms employed by St Luke to denote the coming about of some radical change – in this case the second coming of Christ.

If we love God we need never be alarmed, for perfect love casts out all fear. Whatever lies ahead Christ has already encountered; he has gone in front to prepare the way for us. It is with great trust, then, that we should look forward to the second coming of Christ. For, with his coming, death will be no more, nor mourning nor crying will be any more, for the former things will have passed completely away. In the words of Pope Paul VI, 'We believe that the multitude of those gathered around Jesus and Mary in Paradise form the Church of heaven, where in eternal blessedness they see God as he is, and where, by interceding for us, and helping our weakness by their fraternal concern, they are also associated, in varying degree, with the holy angels in the divine government exercised by Christ in glory. Until this comes about, we must therefore be always ready and prepared. We must watch; we must pray.'

OUR LORD JESUS CHRIST, UNIVERSAL KING
2 Sam 5:1-3; Col 1:12-20; Lk 23:35-43

At the trial of Jesus, Pontius Pilate put to him the direct question, 'Are you the king of the Jews?' And St John's gospel has Jesus replying, 'Yes, I am a king. I was born for this. I came into the world for this, to bear witness to the truth, and all who are on the side of truth listen to my voice' (Jn 18:37). But he also pointed out that his kingship was not of this world. To-day it is only with great difficulty that we can begin to understand the original meaning of the kingdom of God, or the Rule of God. To the modern mind the concept of kingly rule has become associated with authoritarianism and suppression, but not so in OT times. The kingdom of God is nonpolitical and nonnational. In ancient Israel, justice consisted, not so much in applying the law fairly, but rather in maintaining help and protection for the weak, the poor and the helpless. If the justice of God operated in the world it would hopefully usher in peace between nations, between individuals, and within each individual.

Left to their own resources, humans were seen as incapable of attaining this peace and justice, since life was constantly threatened, freedom suppressed, justice trampled underfoot. To remedy this a completely fresh start was necessary, something which God alone could initiate. This new element is what is meant by the kingdom of God, a kingdom which would bring liberation from the forces of evil, and reconciliation between divided peoples. Although Christ denied that his kingdom is of this world, nevertheless his kingship is a very real power, which will be revealed at the end of time. It is interesting that people who are vested with purely earthly power are at a loss when confronted with this power of Christ. Their reaction quite often has been, and still is, to strike out blindly, using abuse, or even physical violence against what they regard as a threat to their power. For power, in a vulgar sense, is by and large recognised only by winning in a confrontation.

We should always remember that Jesus' death and resurrection is the supreme example of evil being overcome by offering no resistance to it in any physical way. In the course of its history Israel learned, through bitter experience, that belief in the Lordship of God contrasted sharply with the world as it was around them. The result was the formation of a new vision of life hereafter, where those who had suffered in the cause of truth here in this world would be rewarded. Jesus himself promised that those who are ready to leave earthly possessions and relatives for the sake of his name will be repaid a hundred times over, and also inherit eternal life (Mt 19:29). Furthermore, Jesus gives another twist to this hope in things to come by saying that a transformation is already taking place: 'Blessed are the eyes which see what you see. For I tell you many prophets and kings longed to see what you see and did not see it, to hear what you hear and never heard it' (Lk 10:23).

Christ spoke of the kingdom of God in parables, in every one of which a mystery lies hidden. For example, to Jews the mustard seed was the smallest of all seeds, the most insignificant of all things. Yet out of it comes a huge tree. God's kingdom comes in a hidden way, even in spite of seeming failure. But, as with the mustard seed, this small beginning holds the promise of a magnificent ending. 'I think that what we suffer in this life can never be compared to the glory, as yet unrevealed, which is waiting for us', St Paul wrote (Rom 8:18). At first sight there seems to be a contradiction between the present and the future in Jesus' references to the kingdom. The kingdom is here and now, we are told, and yet we are asked to look forward and in the Our Father pray, 'Thy kingdom come.' Jesus gives the answer to this. 'The kingdom of God does not come in such a way as to be seen. No one will say, 'Look here it is', or, 'There it is', because the kingdom of God is within you' (Lk 17:20f).

That is to say, here and now, God is at work within each of us, and putting before us a choice, a choice to let Jesus give direction to our lives, a choice which will determine our own future also. For each person Christ's kingdom begins with an inner renewal, a spiritual rebirth. It is only by this personal reformation that we can help in the spread of the kingdom, and also bring about a renewal of the society in which we live. 'I tell you most solemnly', Christ warned, 'unless people are born again of water and the Holy Spirit, they cannot enter the kingdom of God' (Jn 3:5).

THE PRESENTATION OF THE LORD
Mal 3:1-4; Heb 2:14-18; Lk 2:22-40

Priests and religious everywhere are urged to make a spiritual retreat once a year, and I recall a retreat-master on one such occasion passing the slightly cynical remark about all who make retreats, that while engaged in this exercise it was all, 'Glory be to the Father, and to the Son and to the Holy Spirit ...', but soon after the retreat, it was a case of, 'As it was in the beginning, is now, and ever shall be'. And, I think it is a fairly accurate summing up of the relationship most of us have with God, a thing of ups and downs, something as well which is evidenced very clearly in many places in sacred scripture.

Take for example the history of Israel prior to 600 BC, which was a period of affluence, greed, and glaring injustice, accompanied by public displays of religion which were very far from being sincere. Saintly individuals, such as the prophet Jeremiah, who were horrified at what was taking place, and who called on the people to change their ways, were ignored, even physically assaulted as being traitors. Drastic situations require drastic remedies, and so God permitted the ruling classes and their families to be carried off into exile in Babylon, amid anguished cries and bitter protests. While there, these people began to reflect. You might say they were forced into making a spiritual retreat. And it really worked. The exiles began to see the role God wanted of them in a spiritual light. It was a time when prayer, both private and in common, played a greater part in their lives, especially when they came together in the synagogues, institutions which derive their origin from this period. These took the place of the Temple as centres where they could worship and glorify God, be instructed in the Mosaic Law, and have public readings from the Old Testament. Indeed it is claimed that much of the Old Testament which we now have, got its final draft during that period.

But alas, shortly after many of these exiles were allowed return to Israel, this new-found religious fervour began to wane, and like the people making retreats, 'As it was in the beginning' became the measure of their observance once more. This is the background to today's first reading from the prophet Malachi, who was sent by God to call the people to reflect once more on what their priorities in life should be. Malachi is really not the name of a person. It actually translates as 'my messenger'. This unknown prophet was a man profoundly loyal to his religion. He could not tolerate the priests of the day, who were ignorant, grasping and turning a blind eye on the abuses in society. His protest against divorce and mixed marriages was especially stringent. He called on God to cut off from the tents of Jacob, that is excommunicate, anyone marrying the daughter of an alien god, in other words one given to the worship of an idol. Referring to marriage break-down, he said, 'Do not break faith with the wife of your youth. For I hate divorce, says the Lord, the God of Israel' (2:15,16). Malachi was God's messenger to his people, calling on them to amend their ways. And there were to be others, such as Elijah and John the Baptist, up to the time of the coming of Jesus, God's own Son, who would be the fulfilment of Malachi's prophecy about the Lord suddenly entering his Temple.

This Presentation of Jesus in the Temple by Joseph and his Mother Mary is what we recall on this feast today. According to Simeon, this child was set for the rise and fall of many in Israel. For by setting before his people the religious goals they should aim at, and further by putting these into action in his own life, he would force his listeners to look critically at what kind of lives they were leading. In doing so, some people because of their stubborn pride, would actually sink deeper into the mire of their wickedness, while the humble of heart would become more dedicated in their search for virtue, and by trusting in Jesus rise to a new intimacy with God. Pope John Paul has also declared Feb 2nd a new Feast Day. The Feast of the Presentation of Jesus in the Temple is to be a day of recognition of the Consecrated Life of all religious, a life which is a gift of the Holy Spirit to the Church. Many people came into the Temple and witnessed the Presentation of Jesus, but only two, Simeon and Anna, had faith to see in him the future Saviour. It is only when we look at Religious with the eyes of faith that, in this era of growing rejection of God and of things divine, we can hopefully see Christ continuing his presence in the world, in their lives of service and prayer.

THE BIRTH OF JOHN THE BAPTIST
Vigil: Jer 1:4-10; 1 Pet 1:8-12; Lk 1:5-17
Feast: Is 49:1-6; Acts 13:22-26; Lk 1:57-60, 80

During the life-time of Jesus there were four groupings or parties of Jews in Israel: the Pharisees, who stressed allegiance to
the Law both written and oral, and believed in life hereafter; the
Sadducees, mainly from the priestly families, who espoused the
Law, but rejected oral tradition and belief in life after death; the
Zealots, mainly political rather than religious, whose aim was to
drive out the Romans by violence and assassination; and finally,
the smallest and perhaps the most committed religious group-
ing, the Essenes. These latter, never once mentioned in the NT,
turned their backs on Temple worship, and regarded all outside
their group as living lives of wickedness and sin. To prevent
being contaminated they settled in the vicinity of the Dead Sea,
the lowest point in the surface of the earth, a lake with no life
whatever in it, and precious little life in the landscape all around
it, since the whole area becomes a veritable oven in the summer
time. Dividing themselves into sections they took turns at praying, both night and day, and meditating on the Law and the
prophets of the OT, while they also purified themselves by ritual
washings every day.

These were the people responsible for the writing of the
manuscripts known as the Dead Sea Scrolls. The had devotion to
the Torah, the book of the Law, and believed that God would
soon inaugurate his kingdom. It is hardly surprising that many
modern scholars see a link between this community and the
man whose birth we celebrate this day – John the Baptist. He
also was a child of the desert, living a life of absolute austerity –
a stern, forceful character, who did not mince words in telling
people what he thought of them, and yet attracted them to himself
as only deeply spiritual souls can. He too attached such importance to ritual washing that people referred to him as the
Baptiser, or the Baptist. We see from the gospel that the reaction
of people to him was a feeling of uncertainty, the uncertainty
that comes to all of us when we see the way our lives are going.

'What must we do?' – they asked of him. While this manifested
a willingness to change, it also clearly shows that they lacked the
Holy Spirit guiding them from within. 'Love, and do what you
will', would be the motto of St Augustine many years later,

meaning that if a person's heart is caught up in the love of God, he or she will know almost instinctively what is the right way to act. John attempted to bring about this inner change in his listeners' hearts by telling them not to be grasping, not to grumble, not to exact more than a just return from others for the work they did, not to forget those in need. 'Repent', he said, – advice which, if put into action, meant more than merely saying, 'I am sorry for my sins'. It meant changing one's whole life.

God's call to change and be prepared, comes to all of us here and now as well. And we should ask ourselves: (i) are we like the Essenes, who saw themselves as being saved, while the rest were damned; (ii) are we like the Sadducees, who did not really believe in a life hereafter and saw no point in making the effort to change; or (iii) are we like the Pharisees, who saw change as wholly unnecessary, because they thought they were perfect already, and this by their own observance of the Law and all the minor regulations which they added on to the Law?

To everyone, without exception, Jesus addresses the first demand of his public life – the same that John had used so often – 'Repent'. Repent, and believe in the gospel of redemption, not the gospel of the Essenes, the Sadducees, or the Pharisees, but the gospel preached by our divine Lord, Jesus Christ. John was a prophet of the end–time, that is he believed that there is a continual war between good and evil in this world, and that there will come a time when good will finally triumph, whereas evil and all evildoers will be annihilated in a final confrontation. He was also, however, a prophet of doom in that he preached a baptism of repentance for the forgiveness of sin, and punishment for the non-repentant. 'Even now the axe is laid to the roots of the trees', he declared, 'so that any tree which fails to bring forth good fruit will be cut down and thrown on the fire' (Lk 3:9). By instilling fear in his listeners he got them to change. Yet, from the mouth of Jesus himself, John was to receive the supreme accolade, 'Truly I tell you, among those born of women no one has arisen greater than John the Baptist' (Mt 11:11).

SAINTS PETER AND PAUL, APOSTLES
Vigil: Acts 3:1-10; Gal 1:11-20; Jn 21:15-19
Feast: Acts 12:1-12; 2 Tim 4:6-8, 17-18; Mt 16:13-19

The New Testament tells us nothing about the last days of either of the two great saints we honour in today's feast. Early Christian sources, apart from this, reveal little about the actual death or burial of either of them. The only reference is the prophecy of Christ about Peter. 'When you were young, you girded yourself and walked where you liked. But when you are old, you will stretch out your hands, and another will bind you, and lead you where you would rather not go' (Jn 21:18). This he said to indicate by what death he would give glory to God. In ancient times, the phrase 'stretch out the hands' signified crucifixion. There was always support, however, for the tradition that Peter's death took place on the Vatican Hill where the great memorial to him now stands. St Peter's Basilica is without doubt the place of greatest pilgrimage in Christiandom, and has been so right from the time it was first erected in the fourth century, when Constantine was emperor. But, it is probably true to say that most pilgrims who go there today, are more affected by the vastness of it, the Baroque beauty of it, the scale of the decorations within it, rather than by any direct links it presents with the Apostle whose name it bears. In order to get close in spirit to the Apostle one has to go down underneath the huge Basilica to the excavations which were carried out during the period of Pope Pius XII.

There you can discover how this huge building was erected on a most awkward site – on top of a mainly pagan graveyard, which lay on the slope of the Vatican Hill, one of the seven historic hills of ancient Rome. To get a level foundation the original builders were forced to cut away the upper part of the slope, and raise the lower part with earth-fill. The purpose of all this was to ensure that when erected, one particular tomb, until then rather poor and insignificant in comparison with those around it, should lie directly underneath the high altar, which is now some twenty feet above it. For the first few centuries of its existence this grave had no monument identifying it. In fact at some stage a plaster facing brick wall, painted a bright red, was built for some purpose across the graveyard, and destroyed half of Peter's grave. And when you ponder the question, why did the builders go to such immense trouble, and who was it they intended to honour, it is then that you begin to feel the wonder of Christianity.

For the man, to whose memory this vast building was raised close to the walls of the most renowned city of ancient times, was not even a Roman citizen. He was just a poor, unlettered fisherman from an insignificant and, according to the Romans in the first century, a troublesome little country, on the remote boundaries of their great empire. But the thing which set this person apart was the conviction that he was a man of faith, the one who, when Jesus put the question, 'Who do you say that I am?', did not hesitate to answer on behalf of the others, 'You are the Christ, the Son of the living God'. And for him this burning inner conviction was not to stop there; it was something which had to be passed on, even if it meant travelling thousands of miles, even if it meant facing ridicule, condemnation and death at the very centre of the great pagan empire. We have insights from the New Testament into the character of Peter which endear him to us, which make us identify with him, especially in his proneness to fall. But then we take heart from, and are edified by, his humility, his willingness to accept correction, his tears of repentance.

Peter and the saint who shares today's feast with him, Paul, seem poles apart in temperament and personality. Paul was an intellectual, one who rationalised his campaign in advance, and did not hesitate to rebuke anyone, even Peter, should their paths cross. Paul's death, well outside the boundary of Rome, was dignified as befitted a Roman citizen, whereas Peter was stripped and crucified head downwards, before a jeering mob, like a slave without rights, as was Jesus himself. Yet both were great apostles, both gave enduring witness to Christ, both by their heroic deaths won glory for themselves and the Church for which they had made the supreme sacrifice. Their lesson for us is that no matter what we have done in the past – and remember Paul had once persecuted the Church, and Peter publicly denied any knowledge of its founder – if we sincerely try and follow Christ, our Father in heaven will forgive us, and permit us to be with Christ forever in his kingdom.

THE TRANSFIGURATION OF THE LORD
Dan 7:9-10, 13-14 or 2 Pet 1:16-19; Jud 13:23-25; Lk 11:27-28

It is rarely that we have the opportunity to include in our Sunday liturgy the Feast of the Transfiguration of the Lord, which we are celebrating today. It is otherwise in the Eastern Orthodox Churches where it is one of the most important feasts which they observe in honour of Christ. The gospel account of the Transfiguration attempts to describe an event which is cloaked in mystery, an event which spans the interval between two other great mysteries of Christ, his Baptism and Resurrection. We can only approach it with reverence, as did the three Apostles, Peter, James and John, before whose astonished gaze the bodily appearance of Jesus was briefly, but dramatically, changed, and his whole person transfigured. His face shone like the sun, we are told, and his clothes became as dazzling as light. Two figures from the distant past of God's chosen people, Moses, the one to whom God gave the Law, and Elijah, the prophet supreme who championed the Jewish faith against heresy, appeared beside him and spoke with him. Finally, a bright cloud covered the whole place with its shadow, and a voice was heard speaking from within it: 'This is my Son, the Beloved ... Listen to him'.

We may begin to understand a little the significance of all this if we pose the question: 'What did it mean for Peter, James and John?' And St Peter in that Second Reading tells us clearly that they sought its meaning in the prophecies of the Old Testament, because Christ for the Apostles was seen as being the fulfilment of the Law and the Prophets. For example in the Book of Deuteronomy – for the most part a book of the Law – Moses made this prediction concerning Israel's future: 'The Lord your God will raise up for you a prophet like myself; to him you must listen. And the Lord said to me: "I will put my words into his mouth, and he shall tell the people all I command him. Those who do not listen to the words he will speak in my name, I myself will make them answer for it"' (18:15+).

The Apostles would be quite familiar with this passage, as with the promise made at the end of the Book of the prophet Malachi, 'Behold, I will send you Elijah, the prophet, before the great and terrible day of the Lord comes' (3:23). Christ himself would tell the Apostles, on the way down from the mountain, that Elijah had indeed returned in the person of John the Baptist. From passages such as these it became plain to Peter, James and John that the Transfiguration was God's way of telling them that the promises made to Israel in the Old Testament were being fulfilled in the person of Jesus, and that the presence of Moses and Elijah was definite confirmation of this.

We have clear affirmation of this in Peter's own words, so full of beautiful imagery, in today's excerpt from his Letter, 'You will be right to depend on prophecy and take it as a lamp for lighting a way through the dark until the dawn comes and the morning star rises in your minds'. The Apostles, moreover, were themselves given a fleeting premonition of what the immediate future held in store for Jesus. For St Luke tells us that Moses and Elijah spoke about his passing, in other words his departure, his exodus, from this life, which he would accomplish in Jerusalem. Christ would come to his messiahship through suffering, thereby winning many and rich blessings for those who would come to believe in his message. At the end of this gospel account we detect a sense of anti-climax for the disciples when this brilliant vision had ceased. They saw no one with them any more, we are told, but only Jesus – only Jesus, the one they had almost come to take for granted, as so often do we, even now in our own time, after so many centuries during which people have reflected on the significance of Christ's life and message for the world.

Herein lies the lesson of the Transfiguration for us too. Day by day we must try with the eyes of faith to penetrate beyond the ordinary, familiar, externals of our Eucharistic celebration to the glorious supernatural realities that at present remain unseen. For the Eucharist gives expression, as does the Transfiguration, to our hope for human transformation after this life. What happened on Mount Tabor is a demonstration of what we are capable of becoming. But eye has not seen, nor ear heard, neither can the human mind conceive what God has prepared for those who love him. We can only pray that we may be found worthy to be numbered among those who will attain what he has promised.

THE TRIUMPH OF THE CROSS
Num 21:4-9; Phil 2:6-11; Jn 3:13-17

As we celebrate this feast of the exaltation of the Holy Cross, it is very profitable to consider the meaning and significance of the feast, and the extraordinary way in which over the centuries, since Christ's death, an instrument of death has come to be regarded as the source of life and salvation for the world. What was the sign, above all others, of human hatred has been transformed into a symbol of God's infinite love. Prior to the Christian era, the cross was associated in peoples' minds with the most horrific of deaths – a fate reserved only for slaves. It was something to be feared and despised, and was used by political and military leaders to strike terror into the hearts of those under their power. Thus, for example, after the failure of the armed rising of Roman slaves, thousands of these unfortunates were crucified as a warning to the rest not to attempt escape from the degrading existence which was their lot. And yet when God wanted to reveal his love for humankind, he did so – as St Paul today reminds us – through the person of Jesus Christ, his Son, who assumed that very condition of a slave, and accepted the death reserved for slaves alone.

The reason for all this is that love is revealed only by giving, and the most perfect love is shown, not by the giving of things, but by the giving of one's person, in other words by self-sacrifice. 'Greater love than this no man has shown', Christ said at the Last Supper, 'than that a man lay down his life for his friend' (Jn 15:13). What makes Christ's surrender of his life for humanity all the more wonderful is that it took place while the human race was still in the state of sin , that is its members, by and large, were ruled by a state of hostility towards God and one another. And as the Israelites, who were bitten by snakes in the wilderness, were cured by looking at the bronze serpent set up by Moses, just so will all who look for healing and salvation to the Cross of Christ, acquire that inner peace and healing which only God's Holy Spirit can give.

The love revealed in the Cross overcomes the power of sin; it brings forgiveness and reassurance of God's bountiful mercy; it gives us a pledge that death is not the end of everything, but rather the beginning of a new heaven and a new earth. This is the reason why we show devotion to the Cross, why we respect and venerate the Cross, why we join with St Paul in glorying in the Cross of our Lord and Saviour Jesus Christ.

In the Eastern Church, the victory of the Cross was emphasised in a way which seems strange to us in the west. For Christ on the Cross was portrayed in their icons, the oldest religious paintings that survive from the first centuries of Christianity, portrayed as a conqueror, clothed in majestic robes, a figure of glory and power. This too is the Christ described by St John in his Passion narrative, where Christ is always in control, master of each situation, and of his own destiny, who lays down his life of his own accord, and not through force of exterior circumstances. While addressing the Pharisees, Jesus had foretold this quite plainly. 'The Father loves me', he said, 'because I lay down my life in order to take it up again. No one takes it from me; I lay it down of my own free will, and as it is in my power to lay it down, so it is in my power to take it up again' (Jn 10:17f). Moreover, Christ insists that to be his true disciples, each of us must follow in his footsteps, to his or her own personal Calvary, and die to self in order to live to him. For we are the members of a thorn-crowned head.

There are three ways of reacting to suffering in our lives, each signifying a response in ascending order of merit. There is suffering which is not wished, and thus becomes a burden, which weighs down and crushes us. There is suffering which is accepted, thus bringing calm and resignation to the tortured spirit. And finally, there is the suffering willingly undertaken out of pure love, which is the mark of the heroic, the supremely unselfish soul. Seen from this perspective, the Cross is the most complete expression of love. 'I have a baptism to receive', Christ had said looking forward to what he knew lay ahead, 'and how great is my distress until it is accomplished' (Lk 12:50). To atone for the sins of humanity, Christ became a compassionate and faithful high priest of God's religion (Heb 2:16f). The term compassionate implies that, on the Cross, Christ identified with suffering humanity. 'Ours were the sufferings he bore, ours the sorrows he carried' Scripture says (Is 53:4), and when the cross weighs heavily on us, Christ, if we but call on him, is always there to help and sustain us.

ALL SOULS' DAY

When we reflect on the significance of this feast of the Holy
Souls, what strikes us most, apart altogether from the certainty
that death awaits each one of us, is the feeling of helplessness
that takes hold of us, when death snatches away from our midst
those we have known and dearly loved. A veil is suddenly
drawn between them and us, a veil that no earthly gaze can penetrate. We cannot, here and now, see what takes place beyond
this veil; we can only fall back on what our Christian faith tells
us. The grief for those who have departed this life, of people
who do not have that faith, can be as short-lived as that of the
mourners described in the Book of Ecclesiastes. Writing some
hundreds of years before Christ, when there was as yet no belief
in the resurrection, the author poses the question: do virtue and
vice get their proper deserts in this life? Because debate on this
was in a period of transition, for him the answer had to be no.

Concern for the fate of those who have died, he says, can
often be just as brief as that of the mourners who are already
walking to and fro in the street; before, as he so poignantly puts it,
'the silver cord is snapped, or the golden lamp (of life) is broken,
… or before the dust returns to the earth, from which it came,
and the spirit to God who gave it' (12:6f). Even today, this is how
some people react when they have no Christian faith. But we,
who believe and have trust in the promises of Christ, should not
remain without understanding concerning those who have
passed away, St Paul warns us (1 Thess 4:13). Nor should we
grieve like the unbelievers who have no hope – hope, that is, of
resurrection unto eternal life. 'For us, our homeland is in heaven',
the Apostle assured the Christian community in Philippi, 'and
from heaven comes the Saviour we have been waiting for; and
he will transform these poor lowly bodies of ours into copies of
his own glorious body' (3:20f).

To-day's feast reaffirms for us that this transformation, or
purifying process, is one which can also be attained beyond life
on earth. For when the moment finally comes for us to be glorified, then we shall see God face to face, as he really is – a vision
we would not be able to endure, were we to remain in our
present unpurified state. Moreover, St John tells us that, having
departed this life, we are destined to enter into a union with

God, to a degree of intimacy beyond our wildest imagination. For we shall become like God, precisely because we shall see him. The soul then, after death, and before it can enter into the vision of God, face to face, must rid itself completely of selfishness, turn aside from all sin, and be cleansed of any stain left by such sin.

It is from this necessity that the concept of Purgatory arises, and confirmation of its effectiveness came from the mouth of Jesus himself, while addressing the Pharisees on one particular occasion. Forgiveness can be had for every sin or blasphemy, even if directed against himself, he assured them, with one exception, namely blasphemy against the Holy Spirit. Should anyone speak a word against the Holy Spirit, that person 'will not be forgiven either in this world, or in the next', were his exact words (Mt 12:32). That reference to a blasphemer not being forgiven in the next world certainly implies that forgiveness is indeed available in the world to come.

Arising from this, the official teaching of the Church, concerning the holy souls, tells us precisely three things: (i) that all those who die sincerely penitent in the love of God, but without having made satisfaction, by acts of penance, for their sinful ways, all such can be made fit, by Purgatory, for the enjoyment of the beatific vision of God; (ii) that souls undergoing this purification can be helped by our prayers; and (iii) that the most effective way of giving such help is through the holy sacrifice of the Mass. Thus the holy souls, who while on earth joined in the celebration of the Communion of the Body and Blood of Christ, are now comforted and supported by the communion of the saints and of the faithful, remembering them in their hour of need.

Hence, we should always bear in mind that it is truly a holy and wholesome thought to pray for the dead, especially in this particular season, so that they may be loosed from their sins, and enter into the company of the blessed who enjoy the perfect vision of the Almighty God for ever hereafter.

THE DEDICATION OF THE LATERAN BASILICA
Ex 47:1-2, 8-9, 12; 1 Cor 3:9-11, 16-17; Jn 2:13-22

In the year 312 AD, by defeating his enemies in battle, the emperor Constantine the Great became undisputed ruler of the Roman Empire. It was said that Constantine, who as yet was not a Christian, saw a fiery cross in the sky before the battle, and underneath it the words, 'In hoc signo vinces' – 'In this sign you will conquer'. Although he did not adopt the Christian faith for some years afterwards, he put an end to the persecution of the Church, and furthermore, in the year 324 he erected what has ever since been the cathedral of the Pope, the Basilica of St John Lateran. Beside this was a further building, which served as the residence for the Popes for the following 1000 years. St John Lateran was to suffer more than any of the other great basilicas of Rome. Destroyed by the Vandals, levelled in an earthquake, twice burnt down, it underwent numerous restorations.

But in this feast of its dedication, it is not so much a building we are celebrating, but rather that spiritual union or link with the successors of St Peter, that goes back to the early Christian times in Rome. The edifice of St John Lateran is the visible sign of that link. Christians everywhere, and from the earliest times after Christ, have been, and still are, a visible body endowed with invisible privileges. St Paul, sending best wishes to Prisca and Aquila, a wonderful married couple who had been his helpers in many ways, said, 'My greetings also to the Church that meets in your house.' And we should see the Church today as the extension of that Church, down through the believing Christians who met to worship God in St John Lateran. Indeed we might say that the one Church is the entire body of followers of Christ from all ages, gathered together into one.

We must remember as well that all the saints in heaven are part of this one Church also, since we refer to them as the Church triumphant. Nor should we forget the Church suffering, the holy souls who have departed this world, and are being purified in preparation for the vision of God almighty. The thought of all these forms part of our faith, as scripture tells us, 'With so may witnesses in a great cloud on every side of us, we too should put aside everything that weighs us down, especially the sin that clings to us, and keep running steadily in the race we have started' (Heb 12:1). We read in the Acts of the Apostles

(2:46) how the first Christians went as a body to the Temple every day, but also went from house to house for the breaking of bread, the breaking of bread being a reference to the celebration of the Holy Eucharist. Paul writing to Timothy, his disciple, urged the Christians, 'In every place I want people to lift up hands in prayer' (1Tim 2:8), and addressing the Colossians (4:2), he was even more specific, 'Keep on praying, and keep alert as you do so, giving thanks to God'. We might put to ourselves the question, 'Were these counsels of the Apostles, about prayer and worshipping together, intended for the early Christians only, or do they apply to us here and now as well'? In reply what can be said is that God speaks to us from out the pages of the NT, which contain God's inspired word. By this we mean that the writers of the NT, while remaining true authors, committed to writing all those things, and only those things, which according to God's will are necessary for our eternal salvation.

What God is demanding of the members of the Church is, that they continue, to the very end of time, offering up unceasing prayer, as a body together, not only in Jerusalem, not only in Rome, but in every place where they meet. St Teresa of Avila, the great Spanish Carmelite, who was given the title Doctor of the Church, because of her writing on prayer and mystical experiences, declared that 'Prayer is the doorway to great graces from God. If this door is closed, I do not see how God can bestow any favours.' In the holy sacrifice of the Mass, not only do we worship God, but in the fullest way possible we pray for the needs of all the members of the Church, as well as those who have gone to their eternal reward.

In this feast we celebrate the dedication of the first cathedral of the Pope, which is know as the Mother and Head of all the churches everywhere, and in so doing we are made aware of the sanctity of each church, especially our own church in which we are now offering up the same sacrifice of the Mass as was offered 1,600 years ago in St John Lateran. By so doing we are indeed reaping the reward of the promise made by Jesus himself to those who unite in praying together, 'Wherever two or three are gathered together in my name, there am I in the midst of them' (Mt 18:20).